DEBRETT'S NEW GUIDE TO
ETIQUETTE & MODERN MANNERS

Debrett's NEW GUIDE TO ETIQUETTE & MODERN MANNERS

THE INDISPENSABLE HANDBOOK

JOHN MORGAN

HEADLINE

First published in 1996
by HEADLINE BOOK PUBLISHING

10 9 8 7 6 5 4 3 2 1

British Library Cataloguing in Publication Data

Morgan, John
    Debrett's New Guide to Etiquette and Modern Manners
    1.Etiquette
    I.Title II.Debrett's Peerage (Firm)
    III.New Guide to Etiquette and Modern Manners
    395

ISBN 0 7472 1557 X

Typeset by
Letterpart Limited, Reigate, Surrey

Printed and bound in Great Britain by
Mackays of Chatham PLC, Chatham, Kent

HEADLINE BOOK PUBLISHING
A division of Hodder Headline PLC
338 Euston Road
London NW1 3BH

To Belinda

Behaviour is the garment of the mind and ought to have the conditions of a garment. For first, it ought to be made in fashion; secondly, it should not be too curious or costly; thirdly, it ought to be framed as best to set forth any virtue of the mind and supply and hide any deformity; and lastly, and above all, it ought not to be strait, so as to confine the mind and interfere with its freedom in business and action.

Francis Bacon

CONTENTS

ACKNOWLEDGEMENTS

It is impossible to acknowledge everybody who made this book possible. However, I would like to thank the following for their special contribution: Miss Belinda Harley, Mrs Jean Maby, Michael Shaw Bond, Lady Elizabeth Anson of Party Planners, Mrs Sarah Elton and Peter Lippiatt of Smythson, Nicholas Coleridge, Vice-Admiral Sir James Weatherall KBE, Her Majesty's Marshal of the Diplomatic Corps, Major and Mrs Simon Dixon, The Lord Freyberg, Mrs Claire Hamilton-Russell of Farrer & Co, Miss Sandra Boler of *Brides and Setting Up Home*, Miss Eva Lewis of *Tatler*, Mrs William Selka, David Broadhead of Claridges, Miss Lucinda Buxton of the Savoy Group of Hotels, Mrs Michael Fortier, Miss Jan Shure of the *Jewish Chronicle*, Paul de Keyser, Mrs Clovis Meath Baker, Mrs Robin Cohen, The Hon. Mrs Richard Pomeroy, Miss Victoria Mather, Mr and Mrs Thomas Woodham Smith, Peter Hartley LVO of The Lord Chamberlain's Office, Mrs Robyn Murdo-Smith LVO of the Buckingham Palace Press Office, Rev Jonathan Jennings of the Church of England Communications Unit, Father Kieran Conry of The Catholic Media Office, Monsignor Ralph Brown, Mrs Andrea de Swanton of Hennell, Miss Saira Joshi, Lady Celestria Noel of *Harpers & Queen*, Captain Michael Bickley RN, Head of Protocol Ministry of Defence, Colonel JW Trelawny OBE of Headquarters London District, Miss Caroline Buttle of The Jockey Club, Miss Laura Thompson-Royds of The Ascot Office, Mrs Ursula Edmonstone, General Sir Edward Jones KCB CBE, Secretary to The Lord Great Chamberlain, Julian Large, James McGurk of the Central Chancery of the Orders of Knighthood,

Bryan Jones of Kenyons, Miss Anna Harvey of *Vogue*, Miss Kate Reardon of *Tatler*, Miss Drusilla Beyfus, Anthony Gardiner of *Harpers & Queen*, Sandy Mitchell of *Country Life*, Robert Hutchinson, Tom Coles, Giles Eyre, Valentine Villiers, Joint Master of the Chiddingfold, Leconfield and Cowdray Hunt, Mrs Simon Gibbs, Miss Diana Bourne of Holland & Holland, Ben Elwes, Rev William Booth of the Chapel Royal, Mrs Ben Gooder, Mr and Mrs Stephen Bayley, Mrs Naim Attallah, the late Stephen Jones, Miss Nichola Formby, Mrs Susanne Cooper, The Lady Freyberg, The Hon. Annabel Freyberg, Rev Alan Greenbat JP, Jeffrey Blumenfeld of The Jewish Marriage Council, Miss Georgia de Chamberet, Mr and Mrs George Littler, Mrs Charles Woodruff, Anthony Smith, President of Magdalen College, The Lord Palmer, The Countess Alexander of Tunis, Neil Graham of Farrer & Co, Robert Ashby of The British Humanist Association, The Hon. Christina Freyberg, The Lady Kenilworth, Adrian Barnes CVO, The Remember-ancer of the City of London, His Honour Judge Esyr Lewis QC, Mrs Guy Martin, The Natural Death Society, Christopher Mann, Jonathan Wicks, Mark Morris, Nicky Haslam, Mark Riches of Keystone, Miss Sarah Willes of Blues Agency, Miss Kay Crosse of Norland College, Catherine Mansel Lewis of Kuala Nannies, Jeffrey Manton of Barclays Bank plc, Mark Birley, Mrs Mark Littman, The Bath and Racquets Club, Joseph Friedman of Sothebys, The Lady Sarah Baily, Mark Cecil, Mrs Sara Haydon, Mrs Nathalie Hambro, James Maby, Tom O'Connell of the Ritz Hotel, Miss Sophie Morgan Jones of Shortcut, Miss Amanda Cohen, Timothy Glazier, Ivor Spencer.

PREFACE

Debrett's New Guide to Etiquette and Modern Manners is the result of nearly two years' investigation into all aspects of social behaviour, from birth to death and everything in between. The result is a book which, although in the spirit of its illustrious forebears, has been completely re-researched and totally rewritten to deal with the complexities, challenges and contradictions of modern life. The result is, I hope, a book that combines the best of our traditional codes of conduct with acceptable contemporary innovations in everyday behaviour, that will not only guide you through the different aspects of your life but, I trust, will amuse and entertain you as well.

Throughout my research I have been gratified to discover the universal appeal of good manners. Everybody whom I have consulted, from the senior officials of the great offices of state to my own friends and colleagues, has shown enormous enthusiasm, interest and help with the project. Their very positive reactions have proved that good manners make for a kinder, happier and better world.

This is not to pretend that I have not encountered critics. These people argue that etiquette and good manners are outdated. The enormous social changes, especially in relationships between men and women, and the breakdown of traditional family groups have left people with dilemmas that the old certainties are ill equipped to solve. Traditional etiquette, with its subtle nuances and time-honoured forms, is seen by some as at best quaint and charming, at worst ridiculous and snobbish.

To these detractors I suggest that manners and etiquette, like language and fashion, are fundamental means of communication and self-expression. And, as with language and fashion, manners and etiquette adapt effortlessly to social change. I also believe that the best of manners are, in fact, one of the most visible and telling manifestations of civilisation, and without them we pave the way to uncertainty, insecurity and, in the end, a social disintegration that can already be seen in the loutish behaviour of some sections of our society.

This book, therefore, is intended to offer a modern route through the minefield of contemporary manners. It shows how many of our oldest customs can happily exist alongside the more free and informal aspects of contemporary life. It takes account of the very basic concept of human diversity: that what to one man may seem welcome informality may, to another, be grossly offensive. *Debrett's New Guide to Etiquette and Modern Manners* makes every effort to show how acceptable behaviour can exist on different levels and at all times.

Above all, I believe that this book will have succeeded if I show that courtesy and civility are not a matter of snobbery or class (we all know of duchesses who behave disgracefully!). Good manners are purely and simply a way of showing consideration and sensitivity towards others. As such, they are classless. Everyone deserves kindness and respect, and this book will explain the social formulae which will make the conducting of the everyday business of life more rewarding, both for ourselves and for those around us.

John Morgan
London, 1996

PART 1

Rites of Passage

1

BIRTH, BAPTISM AND OTHER CEREMONIES OF CHILDHOOD

Babies, for such small things, enter the world to a great fanfare – not only their own, but the enthusiastic adulation of family and friends as well. They are also, in an age when procreation is increasingly regarded as positively miraculous, trumpeted to a quite unprecedented extent.

BIRTH

Announcement of a Birth

This is traditionally the duty of the father, who must ring any immediate relations who were not present at the birth. Close family should be the first to hear the glad tidings, followed by prospective godparents, friends and colleagues. It is then customary to place a birth announcement in the personal column of newspapers. It is also increasingly usual to leave an announcement on the telephone answering machines of close friends, adding whether or not you are receiving calls.

The choice of wording for a newspaper announcement varies according to personal style, although the proper form is short and elegant.

PROUDPARENTS – On 22 December, to John and Jane, a son.

The inclusion of the year is optional. Some couples like to add the name of the hospital, the infant's name and the mother's maiden name: this, although well intentioned, is not *comme il faut*. Other details such as 'little brother for Andy, Pandy and Mandy' or 'long-awaited grandchild for Don and Doris' are even more inappropriate and should never appear. As for the entry that once appeared in a west country local paper and which included 'thanking all concerned', nothing needs to be said.

The form for single mothers takes the same pattern:

PROUDPARENT – On 30 December, to Susan, a son.

Smart babies are often announced, at the discretion of the social editors and often free of charge, in the Court & Social pages. It has also recently become the custom, immediately on deciding a baby's name, to send out American-style birth announcements (see Chapter 8). These can look very smart. The same cannot be said of a card showing a jolly picture of the new family, with written details on the back. After all, as one mother said: 'I was half gaga at the time, looked absolutely at my worst and am now embarrassed about these images being in constant circulation.'

Registration of Birth

Babies have to be legally registered. In England and Wales this has to be done within forty-two days. In Scotland the period of grace is only twenty-one days. Apart from this slight difference the procedure is largely the same throughout Great Britain. Babies are registered with their local registrar of births. If the infant is born when away from home, it is possible to declare the child locally but register it through the post to the baby's local area. The registering of babies by married couples is very straightforward. Either parent can do the registration, as only one signature is needed. Details of both parents are put on the certificate. Although most children automatically assume the father's surname, an infant can be given the mother's or any other of choice. The position with unmarried people is slightly more complicated. The mother always has to be present. In order for the father's details to be included in the birth entry, he should attend the register office with the mother and sign the register with her, or he can fill in a paternity declaration on a special form from the registrar's office. This needs to be witnessed by a solicitor or Commissioner for Oaths and is brought along by the woman when she attends the registration. Either the mother's or father's name can be used. In some circumstances when a father denies paternity, the mother can take him to court, where it is possible to order DNA tests to prove fatherhood and thus force him to recognise the child as his. On the other hand, if the mother does not want the father's name on the birth certificate a line is drawn through the space for paternal details. Alternatively a mother can also add the man's details later, should circumstances change, such as marriage, and therefore re-register the baby.

Hospital Visits

If you are not an immediate family member it is thoughtful, no matter how happy you are for the new mother, to delay your visit for a day or so, to give time for the immediate family to spend time with their newborn and for the mother to regain her strength. This is to ensure that she, who will undoubtedly be feeling drained by the experience of childbirth, is not overtaxed with visitors. Particularly if she has had a difficult birth, being besieged with callers can make her feel totally exhausted and confused. A mother of great experience recommends that visits from well-wishers should be no longer than twenty minutes.

Presents

As far as the newborn is concerned, it is necessary only for immediate family to bring presents, although friends may give something if they wish. This can range from a practical item for the nursery to something much more substantial and permanent, such as the two million pound trust fund that was recently settled on a very lucky three-day-old baby. Clothes, unless with prior consultation, are not recommended, as most mothers have very strong ideas about how their children are to look.

In all the excitement surrounding the baby, it is important to remember the star performer – the mother. An acquaintance says: 'After a birth, women long to feel feminine again and thus welcome gifts such as delicious soaps, a beautiful nightdress and, of course, flowers.' If sending a present – particularly flowers – rather than taking it in person, it is sensible to check how long the mother will be staying in hospital. Nowadays, this can be a very short time indeed. Some experts also recommend that the new baby's siblings are also given a small present, as their noses are often out of joint after the birth of the new arrival.

Letters of Congratulation

Friends who cannot visit should write a short letter of congratulation to the happy parents. This is always addressed to the mother and could read:

Dear Susan,
I was so thrilled to hear of the arrival of your long-awaited daughter.

She will make a delightful addition to the family and help keep those boisterous boys in order.
With much love,
Freddie Well-Wisher

If time is short, it is just acceptable to send a postcard bearing a suitable image.

Single Mothers

Many women choose to have babies without becoming attached to a man in the conventional sense. Others have accidents. In both cases it behoves family and friends to be extra supportive, as the mother will have to cope with her new family without the traditional help of a spouse.

Complications

If there are complications it is rude to ask too many questions. If a child is born with defects, unless these abnormalities are absolutely horrendous, family and friends must behave in a positive way. If a baby is stillborn or dies shortly after birth, this awful event must be treated as a family death, with letters of condolence sent to the parents.

Breast-Feeding in Public

It is bad manners to expel any liquid from any orifice in public, and breast-feeding is no different. Nevertheless, this habit remains a very sensitive area. During the sixties and seventies, many western women asserted their right to breast-feed in public. The fact that this practice has not become widespread is largely due to the fact that many onlookers (women as well as men of different generations) find the sight embarrassing, even revolting. With this in mind, well-mannered mothers should breast-feed in private. Thoughtful hosts offer lactating visitors a quiet room where they can feed away from the general throng.

BAPTISM

Despite the secularisation of society, a surprising number of babies are baptised. Research suggests that one in four babies is christened into the Church of England alone. However, there can be problems. Although most clergy are happy to baptise babies, many harbour reservations about christening babies of families who do not attend church, claiming that non-practising Christians are unlikely to bring their children up in a truly Christian manner. Others take the more relaxed view that by baptising an infant, the Church has acquired a new recruit.

Many clergymen are reluctant to give private baptisms, preferring to uphold the Church of England's current official line that baptism is a rebirth and a welcoming to the larger Christian communion, and thus infants should be christened during normal Sunday service in the presence of the parish's congregation. Others do semi-private group baptisms of several babies. Policy varies from parish to parish. However, most parents still, quite understandably, want the 'specialness' of a private christening with friends and family rather than a public affair, and there are plenty of vicars who will oblige with a private rite. As in many aspects of contemporary religion, it is down to the discretion of your local incumbent.

Baptism in the Church of England

Within the Church of England, christenings can happen at any age, although the most frequent time is at around three or four months. Clergymen hate leaving it too late, not just for the sake of the infant's soul, but because the older babies are, the heavier, more wriggly and increasingly difficult they become to manoeuvre. It is usual for the ceremony to take place at the local parish church. However, if parents wish for the service to take place at another church, they must first get the permission of both ministers.

In the case of church-going families, the arrangement of a christening is only a formality. However, should the parents never attend church, most clergy will want some assurance that the infant, once baptised, will be brought up in the tenets of the Christian faith. The majority of parishes now insist on some sort of preparation prior to the ceremony: this can range from a single conversation about the meaning of the service to a series of classes or training sessions.

Normally, the local parish priest performs the service. However, some couples wish to have the ceremony conducted by a family member or friend who is in Holy Orders. In these cases it is important to remember that men of the cloth can be as territorial as those of the laity, and thus the local priest's permission will have to be tactfully sought. Also, should a child be christened outside its own diocese, then it is courteous to inform the bishop by letter that this is happening.

There are two main liturgies to choose from. The first is the traditional service from the Book of Common Prayer, which is very beautiful, places a strong emphasis on the renunciation of evil and is preferred by many to the revised texts in the Alternative Service Book. The latter is written in more modern English and is designed to present a more contemporary view of Christianity.

Whichever service is chosen, the central act of the ceremony remains largely constant. Parents and godparents gather around the font with the baby and are asked by the minister to affirm their belief in Christ and the renunciation of all evil. Holding the child, the priest then pours or sprinkles holy water on to the infant's forehead and using the child's new Christian names declares: 'I baptise you in the name of the Father, and of the Son and of the Holy Spirit.' The priest then makes the sign of the cross on the young forehead. Sometimes a lighted candle is presented to the family and specially blessed oils are used to anoint the baby. It is usual for the father to go to the vestry to register the christening. There is always a fee payable for a certificate of baptism, and should the baptism have been a private affair, then a small donation to church funds is welcomed. There is one family who, as their gesture of appreciation, organised for flowers to be delivered to the church for three Sundays after the christening of their newborn. This lovely gesture was much appreciated.

The dress for the christening ought to be special. Women should wear hats and men dark suits. The infant is resplendent in a white gown (this is often part of a family's history) that signifies purity. Sometimes a little white bonnet is also worn. Should you wish to baptise your child in an ancestral gown, it is sensible to remember that in the past babies were smaller than today. Thus your bouncing baby might be too big for the antique: certainly an early christening is advised.

Announcements in the Press
Written announcements of christenings in the Court & Social pages of national newspapers are increasingly rare, although traditionally minded families like to keep up the custom. Typical wording could read:

> The infant daughter of The Earl and Countess of Proudparentland was christened Augusta Boadicea by the Reverend Timothy Tremble at St Margaret's, Westminster, on Thursday 21 December. The godparents are The Hon. Tiggy Tintangel, Mrs Peter Pork-Sausage and The Lord Tickle.

Note, in the case of a male infant, the names of the godfathers precede those of godmothers.

Catholic Baptism
This tends to be a rather more elaborate and lengthy affair than the Anglican rite, although in recent years it has been simplified by innovations from the

Vatican. Although practices vary from parish to parish, the Roman Catholic Church, like the Church of England, now officially discourages the practice of private baptism, although in most cases the choice of baptism during mass or outside it is available (and there are still priests who will perform a private service). One godparent (or sponsor) has to be a Roman Catholic of good standing, and only his or her name is entered in the register. Sometimes there is a hymn at the beginning of the service. The parents and godparents trace the sign of the cross on the infant's forehead. Then follows a reading from Scripture, and a short homily and prayers. After this the infant is anointed with catechumenal oil by the priest. Parents and godparents renounce Satan and profess their faith in God. The actual baptism is then performed. After this the child is anointed with chrism oils and wrapped in a pure white robe, and its father or godfather holds a candle lit from the Paschal candle held by the priest. This elaborate ritual concludes with the saying of the Lord's Prayer, a blessing and the signing of the register. If the service has included an organist, there might be a fee payable to him. The priest does not charge for his services, but an offering is always appreciated. It is most important to keep the baptismal certificate, as it will be needed for future rites of religious passage, such as weddings, and for applications to Roman Catholic schools.

Jewish Procedures

Traditionally, male infants are subjected to an ancient rite called Brit Milah, at which they are circumcised at an official ceremony presided over by a *mohel*. This usually takes place seven days after the birth and is held at home and not at the synagogue. The rite is attended by the parents, grandparents and friends. *Sandeks*, the Jewish equivalent of godparents, will also be present. These may be any Jewish male, and to be asked to fulfil this role is a particular honour in the faith. The godfather holds the infant during the procedure and the father recites a special prayer. The *mohel* is the one who actually wields the knife, as well as reciting prayers and a blessing over a goblet of wine. The baby is then given its Hebrew name which signifies its initiation into the faith. It is considered bad luck to make any reference to the baby's name until after the circumcision. Female infants are spared this religious initiation and are expected only to attend the synagogue on the first Sabbath after the birth, when the father is called up or reads the Torah and the baby is given its Hebrew name. Some Reform and Liberal Jews have stripped the ritual circumcision of some of its ceremony. They may, instead, choose to bless the boy at the synagogue, as is customary with girls.

Men attending a Brit Milah are expected to wear a skullcap (*yarmulke* or *kippah*). Women at very Orthodox rites wear hats. It is usual to take a small present for the baby or some flowers or chocolates. Afterwards there is normally a small drinks party.

PIDYAN HA BEN

In the case of a first-born male child (and where there is no history of pregnancy) there is also a rarely performed rite known as Pidyan ha Ben. This charming little ceremony also takes place at home, and is performed by a *cohen* (priest). The father hands over silver to the *cohen*, who prays for the boy's redemption. There is normally a party afterwards. Pidyan ha Ben normally takes place on Sunday evening and is a relatively smart affair. Again men need to wear skullcaps.

Humanist Naming and Welcoming Ceremonies

Humanists do not believe in God, but in a moral code inherent in human nature. For humanists there is neither an afterlife nor any divine revelation, only an interest in this life and the welfare of others. However, for all their differences with organised religion, the humanists do perform rather touching, tailor-made secular ceremonies, which they are happy to do for people without religious beliefs but who wish to mark life's great milestones with some sort of special rite. The naming and welcoming ceremony for children is held shortly after the infant's birth and is attended by family and friends. There is no established liturgy. Like all humanist ceremonies the rite is specially composed for the occasion. There would normally be a short address welcoming the child into the family circle and society, and espousing humanist ideals. At its simplest the service can be performed by the parents alone, although it is normal to ask a humanist celebrant to conduct the proceedings, for whom there is normally a small fee which should be negotiated beforehand. Humanists do not believe in godparents, as there is no undertaking to supervise the infant's upbringing in a particular faith. However, some couples appoint 'supporting adults' or 'mentors', who are meant to take a special interest in the child's development. There are no conventions of dress at these ceremonies.

Godparents

Being a godparent has become very fashionable and today represents for many childless people – gays, women who have not had children and those who choose not to – a kind of proxy parenting. Prospective godparents are invited to stand by the parents and should themselves have been baptised and confirmed. Traditionally, in the Church of England, a boy infant has two godfathers and one godmother; girls two godmothers and one godfather. In the Catholic Church there is one godmother and one godfather for each child, regardless of sex. In reality, however, in an age of multiple godparenting, whole regiments of adults are dragooned into godparenting one infant. This enthusiasm is all very well, but it often obscures the serious commitment being a godparent brings. Godparents are intended by the Church to guide a child's piety (literally to keep it godly) and to raise the young one in the Christian faith until he or she is old enough to make the promises for him- or herself at the service of confirmation. Outside of this spiritual requirement, being a godparent has also acquired the secular responsibility of enhancing the child's general well-being and development and, most importantly, providing a safety net should disaster strike the child's natural parents. In today's world, with the fragility of the modern marriage, the role of godparent has never been more important. 'You have to be ready to be an ex officio parent, a psychotherapist and the one who will pick up the pieces at the time of trouble,' explains one highly enthusiastic godparent, who boasts nearly a score of godchildren. Thus, prospective godparents must weigh up their commitment honestly and harbour no embarrassment in declining politely the honour of the role, if they feel they might be unable to sustain it.

By the same token parents must resist the temptation to appoint 'trophy godparents' who look impressive in the photographs and sound grand in the newspapers but will probably prove singularly lacking when the chips are down. Parents should also ignore the recent nonsensical idea that the father's best man should automatically be a godfather of the first child. The sole criterion for the selection of a godparent is their suitability for the role. After all, the ability to organise the stripper at the stag party is not the best credential for guiding a child through the Catechism. Parents should also be careful about appointing godparents who are too young. In recent years there has been a trend to choose at least one godparent who, rather than being the same generation as the parents, is nearer the infant in age. The rationale behind this is that godchild and godparent will have more in common. In reality, adolescent godparents often lose interest in their charges.

The godparent is expected to attend the christening, although, should he or she be unable to attend, they can nominate a stand-in. However, in the light of the gravity of the role, this is not really a good start. In the Church of England it is usual for a godparent, usually female, to hold the child at the font until the priest is ready to begin the service. In the Catholic Church, the mother holds the baby throughout.

Christening Presents

Many people claim to be confused about christening presents. Either they don't give them at all, or they give transient items such as clothes or boxed sets of Beatrix Potter, which are much better suited to early birthdays. The perfect christening present is something of a permanent nature, such as a small silver hairbrush, nursery eating implements, a christening mug, a rattle, or a prayer book inscribed with the infant's name and the date of the christening. Jewellery is also very popular for girls, with coral and pearl necklaces being the most traditional. Alternatively it can be an even more long-term proposition, such as a lifetime's membership of a learned institution, a savings account or a cellar of wine or 'pipe' of port put down for drinking when the child comes of age. It is particularly important that godparental presents should be especially lasting. A certain international financier presented his godchild with a pair of specially crafted shoe trees from London's best-known bespoke shoe-maker, with the note: 'These are towards your first pair of shoes when you come of age.'

Christening Parties

It is usual to give a small informal party at home after the ceremony. Private baptisms normally take place in the afternoon, so it is usual to follow them with a tea party. Public baptisms would usually happen on Sunday mornings and thus drinks or a family lunch would be ideal. It is necessary to ask only family, godparents, the priest who officiated (and wife if applicable) and perhaps a few close friends. Whatever food is served, it must include a white-iced (purity again) christening cake, which traditionally, in the case of a first child, is the top layer of the parental wedding cake; alternatively it can be ordered specially for the event. As existing children can become very jealous of newly arrived siblings, it is tactful to provide a small cake for them, so that they do not feel left out. I still remember at the age of four, at my younger brother's christening tea, being presented with my own cake (a jolly iced affair decorated with a blue train) and realising my mother still loved me.

CONFIRMATION, FIRST COMMUNION AND BARMITZVAH
Confirmation in the Church of England
This is usually done between the ages of twelve and fourteen and signifies that the child reaffirms the Christian beliefs made on its behalf at the christening. It is usual for the child to go to confirmation classes with a priest or school

chaplain prior to the service. The ceremony is conducted by the local bishop, and it is common for several adolescents to be confirmed in one ceremony. It is usual for the confirmed to be accompanied by their parents and godparents. Dress is smart all round. The service also means that, as fully fledged members of the Church, they are ready to take their first communion, which can happen at the confirmation service or soon after.

Confirmation in the Roman Catholic Church

This signifies an individual's commitment to become a fully fledged Roman Catholic. The age of confirmation varies in different dioceses, although the most usual age is somewhere between ten and fourteen. Preparation is based in the child's own school or parish. It is usual for the confirmant to chose a saint, who will then be his or her very own mediator with God. The celebration of confirmation is a family event which requires the presence of a sponsor (usually a godparent) to guide the child through the liturgy, which can take place within mass or at a separate service. The confirmants kneel before a bishop, who holds his hands above each child, prays and then traces the sign of the cross on each expectant forehead with chrism oil. It is usual in the case of girls for their sponsor to present them with a piece of jewellery such as a crucifix or a string of pearls. Boys receive a prayer book, Bible or a pair of cuff links.

First Communion (Roman Catholic)

First communion precedes a Roman Catholic's confirmation. This in turn is usually preceded by the child's first confession. First communion is the first time that the Sacrament is taken, and usually happens at the tender age of seven. A programme of preparation for the Sacrament will normally be run by the school or parish. The ceremony is very touching. Girls wear little white dresses and veils; boys a dark suit.

Barmitzvah

This is one of the most important rites of passage in the Jewish religion. It is for boys only and symbolises their arrival at maturity and their acceptance of the teachings of the faith, and stresses their role as fully fledged members of the Jewish community. It is usual to have educational classes before-hand. The ceremony takes place at the synagogue on the first convenient date – usually the Sabbath or *shabbat* (Saturday) – after a boy's thirteenth birthday. During the ceremony the boy pledges to observe the command-ments of the Torah and to be a good Jew both at home and in his community at large. The Liberal wing of the faith has also instigated an alternative confirmation service for boys and girls, which tends to happen in the later teens. However, the majority still plump for the traditional barmitzvah – some having both rites.

Customs, particularly at Orthodox barmitzvahs, dictate the necessity to be thoughtful. If driving to the ceremony, it is considerate to park the car a little way from the synagogue and walk the rest of the distance, as observant Jews do not permit driving on the Sabbath. It is usual for men and women to sit separately. Men wear formal suits and skullcaps. Women generally wear hats (they are essential at Orthodox rites) with a smart daytime suit or dress, and should not expose their arms from the elbow up. Short skirts are inappropriate. Although it is customary for all guests at a barmitzvah to give presents, these are either sent in advance or presented at the celebrations after the service, but never brought to the synagogue. Barmitzvahs are very happy events and it is usual to congratulate the boy and his family after the service.

The barmitzvah is often celebrated at a *kiddush* immediately after the service. It is not uncommon to give a small lunch party on Saturday followed by something much bigger on Sunday. This can range from a formal lunch party to the all-singing and dancing extravaganzas of popular imagination, although there is generally a trend towards less lavish forms of entertainment.

BARMITZVAH OR BAT CHAYIL

This is a barmitzvah for girls and is particularly popular in the Reform and Liberal wings of the church, which are keener on sexual equality than the more traditional Orthodox heartland. For Reform and Liberal Jews, the usual age is thirteen, while twelve is the norm for Orthodox members. The Reform and Liberal ceremony takes place on the Sabbath, while the Orthodox barmitzvah has its own service on Sunday. There is also a party afterwards, but this would generally be less lavish than a boy's celebrations.

2

ENGAGEMENT TO BE MARRIED

Despite record divorce rates and the increasing proportion of people who have lived together for some time, many couples still become engaged to be married. In the past, this act, then known as betrothal, was often considered almost as binding as marriage itself. Today it expresses both privately and publicly a couple's commitment and intention to legalise their bond in marriage.

PRIVATE ANNOUNCEMENTS

Although couples reach the decision to become engaged in many ways, it is still the custom, even in the most modern of relationships, for the man to pop the question (even in leap years). How this is done is a private matter, although one somewhat shy and sensitive young man, too nervous to face a possible rebuttal face to face, wrote to his prospective fiancée a short poem requesting her hand in marriage. She accepted.

Some couples, once they decide to become engaged, keep the news to themselves or let it out gradually and informally to family and friends. However, the traditional manner of informing parents first remains the most polite and practical course of action. This is particularly so nowadays, in an age of greater mobility, when parents might not already know their prospective child-in-law. Remember that an important function of an engagement is to allow the two parental sides to get used to one another, and thus smooth out as early as possible any differences and difficulties.

The usual procedure begins with the man paying a visit to the father of his fiancée, or inviting him to lunch or drinks. By tradition, the young man would ask the older one for his daughter's hand in marriage, but nowadays the situation is more likely to be presented as a *fait accompli*. However, some men do still adhere to the old form. There was one who asked the father of his beloved first so that a family ring could be re-set before he proposed to the girl herself. The meeting with his future father-in-law is traditionally also a time when the prospective groom will disclose his financial status, career prospects and any 'expectations'. Nowadays, in an age of increasingly fragile marriages and easy divorces, the conversation sometimes includes discussion of pre-nuptial agreements. The young man then informs his own parents of his plans to marry.

If the news has been well received on both sides, it is then the custom for the young man's mother to write directly to her future in-laws, expressing her and her husband's delight at the forthcoming nuptials. If the groom's parents are separated or divorced, it behoves them to try and forget their differences for the duration and for the estranged wife to write to the parents of her son's bride-to-be. If the father is widowed, then he obviously has to write. In the letter it is also customary to suggest a date for both sides to get together: this is particularly important if the two families do not know one another. The meeting can take the form of a lunch, a dinner or a weekend stay, and is usually hosted by the groom-to-be's family. This letter should be answered either in the post or over the telephone with alacrity, to demonstrate mutual goodwill. If, for whatever reason, the mother of the groom-to-be fails to write, then it falls to the mother of the girl to make the overture.

Thereafter, it's time to tell family, employers and friends. Technically the young man's mother informs her family and friends, the man's his side and the happy couple all their chums; in reality the news spreads in a much less structured way than this.

PUBLIC ANNOUNCEMENTS

Once family, godparents and close associates have been put in the picture, it is then usual to announce the engagement formally in the Forthcoming Marriages columns of whichever national and/or local newspapers that are likely to have the widest readership amongst friends and associates. *The Times* and the *Daily Telegraph* remain the most popular, although Jewish families also like to place an announcement in the *Jewish Chronicle* and those with strong Hibernian connections appear in the *Scotsman*. The bride-to-be's family normally pays for this, although it is important for them to consult the other side before confirming the wording to the publication, as family circumstances such as parental divorce, widowhood and remarriage all govern how the announcement is worded.

Procedures vary slightly from publication to publication, but the form at the *Daily Telegraph* is typical. The happy couple must give details in writing, either by letter or fax, to the Court & Social Department. The editors will then check the wording of the announcement by telephone before printing. It is vital to be vigilant about correctness, as mistakes are an embarrassing and unpromising start to the new union.

A typical announcement would read:

Mr I. A. M. Smitten and Miss V. G. Sweet
The engagement is announced between Ian, ninth son of Mr and Mrs
Simon Smitten of Haywards Heath, West Sussex, and Violet,
fifteenth daughter of Mr and Mrs Samuel Sweet of Chocolate Hall,
Cambridgeshire.

There are variations to cover different family contingencies, for which publications are now well prepared. For instance, if the groom's parents are divorced and his mother remarried, the bride's are separated but not divorced, then the announcement would read:

Mr L. Love and Miss K. Kissing
The engagement is announced between Larry, eldest son of Mr
Jefferson T. Love of New York and Mrs Frederick Flighty of
Godalming, Surrey, and Miss Katy Kissing, only daughter of Mr
Christopher Kissing of Kensington, London, and Mrs Christopher
Kissing of Middlemarch, Middleshire.

In addition to purely printed announcements in the papers, some magazines also print pictorial tributes. The best known is the full-page portrait of an engaged girl that appears in *Country Life*, although it must be said it is no longer the sole domain of recently engaged girls. Whereas previously the choice of girl was largely governed by family background, it is nowadays guided by her own achievements (and probably her easiness on the eye). Prospective brides wishing to be considered should send a photograph and details about themselves to the editor, who chooses each month's portrait. Alternatively, fashionable photographers who have taken a couple's engagement photographs often submit them.

Once the news is out, it is usual for friends to write to the happy couple, to express their joy at the news. Any associates who harbour misgivings about the match are best advised to keep their own counsel and not attempt to affect events, unless they know something utterly awful, such as the groom's conviction for attempted polygamy in Penge.

ENGAGEMENT CELEBRATIONS

Most couples claim that the announcement of their engagement signals the start of a fun time during which they are the centre of attention of family and friends, the focus of much well-wishing and the excuse for celebrations. These parties vary enormously, depending on the wishes and circumstances of the couple. They can take the form of a small dinner or a large drinks party given by the girl's parents, at which her father will make an informal speech and toast the happy couple. Sometimes both sides join forces so that the widest possible circle of friends and family can meet, although such a gathering is best left until the wedding reception itself. It is also increasingly popular for the couple themselves to host their own informal drinks party for their friends. This is particularly useful if the wedding is to be a quiet one, or if the church is too small for a large congregation, as it enables the couple to celebrate with friends who will not be invited to the marriage service. Timings, dress and conduct depend obviously on the type of party being given. Guests are not expected to bring presents, but ought to write thank-you letters afterwards. Later on in the engagement it is traditional for the bride-to-be to invite her prospective in-laws to dinner or lunch at her house.

CORRESPONDENCE TO ENGAGED COUPLES

Unless you see the couple all the time, it is customary to write a letter of congratulations once they become engaged. Well-wishers who are short of time scribble a postcard – those feeling generous can send flowers. Technically the girl's friends write to her, the boy's to him, although there is no hard and fast rule. It remains a solecism to write to them jointly, even if they live together. It is also still considered bad form actually to use the word 'congratulate' in the letter to a forthcoming bride – as it is seen to suggest a certain unseemly entrapment. 'I was so pleased to hear of your wonderful news' is preferred. There is no similar nuance when corresponding with the future groom, when unabashed congratulations are expected. All letters and presents, but not postcards, should be acknowledged by a thank-you letter. This letter also has the added function of letting people know if the wedding is to be a small family event to which it would be impossible to invite everybody. Two people, as soon as their engagement is announced, become *de facto* a couple socially, and thus are invited everywhere together.

LENGTH OF ENGAGEMENTS

This again varies enormously, depending on circumstances. Although engagements tend to be shorter than previously, few can equal the brevity of one real-life couple's betrothal – two weeks; a day after the wedding the blushing bride gave birth to a bouncing son. Happily, most couples are not in such a hurry and usually plump for between five and nine months. Anything less than six months does not comfortably allow enough time to organise a traditional wedding with all the trimmings.

THE RING

The major present of the engagement is a ring given by the boy to the girl. It is worn on the fourth finger of the left hand, which, according to ancient belief, is said to have a certain vein that flows directly to the heart. Romantic traditionalists still maintain that it should be dashingly produced at the time of proposal and instantly slipped on to the accepting and adoring finger. Although this is still done, particularly in the case of family rings, most couples nowadays choose a ring to the new bride's taste within a few days of announcing their engagement. Even in the case of a hereditary sparkler, it is nowadays much more usual for her to be offered the choice of a new setting, rather than being forced to wear something that looked simply spiffing on Granny back in 1922, but is quite inappropriate for Cassandra in 1997. Other couples like to commission a new design from a contemporary designer, which again takes time. Whatever his choice, the sensitive fiancé does not delay. Most women say that it is only when they start actually wearing an engagement ring that they feel really in the final furlong to matrimony.

Unlike wedding bands, engagement rings should always carry a stone or stones. Diamonds remain the most popular and suitable choice. This is because they symbolise durability, eternity and purity. They are also rare and precious and have the added practical benefit of easy colour-coordination with clothes. Other stones and combinations of different gems are nevertheless perfectly acceptable. Some think incorporating the birth stone of the male betrothed to be particularly lucky, while others ascribe unlucky powers to certain jewels such as opals and pearls. Rubies, sapphires and emeralds remain the most usual, although there is an increasing fashion to utilise much more affordable and often very beautiful semi-precious stones such as citrines, amethysts and

19

aquamarines. The ring itself can be made from any precious metal. The most frequent choice remains eighteen-carat gold, but there is an increasing trend towards platinum. This is thought the most noble, valued and allergy-free of metals and seems to enjoy forty-year cycles in popularity. It was fashionable in the twenties and sixties and is poised for a big comeback for the new millennium.

If choosing a new ring or designing one from scratch, it is advisable to eschew the temptation to be trendy in favour of classical styling that will look good for a long time. Remember always to go for a decent-sized gem.

As the man invariably pays for the ring, it is up to him to lay down budgetary parameters for his fiancée's choice. This can be done quite easily if visiting only one or two shops, by first instructing the jeweller to show only rings within a prescribed price bracket. If a couple intend to shop around then he must let her know how much he is willing and able to spend. Although men are meant to buy the most expensive ring they can afford, little is to be gained by feckless generosity at this stage. In Britain one month's salary is considered the norm to outlay on a ring. In the United States twice that amount is not unusual. A few couples now actually share the cost of the ring. Except in the case of rare stones of exceptional beauty and desirability, engagement rings should not be thought of as an 'investment'.

It is unusual, except in the most trendy of circles, for men to wear engagement rings, although gay couples are known to sport commitment rings as a symbol of their devotion. However, it is common for the bride-to-be to present her swain with a small present of a precious and personal nature. A pair of inscribed cuff links or a watch is the most usual, although the choice is entirely a matter of personal preference. As with christening presents, it should be something of a permanent nature that symbolises an everlasting rather than a transient sentiment.

Family Presents

In addition to presents that the engaged couple exchange between themselves, there are often, particularly in rich families, quite serious presents given by the respective parents. This stems from the time when marriage was seen as a contract of property as much as a romantic attachment, and no self-respecting bride entered matrimony without a dowry or marriage settlement. Nowadays these presents can take the form of a transfer of capital, the setting up of a trust for future offspring, or furniture, paintings or jewellery.

Presents from Friends

Other than actual wedding presents, there is no obligation for friends and associates to provide presents during an engagement. The American consumerist idea of a bridal shower, an informal party given by the bride's best friend (usually the chief bridesmaid), at which girlfriends are invited to 'shower' the bride with items for her new home, has only limited acceptability this side of the Atlantic.

PHOTOGRAPHS

It is usual to commemorate an engagement with portrait photographs of the happy couple. Those who do not commission a photographic record usually regret it later. These photographs ought not, except in particularly talented circumstances, to be snapshots done by friends or family, but should be undertaken by a professional photographer used to such work. Prints are sent to parents, immediate family and sometimes close friends.

CALLING OFF AN ENGAGEMENT

Rather than proceed with an ill-advised marriage, it is always best to call off an engagement, even if it means stopping the marriage machine at the eleventh hour. The procedure depends on the scale of the fanfare that greeted the engagement. For instance, if there was a public announcement in a newspaper, then it is sensible, although increasingly less usual, to publish a small cancellation notice in the same place. This is organised by the erstwhile bride-to-be's parents and would read:

> The marriage arranged between Mr Bertie Been and Miss Gloriana Gone will not take place.

Etiquette does not demand any explanation for breaking an engagement. It is traditional for the girl to announce a broken engagement, first to her family and then to friends. The boy normally tells his side. If the wedding invitations have already gone out, it is usual to send either a specially printed card announcing formally that the ceremony will not take place (see Chapter 8 for specimen wordings), or a short informal note to each guest. The latter model is time-consuming and distressing, and is probably best reserved for only family and closest associates.

It is then customary to return all gifts: those from family and friends and items exchanged by the couple. Although certain women conveniently choose to ignore convention, it is a serious breach of manners and good taste to hold on to the engagement ring. The only exception to this is when a man has ditched his future bride at the last minute or behaved in a particularly awful way, such as when a certain young man disappeared to Argentina two days before his marriage. His fiancée kept the ring, claiming it to be her 'long service medal'.

3

WEDDINGS

One of the great social contradictions of our time is that the less marriage remains the bedrock of society, the more time, money and attention we often lavish on the actual wedding ceremony itself. At one time, weddings, although important, were just one of life's rites of passage. Today they are a major event for most families, providing perhaps the biggest party and dress-up they will ever have.

Nowadays the church wedding, once merely a simple service with a small reception afterwards, is often a pageant, followed by an extravagant party or parties. Although few women can equal the New York bride who entered her wedding not just to a musical and choral accompaniment, but to flocks of live doves and simulated pink clouds, all brides strive to make their day 'special'. Even the civil ceremony, that most anodyne way of tying the knot, need no longer take place in an uninspiring register office; recent legislation allows a variety of locations, from schools to castles, to stage secular weddings of an elaborateness not available to previous generations.

As the modern wedding has grown, it has often also developed into a minefield for the socially insecure and become a logistical nightmare for the organisers. It can also, due to the complexities of the contemporary extended family, be a source of inter-family tension. In the following pages I shall explain that, with a little common sense and a good dose of organisation, these problems can be avoided, thus ensuring that a wedding day is indeed a happy one for all concerned.

THE LEGALITIES

Marriage is as much a legal arrangement as it is a personal one. In Britain the minimum legal age at which two people can marry is sixteen. However, teenagers under the age of eighteen must first receive written consent from parents or guardians before the marriage can take place. This stipulation is waived in Scotland: hence all the romantic associations with Gretna Green. All couples need a birth or adoption certificate and, if either side has been married before, a death certificate or divorce decree absolute.

Prohibitions to Marriage

The law governing who may marry whom is a very complex area, which has been made even more Byzantine by various recent fascinating, if mind-bending, relaxations in legislation.

Couples with close blood or adoptive ties are still prohibited from marrying. A man cannot marry his mother (adoptive mother or former adoptive mother), daughter (adoptive daughter or former adoptive daughter), father's mother, mother's mother, son's daughter, daughter's daughter, sister, father's sister, mother's sister, brother's daughter, sister's daughter. Likewise, a woman is prohibited from marrying her father (adoptive father or former adoptive father), son (adoptive son or former adoptive son), father's father, mother's father, son's son, daughter's son, brother, father's brother, mother's brother, brother's son, sister's son. All these prohibitions also pertain in the case of half-blood offspring and children born outside marriage.

When it comes to the Bloomsbury-like complexities of step-parent and stepchild relationships, various unions are allowed. If both parties have reached the age of twenty-one at the time of the marriage, and if the younger side has not at any time before the age of eighteen lived in the same household as the other party and been treated as a child of his or her family, then the following marriages are allowed: a man may marry a daughter of a former wife, former wife of father, former wife of father's father, former wife of mother's father, daughter of son of former wife, daughter of daughter of former wife; while a woman can plight her troth with a son of a former husband, former husband of mother, former husband of father's mother, former husband of mother's mother, son of son of former husband, son of daughter of former husband.

This liberalisation has also, somewhat bizarrely, spread to the rules governing in-law relationships. For instance, a man can marry the mother of his former wife and the former wife of his son, while a woman can wed the father of her former husband and the former husband of her daughter, if both parties have attained the age of twenty-one and providing (a) in the case of marriage between a man and the mother of his former wife, both the previous wife and her father are dead; (b) in the case of marriage between a man and the former wife of his son, both his son and the mother of his son are dead; (c) in the case of marriage between a woman and the father of her former husband, both the former husband and his mother are dead; (d) in the case of marriage between a woman and the former husband of her daughter, both her daughter and the father of her daughter are dead.

Other relationships in which marriage is now allowed include the following situations: a man can marry his wife's father's mother, wife's mother's mother, son's son's wife, daughter's son's wife. A woman may wed her husband's father's father, husband's mother's father, son's daughter's husband, daughter's daughter's husband. Likewise a man may marry the sister, aunt or niece of his former wife or the former wife of his brother, uncle or nephew.

Whether many of the now allowed unions described above are in good taste is highly debatable. There is one superannuated pop star whose ex-mother-in-law is set to be his new daughter-in-law. As many clergymen have deep reservations about solemnising such unions, no clergyman of the Church of England is obliged to officiate at any marriage under the terms I have outlined above. The reading of banns for such marriages is also deemed inappropriate. They require either a special ecclesiastical licence or a certificate issued to the superintendent registrar (providing the clergyman has first given his permission for such a marriage to be conducted in his church). This area remains deeply personal and often controversial, and each case can only be assessed on its merits at the discretion of the local vicar.

The constant liberalising of the marriage laws, however, has not spread to homosexual unions. Same-sex 'marriage' is acknowledged by neither state nor Church. Only couples of the opposite sex can marry, even if one of the partners has undergone a sex-change operation. This being said, there are increasing numbers of clergy who will unofficially bless gay unions. Again this is at the discretion of the local incumbent.

General Points

Marriage in Great Britain can appear labyrinthine in its legal complexities, but broadly speaking it can be divided between those ceremonies conducted under the auspices of the Church of England on one side; and all other procedures, including the remaining religious denominations and all civil ceremonies, on the other. This is because as the state church, the Church of England is officially authorised to marry people both ecclesiastically and legally, while everybody else needs the participation of the separate registrar of marriages. All churches, chapels, synagogues, temples and civil authorities have codes of eligibility and formal requirements that have to be addressed before the ceremony can be performed. These can involve residential stipulations, declarations of religious affiliation, public announcements and the need to produce licences, certificates and fees.

The law, with few exceptions, validates weddings that take place between eight a.m. and six p.m. only. This is to make sure that marriages happen in daylight, so that there can be no chance of the mistaken identity so prevalent in *bel canto* operas. Therefore, those who have set their sights on a Druid ceremony at Stonehenge on the stroke of midnight on the Summer Solstice will also have to attend a civil service at Salisbury Register Office to legalise their bond.

The only exceptions to this rule are Jewish, Quaker and Scottish ceremonies, which can take place any time, although Jews are forbidden to marry on the Sabbath (Friday sunset to Saturday sundown) and on their big holy days. Certain licences also override the eight-to-six rule.

Church of England

The Church of England, as the established Church, provides everybody with no living former partner the opportunity to marry. Traditionally the marriage takes place in the bride's church, but there are no firm rules about this. For instance, it is possible to be married in a parish other than the one in which you live if you are on the parish electoral roll and a regular worshipper in the one in which you want to be married. Complications can arise when couples choose to be married outside their parish for spurious reasons. The Church takes a dim view of those, often not regular churchgoers, who choose a different church because it will look prettier in the photographs.

Before taking place a marriage must either be announced by the reading of the banns in church, or be approved by a licence. The banns are read out in the churches of the prospective bride and groom on three Sundays (not necessarily successive) prior to the wedding. The wedding may take place on any day within three months of the final reading of the banns. If the couple wait longer than three months the banns must be reread.

A licence may be issued as an alternative only if it is not possible for the banns to be read. There are two types of licence, both of which last for three months:

COMMON LICENCE

This is issued by the bishop of the diocese (or one of his clergy) if a couple require a quick wedding, for example because of a sudden overseas posting, or a wish to avoid publicity. One party must have lived in the parish for at least fifteen days prior to the licence being applied for; it is usually given a day after application. A common licence may also be issued if the banns are not read through no fault of the couple. For example, one vicar had to pay for a couple to travel to London to receive a common licence because he forgot to announce their marriage in church; they were apparently delighted, as the licence is a distinguished-looking document.

SPECIAL LICENCE

This allows a couple to be married in a parish where neither party lives. It is issued by the Archbishop of Canterbury, and only in exceptional circumstances – for instance, if one of the party is ill and cannot move from hospital, or is in prison. A special licence allows the ceremony to take place at a building not registered for marriage in the Church of England, such as a private chapel or hospital, and at any time of the day.

If all else fails it is possible, but extremely rare, to be married within the Church of England using civil rather than religious preliminaries. This involves the granting of a superintendent registrar's certificate (see below) to authorise the marriage when, for some reason, the reading of the banns or issuing of a common licence is not possible, or a special licence has been refused. Circumstances must be exceptional for the Church to allow this. All the above criteria also apply to the Anglican Church in Wales.

Other Religious Ceremonies (England and Wales)

In all religions and denominations other than Anglican, such as Roman Catholic, Nonconformist, Jewish and Quaker, marriage is covered by the superintendent registrar's certificate, rather than by Anglican licence or reading of the banns. The certificate is issued by the civil register office before the marriage ceremony. The participation at the marriage ceremony of the registrar of marriages or someone authorised by him from the register office is also required if the ceremony is to be held at a registered church building of the particular faith. If any of these requirements are not met then the marriage needs to be validated at a separate, preferably preceding, civil ceremony.

The Church of Scotland

All religious marriages in Scotland, whether of the Church of Scotland (Presbyterian) or the Episcopal Church of Scotland (Anglican), or any other denomination, must be registered with the civil registrar. There are no residency requirements in Scotland; the couple must give notice at the register office in the district in which they wish to be married at least fifteen days before the ceremony. After fifteen days the registrar will issue a marriage schedule, which the couple must take to the minister who is to officiate at the religious ceremony. It is not necessary for the civil registrar to be present at the ceremony. At the wedding, the schedule must be signed by the officiating minister, the bride and groom, and two witnesses. The minister will then return it to the registrar within three days for the marriage to be officially registered.

Civil Marriages (England and Wales)

These may take place at the register office, or in any locations granted a licence under the new Marriage Act to hold weddings. Licences are granted by local authorities, and these buildings must be a permanent structure and deemed fit and suitable for the solemnising of the marriage rite. For details of approved places contact the proper officer of your local authority, or the registrar of marriages at your local register office.

Civil weddings are the only ones affected by the Marriage Act 1994, the most recent amendment to Britain's marriage laws. The act is in two parts. The first, which came into force on 1 January 1995, allows couples to marry at register offices or other authorised locations outside the district of their residence (i.e. in places where neither party is on the electoral roll). The second part concerns the new approved locations for marriage, mentioned above; it came into force on 1 April 1995.

A civil marriage, like those of non-Anglican religious denominations, requires a superintendent registrar's certificate. To obtain this certificate both parties must have lived in a registration district of England or Wales for at least seven days prior to giving notice at the register office. If they live in different districts, notice of marriage must be given at the register office in both their areas. Once the registrar has received notification, he displays a marriage notice in the register office for twenty-one days to ensure that there are no objections, after which he issues the certificate and the wedding may take place. As mentioned above, a couple do not have to marry at the register office where they gave notice.

If for some reason a couple cannot wait the expected twenty-one days to get married – for example, if one of them is to be posted overseas – they may apply for a superintendent registrar's certificate with licence (equivalent to the Anglican Church's common licence). This costs twice as much as a normal certificate but allows the couple to marry one clear day after giving notice, instead of waiting the standard time. It is also necessary for one partner to give notice, although this partner must spend at least fifteen days in the district where notice is given prior to applying for the certificate with licence.

In exceptional circumstances a couple may apply for a registrar's general licence (equivalent to the Anglican Church's special licence), which will allow the ceremony to take place in an unapproved place, such as a private home or hospital. There must be a good reason for this, for example, when someone is too ill to marry elsewhere and with little chance of recovery. All civil certificates and licences are valid for three months.

A civil ceremony may be followed by a religious service of prayer and dedication or blessing. This is often favoured by those who cannot marry in a church because a divorced partner is still living. It is meant as a religious 'acknowledgement' of a marriage, and is of a wholly different nature to a marriage proper. For example, the couple enter the church together (see Chapter 5).

Civil Marriages (Northern Ireland)
The law in Northern Ireland governing civil marriages is very similar to that of England and Wales. The major difference concerns the certificate with licence. To obtain this both partners must be resident in their respective districts for fifteen days prior to giving notice of marriage. (If both live in the same district one must have been resident there for fifteen days.) After notice is given the couple must wait seven days before being issued with the certificate with licence, rather than the one day permissible in England and Wales.

Civil Marriages (Scotland)
Notices of intent to marry must be made to the district registrar at the register office at least fifteen days before the wedding. There are no residency requirements. After fifteen days the registrar issues a schedule of marriage, which is held by him if the marriage is to take place at the register office (or given to the couple if it is to be taken to a religious ceremony). All civil ceremonies must take place at a register office and can be solemnised only by the registrar or an authorised assistant. Under certain circumstances the registrar may permit an exception to the fifteen-day rule, allowing the couple to marry soon after notice has been given. Such cases are rare, for instance when one partner is close to death.

Witnesses
All wedding ceremonies, civil or religious, have to be witnessed by at least two people over the age of eighteen (in Scotland over sixteen) and by either

the officiating Anglican clergyman, or, in the event of marriages conducted under the aegis of other religious denominations as well as all civil procedures, by an 'authorised' person. This can be the registrar, his deputy, or a minister nominated by the registrar. In the Church of England the witnesses do not even have to know how to write; they must merely be able to make a mark on the register. At Jewish weddings the two witnesses are normally members of the clergy, as it is felt that they have reached a certain standard of religious observance.

Marrying Abroad

Weddings in a foreign country need to fulfil both the legal requirements of this country and of the nation that will host the happy nuptials. There are many traps, and all couples must make sure they get proper information. It is therefore advisable to organise such an escapade through a travel agency that specialises in overseas wedding packages, and thus should be familiar with international legalities. Those couples doing it for themselves must consult the relevant consulates and embassies. Many British couples have a religious service of blessing when they return home.

Marrying a Foreigner

This can be a can of worms from a practical point of view, as the legalities of marriage abroad can vary enormously from our own. Questions of domicile, change of nationality, work permits, the position of spouses and children in the foreign national's country, the ramifications of divorce, and other complications need to be carefully – and unromantically – sorted out with a solicitor, as well as with the relevant consulate or embassy, prior to plighting the troth.

WEDDING ANNOUNCEMENTS

The procedure is similar to that involved in printing engagement announcements (see Chapter 2). For obvious reasons they always appear after the event. There are generally two types of announcement. The first is a very basic one which is put in the classified section of national and local newspapers. This allows a very restricted content that includes only the couple's names, the date and place of the wedding and sometimes the parents' names. The second is a much more elaborate proclamation which appears in the Court & Social pages of *The Times* or the *Daily Telegraph*. This can include every possible detail of the event, although nowadays it is unusual to include a description of the bride's dress. A typical entry could read:

Captain D. Dreadnought and Miss W. Wyngs

The marriage took place on Friday at the Guards Chapel, Wellington Barracks, of Captain David Dreadnought, Gulfstream Guards, son of Admiral of the Fleet Sir Denis and Lady Dreadnought, and Miss Wendy Wyngs, daughter of the late Squadron Leader Wilberforce Wyngs and Mrs Charles Civyllian and stepdaughter of Mr Charles Civyllian. The Bishop of Barchester officiated, assisted by the Rev. Peter Padre, Chaplain to the Household Division.

The bride, who was given away by Mr Willoughby Wyngs (brother), was attended by Miss Sarah School-Friend, Miss Catherine Cordon-Bleu, William and Wilhelmina Wyngs. Lieutenant Ffyfe-Fyddle-Drumme was best man, and a guard of honour was found by warrant officers of the Gulfstream Guards.

A reception was held at Whites and the honeymoon is being spent in Antarctica.

or, more simply:

The Hon. Charles Swagger and the Hon. Susan Swotte

The marriage took place quietly in London on Saturday between the Hon. Charles Swagger, sixth son of Lord and Lady Simpleton, and the Hon. Susan Swotte, only daughter of Viscount and Viscountess Venezuela.

THE PRACTICALITIES

Once the legal arrangements for a marriage have been sorted out, then it is time to organise the actual practicalities of the wedding. Virtually all weddings, ranging from a register office quickie to the state occasion of a Royal wedding, are divided into two distinct parts: the marriage ceremony itself (whether religious or civil) and the celebration afterwards. Thus bride, groom and their cohorts must carefully divide their thoughts, plans and arrangements between the two from day one of the preparations. It is also advisable to appoint the team of attendants – best man, bridesmaids etc. – as soon as possible.

Convention sensibly suggests that the bride and groom decide on what type of service they want, while the style of the reception is the prerogative of the bride's parents or whoever is hosting the reception. Although life is rarely as simple as that, this practical division of labour and responsibility will help to oil the troubled months that can often precede the big day.

Type of Wedding

The bride and groom must choose the type of wedding that best suits their circumstances, and thus decide whether a traditional church wedding is really appropriate. A religious service is only for couples who to a greater or lesser extent believe in and expect to uphold the Christian views on marriage. Those with no religious leanings should opt for a civil service, which can include the basic procedure of a register office, a more elaborate civil ceremony at a premises licensed for the purpose, or, for those who fancy something more unusual, a ceremony conducted under the aegis of the humanists.

The classic church wedding is also, technically, suitable really only for those marrying for the first time. When one or both parties have been married before, unless widowed, many churches will not provide the full marriage service. However, the Church does offer services of prayer and dedication or blessing, which can have a form very similar to a real wedding, but without actually performing the marriage ceremony. In these cases couples will need to have civil weddings (normally beforehand) as well to legalise their bond (see Chapters 4 and 5).

Although certain Mediterranean peasant cultures consider a pregnant bride to be sign of fecundity, big church weddings – particularly of the full-blown white variety – are positively ridiculous if the bride is very obviously pregnant. Therefore the appropriate scale of wedding is in inverse proportion to the size of the bride. Those couples who don't marry before the pregnancy becomes obvious must content themselves with a simple and small affair, attended by a few friends.

When to Marry

Although civil weddings happen throughout the year, church weddings have distinct high and low seasons. The most popular times vaguely coincide with the annual ebb and flow of the social season. Thus the spring months up until the end of July are popular as the weather tends to be good and people's outlook positive, and, from a purely practical point of view, there are plenty of flowers to decorate the church and fill bridal bouquets, Also, at these times, guests are less likely to be away on holiday. Things then go quiet until the autumn, when there is another flurry of marital celebration in the months leading up to Christmas. The Roman Catholic Church discourages marriage in Lent. The Church of England allows it, but there can be no flowers in the church, it being the season of penitence. However, bouquets may be carried by the bride and her attendants. Marriage on the Saturday before Easter Sunday is also strongly discouraged, and there is some residual superstition about marrying in May. Although many couples still have midweek ceremonies, Saturday, except for Jews, has become the most popular day, particularly for big bashes, as it causes less disruption to the working week and plenty of time to party.

The Time of Day

The time at which weddings take place is largely dependent on the type of reception that is intended to follow the ceremony. In earlier times weddings often took place in the morning – hence the term 'wedding breakfast', denoting the reception afterwards. This is much less usual today, but is still occasionally the form for those who want to have a dance in the evening and allow people time to change. The most usual time for morning weddings is eleven o'clock, although midday is sometimes chosen if the reception is to be a buffet lunch followed by a little dancing.

As weddings have become more elaborate, families have increasingly elected for afternoon affairs, to give the bride (and her mother) as long as possible to spend in the hairdresser's and on perfecting other facets of their appearance. There is one particularly vain and well-known mother-of-the-bride who asked to be woken at two thirty in the morning to allow her twelve uninterrupted hours of pampering so that she would arrive at the church in peak condition. Afternoon weddings also give plenty of time for flowers to be finished and food to be prepared, and mean that those who have to drive long distances do not have to endure an uncivilised early start. Half past two is currently still the most elegant time for a church wedding, although families who are giving a long evening reception that includes supper and dancing often prefer to start the ceremony later in the afternoon. Midweek weddings too are also often staged later rather than earlier, so that guests can stay in their offices longer.

THE RESPONSIBILITIES

Who does what and pays for what is a source of much confusion and conflict for those embarking on a wedding of any scale or expense. It is therefore vital to define the parameters of practical and financial responsibilities immediately a date has been set.

Responsibilities of the Bride

By right and ancient tradition, the bride is the focal point of a wedding, and many of her duties are devoted to making herself and her attendants look marvellous. She appoints her bridesmaids, pages and other attendants. She chooses her dress and the clothes of her attendants, her trousseau and her going-away outfit, as well as booking her hairdresser and beautician. She is also expected to discuss with the organist the music for the service, and to choose the flowers, although at a recent high-profile wedding this role fell to the groom, as the bride was in the Far East making lots of money to help defray the cost of her lavish nuptials.

Responsibilities of the Bridegroom

He appoints his best man and his ushers. He pays for the wedding ring, and all church expenses excluding the flowers and the music (organist, choir and any ancillary performers). He pays for the bride's bouquet, the brides-maids' bouquets, and buttonholes for himself, his best man and his ushers. He also gives presents to all attendants (bridesmaids and pages). In addi-tion, the bridegroom pays for the hire of his car (if necessary) to the church, and any going-away conveyance (if not using his own car). He also organises and pays for the honeymoon (usually). At one time he was also responsible for the entire provision of the happy couple's new home – including furniture, linen, glass and plate. This, thankfully, is no longer the case.

Joint Responsibilities of the Bride and Groom

They choose the church, plan the order of service with the clergyman, supply a list of their friends that they wish to attend the wedding. They also draw up the wedding list of preferred presents, open the accounts at their chosen shops and, if applicable, appoint a wedding list company.

Responsibility of the Bride's Parents

By tradition, they are the big players (and payers) at any wedding. Practi-cally all the responsibility for the preparation for, celebration of and funding of the proceedings is their remit. They place and pay for the public announcement in the press. They draw up, in collaboration with the bride and groom, and his parents, the invitation list. They compose the wording of the invitation, order the plate and engraving, and look after the postage. They pay for the printing of the service sheets, and for the flowers and music at the church, as well as any carpeting and awnings used. They also organise and stump up for all aspects of the reception: this includes food and drink, the wedding cake, the flowers, photographers, toastmaster and any musicians. They arrange and fund the transport of the bridal party to the church. They pay for the bride's dress, her going-away outfit and, in very old-fashioned households, her trousseau. At one time attendants used to pay for their own outfits, but nowadays the cost of clothes for bridesmaids and pages is usually borne by the bride's parents.

This being said, although this traditional structure is the most practical for well-off families, in less financially favoured clans it is now accepted that these expenses may be lightened by contributions from the bride and groom themselves, grandparents and other relations and, in some cases, the groom's family. This has become particularly prevalent in our multiple-marriage culture, in which an ever-obliging father could easily beggar himself celebrating his daughter's repeated attempts at nuptial bliss. Certainly no hard-up parents of the bride should feel in the slightest bit obliged to bankrupt themselves for the sake of providing an elaborate wedding for their daughter. Such lavish displays have always been, and remain, vulgar, sad and inappropriate. Families which allow society magazines to pay for their weddings in return for coverage of the event in its pages are also guilty of a lapse of taste, and indeed of pride.

Responsibilities of the Bridegroom's Parents

Traditionally they have few duties other than simply to supply a list of their preferred guests for the wedding, and to turn up on the day looking delighted and behave charmingly towards everybody. However, as the cost of weddings has escalated and many family fortunes have diminished, and with loss of face no longer quite the social solecism it once was, some parents of the groom do make a contribution to the proceedings. Such offers of financial and practical help are no longer considered bad form, but should be given only in circumstances where they will be really welcomed by the bride's father.

Responsibilities of Attendants

In addition to the main players in the pageant – the bride, groom and their respective families – there are other protagonists who are part of the traditional wedding. All should be chosen for their ability to work as a team.

THE BEST MAN

The best man is a very important figure and should be appointed as soon as possible, as he plays a major role in the arrangements – particularly those pertaining to the groom. He is usually a very close friend or relation of the groom, traditionally and most pleasingly (but not always) a bachelor, and should be highly organised and very well turned out. He should also be a good public speaker, as his speech should be one of the highlights of any wedding reception. Rather like being a godparent, to be asked to be a best man is an honour and a great compliment, and should be treated as such.

The best man should preferably be of the same religion in which the marriage is being celebrated, although adherence to this is less closely observed than previously. It is good manners for a groom to make sure that a man who is rejected from being the best man on religious (or other) grounds is invited to be an usher. Some couples, no doubt in the pursuit of novelty and political correctness, actually have 'best women' – I suppose a 'best person'. This conceit strikes me as positively ludicrous. The idea of choosing a former lover of the bride, or groom, is not advised, as it can lead to a little unseemly tension in the chancel.

The best man has to be the groom's eyes, ears and aide-de-camp. Although his main role is on the actual day of the wedding, when the groom will be too preoccupied to attend to practicalities, the best man has to be involved with preparations prior to the big day. It is very important that he keeps in touch with developments. He needs to know who is coming to the wedding, who is officiating, who the ushers and other attendants are, and to be involved with the planning of the arrangements.

All this information helps the best man with the main part of his responsibilities – actually looking after the groom and making sure he gets to the church on time, in a fit state. Prior to the wedding he has to organise the groom's stag night – or more likely weekend or even week – when the groom and his close male friends gather to celebrate the last few days of freedom with various manifestations of male bonding. The type of party should be entirely in the style of the groom. It does not need to be the Rabelaisian affair of popular imagination, and can be a civilised dinner or a sojourn in the country. Bachelor parties are paid for by the guests, who all go Dutch and pay a set price that also covers the bridegroom's expenses for the evening.

In time for the wedding, the best man has to make sure that every aspect of the groom's appearance has been planned – clothes, haircut and general grooming – and that he will look immaculate on the day. It is most important that all vestiges of polish are removed from the groom's shoes, unless he is to risk marking the bride's dress. The best man also needs to make sure that the groom's packing includes everything he might need, as the wedding is most likely to take place away, at the bride's parents' home. Well-organised best men always write checklists of these items. In addition he has the dubious pleasure of looking after the wedding ring until it is handed over to the groom at the altar. Along the way he has to prepare the best man's speech, which should be well practised, not too long, amusing, but absolutely not smutty. The speech is an opportunity to introduce and give some background on the groom to the bride's side, who may not know him at all. A certain best man charmed all with his delightfully amusing speech that he had composed entirely in rhyme.

Immediately before the wedding, he has to dragoon the ushers, provide them with a seating plan for the family pews, and make sure that the service sheets have arrived. He should also have worked out with the bride's parents and toastmaster the timings of speeches, cake cuttings, departures and other social landmarks of the reception.

His Performance on the Day

He lays out the groom's clothes for the wedding ceremony, and makes sure that his going-away suit is at the place of the reception for the groom to change into. The best man is also responsible for making sure that the bride and groom's honeymoon things are ready – their luggage, tickets, passports, money and sometimes transport to the airport. He collects button-holes or checks they will be at the church, ensures church fees are paid and, in the case of an afternoon wedding, organises and attends, with the groom, a lunch given for the ushers. He calms the bridegroom's nerves, gives him a good lunch (if not lunching with the ushers) and drives him to church. It is customary for the groom and the best man to enter by a side door and not the west door that will see the entry of the bride. He then waits with the groom until the arrival of the bride, when both men move up the chancel steps, where he stands on the groom's right-hand side, while having a final check that he has the wedding ring. Thereafter he has not much of a role in the actual service, other than handing over the ring at the right time and accompanying the chief bridesmaid to the vestry for the signing of the register. At the end of the ceremony he sees the happy couple into their car. He of course appears beaming in all the photographs.

His Role at the Reception

This is largely determined by whether a toastmaster has been engaged. If not, he will be responsible for helping the bride's parents keep everything on track, announcing the cutting of the cake and introducing the speakers. He makes his speech after the groom, thanking him on behalf of the bridesmaids for his toast to them. His final duty is to see the married couple off on their honeymoon and their new life together.

USHERS

Ushers are the best man's regiment, and like the best military campaigns they need to be well organised and smartly turned out. They play an important role in the wedding ceremony by welcoming guests to the church, handing out service sheets and accompanying family and important guests (particularly the bride's mother) to their seats. Although the standard measure is one usher per fifty guests, rather like caterers' estimates of wine it is inadequate. In reality you can't have too many. Usually they are young male friends of both families. It is good to have plenty from the bride's side as well as the groom's to help identify the important players in her family. Girl ushers, although sometimes found, give the church the feeling of a cinema.

On the day, ushers direct the family and guests of the bride to the left-hand side seats and the groom's clan and invitees to the right-hand side. Family (and sometimes particularly close friends and visitors from abroad) always have specially designated places in the front pews. Otherwise there is little protocol, although at very grand and large weddings, where there might be important guests and royalty, their names are tabulated on to cards and given to the ushers. Alternatively front pews are marked off with a red cord extending across the aisle. Good manners expect past lovers literally to take a back seat. Well-mannered ushers always escort unaccompanied women to their pews. After the ceremony they help organise transport (usually rather a performance) for the guests from the church to the reception.

BRIDESMAIDS
Bridesmaids have been around since pagan times, when evil spirits were thought to attend wedding ceremonies. It was felt that by surrounding the bride with similarly dressed attendants of her own age it would be impossible for the malevolent vapours to single her out. Even today bridesmaids, particularly if numerous and on the large side, can give the impression of an armed escort. Therefore when choosing bridesmaids, except for weddings of positively regal proportions, it is a mistake to have more than eight. They are chosen from the bride's friends and near relatives. If the groom has a sister or near relation then it is well mannered and kind to include her. Bridesmaids are always unmarried, although there is nothing to prevent the inclusion of a married woman, who is then known by the stodgy and somewhat unflattering name of 'Matron of Honour'. A typical retinue could include a chief bridesmaid, who should be the same age as the bride and fulfils the equivalent role of the best man. She waits in the back of the church for the bride to arrive, and checks her appearance, particularly the train and the veil, which will make the bride look drunk or mad if it's crooked. She also tries to keep any child attendants in order. During the actual wedding service she looks after the bride's bouquet and gives it back

to her for the recessional. The chief bridesmaid can be supplemented by between two and four other bridesmaids. In addition there can be some child attendants – pages and miniature bridesmaids or flower girls. These seem to be the *sine qua non* of the fashionable wedding procession. Numbers can range from two to six, although to have too many is to court disaster. It is essential to ask permission from the parents first, before approaching the children. Candidates are again chosen from relatives and close friends, but overexcitable or timid tinies are best avoided. For purely aesthetic reasons pretty children are thought preferable to plain ones, and, as they are often required to work as double acts (carrying the bride's train or proceeding side by side), they should be of similar heights. Attendants wear outfits of a design decided entirely by the bride and must follow her wishes implicitly. Pages at military weddings often wear miniature period military uniforms. Bridesmaids, but not pages, carry bouquets, posies or flower baskets provided by the groom, and are always given small extra presents by the groom. This is another ancient custom, surviving from the days when the groom had to catch his bride; rather than actually chasing her over hill and dale, he used to bribe her girlfriends to lure her to a place where he could easily stalk her.

THE CHOICE OF CHURCH
It is usual for the bride and bridegroom to choose where they wish their wedding to take place, and to organise the reading of banns or drawing up of licences. The couple must ask the clergyman if he would be happy to marry them, rather than just assuming he is some local resource. They should also seek his consent if they would like another clergyman to officiate at the service (such as a friend or relative in Holy Orders, or, for those keen on episcopal splendour, a bishop). It is bad manners to approach another member of clergy before consulting with the resident incumbent. On the day, the two generally conduct the service together, with the visiting cleric being responsible for the actual marriage section, an address and sometimes even the blessing. Fees are paid to the parish clergyman, not to the visitor, but it is usual to give him a small present of a permanent nature, such as a piece of silver, a book or a picture.

RELIGIOUS DIFFERENCES
Although the days when young people married largely within their own religions have long gone, the problems caused by unions of different religions have not. Good manners and convention say that the groom must chivalrously acquiesce to the bride's wish – as by tradition the wedding day

belongs to her. However, life is never as simple as that. For instance, should one side be Roman Catholic, the Roman Catholic Church still expects the marriage to take place in a Catholic church, regardless of the bride's denomination.

The modern approach is for neither party to assume that their religion is more important than the other side's. This is vital, both for the happy resolution of the immediate problems over the wedding ceremony, and, more importantly, for the long-term good of the marriage. All protagonists must take a step back and create a solution that best suits all views; remember that the wedding is just the beginning of a married life where religious differences will play a role. Some couples eschew any spiritual components by having a civil ceremony. Others compromise, such as the young Anglican bride who married a Jewish man at a register office, immediately after taking Holy Communion with her family and her friends at a church across the road. Another couple, one Hindu, the other Christian, had two ceremonies on different days; Indian family and friends predominated at the Hindu service, and British guests at the Anglican rite. A more ingenious theological compromise was made for the union of a Roman Catholic groom and a Brazilian Evangelical Baptist bride. They were married in the Church of England, which they felt provided an acceptable middle ground between their distant denominations. Another approach is to assess the degrees of piety on each side. For instance, if religion is very important to one family, their wishes should predominate.

It is also most important to sort out the religion of future offspring at the time of the wedding, as certain churches – e.g. the Roman Catholic and the Jewish faith – are more indulgent about mixed marriages providing they will be able to claim the children. Roman Catholic canon law concerning marriage 'gives permission for mixed marriages to take place' providing 'the Catholic party undertakes to do all in his/her power within the unity of the marriage to have all the children to be born of the marriage baptised and brought up in the Catholic faith, and the non-Catholic party must be made aware of this undertaking.' Likewise, the Jewish community, while disapproving of its members marrying outside the faith, believes its faith to be passed through the mother and thus will more readily accept a gentile husband, so long as his young are brought up as Jews.

MARRIAGE IN THE CHURCH OF ENGLAND

Despite the fragility of marriage in modern society, the Church of England still considers it as a life-long commitment. It expects couples to prepare carefully for their new life. Clergymen arrange to meet in person those whom they wish to marry to discuss marriage, and some very committed clerics invite engaged couples to join special marriage preparation courses, although as these are often in groups, many people are reluctant to join.

The priest will also help with decisions about whether to use the traditional words of the Book of Common Prayer. Dating from 1662, this is considered a rather grand choice, but its lovely and evocative but archaic language is often unacceptable to the modern bride, as it contains the famous 'obey' vow. The second choice is the Revised Version, which was updated in 1928 and, although it is based on the original Restoration format, has language more suited to contemporary times, omitting the contentious vow. The third choice is quite different. Started in the early eighties, it was radically altered by a Church tinged with modernising fever. It reverses the order of reasons for marriage, placing the procreation one third not first. Needless to say, the 'obey' vow (balanced with a 'worship' one from the groom) is optional, and there are liturgical variations for the bride and groom to choose from.

The clergyman will also help you select your readings, hymns and other musical aspects of the service, such as the processional, recessional and anthems. He will ask whether you want the service to include your first communion together as husband and wife, any bell-ringing, floral decorations (often restricted during certain Church festivals), the option of a choir (in my opinion essential) and of course the date of the wedding. He will explain the banns and fees system and ask the bride and groom to fill in the relevant forms. He will also express his views on photographs taken within the church and video or tape recordings of the service, as well as saying whether he will tolerate non-religious music as part of the proceedings. Although it is possible to add a few personal touches to the service, most clergy – quite rightly – take a dim view of those who try and alter it significantly.

Nearer the time of the wedding he will arrange a rehearsal so that all protagonists know exactly what to do and when. He will also have views on confetti. Most resent the mess caused by the paper stuff and might allow biodegradable substitutes such as rose petals or rice. Many, quite correctly, consider the paper variety vulgar.

The Order of Service
Certain clergymen like to perform the actual marriage ceremony very early in the service before any hymns have been sung. Others sensibly allow a hymn between the processional music and the start of the marriage rite. The clergyman then asks if there is 'cause or just impediment' to the couple

being brought together in Holy Matrimony and invites any who agree to come forward. It is not usual to respond to this request, however, whatever your feelings. It is most important that any mobile telephones and watch alarms are switched off at this time. The priest then asks: 'Who giveth this woman to be married to this man?' At this stage the bride's father, or whoever is giving her away, takes the bride's right hand and passes it to the cleric. It is most important that this little gesture is done silently and that there is no chirping up 'I do'. The minister passes on the bride's hand to the groom and then takes the couple through their vows. These should be spoken clearly and slowly. At the same time the best man either puts the ring(s) on the clergyman's prayer book or gives them directly to the groom. He and the bride's father then return to their pews. The bride and groom follow the minister to the altar for prayers followed by hymns and finally the blessing. This concludes the religious part of the service, after which the clergyman leads the newlyweds into the vestry with the witnesses for the signing of the register. While this is going on the congregation is treated to a musical interlude. When the paperwork is done, the beaming bridal party emerge from the vestry to joyful strains, recess down the aisle and leave the church. The most usual order of procession is: bride and groom with attendants, bride's mother accompanied by groom's father, groom's mother with bride's father, with the chief bridesmaid and the best man bringing up the rear.

Wedding Rehearsals

Wedding rehearsals take place in mufti with the officiating clergy and all the bridal party a few days before the wedding, or the evening before if everyone is travelling long distances. The rehearsal is absolutely essential, particularly for elaborate weddings (when more than one run-through may be needed), and is recommended for all nuptials. Brides, especially those with an underdeveloped sense of rhythm, should also obtain a recording of the processional and recessional music to practise walking to at home.

Other Roles on the Day

It is most important that the wedding party should arrive promptly at the church. First to arrive are ushers, who should be at the church around forty-five minutes before the service begins. This is to take care of any last-minute arrangements and to keep things moving as guests enter the church. The groom and best man are the next to arrive (around half an hour before the start). Then come the bridal attendants, followed by the bride's mother, who always makes a kind of mini-entrance shortly before the service begins. The bride and her father are the last to arrive. Although there is endless speculation as to how long the bride can keep the congregation waiting, traditionally the answer is no time at all. However, a few minutes are now acceptable, but anything longer is tense-making and rude.

Usually a girl's father gives her away, although there is no hard and fast rule about this. If the bride's father is dead (or living, but on bad terms with his daughter), then the 'father' role can be split between two others, such as a favourite uncle escorting the bride up the aisle, while her mother waits to give her away. After a bride's father, her mother is the most appropriate person to give her daughter to a future husband, although to ask a mother to escort the bride up the aisle is not done. In the absence of a mother, a male relation can perform the entire escorting and giving away function. This is the usual form for orphaned brides and for those who have completely fallen out with their parents. Problems can also arise if a bride is closer to a stepfather than to her natural father, and thus would prefer the former to fulfil the 'father' role in the service. This is a difficult situation in which compromise is always preferable to confrontation. To this end, some brides split the role, by inviting the stepfather to take part in the service and allowing the natural one to witness the wedding in the register. This is often an imperfect solution. A more sensible one is to allow the service to be the remit of the natural father and provide a major role for the stepfather at the reception, by making the first speech and toasting the bride and groom.

On arrival the bride's mother, accompanied by any of her family who are not in the bridal procession, is conducted to her pew (the front left) by the chief usher. The groom's side are similarly taken to the front right pew, and should be in their seats prior to the arrival of the bride's mother. Immediately the bridal party arrives, the groom is told, whereupon he murmurs a sigh of relief and moves to the chancel steps. Directly the organist strikes up the processional music, the congregation stands and the bridal party moves up the aisle, with the veiled bride to the right of her father in the lead and the attendants following in pairs, carrying the bridal train if applicable. At this stage it is most important that the bride and father do not hurry up the aisle and that the bride adopts an ethereal quality and refrains from beaming at the congregation.

When they reach the chancel steps, the groom stands on the right of the bride, with the best man taking up a position to the right of and slightly behind the groom. The father (or whoever is giving the bride away) stands on her left, while the bridesmaids and pages settle behind the bride and groom.

Although policies vary from church to church, in most wedding services nowadays the clergyman either waits for the bridal party on the chancel steps or precedes the bride with the choir.

The bride then hands over her bouquet and gloves (if worn) to the chief bridesmaid, who will give them back to her later in the vestry after the register has been signed. Some brides, with the help of the chief brides-maid, lift their veil at this early juncture, although it is customary to lift the veil at the last possible moment after the actual marriage ceremony. In the absence of a chief bridesmaid, the bride has to grapple with her own veil and her flowers are handed to her father, who then passes them on to the bride's mother for safe keeping. The service then begins. As the wedding ring is worn on the finger which up until the wedding has carried the engagement ring, the bride removes the latter when she is dressing that morning and pushes it on to the third finger of the right hand. She puts it back again after the ceremony.

The Signing of the Register

This concludes the wedding ceremony and is necessary to legalise the bond. The bridegroom offers his left arm to the bride and escorts her to the vestry. They are accompanied by her parents, his parents, the best man and the chief bridesmaid. It is usual for only natural or adoptive parents to act as witnesses. Step-parents are rarely invited to be witnesses. Five signatures are needed: the officiant, two witnesses – normally one parent from each side (although any adult is allowed) – the bridegroom, and the bride, who always uses her maiden name. While all this is going on, the congregation are treated to a recital of music from the organist, choir, or an instrumental or vocal soloist.

On leaving the church, the bridal party is photographed and the congregation gather around them. Bells are optional, but highly recommended. The best man then helps the bride and groom into their car, and the rest of the bridal party follows swiftly. It is customary for the congregation not to leave until the bridal party have gone. This is to allow the newlyweds time to get to the reception to welcome their guests.

Music

Music is a fundamental component of any wedding and should be celebratory, happy and moving. The clergyman, choirmaster, organist and any musical friends of the couple will be happy to help with the selection, which should be a perfectly balanced mixture of the impressive and the devotional. Of great importance is the technical standard of the organist and choir, and all music must be discussed carefully with the performers before a choice is made. A congregation will be reduced to giggles by an enthusiastic but hopelessly inept musician attempting pieces far beyond his or her technique. Many couples, dubious of a resident organist and choir's capabilities, like to import their own performers. Such moves can cause great offence and need to be handled with diplomacy, although with church organists and choirs increasingly thin on the ground, this is not the problem it once was.

The choice of music for a wedding is personal, but do not reject the old favourites, such as the wedding music from Wagner's *Lohengrin* or Mendelssohn's wedding march, just because you hear them at other people's weddings – these musical chestnuts endure for good reason. On the other hand, it is nice to include personal choices, such as a favourite hymn. But do not be seduced into introducing unusual musical elements into the service just for the sake of novelty. Many couples feel that by importing string quartets, gospel singers or, in one case, a sitar player, they are improving the quality of their wedding. This is quite often not the case.

Soft but anticipatory strains are required as the congregation assembles. These should suddenly give way to something more celebratory as the bride enters the church and proceeds up the aisle. Favourite choices include 'The Arrival of The Queen of Sheba' by Handel, or trumpet voluntaries by Purcell, Charpentier or Jeremiah Clarke. Always make certain that the organist is absolutely sure what he is supposed to play. One hapless bride who had asked an aged organist to play the theme tune from Kevin Costner's *Robin Hood Prince of Thieves* found herself, to the hilarity of the entire congregation, galloping down the aisle to the jaunty strains of 'Robin Hood, Robin Hood, riding through the glen . . .' There can be up to four hymns, which should be rousing old favourites that everybody can join in with, such as 'Jerusalem'. If you intend to include a psalm, which should be more thoughtful in tempo and character, three hymns are enough. During the signing of the register, there should be a musical interlude that can feature a soloist. Suggestions include 'Zadok the Priest' by Handel, preferably with trumpets in the organ loft; 'Let the Bright Seraphim', also by Handel; Parry's 'I Was Glad' (this is sometimes affectionately referred to as 'I Went Mad'); 'Laudate Dominum' by Mozart; or *Blessed be the God and Father* by S. S. Wesley, which contains a lovely soprano solo entitled 'Love One Another With a Pure Heart Fervently'. And lastly the musical climax should be gloriously triumphant as the bride and groom turn to face their congregation and walk down the aisle and out of the church. The best-loved numbers are: the ubiquitous 'Toccata' by Widor; *Crown Imperial* by Walton; and Elgar's *Pomp and Circumstance* marches 1 and 4 and *Imperial March*. It is very important that the organist continues to play until all the congregation have left the church. Bells, if rung, start immediately the bride steps outside the church.

Service Sheets

Service sheets are a guide to the wedding ceremony, and should be printed as soon as the order of service has been decided with the clergyman. Traditionally they are in folded white or cream card that matches the invitation in style, colour and size, although it is usual for them to be printed on a somewhat lighter weight of card. On the front the Christian names or initials of the bride and groom are printed, together with the name of the church and the date of the wedding. Service sheets can vary from simple folded pieces of card with a classic black typeface listing the proceedings to ostentatious booklets bristling with coloured covers and beribboned bindings which contain the entire service in full. As with most things, the simpler option is invariably the smarter one.

Flowers

A similarly restrained attitude to flowers should, but rarely does, apply. Ambitious mothers employ the currently most fashionable florist to festoon the church in and out with vast massed arrangements, fairy bowers and swagged and garlanded arches dripping with every floral confection known – and unknown – to nature, forgetting that a church is a holy place and not the ballroom of a West End hotel. The most important thing to remember is that most churches and cathedrals are beautiful places in themselves and thus any floral decorations should merely enhance the backdrop for the joyous occasion. It is bad manners to start planning and ordering flowers without first consulting the priest, who might have firm ideas himself and will definitely have good advice about his church's architectural quirks and the way the light falls at different times of the day. Some churches will not allow outside florists. Incumbents of very popular churches, who may have more than one wedding happening in a day, will also have devised a squabble-saving policy about flowers, such as brides sharing flowers and arrangers and with it the cost. Flowers can be placed wherever they look good, but the floral focal points are the altar and chancel steps. Remember to place arrangements at head height and above so that they can be seen when everyone is sitting. White and fragrant blooms remain the most popular and appropriate choice.

Photography in Church

We live in an age of photographic fever, when every little human act seems to require instant *reportage*. This approach has now infected weddings, with families ordering a photographic (and sometime video) documentary of the happy day from the moment the bride opens her eyes. However, many churches do not allow photographs in church, and the vicar's consent must be asked before ordering a photographer. If he agrees, then the pictures must be taken as unobtrusively as possible. Flash bulbs are rudely distracting.

Video Cameras

Not content with merely still shots, many couples now like to video their weddings for posterity. In principle, there is no harm in this, unless the actual real point of the service is subjugated in the interest of production values. I know of one instance when the happy couple walked down the aisle twice to ensure the perfect take. This kind of behaviour is in the worst possible taste and debases the whole meaning of the ceremony. Those who wish to video their wedding must first seek the permission of the minister. If consent is refused then it is extremely bad manners to try and smuggle a video camera into the church, as one man did recently in his sleeve. If the priest does agree, good manners expect the filming to be as discreet as possible. Make sure that the cameraman wears morning dress so that he blends in with the rest of the congregation. A certain incumbent of a fashionable church allows videoing, but only from one discreet and secluded spot. Should the cameraman stray from this pre-ordained spot, the organist is under strict instructions to stop playing.

If a clergyman forbids filming, he may allow a compromise solution of having the proceedings sound-recorded and later used in a video (or even CD-ROM programme) that combines the soundtrack of the wedding with a montage of photographic stills and views of the outside of the church and surrounding countryside.

MARRIAGE IN THE ROMAN CATHOLIC CHURCH

Roman Catholic ceremonies tend to be much more elaborate affairs than Anglican rites. This is possibly because the Roman Catholic Church still takes a comparatively rigorous attitude to marriage. A Roman Catholic priest will often insist on between two and six months' notice, so that he can instruct the soon-to-be-married couple about the sanctity of marriage etc. He will also wish to see copies of baptism and confirmation certificates so that he can do his paperwork. As with Anglican weddings, it is usual for the couple to marry in their local church, although special permission can be obtained from the Roman Catholic authorities to marry at another church – such as a private chapel. The actual service does not differ fundamentally from the C of E, other than the fact that it is much more elaborate, if there is to be a nuptial mass. The church currently offers two rites – the Rite of Marriage During Mass and the Rite of Marriage Outside Mass. The former is usual when both parties are Catholics and offers communion to the bride, groom and much of the congregation, although non-Catholics are not expected to go up. The service is long, but solemn and very beautiful. The vows form part of the mass and are inserted into the liturgy after readings from the Scriptures. These weddings are normally graced by lovely music: one leading Roman Catholic family had Mozart's *Coronation Mass* throughout their service at Arundel Cathedral. The Marriage Outside Mass tends to be used when one of the parties is a non-Catholic and when, for whatever reasons, it is desirous to have a shorter ceremony. The marriage vows in a Roman Catholic service are longer than in the Anglican rite, as all names including surnames are used. Also, remember when kneeling in a Roman Catholic church to do it with a straight back and not the Anglican, bottoms-on-pews way.

QUAKER WEDDINGS

Quaker or Society of Friends weddings, like Jewish marriage rites, may take place at any time, but for a wedding to happen, both parties must be members of the Society of Friends, or at least sympathetic to it. They must indicate this in writing to the superintendent registrar when giving notice of marriage. Anyone not in this category may be married under Friends' usage only if the superintendent registrar is supplied with a certificate signed by the local registering officer of the Society of Friends. In addition, the couple must apply to the local registering officer of the society for the marriage to be solemnised. Any non-members need to obtain letters of support from two adult Friends – without these the registering officer will not condone the marriage.

A Quaker wedding takes the same quiet and simple form as regular Quaker worship meetings. Wedding rings play no formal part in the proceedings. There is no music, dressing-up or fuss, and a great deal of silence. Everyone present at the wedding is invited to sign the special Quaker marriage certificate, which is read aloud by the local registering officer of the Society of Friends. The couple and their witnesses must also sign the civil marriage certificate after the service.

JEWISH WEDDINGS

Jewish weddings are very like any other weddings, but often more elaborate. They usually take place on a Sunday, occasionally midweek, but never, ever on a Saturday and rarely on Fridays in Britain. The actual ceremony will vary slightly depending on the denomination (i.e. Orthodox, Reform or Liberal). Apart from the ultra-religious Orthodox rituals, they bear a lesser or greater resemblance to Church of England services when it comes to general atmosphere and procedure, although the music and liturgy are quite different.

Although most British Jewish weddings take place in synagogues, this is not actually required by Jewish law and tradition, which demands only a *chupa* (this is pronounced with a soft 'ch', as in 'lochs'). This is a canopy beneath which the bride and groom stand for the marriage service. Somewhat confusingly, the ceremony itself is also referred to as a *chupa*. In Jewish communities where the climate is kinder, this canopy is often erected outside. Obviously British weather makes this a risk, and it is usual to find the *chupa* in a synagogue, or the banqueting rooms or ballroom of a big hotel.

If the marriage takes place in an Orthodox synagogue, men and women sit separately. At Reform and Liberal ceremonies the sexes are seated together. Unlike many Church of England weddings, Jewish ones begin on time, so it is polite to be seated at least five minutes before the time stated on the invitation. The service normally lasts between twenty and forty minutes. Because it never takes place on the Jewish Sabbath, there are no proscriptions about driving, so cars can be parked visibly.

At Jewish weddings there is often beautiful music. The minister, with or without a choir, will sing one or more of the traditional Hebrew psalms while the groom, together with his father and the best man, waits beneath the *chupa*. The bride is accompanied up the aisle by her father, followed by her mother, the groom's parents and any bridesmaids, page boys, etc. The minister will then recite a brief blessing in Hebrew, followed by an address to the couple. He will then recite two further blessings, after which the bride and groom will be given a sip of wine from a silver cup. The groom places a wedding ring on the fourth finger of the bride's right hand and recites a blessing which is thousands of years old: 'Behold thou art consecrated unto me by this ring, according to the Law of Moses and of Israel.' The minister then recites the *Shevah Berachot*, or seven blessings of God, and the groom treads on a glass covered by a cloth. Although some of the congregants may utter '*Mazeltov*' at the sound of the breaking glass, it is actually incorrect. The glass is meant to symbolise the destruction of the Jews' temple in Jerusalem, and signifies the remembrance of sadness at a time of joy. Thus silence is actually the most appropriate response. The minister will also read out the Jewish marriage contract, or *ketubah*, in Aramaic – another ancient Jewish language – with a brief translation of the major points – names, places and dates of birth and ceremony – into English. The bride and groom will also sign their civil marriage certificate. The ceremony ends with photographs on the steps of the synagogue.

Dress

Don't expect ethnic dress at a Jewish wedding. Usually the bride wears the traditional English white gown, head-dress and veil. The groom will normally wear morning dress, or a dinner jacket for a late afternoon or evening wedding. At very Orthodox weddings, the bride's dress might be particularly modest, with a high neckline and long sleeves.

GUESTS

Women guests at Orthodox synagogue weddings should cover their shoulders and arms. At Reform and Liberal ceremonies it is more acceptable to wear a strappy or sleeveless gown intended for the reception to follow, but it is decorous to cover the shoulders for the duration of the religious proceedings. The conventions on hats and head coverings can be confusing. Traditionally all women's heads should be covered, but in practice the rule is rarely enforced, with a lot of Jewish women turning up bare-headed. Jewish weddings, like all nuptial events, take their sartorial tone from the type of wedding, the time of day and the sensibilities of the family. However, if in doubt, it is never incorrect to wear a hat.

Men, on the other hand, must always cover their heads in the synagogue. They can wear either a hat or a skullcap (*kippah* or *yarmulke*), which can be bought in advance or borrowed at the synagogue before the ceremony. Any other hat is also acceptable, providing it covers the crown.

As a rule of thumb the dress at a Jewish wedding is also dictated by the type of party which follows the ceremony. Traditionally in the Anglo-Jewish community this will be a formal dinner with dancing, so the invitation will state black tie. In this case, despite the ceremony taking place in the afternoon, dress will be cocktail, dinner or evening dresses for women and dinner jackets for men. The scale of the women's dress is dictated by the lavishness of the proceedings, so a few enquiries will probably be necessary.

However, sometimes the ceremony takes place earlier in the day and is followed by a formal lunch or afternoon reception. In this case women should wear afternoon clothes, such as a suit or a dress and jacket, with a pretty hat that can be worn for both ceremony and reception. Men wear lounge suits.

The Reception

Jewish wedding receptions can be spectacular events, although the trend in recent years has been towards more understated gatherings. At most, as well as the usual bridal-type speeches, grace will be intoned before and after the meal, when male guests will be expected to cover their heads. At very Orthodox weddings, there will be separate dancing, and perhaps separate seating at dinner. Even at relatively secular receptions, there may be Israeli-type *horah* dancing, where women and men dance in separate circles. You can either join in, or just clap enthusiastically.

The Wedding Present
Most Jewish couples have wedding lists nowadays, and the usual criteria apply. However, cards and wrappings with Christian imagery such as wedding bells, crosses and church spires are to be avoided, as many Jews, particularly very religious ones, will find such oversights offensive and insensitive. Confetti is never thrown at Jewish weddings.

Thank-you letters, while remaining a solecism after C of E weddings, are more acceptable. A bunch of flowers with a note seems to be particularly appreciated.

GREEK ORTHODOX WEDDINGS
Greek Orthodoxy has become increasingly popular in recent years, with many people with no Greek heritage converting to the faith. The ceremony is very beautiful, but there is little participation from the congregation, which is left standing for long periods.

The weddings normally take place in the afternoon. It is usual for the groom to await his bride at the door. The bridal couple are then led to the *soleas* – an area in front of the altar – where by tradition the service takes place. Here there is also the *soleas* table, on which are placed a Bible, a dish of sugared almonds, a tray holding wedding rings for him and her, and most romantic – and idiosyncratic – of all, a pair of ceremonial crowns. This scene is enhanced by children holding decorated wedding candles to augur brightness and to let the happy couple's previous sins melt with the wax.

The ceremony begins with the Service of the Rings, in which the priest blesses the rings and places them on the couple's hands. Then the best man and the groom's other supporters swap the rings around three or four times, making sure that the correct ring ends up on its proper hand. Next the Service of the Crowns begins, during which the priest holds the crowns above the heads of the bride and groom. He does this with his arms crossed, and makes three blessings, uncrossing and recrossing his arms after each intonation. The crowns symbolise the glory the Church bestows on the marriage and that the happy couple will indeed be king and queen of their own home. This little ritual is then repeated by the best man, who stands

51

behind the bridal couple exchanging their crowns in between blessings. This is followed by prayers, lessons and the blessing of the Common Cup, from which the couple must drink three times. The bridal couple are then led around the table three times by the priest, while he chants the Hymn of St John Damaskinos. The sacrament is then complete.

The ceremony over, relations gather round the newly-marrieds to offer their congratulations and to kiss the Bible and the crowns. There is no need for the ordinary guest to get involved with this.

Afterwards there are always great festivities, usually a reception and dance at which the bride and groom perform the traditional wedding dance and the sugared almonds are handed around to the unmarried women to ensure that they too will soon find a groom. Legend has it that if a girl puts the sweetmeat under her pillow, she will indeed dream of her intended.

Couples have to fulfil civil requirements too. In some cases it is possible to sign the register at the church after the ceremony, but most people have a register office wedding shortly before the church one.

SECULAR WEDDINGS
Register Office Weddings

The form of these is suitably short, sharp and secular. Bride and groom, in front of the registrar and in the presence of two witnesses, declare that they are free to marry and wish to take each other as husband and wife. Thus the legal contract is made and the registrar pronounces the couple man and wife. The service only takes about ten minutes and it is not even necessary for the groom to slip a ring on to his bride's finger, although rings can be included in the brief proceedings at the discretion of the registrar.

It is not sensible to be late for a register office wedding, unless the couple concerned want to miss their spot. Nor is it advisable to have more than the minimum number of guests, as there is usually little room available. It must be remembered that register office weddings are a private business and thus not to be confused with the public and social significance of big church weddings. It is also an utterly secular service and thus any attempts to mimic the trappings of a church wedding – white dresses, bridesmaids and top hats – are in poor taste. The bride may carry a small bouquet and the groom wear a buttonhole, but that is all. A kind of understated chic should be the watchword at all times.

Depending on the time of day, it is usual to have a small celebration afterwards, such as a lunch or drinks party, where it is customary to toast the bride and groom. Long speeches, no matter how amusing, are out of place.

Couples who wish to have a larger party should hold a separate gathering to celebrate their bond. This is usually hosted by the couple themselves, although it is quite acceptable – and rather nice – for a relation or friend to give the party for them.

A long white dress is totally inappropriate at a register office wedding. The same is true of morning dress for the groom. A smart pale suit, perhaps with hat and bouquet, is the smartest choice for women. Men should wear a dark grey suit, perhaps with a buttonhole. The guests' sartorial style is complementary.

Other Civil Ceremonies

It is hardly surprising that many couples, dissatisfied with the almost clinical aftertaste that a standard register office leaves in the post-nuptial mouth, are going in for one of the new secular civil marriages that can take place at licensed buildings other than register offices and places of worship. These weddings are uncharted social seas, with no precedents of form or etiquette for people to follow. Thus they are subject to all manner of unfortunate lapses of taste.

The most important consideration is to remember that it is vital to choose a place that already has a sense of occasion such as a grand house or hotel, many of which now have licences. This is because the actual marrying procedure is the same as the one used for any civil marriage, and thus it is the trimmings rather than the heart of the matter that will create a day to remember. Music is also very important, but restricted. It is allowed while waiting for the ceremony to start, and from the moment that the 'signing' begins. The choice is purely personal, but anything of a remotely religious nature is forbidden, as it is completely inappropriate. One idea is to have arias or scenes from opera that portray marriage in a felicitous way. A more intimate approach can be achieved by a small chamber ensemble. There is nothing to stop jazz lovers having their favourite numbers, but it is to be remembered that very populist touches can render an already rather new and not very smart marriage model somewhat tacky. Themes likewise have to be handled with care. Any resemblance to religious ceremonies and blessings is not permitted.

One advantage of these weddings is that the reception usually happens in the same place, so there is none of the hiatus associated with church weddings as bridal party and guests scramble from the place of worship to the place of fun. Particular attention should be given to the party to make up for any shortcomings that might have become apparent in the ceremony. Therefore flowers, food and drink must be absolutely top-notch. The structure of the reception – the speeches, cake-cutting and going-away – can be the same as after a conventional church wedding, although somehow an informal cocktail party with a toast to the bride and groom is altogether more elegant and appropriate.

Questions of what to wear are also causing confusion. As with good Jewish weddings, the choice of dress should be determined by the time of day, the location and the type of party. Thus an early-afternoon wedding will call for lounge suits for men and smart day clothes for women. A late-afternoon/early-evening affair can have men in black tie and women in evening dresses.

HUMANIST WEDDINGS

Humanist weddings are the new nuptial buzzword. They are multiplying by fifty per cent every year and are increasingly popular with people who have ideals and aspirations that owe nothing to religious affiliations, but who want to enter into committed marital relationships with public ceremonies to mark their rites of passage.

Not to be confused with paganism (also said to be on the increase), humanist weddings remain totally secular but are designed to offer couples an opportunity to declare their love for each other and their future hopes in a more convivial environment than the austere and uninspiring atmosphere of the local register office.

The ceremonies are quite distinct from the procedures offered by organised religion and the state, and are specially designed to suit individual circumstances. They have a strong emphasis on the humanist view of marriage as 'a commitment that involves mutual love and respect' (which sounds very like any other wedding to me) and on the expression of the personalities of the participants. Moreover, they have a non-judgemental openness and flexibility that suits the modern *Zeitgeist*. Humanist ceremonies are ideal for couples with no religious views; those with religious complications so intractable that a common ground is needed; those who want to remarry after divorce, but whose church forbids it; or those who already have children and/or are pregnant. Humanism also warmly embraces gay couples who wish to commit themselves to a long-term relationship with what is called in America a 'same-sex affirmation'.

However, it is important to remember that rites performed under the humanist aegis have no legal status whatsoever. Those who want, and are entitled to, this recognition of their bond need also to have a civil wedding at the register office.

The usual form is that after the civil formalities have been completed, but in a completely different location from the register office, the humanist wedding is conducted by a celebrant, trained and licensed by the British Humanist Association. This rite includes vows phrased in the couple's own terms, music of their choice, readings and any other *divertissements* they consider necessary to plighting their troth in front of their peers. People have exchanged vows in hot-air balloons, in shaded gardens, by majestic rivers and on clifftops, which must say something about the precarious state of modern marriage. The new Marriage Act also allows these ceremonies to be conducted in some of the specially licensed premises approved for civil marriages. In these cases, the registrar and the superintendent registrar come to perform the ceremony. Interestingly, the reception can take place only after these officials have completely left the premises. Understandably there are no dress conventions for humanist weddings, and guests come attired for a party in the style of their hosts' choosing. It is usual to give presents in the traditional way. The same criteria apply to invitations.

WEDDING INVITATIONS

These should be sent out in good time (no less than six weeks before the event – between ten and twelve is now usual). They should be of the very best quality (i.e. always engraved, never, ever thermographed), and ought to reflect the style of the family, event and occasion. Full details are given in Chapter 8.

The invitation list for practical reasons is usually compiled by the bride's mother. It is invariably a problem. Traditionally this list is shared by both parental sides. However, nowadays there is usually quite a large contingent of friends and acquaintances of the happy couple who are not known to the respective parents. Also, there is less emphasis on duty invitations, as brides would rather invite their secretary, who they see every day, than a distant aunt they have not met since school times. This being said, the essence of good manners is not to upset others, and the well-mannered bride should try to some extent to modify her own feelings in favour of others – even on her big day. The parents of the groom should remember, unless the wedding is an entirely shared event – both financially and practically – that the day belongs to the bride and her side, and thus should not be too demanding. At the same time, bridal parents should not abuse their roles as hosts by setting unfairly low limits on the groom's contingent.

Most people start out with lists that are far too long and thus need heavy pruning. Nowhere, even a cathedral, offers infinite space, and the guest list, which should be a balanced picture of the bride and groom's lives and those of their respective families, will bring disappointment to some. Families faced with a small church get around this by inviting only family and close friends to the service but giving a bigger reception to accommodate everybody else. Some even stage a third party so that everybody can get a slice of the action. All these alternatives are correct, but, when doing their calculations, wedding givers must allow for up to a twenty-five per cent refusal rate, and compile a 'B'-list of guest substitutes. Friends who are not invited to weddings have to accept their exclusion gracefully. It is in the worst taste to request an invitation for a wedding. It is also ill-mannered to ask if you can bring a boy- or girlfriend (unless you are in a long-standing relationship with them) who is unknown to the bride's mother and thus not included in her calculations.

Courtesy Invitations
It is good manners to send invitations to the vicar and his wife and all other clergy and officials linked to the event. It is also courteous to invite people who for reasons of great distance or illness will not be able to attend the wedding, but who would like to be there in their thoughts. The parents of the groom are sent an invitation as a formality. Invitations also go to all the bride and groom's attendants (bridesmaids, best man and ushers, etc.), but convention does not expect the groom to receive one.

The Squalling Child Question
It is the prerogative of the bride and groom to decide whether they want small children at their wedding. No guests should make the mistake of assuming that their offspring are included in an invitation sent to them. Traditional etiquette clearly states that if no mention of family is made on the card, then no small ones are expected. Many choose to ignore this old rule. And although children can add charm to a country, 'family-style' wedding, they can be annoyingly inappropriate at a metropolitan marriage, particularly a very formal affair. Babies are even worse.

However, such exclusions are difficult to justify if the bride is attended by a kindergarten of tiny attendants. Many modern parents, somewhat irritatingly, seem inseparable from their little darlings. Others, who work long hours in the week, see the weekend (now the most usual time for weddings) as precious family time. They resent being apart from their offspring and are likely to slip away quickly from a wedding to get home and relieve baby-sitters.

It is therefore recommended to decide on a child policy and stick to it. Many find it useful to enclose a short note explaining the form, such as: 'We are unable to accommodate children'; 'Children will be welcome, but we are unable to offer any special arrangements'; 'Much as we would like to invite all the children of our friends, due to space it is possible to accommodate only the offspring of close family'; or 'We have arranged crèche and child-minding facilities for the duration of the service'. If special provision is promised, it must be delivered on the day.

Parental Marital Complexities

The modern extended family with its contingent of new spouses, stepparents and sundry 'significant others' can turn a wedding invitation list into a social tinderbox. This reached dangerous and ridiculous proportions at a recent wedding, when each of the parents was divorced and all insisted on bringing their new spouses. There was no actual physical violence, but the malevolence was palpable.

In such situations there are two vital guiding principles to remember. First, to be invited to a wedding is an honour, not a right. Second, the wedding day belongs to the bride, and thus her wishes are paramount.

Step-parents following widowhood, particularly those who have helped to bring up the bride or groom, present no problems, because in social terms they automatically take on the role of the deceased parent. The position is less clear with stepparents following divorce. As most weddings are given by the blood parents, reunited for the family nuptials, the position of the second wife/husband can feel like social Siberia. Thus it is important, if these people have contributed in any way, either emotionally or financially, to the upbringing of the bride or groom, that their feelings are respected. Although they have no official part in the marriage ceremony or celebration, some brides confer on them a special role in the service, such as reading a lesson. Even if they are to take no role in the proceedings they must be invited. The gracious mother of the bride will also ensure that a suitable escort is included on her guest list (perhaps the person in question's sibling) and that they are assured of a good seat in the church. Another solution is to make the second spouse feel wanted and important at the reception by allocating them a table to host. Alternatively, in the double-father situation, one man can give the bride away at the church (usually the natural one) and the other speak at the reception. These solutions, of course, presuppose relatively amicable relations between all parties.

Invitation list complexities are further muddied by the position of new spouses who have little or nothing to do with the happy couple or the wedding in hand. In virtually all cases, unless all parties get on absolutely famously, subsequent wives, husbands, lovers and companions who have little or no part in the rearing of either bride or groom should have a very limited or non-existent role at their wedding. Whether or not they are invited should be governed by the tinderbox principle. Although technically wives should be included on their husband's invitation, second wives who were actually responsible for the break-up of the first marriage and for causing actual hurt to the bride's mother can, conceivably, if not quite correctly, be left off the guest list. However, those who came into the father of the bride's life subsequently (and independently of the first wife) should be invited, but given no special treatment (seating at church or reception). Mothers of the bride should not follow the example of one rather catty woman, who sent an invitation to her ex-husband's new wife with 'for information only' written neatly next to a crossed-out 'R.S.V.P.'.

By the same token, second wives need to be philosophical about being omitted from the guest list, and, if invited, should not feel in the slightest bit embarrassed about declining. For that day, her husband returns to his old life, to celebrate the rites associated with it, and the well-mannered second wife must accept this. However, he, in response to a wife who has behaved gracefully and avoided a potentially embarrassing situation, must make it up to her afterwards, by taking her away for a weekend or giving her a transient present – something of a permanent nature such as jewellery is inappropriate.

When it comes to unmarried couples, the issues are even more complex. As a general rule of thumb, established and long-standing partners are treated as *de facto* married spouses. New ones are not.

WEDDING RECEPTIONS
Planning
Wedding receptions are traditionally held at the bride's parental home. This dates from the time when girls lived at home until married, when brides automatically married at their local church and people who gave big weddings normally lived in big houses too. Today the picture is less cut and dried. Nowadays receptions take place in hotels or clubs; in houses lent by friends; in marquees built to augment houses unused to massed gatherings; in various locations ranging from the most conservative St James's club to a cave transformed into a grotto. All these options will need to be booked very well in advance, particularly during the prime wedding months.

All but the simplest receptions will require a caterer or wedding organiser, who will either come with the location or have to be engaged independently. Unfortunately many places often give you no option but to use their own invariably dreary caterer. It is usually best to engage a firm by personal recommendation, or one that has catered an impressive wedding you have attended. Always ask for references if unsure. Fashionable caterers will need to be booked months in advance. Hugely elaborate weddings often require a team of specialists.

Perhaps because people give and go to far fewer big parties than before, the scale and variety of wedding receptions have escalated enormously. Traditionally wedding receptions fall into two categories. The first is the wedding breakfast, which is a sit-down lunch following a morning wedding, with a top table and a heavy emphasis on *place à table*. This is nowadays less popular, and can cause intractable problems for families extended by separation, divorce, remarriage and new companions. The second is the stand-up afternoon reception after a two thirty or three o'clock service. This has always been the preferred form for metropolitan weddings. It is also the most elegant option, and, in my opinion, the one that provides the greatest feeling of a special occasion, as the participants are dressing up and drinking up at times not usually associated with such activities.

However, many brides like to extend the festivities into the night by having a late-afternoon service and providing a reception with dinner and dancing thereafter. This social hybrid extravaganza, although well meaning and increasingly popular, brings with it many problems but no established social form that people can gracefully fall into. For instance, guests do not know whether to come dressed for a formal daytime event or an evening dance, and many – particularly the young – come attired in arresting combinations of the two. When do the speeches take place? I suggest after everyone is seated and before the cake is cut, but others like to leave it until after dinner, when guests are feeling more mellow. The timing of the happy couple's cake-cutting and going away is also problematical. Is the cake cut at the end of the reception or the dinner? I suggest the former. Do they leave after the dinner to joyful cheers, only to return after half an hour languishing in a local hotel, or do they stay to lead the dancing and disappear later? The answer is that the couple change at around nine thirty and depart for their honeymoon at ten, leaving the revelry to continue into the early hours. In reality few want to leave that early and stay too long, so that their big day ends in an exhausted whimper rather than a joyous cheer.

The best, but most expensive, solution is to eschew the all-purpose single event in favour of two distinct parties – a traditional wedding reception (which follows the time-honoured format and ends with the departure of the bride and groom) and a dance held some hours later to give everybody time to change. Two different invitations are issued, thus providing the opportunity to include people who were not included on the church list. The event can take the form of either dinner and dancing (usual in London), or just a dance preceded by local dinner parties in private houses (popular in the country). The bridal couple magically reappear in evening dress and dance the night away before leaving, either at a special going-away ceremony around midnight or by quietly slipping away at some point in the early hours. These dances can be as lavish as the pocket allows, and include entertainments, fireworks and a breakfast. The music should, like all aspects of any wedding ceremony, be appealing to all generations.

Those whose circumstances do not allow two parties but who still want dancing can have a midday wedding, followed by either a buffet or a sit-down luncheon, with cake-cutting and speeches afterwards. After this a band starts playing and proceedings generally melt into a kind of *thé dansant*, with the bride and groom circulating and leading the dancing. They leave for their honeymoon at around five, but the dancing will continue until around seven.

Catering for Stand-Up Receptions
DRINK
The wedding reception drink is unequivocally champagne. It should be served in copious quantities, but need not in any way be vintage, unless the father of the bride is in a position and state of mind to be very generous. There should be some very good, not too heavy, white wine for those who don't feel like 'fizzy' drinks, and two or three semi- or non-alcoholic options, including plenty of mineral water. At an afternoon reception tea should also be served towards the end of the proceedings.

FOOD
Food should be as if for a very special cocktail party, and include various canapés etc., which are handed around during the reception. Tiny sandwiches with delicate fillings such as cucumber, chicken and smoked salmon should also be available. If the wedding has taken place in the morning, or in the late afternoon to be followed by a dance, it is also usual to offer a more substantial cold buffet.

Sit-Down Receptions
These are more complicated affairs, and differ from a standard stand-up reception because the sit-down dinner requires days of agonising over the seating plan. The old idea of a rectangular high table is increasingly unfashionable and has been widely replaced by everybody sitting at round tables. This is not only less formal, but also conveniently circumnavigates

the problems of seating today's extended families. For those who do want one, the time-honoured seating plan, from left to right, is: chief bridesmaid, groom's father, bride's mother, groom, bride, bride's father, groom's mother and best man. This *place à table* can also be used on a circular table. Round tables are also an expedient way to make stepparents and second spouses feel wanted and useful, as they can be designated their own patch. Whatever you choose, remember that early, frank and sensible family discussions will avoid embarrassment later.

The Receiving Line

This is another old-fashioned wedding custom that, also due to the marital complexities of the modern family, is less favoured than before. This is a shame, because a receiving line ensures that all the guests (usually a very disparate group) get to meet and congratulate the happy couple and their respective parents. It is usual for the line to be at the entrance to the reception, providing this does not require guests to wait outside. The traditional line-up, in order of meeting, is: the bride's parents, the groom's parents, the newlyweds and sometimes their senior attendants (best man and chief bridesmaid). Guests are announced by a toastmaster at the door. It is most important that one and all keep their salutations short and sweet to avoid the inevitable queue taking on the feeling of an airport departure lobby. Guests traditionally do not receive a drink until they have finished the line, as holding a glass and shaking hands can be an awkward combination. However, clever organisation can provide guests with a drink when they arrive and are waiting, a waiter with a tray before the receiving line to take glasses, and another at the end to replace them.

The Informal Receiving Line

Some newlyweds, in the interest of inter-extended-family diplomacy, have an informal and scaled-down receiving line that comprises just themselves. I think this a poor solution and would suggest that, in such circumstances, families should revert to the pre-war custom of the bride's mother alone greeting guests (after all, she *is* the hostess) and the bridal party standing in a prominent position in the centre of the room, so that guests, after taking a drink, can rush up to them to say hello.

The Wedding Cake

Traditionally this is a two- or three-layered fruit – or plum – edifice, which is elaborately decorated and iced with sparkling white (purity again) royal icing. Nowadays brides often opt for something that more suits the modern palate, such as chocolate cake or the French *croque en bouche*. This is all very well, but a plum cake remains the correct option, as its high fruit content has since ancient times been a symbol of fertility. Also, on a practical note, people often complain that sticky confections such as chocolate cake are tricky to eat standing up in their best wedding clothes. The wedding cake is the focal point of all bridal buffets and needs to be displayed prominently.

Staff

A wedding reception of any size will need plenty of staff to ensure it runs smoothly. Although a good caterer should be versed in all serving requirements, remember that you will need someone to open the door and take coats; people to look after the coats; a photographer; a toastmaster (optional) to announce guests and run the proceedings; lots of waiters and waitresses to hand round food and drink; as well as someone to help with the children, if present. Country weddings will also need car park attendants. All weddings that make a display of the presents (a habit that is thankfully virtually extinct) will sadly need a couple of guards.

Flowers

Flowers for a reception should be big, bold and prominent. They should manage to be stylistically in tune with the bridal bouquet, while also being in keeping with the style of the reception rooms. As with the church, there are strategic sites where flowers are needed to make an impact. The first is at the entrance, where people arrive. One rather rich family asked a fashionable florist to transform the hall of their house, where the reception was being held, into a kind of floral grotto, lined with yellow and gold hydrangeas, stephanotis and roses: the effect was fragrantly magical. Another delicious effect was achieved by a family whose florist strewed fresh herbs (rosemary for remembrance, myrtle for love, etc.) on the marquee floor. As the tent warmed up and people trod on the sprigs, the scent was released into the atmosphere. Other important places are around the cake, and on buffet tables, which look most attractive if decked with flowers and foliage. Marquee pillars also respond well to being entwined with greenery and hung with blooms. At a sit-down reception all tables must also have flowers.

Music

Reception music is very important and often overlooked. Guests will have left a church brimming over with music, choirs and bells, and the suddenly sepulchral sensation of arriving at a silent reception can be a bit of a let-down. Therefore, it is thoughtful to have a little music, if not in the actual room where the main reception takes place (where the decibel level might be too much), at least in the entrance as guests enter the building. The choice of music is entirely personal but should be very jolly. Army receptions sometimes have a small military band, which are always fun. String quartets and jazz bands are acceptable if a little ubiquitous. A harpist is a waste of time and a pianist too redolent of a cocktail bar. Piped music is absolutely out of the question.

On the Day

Whatever time of day, or form the celebrations take, it is important that there is not too much hiatus between the ceremony and the reception. The nicest receptions are those that guests can walk to after the church, but this is unusual. The bridal party needs to be there as quickly as possible to give time for photographs and to be in its place for the arrival of the first guests. If time is short, photographs will have to be abandoned until later in the proceedings.

Guests should allow a decent, but not protracted, interval for this to happen, and arrive gently at the reception. If there is a formal receiving line, they wait quietly in a queue. It is very important to keep the receiving line moving, and guests must not linger with the bridal party. However, once in the mêlée, it behoves guests to be as sociable as possible, in order to avoid the curious sense of awkwardness that sometimes descends on wedding receptions.

Speeches and Toasts

Whatever social form a reception takes – whether stand-up or sit-down – its ritual always includes speeches and toasts. These form the heart and the theatre of the reception and should always be properly planned, rehearsed and timed. They should also be not too long, tender but not sentimental, and if possible funny but never smutty. The first is given by someone who has known the bride for a long time: a relation, old family friend or, nowadays in many cases, her brother or even her father. This speech centres on the bride and is a way of introducing her to the groom's side, in the same way that the best man's oration presents the groom to her side. It ends with a toast to the bride and groom. The bridegroom then replies. He thanks his new wife's parents for the splendid party and for having a lovely daughter and allowing him to marry her. He also thanks the guests for coming to celebrate his marriage and for their presents. He concludes by proposing a toast to the bridesmaids. The best man then stands up and responds to this with his speech, in which should be a light-hearted but never embarrassing *vignette* of the groom. He also reads out a couple of the more amusing telemessages from those who can't attend. Nowadays it is unnecessary to wade through tedious telemessages from distant aunts, although it is considered polite to acknowledge these missives as a group.

The Cutting of the Cake

This is another traditional highlight of the wedding reception, and is announced by either the toastmaster or the best man. Silence falls and the couple move towards the cake, pose by it for the photographer and then sink a knife (or at military weddings a sword) into it. The caterers then swiftly slice it up and hand round to all and sundry. Everybody must eat at least a little of the cake – those who cannot bear fruit cake merely nibble at the icing. There is still a tradition for the top layer of the cake to be saved for the christening of the first child.

DEPARTURES

The departure of the bride and groom has, in many cases, become symbolic rather than real, with happy couples leaving their reception only to reappear later to rejoin the fun. This being said, the traditional goodbye, with the newlyweds really disappearing on their honeymoon to start their new life, remains the most romantic, stylish and correct exit. Strange as it may seem, the happy couple must not overstay their welcome, even at their own wedding reception.

It is usual for them to slip away to change shortly after cutting the cake. The best man should have loaded the car and made sure they have all the necessary travelling papers. The toastmaster (or, in his absence, the best man) announces that the bride and groom are about to depart, and the throng moves with invariable excitement to the door to await the departure. It is normal for the newlyweds to emerge rather glamorously in film star fashion (a staircase always helps). Gimmicks such as the bride who slid down the staircase only to land in a heap are not recommended. As she leaves, the bride kisses her mother and other family members farewell and then throws her bouquet into the crowd. This is a relatively new custom imported from America (British convention does not dictate such floral abandon). However, it would be a churlish bride who did not oblige, as superstition has it that she who catches the bouquet will be next at the altar. The wedding is now over, and guests must soon depart, thanking their hosts as they go.

THANK-YOU LETTERS

By old tradition it is a solecism to write to thank the bride's mother (or whoever hosted the wedding). However, many people do, and those who receive such letters claim to appreciate the gesture greatly.

TRANSPORTATION

This can be a logistical nightmare, particularly at country weddings. In all cases the bridal party – the bride, her father (or whoever is giving her away), mother, and all the bridal attendants (bridesmaids and pages) – will need special big cars to take them to church. These are usually hired with chauffeurs, as few families today have cars (or other conveyances) grand enough for the purpose.

Often the same car that brought the bride to the church takes her with her new husband to the reception. The bride's parents and attendants are put into the others to get them to the reception ahead of the guests.

It is not usual to hire a special car for the groom, as he is usually driven to the church by his best man.

Afterwards the bridal couple usually go away in their own car, but failing this, taxis or other hired vehicles are also popular. These can range from open landaus to vintage cars to more singular conveyances, such as the sedan chair that recently whisked two barrister newlyweds from the Temple.

At country weddings – or town ones where the reception is a distance from the church – it is usual for the bridal family to make provision for the guests' transportation as well as their own. For country weddings it is usual to include detailed maps, directions to the church, and times of local trains, and to lay on taxis from the station. Other families hire buses to move guests around. Really thoughtful hostesses will also try and arrange lifts. The cost of transport to the wedding (except in the case of the super-rich, who sometimes organise all travel including long-distance air travel) is borne by the guests.

ACCOMMODATION

At town weddings this is not an issue; however, country weddings, particularly remote ones, will need accommodation organised. Any visiting member of the bridal party must be put up at home, and not be expected to languish at a local hotel. The groom's side, however, sometimes like to make their own arrangements, and obviously bride and groom do not spend their wedding eve night under the same roof.

Traditionally in the case of large country weddings, as soon as a forthcoming marriage was announced, local friends and neighbours used to rally round and offer to host house parties for guests. Sadly British country – and indeed county – life is not what it was, and although the custom continues, it is now not unusual for guests to have to fend for themselves in hotels and guest houses. In such cases, bridal families must be as helpful as possible with suggestions, perhaps including with the invitation a list of various types of local hostelries, with indications of convenience, cost and telephone numbers. Hosts are not expected – except in the most lavish of arrangements – to foot the bill.

THE PHOTOGRAPHER

All families want a photographic record of their wedding, and some also order a video recording. Such professionals need to be chosen with care. When booking a photographer, make sure that he is a 'social' photographer, skilled at effortlessly blending into the proceedings as well as recording the event and catching its flavour. Bad photographs can be an immense let-down, and so it is silly to take risks by engaging someone without a suitable track record, or who has not been recommended by a friend. As with caterers, it is vital to book early for fashionable photographers, particularly during the summer high-wedding season. Always ask for more than one quote, as packages vary considerably. Once you have decided on your snapper, give him a written brief as to exactly what aspects of your day you want to be photographed. There are various set-piece arrangements for wedding photographs, although most couples today also want more informal snapshots to paint an atmospheric picture of the day. It is also important that the photographer wears morning dress or a decent suit to blend in. The same general guidelines apply to video, but with a special emphasis on discretion.

WEDDING DRESS
The Bride

Most brides choose to wear a dress that has little to do with contemporary fashion, but which evokes the timeless appeal, semiotics and aesthetics of the wedding ceremony. Thus all but a few still opt for a long white, cream or ivory dress that takes its inspiration from late Victorian or Edwardian styles. With it is worn a veil, generally of lace or tulle, secured by a circlet of flowers or pearls or sometimes a diamond tiara. Lace veils and tiaras are treasured in old families and are worn by successive generations of brides. These can be supplied by either the bride's or the groom's family. However, these adornments, together with the bride's bouquet, are the only contribution that convention allows the groom's side to give. The addition of a blue garter completes the lucky combination of 'something old, something new, something borrowed, something blue'.

Bridesmaids and Pages

These attendants wear outfits chosen by the bride to enhance her dress. Traditionally they were paid for by the bridesmaids themselves and it was thought bad form to expect them to run to expensive dresses. However, now that these costs are frequently swallowed up in the general bridal budget, they can be as fanciful as the bride desires. Bridesmaids carry bouquets or posies provided by the groom. Pages' outfits can be hired, but really should be made specially for the occasion. Again their design invariably takes its inspiration from the past and is intended to complement the bride. The most popular styles range from Little Lord Fauntleroy to miniature military uniforms.

Guests

As one of the last great dress-ups in an increasingly casually attired national life, what to wear presents as many problems as it does pleasures to those unaccustomed to wearing formal clothes. Dress for a wedding is never stipulated on the invitation, but is passed by word of mouth and follows the lead of the bride's parents. At traditional church weddings in Britain, it is still expected that men will wear a black morning coat (grey is somewhat less acceptable than previously), with striped or checked grey wool trousers and a waistcoat which can be either double- or single-breasted and in a plain or patterned cloth. The tie can be old school or regiment, or alternatively in a heavy woven silk. Men usually make mistakes with their shoes, which should be formal black leather lace-ups polished to military perfection, not the Gucci loafers seen at certain types of London wedding. Shirts, which can be either white, cream or coloured, should be worn with a stiff separate collar attached with studs. The shirt should have French – i.e. folded-back – cuffs, secured by cuff links. Wing collars have no place at a wedding, and are quite inappropriate. Nowadays top hats and gloves are optional, although technically no well-dressed male wedding-goer is properly kitted out without them. Many men merely carry a hat, rather than wear it, which is sad, although all should appear bare-headed for the photographs. The type of hat is also important, with old black silk being far smarter than new grey furry ones. Gloves should be yellow chamois (black coat) or grey suede (grey coat). Fresh flower buttonholes always look right for a wedding, but carnations now have rather unstylish associations and should be eschewed in favour of a single rose or perhaps even the exotic charm of an orchid. Greenery – particularly the ferny type – is deeply vulgar and should never be seen.

Men who do not possess morning suits can either hire them or wear a dark-grey suit with a shirt and tie. With the suit a man would wear a normal formal shirt – i.e. soft turned-down collar and French cuffs worn with cuff links. Rules governing buttonholes are the same as with morning dress.

Shoes should be black, formal and immaculate.

Women of course have greater freedom, and a wedding gives a glorious opportunity for female display. As weddings tend to be happy occasions, bright or pastel colours are best. White, cream and its near relations are probably best avoided by all except the bride and her attendants. Black, although increasingly popular, is not suitable and should be used for accessories only. Green too can be tricky, as some people think it an unlucky colour. Generally speaking, some sort of dressy suit best fits the bill. Hats are always worn, and can be as fanciful and extravagant as the wearer wishes. Accessories such as handbags, shoes and tights should be carefully chosen and of the very best quality. Should a woman turn up in the same outfit as another – even a member of the bridal party – she must behave with utmost nonchalance at all times.

PROBLEMS WITH WOMEN'S HATS

Many women, unaccustomed to wearing hats, find them difficult to cope with after the service and can be seen trying to secrete them under chairs or in other inappropriate places. This is quite wrong, as well as being tough on the hat. Hats should be worn throughout any daytime reception, whether it be an afternoon stand-up or a lunchtime sit-down. The only exception to this is when the reception is an evening one and there is no time to go home and change. In this case women must remove their hats. Thoughtful hostesses leave plenty of hairspray and other tools to rescue flattened hair. Women sporting wide brims are advised to keep social kissing to the bare minimum.

Going-Away Clothes

A bride's going-away outfit, like her wedding dress, must not disappoint. It should, however, be chosen to integrate with the rest of her wardrobe. Thus an elegant suit or dress worn with a hat is usual for town weddings. At country affairs the outfit can be more casual. The groom wears a suit.

WEDDING PRESENTS

Present mania grabs one and all at wedding time and care must be taken not to allow the whole thing to be slightly tainted by the same consumerist frenzy that has reduced Christmas to an annual orgy of conspicuous consumption.

The Wedding Ring

The wedding ring is the most important wedding present. Without it no marriage is complete, as it is considered the first pledge of true and undying love. It should be made of precious metal, such as eighteen-carat yellow gold or platinum, and be perfectly round to symbolise eternity. Some of the 'higher churches' will not perform a marriage service if there is a break in the ring or if it is misshapen in any way. The width of the band is entirely a matter of personal taste and depth of pocket. Modern trends towards having the ring set with diamonds are in poor taste, although the old-fashioned custom of having an inscription of the couple's names or initials, date of the wedding, a motto or even a message engraved on the inside remains romantically appropriate.

The ring is given by the groom to his bride at the heart of the marriage service, when it is slipped on to the fourth finger of her left hand. Once placed on the finger a wedding band should never be taken off. The engagement ring acts as 'keeper' ring (keeping the wedding band nearest the heart) and can be removed at any time. Before the service it is temporarily moved to the bride's right hand and then returned to the left on the way to the reception. In Britain it is customary for the bride alone to sport a wedding ring and although some brides have adopted the Continental habit of presenting the groom with his own band during the vows, this custom remains not quite *comme il faut*. The innovation also requires the clergyman to make changes to the standard Anglican wedding service to accommodate it.

Family Presents

It is usual for the happy couple to receive important presents from their new in-laws, such as a piece of family jewellery, antique furniture or even a house.

Presents for Attendants

The bridegroom gives presents that suit his means to all the bridesmaids – traditionally this is a piece of jewellery that they wear for the ceremony, but today can be anything at all of a 'memento' nature. The bride makes sure the pages have a small present, such as a pen, or a stud box engraved with their name. Best men and ushers technically do not receive presents, but only the most ungrateful of grooms would not show his appreciation in some way.

Presents from Guests

The old form declared that guests who attend a wedding must also give a present. This still applies today. Somewhat unromantically, but eminently practically, most couples establish a list with two or three local department

69

stores or specialist shops, or a special wedding list company. These list the exact presents, ranging from the practical to the fanciful, that the bridal couple hope to receive. The list, or lists, should include presents to suit every pocket and give several guests the opportunity to club together for large items such as a dinner service. There is no obligation for guests to buy from this list, although doing so ensures that your present will not be unwanted or duplicated and that its wrapping and sending will be taken care of. It is customary to ask, on accepting the invitation, where a couple's list is, as it is not done for details of lists to be sent out with invitations. It is acceptable to circulate a list of the details to close associates so that they can spread the news. It is bad form for couples to request cash presents, although acceptable for them to receive them.

Home-Based Lists

These are awkward things and are not recommended unless the bride and groom insist on unusual presents from a variety of different sources. They are tedious to administer (usually this onerous task falls on the bride's mother, who already has enough to do) and tiresome for guests, who then have to apply for the list, choose something, return it with their choice crossed out and then find, buy, wrap and send the thing.

Prior to the wedding, the presents are sent to the bride's house, and after the wedding to the new marital home, if applicable. It is usual to include a card wishing both bride and groom every happiness in their married life and to write your name clearly, so they know who to thank.

Thank-You Letters

As wedding presents stream in most irregularly from the minute the engagement is announced until well after the event, bridal couples must keep a detailed record of what they have received and from whom. Good manners demand that every gift requires a letter of thanks to the donor. It is usual for this task to be shared by the couple. This has two benefits: reintroducing each to the other's circle, and sometimes establishing exactly how the new wife wishes to be styled.

The habit of actually taking the present to the wedding is increasing, but remains a very unsophisticated thing to do. However, hostesses must be prepared for this and should have a small room put aside in which to store the booty.

The somewhat primitive habit of displaying presents at the reception is, thankfully, dying out at all but the most provincial of affairs. Such a display is not only ostentatious but absolutely ridiculous in an age when most couples, if not already living together, at least have their own places and will not be starting a home from scratch. Families who insist on a display are strongly advised to hire security guards and take out special insurance.

Unwanted Presents

Unwanted presents are the *bête noire* of any wedding. However, the list system has greatly curbed expensive mistakes. Also, if couples circulate their wedding list arrangements to close friends and family, they can give guidelines such as, 'We are already lucky enough to have ample furniture, silver and basic kitchen equipment.' However, mistakes do happen. Simple duplicates can either be stored until the first one wears out, or exchanged (with the knowledge of the giver). Unwanted horrors are more difficult. Good manners, rather than personal preference, have to win the day, and hideous gifts from sensitive friends will have to be either lived with, stored away or, if you rarely see the person, discreetly sold at a much later date. After three years your conscience can rest easy.

4

SEPARATION AND DIVORCE

Once a recipe for social suicide, separation and divorce are nowadays almost as common as marriage itself. As such, they are gradually encoding a pattern of behaviour – even an etiquette – of their very own. Some might argue that good manners play a very small part in such sad and often acrimonious happenings. But they would be wrong. Good manners, in these situations as in all others, are invaluable.

Marital break-up, despite its familiarity and easy availability, remains a sad business. Marriage, unlike a private arrangement such as living together, is a public rite, and its breaking up is subject to complicated legalities and wider personal, material and social complications. These all need to be carefully considered before a decision to split is made. With any divorce there are two distinct parts: first, the actual dismembering by law of the marriage bond; and second, the ancillary proceedings that sort out arrangements for both money and children. These are both major concerns. All would-be divorcers should peer purposefully over the precipice and decide whether it is worth paying the price, not just financially, but emotionally too.

THE DECISION TO SEPARATE
When a couple have taken the difficult decision to separate, it is important to let family, friends and colleagues know as soon as possible. Some couples naïvely believe that marital breakdown is nobody's business but their own, disregarding the fact that ignorance and speculation can only make life more difficult for themselves and those they love, particularly children.

The usual convention is to tell people informally, either in person or by letter, taking particular care in the case of members of an older generation, to whom divorce might be particularly upsetting. As with engagements to be married, it is courteous and sensitive to inform family first, to spare them the embarrassment and hurt of hearing the news from a third party. Lengthy explanations are unnecessary, while histrionic moral justifications and desperate entreaties for sympathy are in poor and embarrassing taste. One woman cleverly got around the problem of her sudden separation by merely sending out change of address cards for herself. Her husband's name was very conspicuous in its absence from the announcement. Christmas cards are another much-used, if slightly inappropriate, device.

It is important to remember that a decision to separate is quite different both personally and socially from one to divorce. Separation should never be seen automatically as a prelude to a divorce. Couples remain married in the eyes of the law and society while merely separated and must behave if not as a united front then as a dignified one. Recriminations in public are (as in all circumstances) to be avoided, as are entreaties to family and friends to take sides. Associates for their part must continue to view a separated couple as still a couple and not suddenly as two singles. Help and support from all may assist reconciliation. Those who associate themselves too markedly with rival camps can end up with egg on their faces if the couple do reunite.

THE POSITION OF CHILDREN

Children are invariably the biggest losers in any marital break-up. Whereas few these days would recommend the old-fashioned custom of deeply unhappy and frustrated couples staying together for the sake of the children, modern manners do insist that children must be treated honestly and sensitively and thus be spared any unnecessary suffering. Once, however, the decision has been made, it is important – and courteous – to tell children (unless they are too small to understand) what is going on as soon as possible. Ideally they should be informed in private by both parents together. As children often blame themselves for their parents' unhappiness, it is most important to stress that they are not responsible for the break-up and that their parents still love them dearly.

It is kind to children not to subject them to a character assassination of either party, no matter how grimly acrimonious the parental circumstances may be. It is also cruel to expect them to take sides. Many are the children, particularly of the post-sixties divorce boom, who have grown up with very warped ideas about the opposite sex, marriage and, indeed, any personal commitment. The practical arrangements of the separation and visits should also be explained, so no child suffers the numbing panic of feeling he or she is never going to see a beloved parent again. Do not discuss finances with them during negotiations.

THE POSITION OF FAMILY, FRIENDS AND COLLEAGUES

In an age of greater honesty about human frailties, moral judgements are now replaced by feelings of mere sadness (and occasionally relief) on the part of family, friends and colleagues when they learn of a separation of those near to them. For them the announcement of a separation is more likely to come as a confirmation than a revelation. It is vital for associates to remember that a separation is not the same as a divorce, and thus they should try not to take sides but rather aim to behave well to both parties. Decisions about personal loyalties, unless one party has behaved so disgracefully that a reconciliation is out of the question, are best left until after a divorce.

However, it is a mistake to go on as if nothing has happened. Only the most insensitive hostess would invite an estranged couple to the same party, unless the break is known to be thoroughly amicable. Thus during a separation, although a woman is still correctly styled by her married name, i.e. Mrs Charles Still-Married (though increasingly separated women prefer to be styled by their own name, i.e. Mrs Jane Still-Married), she is invited singly to dinner parties and other small social gatherings. Particularly if she has been left for another, it is important to arrange a little attractive – and unattached – diversion for her. At large formal and family events, such as weddings, when it is impossible not to invite both sides, she is sent an invitation in her own right, with a small accompanying letter saying that her estranged husband has also been invited: this gives her the opportunity to decline if she wishes. The same applies to the husband. On the day, care must be taken to avoid problems by trying to keep couples on bad terms apart. Clever hostesses always seat such people out of each other's sight lines and even delegate a diplomatic friend to keep an eye out for impending altercations. However, only the most ill-mannered couple will allow personal bitterness to mar someone else's happy day.

LEGAL ADVICE AND PRACTICAL ARRANGEMENTS

It is wise, if somewhat pessimistic, for both parties to take legal advice as soon as they separate. Although the ideal purpose of a separation is to reconcile a marriage, it often does lead to divorce, and all parties need to know exactly where they stand. Practical arrangements will also have to be made regarding banks, building societies, investments, shopping accounts, insurance and medical matters. Forward planning, such as the rewriting of wills, covenants and settlements for children, should be considered with your legal advisers. A good solicitor will also advise on marriage guidance and recommend counsellors, as seeking early assistance improves the chances of reconciliation.

THE RECONCILIATION

If a separation proves a success and a couple decide to get back together again, the event must be made known as soon as possible to family and friends so that they can readjust the social goal posts. As at the beginning of the separation, children must be told clearly, frankly and joyfully that their parents are reunited. Some families find it useful to mark the event with a small celebration; others go on a short holiday *en famille* to reassert the marital bond. Larger parties for friends are out of place; however, associates can feel free to revert to inviting husband and wife as a couple to gatherings. In all social circumstances well-mannered guests should behave as though the separation never happened.

THE DECISION TO DIVORCE

If separation leads to divorce, then good manners and common sense decree that couples should adopt as businesslike and courteous a position as possible in the circumstances. Solicitors, if not already organised, need to be engaged, and family, friends and associates must be told as soon as possible. Obviously particular care needs to be taken when informing children, who need to be fully and gently familiarised with what is happening. In many cases professional counselling might be useful.

CHOOSING THE RIGHT SOLICITOR

The legal profession has abandoned the old confrontational attitude to divorce in favour of a more constructive and conciliatory approach. Sensible solicitors will never push a couple into a hasty divorce unless they are convinced that the marriage is irretrievably broken down and the two parties actually *really* want to divorce. Indeed, most will aim for reconciliation and recommend counselling early on, taking the pragmatic view that even if it does not save the marriage, it might reduce recriminations during the divorce and even contribute to a more favourable *modus vivendi* afterwards.

The choice of a solicitor, rather like a doctor, is a very personal one. It is vital from the start to feel that he or she is on your side and that he or she is a specialist in family law/matrimonial matters. As the majority of divorces today are instigated by women, there are now a large number of excellent female divorce lawyers, who, rather like women gynaecologists, are often more favourably inclined towards women's problems. Whichever sex you feel happier with, the best way to find a solicitor is by recommendation, either from a friend who can give a personal reference, or from a lawyer who has successfully handled another legal aspect of your life. Failing this, consult a member of the Solicitors' Family Law Association, which binds its members to settling divorces as amicably as possible.

A good solicitor will be frank about the individual ramifications of a divorce. He or she will explain exactly where you stand, and will also try to make sure that while getting the best possible settlement for his client, he will not, unless he is of the 'fighter' temperament, jeopardise future relations between a couple, family, friends and business associates for the sake of another few thousand pounds. All couples must realise that life does not end with divorce. Their paths are bound to cross, whether it be picking up their children from school or running in to each other at the wedding of a mutual acquaintance.

GROUNDS FOR DIVORCE

The law concerning divorce is at a crossroads. Currently the sole ground for divorce is the irretrievable breakdown of a marriage. This collapse has to be evidenced by one of five facts. These are: (a) adultery; (b) unreasonable behaviour such as drink, drugs, gambling, violence, extravagance, meanness, neglect, refusing to have sex or children, excessive sexual demands, mental instability, homosexuality or persistent nagging; (c) desertion; (d) two-year separation with both partners' consent; (e) five-year separation without consent.

However, the new divorce bill passed by Parliament plans to change the divorce law radically. In it, although the irretrievable breakdown of a marriage will remain the only ground for divorce, the five facts will be abandoned in favour of a statement of marital breakdown. In this way the concept of fault will be abandoned. After this statement is filed, the new law stipulates a 12-18 month period of reflection, in which the couple decide whether their marriage is beyond repair while simultaneously negotiating financial settlement and arrangements for children. The intended result is less acrimonious – if more pedestrian – divorce proceedings.

THE PROCEDURE

The invariably rocky road from filing the first petition to the granting of the degree absolute is for your solicitor, rather than this book, to explain.

However, divorcing requires a great deal of paperwork, and those going through the procedure must be assiduous in supplying often very personal, yet essential, information. They can, though, feel assured that, as divorce is viewed as entirely a private matter, these papers are seen only by the solicitors and judges involved, all of whom are sworn to secrecy unless the divorce is defended. A similarly discreet approach is highly recommended to friends who have been privy to confidences.

During the procedure, orders for maintenance and the division of property and other assets, as well as practical and financial arrangements for the children, will be negotiated and agreed between the partners, or, in the case of disagreements, adjudicated by the courts. The procedure is based on a cards-on-the-table approach. Thus it behoves couples to be as honest as possible about money matters, and not assume by concealing assets that they will end up with a better deal in the end.

ARRANGEMENTS FOR CHILDREN

When children are involved, divorcing couples must, as the courts do, put the well-being of their young before their own interests and eschew short-term reactions in favour of a long-term view. They must also resist the obvious temptation to manipulate their children for their own ends and strive not to turn their children against their former partners. Furthermore, no matter how bitter the circumstances, they should avoid acrimonious scenes and emotional tension in front of their young. No family wants to be in the position of the children of a certain clan, who were obliged to engage a bodyguard at a wedding, to protect their mother from their father, a full fifteen years after they had divorced.

It is also deeply unattractive, as well as selfish, to mix financial matters with arrangements for children. Wronged women must resist the frequently used (and rather common) tactic of denying access to children until the father has stumped up a certain settlement. They should also remember that the old idea of custody has been abandoned in favour of a notion of joint parental responsibility, in which both parents have equal rights over their children, irrespective of the actual practical arrangements made for them. Courts are reluctant to make orders other than when it is in the interests of the child, and are keen for parents to work out the arrangements for themselves. Denying access can also backfire, as the rare visits by the father to his offspring can become such special occasions that life with the mother is just a succession of long, tedious intervals.

Parents must also resist the temptation to quarrel, particularly in front of their young, over the many practical arrangements that have to be made for children, such as where and with whom they are to live. Education is often a source of much inter-parental squabbling. This is rarely due to cost, but often because of very different educational aspirations on the part of parents: the most usual scenario being a father who wants a traditional public school boarding education for his children and a mother, already feeling somewhat robbed by life, who wishes the children to remain at home with her. In certain cases these disputes conceal a more sinister hidden agenda, in which one parent (usually the father) gradually aims to break his children's ties with their mother and thus diminish her influence over them by insisting his offspring attend distant and inaccessible boarding schools. This behaviour, unless the mother is unfit to bring up her children, is obviously quite out of order.

In all circumstances the courts will always attempt to make the best decision for the child. In certain cases, where there is conflict but both parents have a good case, the courts will strike a compromise on the age when a child will be sent away. An example of this is the case of the eight-year-old son of a peer, who will one day inherit the family title. The father felt that such circumstances demanded a public school education for his heir. The mother said he was too young to board. The court compromised by ordering day school until the age of thirteen and boarding thereafter. Obviously rulings depend on the children themselves, and each case is considered individually.

Just as the courts will intervene to sort out practical arrangements for children in the case of parents who cannot agree, they will do the same if similar discord affects the financial arrangements. Again the needs of the children are considered more important than those of their parents, although they will obviously be linked to the parent who will be doing most of the caring. The main considerations are to ensure that children will have a proper home to live in until they complete their education and that they are adequately maintained, if not quite to the standard to which they were accustomed, then at the best possible level.

SEPARATION WITHOUT DIVORCE

Many couples decide not to proceed with a divorce and choose to remain married but separated. A separation agreement may be drawn up, setting out the terms on which the couple are to live in the future. In this way clarity can be obtained, financial arrangements agreed and the possibility of a future reconciliation preserved.

It should be noted that a separation agreement cannot be forced on either party. There is no court procedure (except for judicial separation, below) and therefore both parties must co-operate if a separation agreement is to be drawn up. Legal advice should be sought on the terms to be agreed.

JUDICIAL SEPARATION

It is possible (but relatively rare) for couples to become legally separated in a process known as judicial separation. A petition for judicial separation is made in the same way as a petition for divorce, and the courts have the same powers to grant orders that they do in divorce proceedings. The only difference is that at the end of the day the couple will still be married, although in every other way, including a final distribution of their assets, they will be separated. A judicial separation might be appropriate for couples who for religious reasons do not wish to get divorced or for couples who are elderly and there is no question of remarriage on either side. Again, legal advice should be sought.

THE DIVISION OF ASSETS AND PROPERTY

This is usually the time when divorce can become nasty, as couples try and recompense emotional trauma with material gain. Although Zsa Zsa Gabor might recommend returning the ring but keeping the stone, unseemly squabbles on the part of the once happy couple are both unmannerly and unproductive. These are best left to the law, which enjoys such problems and is trained to work out cash settlements, maintenance awards and allocation of capital. As one socialite was heard to opine: 'I've always tried to be as charming as possible to my exes [she is currently on husband number three], but have always made sure that I have engaged the best solicitor I could afford. In this way I have managed to win personally, socially and, most important of all I'm afraid, financially.'

Although it is true that the longer a woman has been married the greater her entitlement to the marital assets, the commonly held view that a woman is entitled to half her former husband's wealth is utterly misfounded. Even the ex-wives of the super-rich may end up with less than ten per cent of their husbands' money (including their housing needs). Nor can an ex-wife automatically expect to be maintained *ad infinitum*, as was previously the case. The courts are ready to stress that men should not be seen as a meal ticket for life, are keen to get women back to work, and will often work out 'an earning capacity' for a divorcee, whether or not she seeks employment. Those who consider this sexist should remember that the same model applies even more stringently when a hard-up man is divorcing a well-off woman.

Financial settlements are based on need, and may work in favour of women if their assets are less than those of their husbands and they still

79

have to bring up children. Both parties will need somewhere to live, a car, and enough money to pay off existing debts and start again. Although the idea is that divorcees should be kept in the style to which they are accustomed until they remarry, there is invariably, except in the case of the very rich, a visible drop in living standards. Friends are asked to be understanding in such circumstances.

Types of settlements vary enormously, depending on the circumstances of the couple. However, one thing is certain – a full and frank disclosure of finances is the only way to prevent an acrimonious and embarrassing spectacle. Attempts by rich husbands or wives to hide money quickly abroad and then plead poverty to their spouse in front of the judge are not recommended, as all such tactics achieve are more acrimonious and costly proceedings.

Settlements range from regular maintenance payments to 'clean break' one-off sums. The latter is infinitely preferable, particularly after short marriages, childless unions, and for very well-off people, because both parties know where they stand financially and are able to get on with their lives without being encumbered by unhappy emotional baggage. Levels of settlement vary according to whether a woman is a 'fully entitled wife' – a woman of mature years who has brought up a family and whose efforts have contributed to her husband's success – or a 'semi-entitled wife', where the marriage has been short, who might have her own means, a handsome inheritance or a successful job. Awards are further complicated by many factors such as whether either party is entitled to present and/or future income from family discretionary trusts. Provision for pensions is also an increasingly important factor, particularly when either party is approaching retirement age. Also the new legislation plans to allow pension-splitting on divorce, in appropriate cases.

Children's Maintenance

It is usual in divorce proceedings to try and agree what maintenance should be paid (usually to the mother) for the benefit of each child of the marriage. Such discussions are usually intrinsically linked to overall settlement discussions. If maintenance cannot be agreed, the party seeking maintenance for the children (usually the wife) must apply to the Child Support Agency for an assessment. Once the assessment has been made, it might be necessary to apply to the court (there is a ceiling on maintenance that can be claimed from the Child Support Agency) for a top-up order. An application to the court must also be made for all other forms of financial provision for the children, including but not limited to school fees, lump sum payments, secured maintenance payments and matters relating to trusts, etc.

The Division of Tangible Assets

The division of tangible assets such as houses and possessions adds even greater complexity to the mere arithmetical allocation of the financial settlement. If the marital house is in both names, then technically its worth should be split down the middle. However, in practice things are invariably more complicated, and become even more problematical when a property is in the name of one spouse only. In these cases legal advice should be sought by the other partner. One solution is to sell up and start again, but many people, particularly with children still to rear, or in ancestral situations, become deeply attached to family houses and are reluctant, or unable, to do this. Negative equity situations can also bring complications. A sensible solution, particularly for those who own more than one place, is maybe to follow the example of one couple, intent on settling amicably, who awarded the town house to the husband and the very nice farmhouse to the wife, who, using the country place as security, was able to buy herself a little *pied à terre* in town.

When it comes to other effects, as a rule of thumb, possessions usually revert to the side of the marriage that provided them, particularly in the case of inherited furniture, art works and silver. However, if one side is awarded the custody of children, the house and contents are often included in the divorce settlement in the entirely sensible interests of family continuity. Again, couples must resist vindictiveness and try and allow their decisions to be guided by notions of the greater good rather than personal revenge. Possessions acquired before marriage are the easiest to allocate, as they usually revert to their original owners.

The Division of Goods on the Marriage List

Even if a marriage collapses soon after the wedding, there is no need for the couple to return the wedding presents. The wedding ceremony is a *fait accompli*, and all goods and chattels involved are treated likewise. It remains merely for the once happy couple to split the booty between them: it is usual for the bride to keep the presents given by her side and for the groom to do likewise.

The Division of Presents Given Between a Couple

Technically these should be returned; however, modern manners allow 'once a present, always a present', and most couples quite rightly decide to hold on to mutual gifts, unless they want no tangible reminder of their ex. In areas of conflict, particularly very valuable offerings such as jewellery, paintings or important pieces of furniture, a sensible solution is for both sides to eschew the presents themselves and put them in trust for their children. One couple, frustrated and exhausted by wrangling, took this to its ultimate conclusion by selling everything and dividing the capital between themselves and their offspring. Thus they were able to start their new lives with an entirely clean slate, and the children, although losing the stability of their family life, could feel secure with their nest egg.

Family Heirlooms

These are the only exception to retaining presents, and no matter how fabulous should be returned to the family to which they have always belonged. After all, only the most mercenary girl will want to wander around in a tiara that has such unhappy associations. Sometimes, as part of the negotiations, women are compensated for handing back ancestral baubles. However, there will be situations, when families are asset rich but cash poor, in which the courts might insist that certain effects, unless they are national treasures, are sold off to provide adequate income to support the divorced spouse and any children.

Family Estates, Companies and Trusts

Many are the disappointed divorcees who have cut ties with a great family in the hope of getting a slice of their vast wealth only to end up with a small cottage and/or a modest income. This is because, although rich on paper, this type of wealth cannot be realised without selling assets. Such a course of action is thought unacceptable and may in practice be problematic, particularly in the case of historic estates, because it can jeopardise many people's livelihoods, attract considerable tax liabilities and threaten the property's survival. Many houses are held in trust and simply cannot be easily sold or mortgaged. In these cases, as in all divorce matters, settlements are assessed on practical considerations and need, rather than grand expectations, and once proud chatelaines of great houses have to cut their cloth accordingly.

COMMON-LAW WIVES AND COHABITING SAME-SEX COUPLES

The former, due to their growing numbers, are increasingly recognised by the courts, but are not protected in the same way as legally married women. Settlements tend to be assessed on the direct contribution of each party throughout the period of cohabitation. Children's maintenance will be assessed in the same way that it is determined in a divorce. Financial provision is, in the absence of agreement between the parties, sought first from the Child Support Agency and thereafter through the courts for additional help and a variety of other orders, such as for school fees and capital sums. Cohabiting couples of the same sex who split and have recourse to law are assessed on their individual financial contribution during the relationship. A financial agreement should be considered in some circumstances.

ANNULMENT

It may, in a very limited number of circumstances, be possible to apply to nullify the marriage. The grounds for doing so are extremely restricted and include facts at the time of the marriage such as the parties not being respectively male or female; one of the parties being already lawfully married; or various conditions not having been satisfied, e.g. that one of the parties was under sixteen.

If the marriage was celebrated after 31 July 1971, it may be voidable on one of six grounds. These include one party's incapacity to consummate the marriage; one party's wilful refusal to consummate the marriage; one party suffering at the time of the marriage from venereal disease in a communicable form; the woman being pregnant at the time of the marriage by some other person than her 'husband'.

There are quite strict rules about when certain grounds apply, and legal advice needs to be sought at an early stage. Catholics may wish their marriages to be annulled under Catholic law (see Chapter 5). Advice should be sought from your Catholic priest, who will take you through the specific grounds for nullity. These are different from the grounds applicable for a decree of nullity as set out above.

THE SOCIAL COMPLICATIONS OF DIVORCE
The Position of a Mistress or Lover

Mistresses and lovers should be aware that they can still be cited as co-respondents in divorce proceedings. This can be extremely embarrassing, although a good solicitor will try to avoid bringing them personally into proceedings by not naming them specifically but asking them instead to sign documents confirming their involvement. It is also worth bearing in mind that when assessing the financial settlement of a divorcing couple, the assets of the mistress/lover if they intend to co-habit or remarry can be brought into account.

Throughout the divorce proceedings, the mistress or lover must behave, regardless of personal feelings, generously and with tact and discretion towards the estranged couple. It is in bad taste, as well as being unproductive, to heap flames on the marital fire as it burns, and it remains in absolutely the worst taste to allow children – particularly very small ones – to discover their parent in bed with anyone other than the official spouse.

The Social Position of a Man Who 'Comes Out of the Closet', Ends His Marriage and Produces a Boyfriend

This is very much a phenomenon *de nos jours*, and a testing one for all those concerned. Despite ever-relaxing attitudes to homosexuality, men who leave their wives for another man (and the lesbian equivalent) can be subjected to a huge amount of opprobrium. One man was sent hate mail from people who had been his friends for years, and even received a sinister little package in the post containing three pink feathers. This behaviour is bigoted and unproductively cruel, particularly to a man who has had to cope not only with the collapse of his marriage but also with coming to terms with a different – and for him, long suppressed – sexuality. As one philosophical woman, whose husband had found sudden, surprising and lasting passion with a male Swedish lift engineer after twenty years of uneventful heterosexuality, sanguinely pointed out: 'I would rather this happen than him having a sordid secret life, and quite frankly, because it's a man, I don't feel as if my role has been completely usurped by another woman.' However, this reaction applies only to around half of all women who find themselves in these circumstances. The other fifty per cent consider it worse. Nevertheless, whatever the individual details, it behoves protagonists to face up to the facts frankly and fairly and for friends to try and be supportive and accepting to all concerned.

The Social Position of Divorcees

Rather remarkably, the old idea, particularly popular in the fifties, still persists that divorcees are dangerous and automatically man/woman-hunters and marriage-breakers in the making. In reality, it is more likely that people emerging from a difficult divorce might be rather 'off' the opposite sex, and would prefer a period without attachment. By the same token it is also misguided to assume that an estranged person is desperate to fill the void, and thus should be paraded in front of as many available strays as possible. The good friend does not encourage rebound affairs, particularly with other divorcees. It is ultimate bad manners for men to make passes at divorced friends in the mistaken belief that they must be desperate.

The Change of Name

There is no change to a man's name after divorce; however, women's names do alter. The most usual form, once a divorce is absolute, is for a woman to retain her married surname, but discard her husband's first name and substitute it for her own. Thus Mrs Henry Footloose-Fancy becomes Mrs Felicity Footloose-Fancy. As one very worldly woman once told me: 'It is very important for a woman to have been married – or at least to be seen to have been married – even if it was only for five minutes.' However, some young women who have enjoyed rather cursory marriages and fancy a fresh start, or who are widely known either professionally or socially by their maiden name, totally revert to 'Miss'. In this way Mrs Henry Footloose-Fancy becomes Miss Felicity Free.

The position of peeresses and other women divorced from men of title is more complex, as anyone who has met the posse of elderly duchesses who make up the extended family of one celebrated ducal line will know. The former wife of a duke remains a duchess until she remarries, but her title is preceded by her first name to distinguish her from succeeding models. Thus the Duchess of Daredevil becomes Davina, Duchess of Daredevil. However, it is important to point out that this is only a name and no longer an indication of status, and as such, a divorced duchess is no longer a peeress and thus not entitled to the formal prefix of 'Her Grace' (except as a courtesy from employees). In conversation she is still addressed as 'Duchess'. Former wives of all other peers (marquesses, earls, viscounts and barons) also retain, as a courtesy, their married titles until they marry again. Again the wording is changed to distinguish them from successors, and is stripped of formal noble embellishments such as The Most Hon. (marchionesses) and The Rt. Hon. (countesses, viscountesses and baronesses). Thus the Marchioness of Madly-badly becomes Helena, Marchioness of Madlybadly. This form is used on envelopes, cards, etc., but in conversation she is still styled as Lady Madly-badly. Former wives of baronets were never peeresses and merely become Clare, Lady Clever, and divorced wives of knights remain Lady So-and-So until they remarry. Some ex-peeresses even try to keep their courtesy titles when they remarry a commoner. Although there is nothing technically illegal about this, as was decided in the famous Edwardian case, Earl Cowley v. Countess Cowley, it remains in the worst taste.

Taking Sides and Divided Loyalties

Friends of an unhappy couple often find themselves in the invidious position of being forced to take sides, as they almost invariably are closer to one partner than the other. The secret here is to adopt a low-key approach and avoid fanning the flames of discontent, particularly during the divorce proceedings. This is especially important in cases of divided loyalties, where an individual is actually the friend of one party, but whose sympathy lies with the other, because the friend has behaved badly. It is also important to remember that no outsider can ever really know the true relationship between a couple. Thus they must never say: 'Oh, but you made such a lovely couple and seemed so happy together' or, 'But he was so charming.' As one divorcee was heard to sigh: 'It is quite often the most charming ones who turn out to be the wife-beaters.'

5

REMARRIAGE

Although Britain has a long way to go before equalling the American enthusiasm for serial matrimony, remarriage is an everyday rite of passage of modern life. As one worldly socialite was heard to opine: 'Marriage being what it is today, the second wedding is *the* wedding, the first one merely a rehearsal.' Cynical as this remark sounds, it does illustrate a private and social need for couples to celebrate their repeated attempts at marital happiness.

THE RELIGIOUS VIEW
The attitudes of the main religions vary enormously, from the deeply rigorous – in the case of the Roman Catholic Church, with its traditional emphasis on the sanctity of marriage – to the very accepting – on the part of the nonconformist community, which, as it does not consider marriage a sacrament, makes it possible to marry several times. The Church of England finds itself in the middle and occupies a somewhat invidious theological no-man's-land. Although its doctrines on marriage echo the Roman Catholic ideal, the state, which as the established Church it serves, accepts divorce as a fact of life and law. Thus the Anglican Church is faced with a dichotomy that is difficult to resolve and which becomes ever more thorny when it is remembered that the Church of England owes its very existence to the breakdown of the marriage of Henry VIII and Catherine of Aragon.

The Church of England

The official view of the Church of England is that no one with a partner still living can remarry. However, in reality the approach is much more flexible and offers those of the Anglican faith other options. These vary considerably and are almost entirely dependent on the views of the clergyman concerned.

Each case is considered individually on its merits. Some clergy, if satisfied that a full remarriage is possible, will conduct a complete marriage service with vows, veils and all the other traditional trimmings. This union, as is it performed by the established Church, also has full legal status.

Most, however, still recommend a service of prayer and dedication or a blessing instead. This has no legal status and is usually conducted after a civil ceremony at the register office. The service, although often very similar to a wedding, eschews vows in favour of promises composed of words that are very similar to those in a full marriage rite. Also, as the couple are technically already married before they come to the church, they normally enter together instead of the bride being 'given away' in the traditional manner. The style of service is by mutual consent of the protagonists and the vicar, who will tailor the proceedings according to his own convictions and will advise as to the level of sobriety or flamboyance that he considers appropriate. Holy Communion may also be taken if the couple wish to receive it and providing the clergyman agrees.

OTHER LEGAL POINTS

The legal status of divorced people is very important. When considering a full remarriage, an Anglican vicar will need to see divorce papers to prove that both parties are free to remarry. He will not recognise a Catholic annulment or a Jewish *get*, as these are purely religious judgements. This is because, as an agent of the established Church, an Anglican vicar acts as registrar. However, in the case of a civil annulment, he will unconditionally accept the verdict reached by a court of law.

If a clergyman has consented to perform a full marriage service, banns are read on three Sundays during three months prior to the wedding. Banns, however, do not precede a blessing or service of prayer or dedication, and should not be requested in such cases.

The Roman Catholic Church

The Roman Catholic Church maintains a strict discipline about remarriage. An individual can enter into a second marriage only if the first spouse is dead or if the first marriage has been annulled by the Church. Civil divorce is regarded as a purely secular procedure with no effect on a marriage that has been recognised as valid by the Church.

An annulment of a marriage can take place only if it can be shown that the proper procedures for marriage were not observed, or if one or both of the parties can be proved to have entered the marriage either without free will or without serious intent or commitment. Previous marriages that have taken place in a non-Catholic church or register office without special permission can also be declared void. The annulment process can take a long time and is done by the diocesan court or tribunal; it does not involve a public hearing or verdict. It is handled in the first instance by the parish priest or the plaintiff.

In the case of a successful annulment, the situation would become apparent to the priest dealing with the paperwork for a second marriage, and the appropriate manner of remarriage would have to be decided. No plans for a second marriage should be made until an annulment process has been completed.

A marriage can also be dissolved in the case of non-consummation. This is also dealt with in the first instance by the parish priest.

Grounds for annulment are complex because of the large number of different factors that can have a bearing on the validity of the marriage. Reference should again be made to the parish priest in the first instance. Before an annulment process can begin there must have been a civil divorce and the completion of all litigation regarding children and property.

The Jewish Faith

Divorce amongst Jewish couples, once a rarity, is now a frequent occurrence. Jewish law provides its own specific procedure to dissolve a marriage. This is called a *get* and is a special document, hand-written in Hebrew or Aramaic. The term is also used to refer to the divorce proceedings as a whole. It is required, in addition to civil divorce, to terminate a marriage in the eyes of the faith. Without it no Jewish couple can remarry in Orthodox Jewish law during the lifetime of their partner, although the Liberal and Reform wings of the faith take a more relaxed view.

A *get*, except in exceptional cases, requires the mutual consent of husband and wife. The Jewish faith, although disapproving of divorce, reasons that if two people marry of their own free will, then they can be divorced in the same way. Complications arise when one side wants a split and the other does not. In these cases the Beth Din, a religious court which presides over and processes Jewish divorces, will try to sort things out and help both parties dissolve their marriage in an amicable fashion. In difficult circumstances the parties can, by consent, insert a *get* clause into their civil divorce: this provides for the *get* procedure to be completed within a specified time. Another approach is the pre-nuptial agreement, PNA. At the time of writing, the Jewish community is considering the introduction of PNAs, which would be signed at the time of marriage and would make provision for mediation should a marriage later fail.

A *get* can be applied for at any time during the divorce proceedings, but an early start is recommended. After preliminary appointments with the Beth Din, a date is made for the actual writing of the *get* document. The husband arrives and formally instructs a scribe to write the document on his behalf. (If he cannot attend it is possible to use an agent provided by the Beth Din.) Two witnesses are also asked to sign. The writing of the paper takes about two hours and is then checked by an official. The husband (or his agent) then hands over the *get* to the wife. As she accepts it, their marriage ends. As a valid *get* is totally reliant on the free will of both parties, even at this eleventh hour a woman can refuse the document and thus make the *get* instantly void.

SECULAR REMARRIAGE

This provides few problems and is therefore the most usual choice for those remarrying. Register office and other licensed premises are happy to remarry those who are widowed or legally divorced. The procedure is the same as for first marriages. The same is true of the humanist position.

THE STYLE OF WEDDING

Subsequent weddings are by tradition much smaller and more low-key events than the white and wonderful events associated with those marrying for the first time. However, in recent years, as divorce has become more acceptable and marriages more multiple, couples have increasingly opted for more elaborate parties. Thus today most remarriages fall into two distinct categories.

The Small Wedding

This remains the most usual and appropriate option. It is particularly suitable for those who have had several stabs at nuptial bliss or anybody who wants the minimum of fuss and complications. It usually takes place in a register office, quietly, simply and in the presence of only a few people. The bride wears a very smart suit. This is never white. Traditionally pastels were considered the most suitable, but this is no longer entirely the case: many women feel they want to start their new life with a bright and confident colour. She should wear a hat and can carry a *small* bouquet. The groom sports his best dark-grey suit, with a collar and tie and a buttonhole containing a single bloom, devoid of foliage or foil. Those present take their sartorial cue from the bride and groom, but should be seen to make an effort.

This type of ceremony usually takes place in the morning and is followed by a small lunch for close friends and family. Speeches in the traditional manner are inappropriate, but it is usual for a close relation or friend of the bride and groom to say a few words and toast the happy couple.

Couples with lots of friends often like to give a larger party as well. This is usually an evening drinks party and can take place on the day of the wedding if they do not disappear on honeymoon. It is the custom for the couple to host their own festivities, but it is also quite appropriate and fun for it to be given by friends or family in their honour. Often, in the case of remarriages, couples have quite spread-out festivities. One couple who had a lunch, a cocktail party and a small garden party over the space of six weeks were also celebrating the confirmation of their first pregnancy by the time they had their last party.

The Big Wedding

Many couples of 'the second wedding is *the* wedding' school go for more lavish festivities. This approach is particularly appropriate if only one partner has been married before and the unmarried side, quite understandably, expect a major celebration. It is also favoured by those whose first wedding was a small affair, and who feel they deserve something better the second time around.

The form these large arrangements take depends on various components the protagonists wish to include. A typical format would be to have a register office ceremony in the morning, followed by a family lunch, a blessing in the afternoon and a large party or dance in the evening. This can be extremely complicated from the logistical point of view. It will be necessary to synchronise bookings of both register office and church, print more than one set of invitations and allow time and space for bride and groom to change if they are to wear different outfits for the blessing. Simpler alternatives for those who want no religious component in the proceedings are either to leave out the blessing so that everybody can have the afternoon to rest and change, or to have a register office wedding in the late afternoon, followed by a big party.

THE STYLE OF THE SERVICE OF PRAYER AND DEDICATION OR BLESSING

The style of the proceedings takes its cue from the beliefs of the clergyman concerned and, as with all weddings, the bride. Her approach should be governed by her individual circumstances. As a general rule of thumb, girls who are being married for the first time can expect a white dress, bridesmaids, bells and all the other trappings of a first-time bride. Widows, although not expected to wear the delicate shades of mauve or grey of previous generations, must not turn up bedecked in orange blossom and tulle veils. Instead a smart but relatively simple long or short dress worn with a hat or plain head-dress is appropriate. The bouquet and floral decorations should be less elaborate than for a first-time bride. Widows can choose if they want to be given away in the ceremony. While this is permissible for young widows, many older ones, quite understandably, opt for merely being escorted up the aisle by a male relation or friend. Widows should not have a procession of brides-maids, although a matron of honour is acceptable. A widow removes her previous wedding ring on the morning of her new marriage. Divorcees should also exercise restraint. A virginal white dress, while acceptably stretching a point with a first-time bride, is positively ridiculous when worn by a divorcee. Ivory and other off-white shades are more appropriate. Like widows, divorcees should eschew the maidenly paraphernalia of bridesmaids, veils and vast bouquets, although, if the first marriage was merely a civil affair, with no vows spoken before God, ministers are often more indulgent about such vestal accoutrements.

The groom and best man's clothes are largely dependent on the style of the wedding. But as a general guide, whereas dark suits are suitable for a register office, morning dress, unless there is no time to change, is still the order of the day at church services. The rules governing the dress of guests at subsequent weddings are the same as at first ones.

THE ROLE OF CHILDREN OF A PREVIOUS MARRIAGE

Children from a previous marriage must be included in the wedding ceremonies of their parent and his or her new spouse. They must be present at the register office and be given roles at any religious rites. It is also important for them actually to see their parent marrying the new spouse, so that they can really believe it. The most usual thing is to ask them to be bridesmaids or pages (if applicable). One man even invited his two young sons to be twin best men. They should also appear in the official photographs. They ought to be invited to the reception and, if old enough, be asked to host a table.

THE RECEPTION

The reception after a Service of Prayer and Dedication or Blessing can take the time-honoured form of a traditional wedding, with speeches, toasts and tiered white cake. This is particularly suitable if one of the partners is marrying for the first time. However, if both parties are divorced or widowed and have done it all before, it is often more appropriate to stage a more grown-up party that includes dancing, a cabaret or another form of entertainment. One remarrying couple engaged a chamber opera company to perform several matrimonial vignettes from the operatic repertoire. Another had a cabaret and a conjuror. At these types of receptions, only the bride and groom receive their guests. However, whatever the choice of entertainment, there must be one moment that remains resolutely matrimonial, such as a short speech. This differentiates a wedding party from an ordinary gathering. The bride and groom can go away in the traditional manner.

INFORMING PREVIOUS SPOUSES OF INTENTION TO REMARRY

It remains good manners to inform any previous spouse as soon as possible of your intentions to remarry. Regardless of how acrimonious a split might have been, it is unnecessarily hurtful for an earlier wife or husband to learn of a successor from a third party, by hearsay or from a public announcement. The traditional way to impart this news is by letter. In most cases this remains the best option.

By the same token, the old spouse must graciously accept the new state of affairs. He or she is not invited to the new wedding, should not be obstreperous about allowing children to attend, and should definitely not be tempted to use it as an excuse for revenge. There is one story of a former wife making an entrance at the reception following her divorced husband's second marriage. In theory she was there to pick up her sons. In reality she used it as an opportunity to turn up looking glorious and to spend an animated half-hour working the room, before she was frog-marched out.

PUBLIC ANNOUNCEMENT

No public announcement in the newspapers should be made until both parties are free to marry legally, and until all previous spouses and family members have been informed. The style is largely the same as for a first engagement or marriage, although it is usual for a divorcee to be styled by her previous married name:

Mr Frederick First and Mrs Samantha Second
The engagement is announced between Mr Frederick First, fourth son of Commander and Mrs Frank First of Camberley, Surrey, and Samantha, only daughter of Sir Samuel and Lady Sagge of Dewsbury, Yorkshire.

Widows are also styled by how they were known during their marriage. It is good manners to mention the dead husband in either the engagement or wedding announcement:

Mr Flavio Quadros da Silva and Mrs Vivian Vain Fourtt-Tyme
The wedding took place on Saturday 4 June in London of Senhor Flavio Quadros da Silva, second son of Senhor and Senhora Haroldo Ribeiro da Silva of Rio de Janeiro, Brazil, and Clarissa, widow of Mr Vivian Vain Fourtt-Tyme.

WHO TO INVITE

Remarriage is a completely new beginning and the invitation list should reflect this. This is particularly important in the case of divorced people. With the exception of family and closest friends, few associated with the old life should be invited. The list should be comprised of the twin worlds of the new bride and groom and should carry no dead wood from the past. This being said, it is vitally important to include those who were supportive during the darkest hours of the preceding divorce.

The case of widows and widowers is more complex. Often, because their marriage was ended by bereavement rather than by acrimony, they retain close ties with their late spouse's family. In these cases, although they are under no formal social obligation, it is understandable that they may wish to invite them to a subsequent wedding. After all, these people may have grandchildren participating in the ceremony. By the same token, the dead spouse's family are not obliged socially to accept the invitation, but if they do, their presence should be relatively discreet.

The position of divorced parents can also be an extra strain on a bride perhaps still trying to get over the bitterness of her own marital collapse. In these cases, as with first weddings, a thoroughly pragmatic approach must be taken. Divorced parents, if reuniting for the day, must put their personal differences aside, Step-parents should be made to feel wanted, and anybody who harbours ill-will about the new match must keep their own counsel.

WEDDING PRESENTS

This is a vexing problem. The scale of present-giving depends on the individual circumstances of the bride and groom. If one, particularly the bride, is marrying for the first time, then she should be accorded the full nuptial generosity associated with a first bride. If, however, both protagonists are widowed or divorced, then a little circumspection is the order of the day. It is cheeky of an already well-equipped couple to establish lavish lists at department stores and specialist shops in the hope of a second bonanza funded by family and friends. Such couples should content themselves with gifts of a more token gesture, particularly from friends who shelled out substantially the first time round.

PAYING FOR THE WEDDING

It is traditional for a widow to pay for her own wedding, although nowadays this cost is often shared between her and her new groom. If both sides are divorced it is increasingly usual for them to fund if not the entire wedding, then at least a significant part of it, rather than expecting parents to stump up a second or third time. One happy compromise is for the couple to host their own wedding, but for their parents to throw another party to celebrate the new union. However, it must be remembered that no matter how small their financial contribution, parents are afforded the traditional courtesies, such as the front left-hand pew at a church service. In the case of a previously unmarried girl marrying a divorced man, it is largely expected that her parents will give the wedding in the traditional way that is the prerogative of the first-time bride.

6

DEATHS, FUNERALS AND MEMORIAL SERVICES

INTRODUCTION

Since ancient times much pomp and ceremony has characterised the rituals of death. This is because, as far back as the primitives, it was felt that the dead were embarking on a long journey and that their family and friends wanted to send them on their way in the very best possible fashion. It is only in our increasingly secular times, when death has become something to be ignored, avoided and indeed feared, that these most final and utterly inevitable rites of passage are often, quite wrongly, skimped on.

This is not to say that it would be desirable to return to the Victorian fascination with the paraphernalia of death, when a 'handsome' funeral, consisting of a cortège of horses clad in long velvet cloths pulling a hearse nodding with black ostrich plumes, was considered essential to honour the dead. Today the sophisticated funeral is characterised by a simplicity that would have floored our forebears. However, it is important that no matter how simple the ceremony, it must be a proper and solemn rite that not only does justice to the departed, but also acts as a focal point for the bereaved and thus helps them to come to terms with their loss and grief.

THE LEGALITIES OF DEATH

Every death in England and Wales must be registered by the local registrar of births and deaths in the district in which the person died or in which the body was found (rather than the district in which he lived), although in Scotland a death may be registered either where the person died or where he lived. To register a death the registrar must be provided with a medical certificate, on which the cause of death is recorded. The medical certificate can be issued and signed by any doctor who has 'attended' the deceased person before death – i.e. treated him at some point during his illness. If the doctor has not seen the patient within fourteen days prior to his death then he must report the death to the coroner in the area where the death took place. However, in certain cases when a doctor has attended a patient throughout a long illness, and where there are unlikely to be suspicious circumstances, this fourteen-day rule is sometimes waived by the coroner, who will advise the registrar that he has given his permission for the attendant doctor to issue a certificate.

If for some reason the attendant medical practitioner is unable to issue a certificate as to the cause of death, then the death cannot be immediately registered and is reported instead to the coroner. A doctor will also report a death to a coroner under the following circumstances: if the cause of death is unknown; if the death is violent, sudden, suspicious or unnatural; if a patient dies in hospital during the course of an operation; if the deceased died because of industrial disease or poisoning. A member of the public unhappy about the circumstances of a death may also inform the coroner, and the registrar will report to the coroner if he lacks enough information to register a death.

The Coroner

The coroner (called the procurator fiscal in Scotland) investigates any death which is reported to him. If, after a post-mortem, he discovers that the death was due to natural causes, then he reports it to the registrar, who can then register it in the normal way. If the death is not natural, the coroner is obliged by law to hold an inquest – an inquiry to establish the facts of the case. In these cases an interim death certificate can be issued to allow for releasing of funds from the estate, and other legal purposes, including funeral arrangements. Coroners are judicial officers quite independent of central and local government. They have to be available (or arrange for qualified deputies to be available) at all times.

Registering a Death

A death should be officially registered within five days; if necessary, however, up to fourteen days is allowed, providing the registrar is informed that there will be a delay. The registrar must be supplied with the medical certificate of the cause of death when the fourteen-day extension is utilised. In Scotland a death should be registered within eight days. If a death has been referred to the coroner it can be registered only after the coroner has authorised the registrar to do so. The delay may be a year or more if an inquest is held.

If the death occurred at home or in a house then registration may be carried out at the registrar's office by any of the following people, in order of priority: a relation (blood or marriage) of the dead person who was present during the last illness; an individual, other than a relation, who was present at the death; an occupier of the house where the person died; the person responsible for arranging the funeral (not the undertaker, who is not permitted to register the death, except sometimes in the case of deaths of foreign nationals).

If the death occurred elsewhere, then the order of priority of those who may register the death is as follows: any relation of the dead person; anyone present at the time of death; the person who found the body; the person responsible for arranging the funeral.

The following pieces of information are required by the registrar when a death is registered: the date and place of the death (in Scotland the exact time of death is also required); the deceased's home address and full name (including maiden name in the case of a married woman); the date and place of birth of the deceased; the occupation of the deceased; the name and occupation of the husband (late or living) if the deceased was a married woman or widow (in Scotland the name and occupation of the wife is required if the deceased was a married man or widower); the date of birth of any living husband or wife of the deceased. In Scotland the registrar also requires the name and occupation of the dead person's father and the name and maiden name of the mother, and whether or not they are still alive.

THE FUNERAL ARRANGEMENTS

Immediately upon a death, someone has to take charge of organising the funeral. If the widow/widower is too distraught to perform this task, then the role falls to a sibling, child or even the family solicitor. Although there is a slight fashion for DIY funerals, few are arranged without the co-operation of an undertaker or, as they like to be known, funeral director. It is vital to choose a reputable firm. Anybody can set up as an undertaker, so it is very important to select a company by personal recommendation and/or which belongs to the National Association of Funeral Directors or the Society of Allied and Independent Funeral Directors. Your chosen firm should be engaged as soon as possible after the death, and will expect to take on the entire responsibility, after registration by an executor or the next of kin, of looking after the body. It will arrange for the body to be taken to a chapel of rest, if requested. The undertaker will also make all the arrangements for the funeral service, even introducing the bereaved to a local priest if they are not already acquainted with one. In general, the undertaker will relieve the bereaved of all the considerable bureaucracy that a funeral entails. He will arrange for the payment of all disbursements, such as the cemetery or crematorium, minister, doctor, organist, choir, and so on. Members of the National Association of Funeral Directors are bound by a code of practice to issue an itemised estimate and account.

The undertaker will also advise on the type of coffin. Although the best coffins are solid wood and with splendid brass fittings, many people who are cremating their dead opt for a more economical veneered version. He will also suggest whether the deceased should be embalmed. This is the process in which the body is transfused with embalming fluid. It has several constituent parts but in essence is made up of formalin, lanolin and a pink dye that will permeate the small capillaries in and around the face and also the extremities. The chemical cocktail restores a more lifelike appearance to the tissue and temporarily delays post-mortem changes. It is strongly advised if the body is to be viewed or returned to the house prior to the funeral. The lavish use of cosmetics, unless the body has been disfigured by illness, cause of death or the post-mortem, is to be assiduously avoided. What the deceased is to wear must also be considered. Many people are buried in their own clothes, others sport a funeral gown supplied by the undertakers to match the interior of the coffin. Old soldiers sometimes march to the end of the road in uniform. One woman, a war widow, was committed *à la* Miss Havisham in her wedding dress. It also has to be decided whether jewellery is to remain on the deceased. In most cases it is removed and kept for family and descendants. It is also possible to place mementoes in the coffin such as photographs, love letters and flowers, but in the case of cremation, these must be combustible.

THE STYLE OF FUNERAL

The style of funeral should be very much in the manner and taste of the deceased. Many people leave very detailed instructions about the type, content and spirit of their send-off; others leave it to the discretion of their loved ones. This being said, the modern funeral, except in the case of celebrated East End villains, should be low-key, dignified but moving. Nowadays, due to the pace of life and the speed at which funerals are often organised, it is likely to be a smaller, more private gathering than in earlier times. The major event today is often a memorial service, which can be held weeks or even months after a death (see p. 114). Traditionally funerals are public events that anyone can attend, so if you want only invited friends and family there it is sensible to include the words 'funeral service private' in the death notice. Another solution for families expecting a big turn-out, but who do not consider it appropriate to have a memorial service, is to hold the funeral in a large church, but follow it with a small cremation or burial attended by only close family and friends.

The most usual time is mid to late morning, as this gives people time to drive to the place of the funeral and leaves plenty of daylight (particularly important for the elderly) to return afterwards. The ideal sequence for a conventional funeral could be: service at eleven o'clock, committal at noon and lunch at one. At one time committals were followed by quite lavish funeral breakfasts. This is now rarely the case, as the modern simpler and less formal funeral makes it difficult to gauge numbers accurately. At small private funerals receptions normally take the form of family lunches, or, in the case of larger affairs, some sort of buffet.

Traditionally, the cortège or funeral procession would make its stately progress from the deceased's house with the hearse in front, followed by several large black cars carrying the principal mourners. Although this still happens, now quite often the undertaker will proceed directly to the church, cemetery or crematorium, with the rest of the party meeting it at the destination. Either is correct, but the traditional form shows greater respect and has more of a sense of occasion.

Once at the church, crematorium or wherever the ceremony is taking place, it is usual for the undertaker to lead the procession. The coffin is normally carried on the shoulders of four of his staff, although sometimes strong male members of the family can also act as bearers. Sometimes, at very formal funerals, pall-bearers also walk alongside the coffin. This dates from a time when these attendants carried the pall (a heavy cloth canopy over the coffin).

In cases where there is to be a church service, the coffin is carried in and placed on a trestle in front of the altar. Sometimes, in the case of Roman Catholic services, some other denominational rites, and the occasional grandee's funeral, the coffin is taken to the church earlier in the day, or even the previous evening, to lie in state. Most funeral services are short, around half an hour, although in the case of well-known members of a congregation, prominent people, Anglican funerals with full Eucharist, and Catholics enjoying the splendour of a full funeral mass, they can take over an hour.

In most cases the congregation normally assembles before the arrival of the coffin and the chief mourners. They rise as the coffin enters. It is usual for the front right-hand pews to be reserved for the bereaved family, with the widow, widower or other senior mourner taking the seat nearest the aisle. If members of the deceased's family are carrying the coffin, they too take aisle-side seats. If mourners are to be listed, this task can be fulfilled either by the family or by the undertaker, who can supply pew cards or a special name-taker to greet mourners at the door.

At very traditional funerals the old order of mourning precedence is still observed. A widow, accompanied by her eldest child, follows her husband's coffin, with any other children immediately behind. The dead man's parents are next, followed by any of his siblings. The form is the same in the case of a widower. Where there is no surviving spouse, children by old custom proceed according to age, with the eldest in the lead. However, in most cases nowadays brothers and sisters would walk side by side. A childless widow may follow the coffin with a brother or other near male relation. At a child's funeral, its parents walk together after the coffin, with any brothers and sisters following immediately behind. At an infant's funeral the parents may even wish to carry the coffin themselves. The form is slightly different at crematoria, where the coffin is awaiting the arrival of the mourners. In these cases a general throng often follows the family and close friends into the chapel.

At the end of the funeral, the congregation waits for the family to leave the church first, as at a wedding. In the case of burials, after the service the bearers will carry the coffin to the grave for the committal. This is usually quite short. The clergyman, family and friends gather around the grave for the final farewells. In Scotland the coffin is often lowered into the grave by the family mourners. It is usual for the chief mourner to cast a small clod of earth into the grave. Others can throw in flowers. At Jewish funerals there is a strict protocol of who can go to the grave, and quite often these mourners actually help to fill in the grave afterwards.

Flowers

There are far fewer flowers sent to funerals than previously. Many death announcements in the press specify that either no flowers or merely family flowers are expected, and suggest charitable donations instead. These requests should be rigorously adhered to. If, however, no floral prohibition is expressed, then it remains a thoughtful gesture to send some sort of tribute, particularly if you cannot attend the funeral. The style of arrange-ments are today much less elaborate than before, with simple posies and flat spray arrangements being preferable to massive crosses and wreaths. Indeed today wreaths are usually only for corporate or cenotaph use. The most suitable colour remains pure white. Pastels are also acceptable but not nearly as elegant. If the deceased was known to have favourite colours or blooms, then these can add a personal touch. Senders should also, if possible, write their own accompanying card, rather than leaving it to possibly semi-literate floral assistants. The card should be quite plain and white. Remember that funeral flowers are a tribute to the dead and not a comfort to the living. Thus the card should read 'In loving memory', and not 'In deepest sympathy', or bear a more personal message, such as 'Darling Mummy, I shall miss you for ever'. The envelope should be addressed to the deceased. These flowers are normally sent to undertakers. Family flowers are always placed on the coffin.

Personal preference of the deceased should also be borne in mind when instructing the undertaker about the floral decoration of the church or crematorium. For instance, if the deceased hated yellow, it would be thoughtless to festoon his or her funeral with daffodils. It is also strongly recommended to be quite clear in your instructions. One top undertaker recounts how, having followed the request of a Greek shipping tycoon to fill his chapel of rest entirely with flowers for a family funeral, he was told to replace them all at the last minute, because the magnate had not made it clear that only white blooms would do. The logistics of the whole operation, which happened over a bank holiday, were so complicated and costly that the managing director of the country's biggest florist had to be dragged from the golf course to mastermind it personally.

Charitable Donations in Lieu of Flowers

Whereas the expenditure on flowers has decreased, the incidence of charitable donation in lieu has escalated enormously. This is for several reasons. Ecologically minded people feel that it is wasteful for flowers to be ordered and often thrown away after a funeral; hospitals, the traditional repository of post-funeral flowers, no longer have the staff to distribute them around the wards. Others frankly feel that the money can be put to a better cause. Usually these donations go either to the medical charity associated with the illness from which the deceased died, or towards the hospital that nursed him. Now, however, there is an increasing trend to establish a memorial fund or trust in the dead person's name. These endowments can be used for medical research, educational scholarships or any good cause that the deceased held dear.

Service Sheets

These are necessary for all formal services. They resemble service sheets for weddings and should be simply produced on good-quality paper or light card. As well as outlining the order of service, they act as a memorial record, as the name of the deceased, with any titles and honours, is printed on the front, along with his or her dates of birth and death and the date and place of the funeral. A black cross is also often used. All psalms and hymns should be printed in full, so that people do not need to keep referring to either hymnals or prayer books.

PRIVATE AND PUBLIC ANNOUNCEMENTS

At one time special invitation cards were often printed for funerals. This is no longer the case. News of a death in a family is normally given immediately over the telephone to family, close friends and business associates, or by a short letter, telemessage, or even a recorded message on an answering machine if more appropriate. This task normally falls to the individual who is organising the funeral, but can quite reasonably be delegated to another member of the family. In the case of an individual dying of a terminal illness it is usual to give prior warning of the impending end.

The majority of people, however, learn of a death from an announcement in the press. This remains essential, as it is usually the only way that those outside the immediate family, social and professional circles learn of the sad news. Indeed, scanning the death announcements of the national press becomes quite a regular pastime for people when they reach a certain age. Death announcements will often give details of the funeral as well.

Death Notices

Death notices are just that. They ought to express the facts simply and clearly. Attempts at sentimentality or pretension should be avoided, as they are in poor taste. They should be short and factual and not attempt to be a miniature obituary. Most papers will insist that a standard form of announcement is used. They also operate a call-back system for entries sent in by post, to eliminate hoaxes, and rarely accept bookings by telephone. Announcements are not published unless they are confirmed.

At its simplest a death notice can read:

LATEMAN – On 1st April, Andrew Bryan.

In the case of a peer, it would read:

LATEMANLAND – On 1st April, Andrew Bryan Charles, 5th Baron.

However, announcements are usually longer and can also include information about how the deceased died (e.g. 'peacefully/suddenly') and where, the age, mention of spouse, partner or children (e.g. 'beloved husband of Cassandra'), address and sometimes past address (e.g. 'of Middleshire' or 'formerly of Hong Kong'), date, place and time of funeral, and directions about flowers and charitable donations. For convenience sometimes the name and number of the undertaker is included for enquiries. At one time it was usual to include the deceased's actual address (e.g. 'at 707 Eaton Crescent'), but a rise in burglary has, quite sensibly, largely made this inclusion inadvisable.

Here is a typical announcement that sets the right tone between imparting information and showing respect for the dead:

LATEMAN-SMITH – On 18th November in hospital, Adrian Lateman-Smith, second son of the late Sir Charles and Lady Lateman-Smith of Leicestershire, and beloved husband of Alice Lateman-Smith. Funeral service at St Mary's Church, Belgrave Square, on Tuesday 22nd November at 11 o'clock. Interment at the Westminster Cemetery.

If details of the funeral and committal arrangements are not known at the time of the death announcement, then a separate announcement should appear when they are confirmed.

Obituaries

Obituaries are placed at the discretion of newspaper obituary editors. They, unlike death notices, cannot be bought, although there is nothing to stop you suggesting candidates or even preparing an obituary and sending it in for consideration. The qualifications are that the deceased was distinguished, had been eminent in his or her field and had in some way contributed to the greater good. Being an upstanding citizen, beloved by family friends and colleagues, no matter how laudatory, are not enough criteria for inclusion. The best obituaries are in fact mini-biographies that not only paint a vivid picture of the person, but also provide a potted social history of our times.

LETTERS OF CONDOLENCE

These are very important and should be written immediately on learning of a death, unless there is a request to the contrary in the death notice. They should be sympathetic but not sentimental (see Chapter 8). They should make at least one positive reference to the deceased, but should be largely directed at the bereaved. It is also helpful to confirm if you wish to attend the funeral.

Offers of help should be given only if the writer genuinely intends them. Only the coldest of people will not wish to do something. However, it should also be remembered that sorrow is sacred and to intrude on private grief remains bad manners. Thus, although it is good form to write a condolence letter, it is bad form to keep ringing up and calling on the bereaved, unless such attentions are obviously welcome. On the other hand, it is equally thoughtless to avoid the bereaved out of embarrassment, or to forget to offer sympathy when meeting them in public by chance. Also, never assume that the bereaved will get over their loss quickly. Often the grief gets worse once the initial shock has worn off. Thus the support and understanding of friends may be needed months after the funeral, rather than just after the actual death. Godparents obviously have a vitally important role if a child has lost a parent, and must remember the promises they made at the font.

Black-edged paper is no longer used for condolence letters and is thought pretentious and mawkish, although very jolly coloured stationery is quite inappropriate. Manufactured condolence cards bought from newsagents are in poor taste and should never, ever be sent. The old custom of bereaved families ordering special stationery with a narrow black border for their period of mourning has died out, as has closing curtains and blinds at the front of the deceased's house until after the funeral.

Titles and Names After Funeral

Remember that someone is not *socially* dead until after their funeral, when they become the late So-and-So. Thus when addressing an envelope for a letter of condolence to the eldest son of a recently departed peer, remember to use the son's courtesy title after the funeral has taken place.

Answering Letters of Condolence

All letters should be answered in person as soon as possible after the funeral. This can take months, and some people like to print interim notices in the newspapers, reading:

> Mrs Stephen Sorrow thanks everyone who sent flowers, letters and charitable donations following the death of her husband, Mr Stephen Sorrow. She will reply personally to all of them soon.

Alternatively, this acknowledgement can be specially printed on a card and mailed to all concerned. In cases of the death of a well-known and popular public figure, where the response has been too vast to make a personal letter to each and every individual possible, or for reasons of health or similar considerations, a specially printed card (or press announcement) is an acceptable and expedient option. An example could read:

> Due to the overwhelming response to the death of her late husband, Field Marshal Sir Henry Bluff-Hero, Lady Bluff-Hero is unable to answer

personally all who kindly wrote, sent flowers or gave generously to the White Woodcock Trust. Instead she hopes that this acknowledgement will be accepted as an expression of her very deep appreciation.

DRESS

The days of carefully conceived mourning dress, when women wore a succession of sorrowful shades beginning with all black and then gradually moving through grey, lavender, purple and black with white, are long past. With them have gone other sartorial indications of mourning such as crape veils, black armbands and black lozenges sewn to the sleeves of clothes. However, it is still appropriate and expected that the dress of all those attending a funeral should be sombre. Bright ties are particularly inappropriate. Thus men should wear dark suits, except in the case of grand funerals, when morning dress with black waistcoat and tie is still sometimes appropriate. Morning dress is also often worn by those reading the lesson and taking other important roles in the service. Women should wear simple clothes in black or another subdued shade. Remember that clothes that appear quite dark in normal circumstances might appear much brighter in the gloom of a funeral. Hats are now optional, but are still recommended. Jewellery should be discreet.

RELIGIOUS RITES
Church of England
There are two authorised types of funeral service available within the Church of England. These are the very beautiful and moving words found in Cranmer's Book of Common Prayer; and the updated Alternative Service Book, which is written in more contemporary language. There are different versions for adult and child funerals. (In addition, there is one joint Church of England/Roman Catholic service available in crematoria and cemetery chapels.) The choice of service is made by the family of the deceased, together with the clergyman, who will generally be happy for special prayers and readings to be incorporated in the service. It is usual for lessons to be read by family or friends. Particular care must be taken in the choice of music, which should be moving and uplifting but not cloying. Purcell's *Funeral Sentences* are especially touching.

The service may take place entirely in the church, with a minimal ceremony at the graveside or in the crematorium. It is also permissible to dispense with the church entirely and hold the whole service at the graveside or in the crematorium chapel. A mixing of these two alternatives is common. The ancient custom of women not attending the graveside ceremony is now mostly redundant; it was never a Church of England tradition, but is still observed by Orthodox Jews and Muslims.

Church of Scotland
A funeral service may be carried out anywhere – on a mountaintop, in a house – providing the minister agrees and providing any necessary permission has been sought from the local authority. There are a number of alternative services in the Book of Common Order, though none of them has to be rigorously adhered to. It is a matter for the family and the minister.

Roman Catholic
Roman Catholic funeral rites have been revised recently. It is usual for the undertaker to liaise with the priest responsible for the deceased. Although traditionally cremation was considered not *comme il faut* by Catholics, today there is a choice between burial or cremation. The mourners will also choose if the body is to be taken into the church or directly to the cemetery and whether (in the case of the body being taken to the church) there is to be a funeral or requiem mass or a more simple service. In the case of burial, it is usual for the body to be taken into church. This can happen directly before the funeral mass or service, or, if the family wishes, the night before. In this case there may be a vigil mass (for those who are unable to attend the next day) or just a simple service as the body is brought into the church. The funeral mass in church will be arranged jointly by the family and the priest, who will discuss music, readings and so on. Cremation may also be preceded by a service or mass in church, or by a short service at the crematorium chapel. The word requiem is still in common use, even though it refers to the first words of the old Latin ceremonies now no longer generally held. It is still possible to have a Latin mass, but it must be remembered that not all Catholic priests read or speak Latin, so it is advisable to check to avoid risking the proceedings being ruined by mispronunciation. The Roman Catholic Church offers a wide variety of prayers that can be used in the funeral service, reflecting the particular situation of the deceased.

Jewish
The Jewish way of death is quite different. Orthodox Jews are very strict about observing their faith's funeral rites, the Reform and Liberal wings less so. Many dead Jews have watchers from an organisation called Chevra Kaddisha (Holy Friends), who prepare the body, and stay with it day and

night, reciting prayers and psalms, until the funeral. Jewish funerals are conducted without delay, although they are not permitted on the Sabbath or festival days. There is no embalming, viewing, expensive coffin or flowers. The body is clothed in only a simple burial shroud. Cremation is not acceptable to Orthodox Jews, but is becoming more practised by less strict wings of the faith. Jewish funerals are usually conducted by special Jewish burial societies or by commercial undertakers under strict rabbinical control. The funeral will take place in the burial hall of the local Jewish cemetery, where the Kaddish (or mourner's prayer) is said. Men wear skullcaps and women's heads should be covered. Sometimes in the very Orthodox community women stay at home rather than coming to the funeral. In other cases only specially designated mourners go to the grave: the spouse, the parents, children and siblings. At the committal another Kaddish is spoken by a close male relation. After it the male members of the family normally fill in the grave. The usual form is for them to throw in three big shovelfuls of earth and then for the other men to join in. Mourners wish the bereaved family 'long life'.

After the funeral all Orthodox and many Reform and Liberal Jews go into mourning for a week. This is called sitting shiva. It takes place at the house of the bereaved and is attended by family and friends. There are prayers from the rabbi each evening (at very Orthodox shivas the praying can go on all day), and mourners are meant to eschew any physical comfort for the duration and sit on hard low chairs. There is even a tradition of ripping clothes. Gentiles must remember that it is a solecism to bring flowers as a gesture of sympathy. On leaving a shiva it is customary for each mourner to say: 'I wish you long life' to the bereaved family.

Quaker

Funeral services within the Society of Friends take place in the spirit of the society's regular services of worship – they are simple, unelaborate, and involve periods of silence. There are no restrictions on when or where a funeral may be held, or on who may attend. Most deceased Quakers are cremated, although there are several exclusively Quaker burial grounds around the country.

SECULAR SERVICES

Many people of no religious affiliation prefer to have a secular ceremony on their death. This is perfectly acceptable, but if the body is to be committed without a religious service, it is polite to tell the local parish incumbent beforehand. It is also customary to inform the undertaker and the cemetery or crematorium authorities as well at the time of organising the funeral. Some people have no ceremony whatsoever, with the coffin being lowered into the earth or winging its way to the cremator in complete silence or to a short burst of music. Most, however, expect a more respectful farewell and appoint an officiant who prepares and conducts the ceremony. This can be a partner, relation or friend, or a professional celebrant from one of the secular or free-thought organisations such as the National Secular Society or, more fashionably, the British Humanist Association. A non-religious service can take any form. Normally the officiant will introduce and outline the ceremony, which will contain the deceased's favourite readings of poetry or prose, the playing of music and tributes from family and friends. There is usually a period of silence, while mourners can remember the dead and the religious may offer silent prayers. Most non-religious funerals are cremations. Humanists like to stand as the coffin disappears. The officiant usually hides the crucifix, and as the curtains close around the coffin, the body is committed 'to its natural end', rather than 'to the life everlasting'.

ALTERNATIVE PROCEDURES

The rise of HIV-related deaths has meant an increase in funerals of the young. Many of these people are, quite understandably, disenchanted with the traditional deities and want to do things their own way. Their services tend to be secular and have no recognised liturgical form. The service is rarely taken by an incumbent, but the deceased's partner often coordinates a series of readings, favourite music and reminiscences from friends gathered. There are often touching little rites such as each mourner placing a flower on the coffin or lighting candles.

The other new trend is the eco-friendly funeral. This is becoming quite fashionable among people who feel uncomfortable about using up rain forests to build traditional coffins, and about polluting the atmosphere by cremating the dead. For these eco-enthusiasts there are now two main options. The first is to be buried in their own garden or land in an eco-friendly cardboard coffin made from recycled paper. These tend to be rather spartan things, but can be decorated and lined by the bereaved, an activity which is, apparently, a satisfactory grief therapy. True aficionados dispense with the coffin entirely and meet their maker encased in only a simple woollen shroud. This approach, although particularly suitable for those endowed with aristocratic acres, is perhaps not so practical for those with more modest estates, who can find the resale value of their property affected by their little secret at the bottom of the garden. For them there is a new breed of green burial ground, designed to resemble a completely natural landscape, with groves and trees and open pasture, rather than a conventional cemetery. There are no gravestones, but the final resting places are marked by trees (oaks are particularly popular), which draw sustenance from the corpses as they decompose. Enthusiasts feel that it is an apt and tidy way to return the human body back to nature.

STILLBIRTHS, COT DEATHS AND THE DEATH OF CHILDREN

These are the most tragic bereavements, and must be given full dignity and mourning. Until quite recently a stillborn baby was not viewed as a real person who had died. Dead babies were whisked away from sedated mothers, and families and friends were encouraged to remove or destroy all reminders (such as baby clothes) of the lost life. Now dead babies are fully mourned by their parents, friends and family. One mother whose child was stillborn keeps a tiny lock of its hair in a small locket, and says that its presence was one of the most important factors in assuaging her grief. Letters of condolence from family and friends are also very helpful. Flowers, unless the family has requested to the contrary, should also be sent.

The Funeral

These tragic deaths should be given full funeral rites. They are normally buried in small white coffins. Often hearses are not used. Some crematoria make a small charge for the use of the chapel; others expect no payment. In the case of a burial, the grave has to be bought. This can be expensive, and it must also be remembered that the grave can be for several interments and not for the exclusive use of the child. Some cemeteries have a special section reserved for the burial of children. The charge for this plot varies. The bills levied by undertakers also vary. Some make no charge other than for the transportation of the family to and from the cemetery or crematorium. Others, however, do charge, particularly for more elaborate procedures. The funerals of children, and particularly babies, are normally small, private events attended only by family and closest friends.

BURIALS

Burials, although less common than before, are still often the preferred choice of traditionalists. A burial cannot proceed without a 'disposal' certificate, issued by the registrar, or its equivalent from the coroner (known as the Coroner's Order for Burial) if an inquest into the death is to be held. The disposal certificate is issued at the time of registration, but will be provided only on receipt of the Certificate of the Cause of Death. The funeral director will take the disposal certificate to the directors of the cemetery or vicar of the churchyard where burial is to take place. (In Scotland there is no disposal certificate; the certificate of registration of death serves the same purpose.)

Anyone of any religious denomination who is resident in a parish is entitled in theory to be buried in the parish churchyard. In practice, however, most churchyards are full, and the dead are now buried in burial grounds elsewhere. Anyone who dies within the parish, and is a close relation of people previously buried there, is also entitled to a plot. The vicar and the parochial church council may grant permission for someone without this entitlement to be buried in the parish. A fee is payable in all cases.

Normally the vicar chooses the site of the grave, but plots may be reserved by obtaining a licence called a 'faculty' from the diocesan registrar. This entitles you to exclusive use of a plot in a graveyard, but not ownership of the space, which, for sensible reasons, remains the property of the Church. A faculty must be applied for prior to death, as it takes time to process. The faculty must be shown to the vicar before the funeral – again, this will be the job of the funeral director. If the grave is to be the last resting place of other members of a family, then the incumbent will charge a fee for all interments in a grave reserved by faculty. It is no longer the custom to be buried inside a church.

Some parish graveyards have no space left for new burials, in which case the local authority is obliged to find space in a cemetery. As in a churchyard, a grave in a cemetery can be reserved prior to death by applying to the cemetery office for a deed of grant. As space is increasingly limited, many cemeteries will now only lease a grave space for periods of forty or seventy-five years, depending on local by-laws. Indeed, all local authorities can only sell the exclusive rights for up to a maximum of a hundred years. All burials have to be registered with either the parish church or the cemetery.

It has been known, and is increasingly popular, as mentioned above, for people to be buried in their back gardens, which is perfectly legal, although a licence must be obtained from the local environmental health department – the authorities must be satisfied that the site will be looked after and will not pose a danger to water supplies, etc.

CREMATIONS

Nowadays nearly three-quarters of people are cremated. However, because it is so final, its procedures are more complicated. Consequently, there is much form-filling. The death must be registered to obtain a disposal certificate, which is issued by the registrar after presentation of the attendant medical practitioner's Certificate of the Cause of Death. If the coroner is involved, he will issue Form E for cremation and his officer will inform the family that they may now go and register the death; they will be given death certificates (or copies of the entry) at this point only. Form E replaces the disposal certificate and Forms B, C and F, and is normally collected from the coroner by the undertaker.

Apart from Form E or the disposal certificate, the crematorium will require an application for cremation, which is completed by a near relation or executor, a signature from the applicant relating to the disposal of the cremated remains and a notice of cremation from the undertaker.

The family have five days in which to register the death after the coroner's office has advised them to do so. It does not have to be done before the funeral can take place. In many cases when the death appears to be uncomplicated, the coroner's officer will advise the family that they can make prior funeral arrangements. Thus, in theory, a booking can be obtained by the local undertaker pending the issue of Form E.

In the case of a normal death not involving the coroner, two doctors have to see the deceased after death. These medics do not need to be in any way related or connected with the deceased or each other. They issue, in turn, Forms B and C. Form F is signed by the referee at the crematorium and the registrar issues the disposal certificate. If the death has been referred to the coroner then he will issue a separate certificate for cremation when he has finished his enquiries. This certificate takes the place of Forms B and C and the green disposal certificate.

Traditionally there was always a church service before a cremation, with only close family and friends going to the crematorium for the committal. Nowadays it is quite usual for the whole funeral service to be conducted at the crematorium chapel. In these cases the hearse goes directly to the crematorium chapel, where the coffin is placed on a catafalque. Mourners either follow it into the chapel, or await its arrival in their pews. In the latter case, they stand as it enters.

The service ends with the committal (optional for those who find the final exit distressing), when the coffin disappears behind a curtain, on a descending catafalque or through a hatch in the wall. Each coffin is placed in the cremator and burned individually. Those who harbour dark but invalid fears of unscrupulous undertakers recycling coffins, or who want to spend the last possible moment with the body, can actually witness the coffin being charged into the cremator. The process takes around two to three hours, after which the ashes are pulverised and returned to the mourners.

The Ashes

Once the cremation has taken place the ashes have to be dealt with. This may sound simple, but it too has its complications. It is not important to make the decision regarding the ashes at the time of arranging the funeral, as the crematorium cannot act unless they have been given the written instructions of the Application of Cremation. These can be and are often received after the cremation has taken place. However, it is important to think carefully about what is to happen to the last vestiges of the deceased. Whereas ashes can be scattered at any time, it is impossible to gather up lost ashes for other purposes later. The most common solution is to scatter them over the grounds of the crematorium, in specially designated, but unconsecrated enclosures known as Gardens of Remembrance. This can be somewhat messy, and some crematoria recommend that the ashes should be buried in a little clump by a rose bush, or placed under a small square of turf, which is cut from a lawn and then replaced over the ashes.

Failing these simple and immediate solutions, ashes may be taken away and scattered or buried elsewhere. In this case the crematorium will issue a cremation certificate. If the ashes are to be buried in a churchyard, this certificate must be given to the vicar; if in a cemetery, it must be given to the director of the cemetery. Alternatively the ashes may be scattered in a favoured place, such as a beauty spot or at sea. Permission must be sought in some cases, for instance from the owner of private land. Always remember when scattering ashes to make sure that you and other mourners stand with any wind behind you.

Others, quite understandably, prefer a more lasting epitaph for their loved one's ashes. In these cases ashes are either kept on display or, more usually, are buried in a family grave or set into the wall of a mausoleum for a more permanent memorial. For these purposes ashes are placed in a small casket. These vary from the basic and functional to more elaborate reliquaries. The smartest and most appropriate choice is a small but well-carved wooden box, bearing a brass plate inscribed with the name and the dates of birth and death.

MEMORIALS

Although some important tombs are still built (such as the mammoth lead-lined sarcophagus that was constructed as the final resting place for an ancient grandee at his ancestral Scottish castle), the days of lavish memorials and monumental tributes to the mason's skill, so beloved of our ancestors, are long since over. Nowadays both churchyards and municipal cemeteries place restrictions on the size and scale of memorials, and modern taste suggests that only the simplest of stones are appropriate. It should also be remembered that neither reserving a grave by faculty in a churchyard nor buying an exclusive burial plot in a cemetery entitles those left behind to erect a memorial. Permission has to be obtained from the relevant authorities and a fee paid.

Depending on the soil, several months must be left after a burial for the ground to settle. Most undertakers are also monumental masons, but if you employ a separate firm, make sure that it is, as with an undertaker, either by private recommendation or a member of the National Association of Memorial Masons. The cost of the memorial obviously depends on its size, scale and elaborateness, although the smartest (as with stationery) are always the simplest. The inscription should also be suitably plain and must be approved by the clergyman in the case of church burials. Most, quite rightly, take exception to slangy, colloquial or deeply idiosyncratic inscriptions, although family mottoes can make a personalised but dignified impression.

Those who have been cremated can be remembered by having their name, date of death and perhaps a short epitaph written in the book of remembrance at the local crematorium. This, however, is somewhat municipal, and many prefer to erect memorial plaques, which can be placed in special colonnades for ashes called columbaria at the crematorium or wherever the ashes are interred.

MEMORIAL SERVICES

Memorial services are quite different from funerals, as they celebrate the life of an individual rather than commemorating his or her death. At one time they tended to be reserved for only the great and the good. Today many far less illustrious people have them. There are no rules governing memorial services – or services of thanksgiving as they are commonly called in Anglican churches. Roman Catholics often stage memorial masses. Jews sometimes give memorial gatherings, either at the synagogue or at the stone-setting ceremony that takes place at their burial grounds some months after an interment.

There are no residential qualifications needed – it is up to the clergyman of the relevant church or chapel to give permission for a memorial service to be held. Certain churches have associations with different *métiers* or branches of the armed services. The service is arranged by the clergyman and the family of the deceased. It would generally contain prayers, hymns, music and also some non-religious facets such as commendations and readings from literature or poetry. There is no standard memorial service in the Book of Common Prayer.

As at funerals, the front right pews are reserved for the family of the person being commemorated. Any representatives of the Royal Family are usually assigned the front left pews. They are the last to enter and it is customary for the congregation to stand. The Monarch never attends non-family funerals, unless they are state funerals such as that of Sir Winston Churchill, where the Queen graciously gave precedence to the hero's widow, Lady Churchill.

Dress should be sombre. At very grand memorial services some men still wear morning coats, with white shirts, black ties and, most importantly, black waistcoats. This very formal appearance is rare these days, with dark grey or black suits now the most usual and suitable dress. This being said, a plain black silk grenadine tie should be worn. Women wear dark clothes. Black is obviously the most traditional and appropriate choice, but any subdued hue is now acceptable. However, at certain services that commemorate a long and happy life rather than a sudden tragic end, less sober clothes are now often acceptable. Hats are optional but still recommended, particularly in church.

The service can be held any time after the death of the person being remembered, although several months after death is usual, as this gives time for family and close friends to get over their initial grief. However, in the case of a foreign national or resident abroad, whose funeral might take place far away, it is sensible to have the memorial service sooner rather than later, so that friends and colleagues are able to comprehend and grieve for the loss of their friend.

Private Announcements

Although announcements of memorial services are usually placed in newspapers, it is also still usual for whoever is giving the service to write to close friends and family, inviting them to attend. In the case of very large services, when there are many people who the bereaved would like to be present, it is advisable to print an invitation or circulate a letter announcing the service. These should always be replied to. At large memorial services, where a huge turn-out is expected, it may also be necessary to issue numbered tickets.

Public Announcements

Announcements for memorial services are normally placed in national or local newspapers. *The Times* and the *Daily Telegraph* are particularly popular. A typical announcement would read:

> LATEMAN – A memorial service for Mr Andrew Bryan Lateman will be held at St Mary's Church, Westminster, on Tuesday 4th June at 11.30 a.m.

or:

> LATEMAN-SMITH – A service of thanksgiving for the life of Sir Anthony Lateman-Smith will be held at Midchester Cathedral on Friday 6th June at noon.

In the case of notable memorial services the Court & Social pages sometimes print very detailed entries afterwards, in which full particulars of the service are given, together with a long list of everyone present. In these cases the newspapers send their own reporters.

PART 2

Social Life

7

ROYAL, DIPLOMATIC AND OTHER FORMAL OCCASIONS

ROYAL OCCASIONS

People often behave in strange ways when they meet Royalty. The normally gregarious become tongue-tied, the shy garrulous, and a lot of people unappealingly obsequious, or overconfident and pushy. This is a shame, because royal, diplomatic and formal gatherings, both great and small, although invariably conceived for a special purpose, are, like any other party, given so all those present can enjoy themselves.

Over recent years royal entertaining has become much less stiff than in earlier times. The Queen and the Royal Household are always finding new ways to make their procedures more friendly, while still retaining the *sine qua non* that sets royal and state occasions apart from other happenings.

Added to this, the Royal Household is trained to guide guests every inch of the way. This starts from when they receive invitations (which always give any special instructions on dress, arrivals, etc.), includes their entire stay at the Palace, during which there are plenty of people to help, and only ends when they leave the Palace precincts. All members of the Royal Family have their own staff. Advice can always be sought from the relevant private secretary, lady-in-waiting or equerry, all of whom have offices within the royal palaces and will be in attendance at every event that falls within their remit.

Nevertheless, royal and state occasions are probably the most formal and prescribed form of entertainment that most people will ever attend, and as such they provide guests with a variety of social eventualities and special protocols that they do not encounter on an everyday basis. In this chapter I shall explain the main points that any member of the general public needs to know. But in this area, as in all aspects of sophisticated social behaviour, remember that if in doubt, basic good manners and common sense will always carry the day.

Meeting Royalty

Meeting the Royal Family (never referred to as 'the Royals' or 'the Royalty') often throws the *ingénue* into a flap. On being presented and taking leave of a member of the Royal Family, it is usual for men to bow and women to curtsey. Not to do so is churlish. The important point to remember is that these gestures should not look overdone or affected. A bow should come from the neck not the waist. Low sweeping curtseys, although usually well meant, are best reserved for the amateur dramatic stage and can be the subject of some amusement within royal circles. Opt instead for a brief bob with the weight on the front foot. Do not offer to shake hands. If the royal hand is proffered, take it lightly and briefly.

Addressing Royalty

The Queen and Queen Elizabeth The Queen Mother should in the first instance both be addressed as 'Your Majesty'. Thereafter it is correct to refer them as 'Ma'am'. It is very important to remember that this should rhyme with 'jam' and not, as it is often pronounced, 'smarm'. (By the same token, equerry should be pronounced like 'berry', with a particularly languid touch to the double consonant.)

The Duke of Edinburgh, as a prince in his own right, is firstly addressed as 'Your Royal Highness' and thereafter merely as 'Sir'. The same form applies to The Prince of Wales. The Princess Royal and other members of the Royal Family are addressed as 'Your Royal Highness' on first meeting, and after that 'Sir' or 'Ma'am' depending on their sex.

How royal spouses are addressed depends on their sex. Wives automatically assume their husband's status and should be addressed as 'Your Royal Highness' and thereafter as 'Ma'am'. However, the poor men, unless they have sufficient rank in their own right, are not referred to as 'Your Royal Highness' or 'Sir', and are not accorded a bow or curtsey by those they meet.

Conversational Descriptions of Royalty

Needless to say, 'she' is the cat's mother, and equal care must be taken when referring to a member of the Royal Family in his, her or others' presence as when addressing them in person. The Queen is known as either 'Her Majesty' or 'The Queen'. Her mother is never referred to as just 'The Queen Mother', but as 'Her Majesty' or 'Queen Elizabeth The Queen Mother'. A royal prince is called 'His Royal Highness', followed, if necessary, by the relevant title, such as 'The Duke of Edinburgh' or 'The Prince of Wales'. Referring to these men as merely 'Prince Philip' or 'Prince Charles' is really only for those who know them quite well and appears pushy in individuals who don't. The prefix 'The' is reserved for children of the present and any previous Sovereigns, such as 'Her Royal Highness The Princess Royal' or 'His Royal Highness The Prince Edward'. In the latter instance the definite article is rarely used in conversation. For just a relation it is 'His Royal Highness Prince Michael of Kent' in all circumstances. It is also not quite done to refer to family relationships. For instance, The Queen's father should be referred to as 'King George VI, His late Majesty' or 'the late King' rather than 'your father'.

Rules of 'You' and 'Your'

There is a difficult balance to achieve between being suitably respectful and appearing stilted. The correct form is never to refer to a royal person as 'you', but to substitute 'Your Majesty' or 'Your Royal Highness', depending on their rank. Thus, when meeting The Queen at the Royal Enclosure at Ascot, it would be polite to say: 'I trust Your Majesty is having a good day's racing,' or when talking to The Prince of Wales about one of his patronages: 'I understand Your Royal Highness will be hosting another party for the RSC at Buckingham Palace later this year.' These 'Your's should be religiously used when making a formal announcement or speech, but can nowadays in conversation be employed sparingly to avoid too obsequious a manner.

Rules About Asking Questions

This too has been subject to much greater laxity in recent years. At one time it was considered rude to ask royalty a direct question, such as 'What does Your Majesty think about blah blah problem?', to introduce new topics into a conversation or, unless an intimate, even speak until spoken to. This was obviously intended so that the Royal Family would never be quoted as saying anything too contentious or be put in an embarrassing position, and could themselves guide the conversational proceedings as they wished. This is no longer the case, particularly at less formal events where such an approach would be both anodyne and deeply heavy-going for the modern mind. However, it must not be forgotten that, for all the new informality, the royal personage remains firmly in the driving seat of any social situation and others should not behave in a bumptious, pushy or cheeky way.

Making Introductions to Royalty

Subjects are always introduced, or rather presented to royalty, never the other way round, by saying: 'Your Majesty, may I present Sir Timothy Tutting.' Notice that only Sir Timothy's name is used and not The Queen's.

The Form with Foreign Royalty

Foreign kings, queens, princes and princesses are treated in the same way as members of the British Royal Family. However, other countries have different ruling houses, including an imperial set-up in Japan and a reigning princely one in Monaco. An emperor or empress is addressed for the first time as 'Your Imperial Majesty' and thereafter as 'Sir' or 'Ma'am', and is referred to as 'His [or Her] Imperial Majesty'. Reigning princes or princesses are addressed as 'Your Serene Highness' and then 'Sir' or 'Ma'am', and are referred to as 'His [or Her] Serene Highness'.

Royal Invitations

Invitations from The Queen or Queen Elizabeth The Queen Mother are not like other invitations. They are commands. They are not declined unless there is a very good reason, such as illness, or a long-standing family commitment, such as a wedding, or a business arrangement that would gravely let others down. They should also be replied to as commands, in writing, by first presenting the guest's compliments to the member of the Royal Household who sent the invitations. Then, instead of writing the usual 'have great pleasure in accepting', the wording must read: 'have the honour to obey Her Majesty's command to'.

Thus a typical reply would read:

Mr and Mrs Michael Mighty-Worthy present their compliments to the Master of the Household and have the honour to obey Her Majesty's command to attend a luncheon at Buckingham Palace on Friday, 6th April at 12.30.

However, invitations from other members of the Royal Family are just that, and not royal commands, and should be replied to in the usual way (see Chapter 8). The reply should be sent to the Private Secretary or other member of the Household who proffered the invitation, and not HRH in person.

Royal Events

The Royal Family does a huge amount of entertaining, including the well-known garden parties held each July, investitures, state banquets and receptions, the annual party for winners of the Queen's Award for Industry as well as, from time to time, a range of informal lunches and cocktail parties.

STATE BANQUETS

As the once grand levees, drawing rooms and state balls are now only a memory, the few main royal set pieces are very largely to do with state rather than society. The biggest and best remain the state banquets, which are usually given to commemorate a visit of another head of state. The banquet is usually held on the first evening of the visit. Guests include members of the Royal Family, senior members of the Government and other political parties, high commissioners, ambassadors and others with important associations with the country being entertained. They are large, formal and splendid affairs. They take place either at Buckingham Palace (which The Queen thinks of as the office) or at Windsor (which she considers home, but which is temporarily out of action due to fire damage), or sometimes at Holyrood House in Scotland.

The invitation is a formal command issued by the Lord Steward of the Household. It is replied to as a command (see p. 122 above). As with all royal invitations it will carry the most comprehensive information about time, place, what to wear and where to arrive. The envelope will also contain a presentation card. As security is becoming ever stricter, it is important to remember to take both cards. The invitation card gets you in and the presentation one makes sure that you are properly announced.

Dress

Dress is very grand and often a handsome sight. Men wear white tie or full dress uniform and foreign nationals turn up attired in the top rank of their national dress. Full decorations, although at the discretion of the owners, should always be worn. Not to do so is rude, particularly when a guest of the royal house that bestowed them. Women wear long dresses, which should, if sleeveless, be accessorised with long gloves. Tiaras and other important pieces of jewellery are worn.

A state banquet, as with all formal royal occasions, is not the place to wear overtly avant-garde or unconventional dress. A gold lace mini dress amongst a sea of immaculate long gowns is likely to make the wearer feel uncomfortable rather than stylish, as the function of fashion at these gatherings is to reinforce not disrupt the formality of the proceedings.

123

The Procedure

It is very important not to be late, and those who do find themselves delayed should ring. It remains unspeakably bad form to arrive after the Sovereign. Once in the palace, the guest will find everything is very organised, with members of the Royal Household circulating to make sure that no one gets lost.

Footmen will guide guests to the first reception, which at Buckingham Palace is usually in the Green Drawing Room, where they will be greeted by the Lord Chamberlain and the Mistress of the Robes. After that they are given a drink and wander around the Picture Gallery. From there guests are coaxed into the music room, where they will be presented to The Queen, The Duke of Edinburgh and the visiting head of state and his or her spouse. It is most important not to jostle at this stage. The form is merely to hand over your presentation card to the Lord Steward of the Household, who will then present you to your hosts. As at a wedding reception line, it is vital to keep moving and not engage Her Majesty or her party in protracted chitter-chatter – that comes later. After presentation, guests make their way to the ballroom, where with the assistance of the staff and a table plan they find their places. Nobody sits down until the royal party has processed in and taken its seats.

This procession is led by the Lord Chamberlain and the Lord Steward, followed by The Queen accompanied by the visiting head of state, the Duke of Edinburgh with the visiting consort, Queen Elizabeth The Queen Mother accompanied by the Archbishop of Canterbury, and so on in descending order of precedence.

The Queen sits at the top of a horseshoe-shaped table, with the visiting head of state and other members of the Royal Family. The table is bedecked with flowers and a magnificent array of silver, porcelain and glassware taken from the many sumptuous services in the royal collection. The footmen wear scarlet livery bristling with gold braid, although sadly their hair is no longer powdered.

Dinner is then served. Although there is a long menu comprising soup, fish and meat, pudding and dessert, the food tends to be plain so that a wide variety of tastes, races and religions can be suitably fed. Those with very specific dietary requirements must let the Royal Household know in advance. It is in the worst taste to make a fuss, particularly at a state banquet. Throughout dinner there is very jolly music provided by a band from the Household Division, which greatly adds to the amusement of the evening.

Speeches and toasts used to be left to the end of the dinner, but more recently, in the interests of conviviality, they are given after dessert (the fruit course) or before the food is served. Silence is called, and The Queen stands and gives a speech that welcomes the visiting head of state to Britain. She toasts him as everybody stands and raises their glasses then sits again. The guest of honour then returns the favour with the Loyal Toast. The throng once again stand, intone, 'The Queen' and sit down again. At the end of the banquet Scottish pipers parade and pipe around the tables. Then the company rises as The Queen and her party leave the ballroom. This does not mean that the evening is instantly over. Coffee and liqueurs are served to guests. There is a story of one state banquet at which Her Majesty was having such a good time that she officially left the banquet with her foreign guests, only to return to the party after they had retired for the evening.

A thank-you letter is not obligatory, although one can be sent to the Lord Steward of the Royal Household, in which you 'kindly ask' him to 'pass on our thanks to Her Majesty The Queen'.

THE STATE OPENING OF PARLIAMENT

The State Opening of Parliament is one of the great set pieces of the royal and parliamentary year. Here the trinity of the British state – the Sovereign, the House of Lords and the House of Commons – come together for the ceremonial opening of the new session of Parliament. It usually takes place in October or November. A state opening also happens when there is a new parliament after a general election. The Queen comes to the Palace of Westminster, and from the throne in the House of Lords reads a speech prepared by the Cabinet which outlines her Government's plans for the next year. The State Opening is one of the few occasions when all three parts of Parliament meet – the Queen on her throne, the Lords ensconced on their red benches and the Commons behind the bar at the back of the chamber. The bar does not refer to one of the many convivial drinking dens in the Palace of Westminster, but to a bar which is to be found in each chamber and which marks the boundary of the House. MPs cannot go beyond the bar in the Lords when the House is sitting. The Lords respect the privacy of the Commons in the same way.

The State Opening of Parliament is a very formal, dignified and splendid but happy event. The procedure starts with The Queen arriving at the Sovereign's Entrance to the Palace of Westminster in the Irish State Coach. She is then conducted to the Robing Room, where she dons the Royal Robes and the Imperial State Crown. In the meantime a member of the Commons goes to Buckingham Palace to act as a symbolic hostage to guarantee the safe return of the Sovereign. Once robed, The Queen joins an elaborately attired procession awaiting her in the Royal Gallery and then proceeds in state into the chamber of the House of Lords. She takes her place on the throne. There is then a great deal of ceremonial, which culminates with the Gentleman Usher of the Black Rod proceeding in a stately fashion to the door of the House of Commons, which is slammed in his face and opened only when he knocks three times with his ebony stick and thus summons MPs to the ceremony. The Commons, affecting an air of insouciance – by tradition they show disdain for the pomp and circumstance of the Lords – saunter to the bar of the House of Lords to hear the Queen's Speech.

Space is in extremely short supply and highly subscribed. The chamber and its galleries are reserved for members of the Royal Family and their guests, the Lords Spiritual (the archbishops and bishops), the Lords Temporal (dukes, marquesses, earls, viscounts and barons in order of precedence), judges from the High Court of Justice, and various dignitaries including members of the diplomatic corps. Other guests must sit in the Royal Gallery where it is possible to see the procession go through to the chamber and return again after the event. Places are allocated by a ballot offered to peers and held by the Lord Great Chamberlain shortly before the State Opening, the outcome of which is keenly awaited. Those who have been lucky receive admission cards which must be brought on the day. It is also possible to obtain pavement tickets from the Lord Great Chamberlain's office. These give a good view of the arrival of the Queen and other grandly dressed people but are only for real enthusiasts who don't mind standing for long periods.

The dress, as befits such an important occasion, is formal. In the chamber peers wear their scarlet robes over suits or service dress. Peeresses wear evening dresses ranging from stately gowns that Queen Mary would recognise to more strappy numbers that look as if they have come straight from Annabel's. Tiaras are also worn. The eldest sons and daughters of peers (who are allocated standing places in the Eldest Sons' Box) wear morning dress or day dress and a hat. In the Royal Gallery men wear morning dress, service dress or a dark suit. Women wear day dress with a hat, which should be small enough not to block the view of others. The Commons and their cohorts wear suits of disparate quality. Needless to say, some of their number make a point of looking particularly sartorially uninspiring. After the State Opening there are many lively lunch parties throughout the palace.

TROOPING THE COLOUR
Trooping the Colour celebrates the Sovereign's official birthday and the long and strong connections between the Royal Family and the Household

Division. It is *always* known as Trooping the Colour, *never* Trooping of the Colour, and usually takes place on the second Saturday in June. The parade is based upon a ceremony used for guard mounting from Horse Guards Parade in the eighteenth century and was first performed for King George III. Officially and properly known as The Queen's Birthday Parade, it consists of part of the Household Division in a ceremonial review by their Colonel-in-Chief, Her Majesty The Queen. This splendid and stirring spectacle consists of the seven regiments of the Household Division – the Life Guards, the Blues and Royals, the Grenadier, Coldstream, Scots, Irish and Welsh Guards – ceremonially marching the Colour (the flag of the particular regiment being trooped) in front of The Queen and other members of the Royal Family around and around Horse Guards Parade. This is performed to the rousing accompaniment of slow and quick marches provided by the massed bands of the Household Division. There is a huge amount of standing up and sitting down. The usual signals for standing are: at the arrival of Queen Elizabeth The Queen Mother; when The Queen arrives in her phaeton made for Queen Victoria in 1842 (she no longer takes the salute on horseback); at the several strike-ups of the National Anthem; and every time the Colour passes in front of you. The effect can sometimes be like a rather well-dressed Mexican wave. It is customary for men to doff their hats as the Colour passes.

The Trooping is very popular, and its audience is drawn not only from those with a direct military connection, but also from diplomats (including defence attachés of the various embassies), civic officials, Members of Parliament and interested members of the public. Tickets are allocated by ballot and are limited to two per application. Applications should be made in writing before 1 March to The Brigade Major (Trooping the Colour), Headquarters Household Division, Horse Guards, Whitehall, SW1A 2AX. Always enclose a stamped addressed envelope and state whether, if you are unlucky in the ballot, you would like to come to one of the two reviews that are held on the preceding Saturdays. The first is usually taken by the Major-General commanding the Household Division, and the second by the Colonel of the Regiment of the Colour that is to be trooped, which is often another member of the Royal Family, such as The Prince of Wales in the case of the Welsh Guards, or the Duke of Kent when it is the turn of the Scots Guards.

Dress
The choice of dress depends on where you are sitting. Directions are printed on the ticket. However, the majority of men wear morning dress or a

suit. Women wear formal day dress, coat or suit with not too large a hat. As Horse Guards is extremely large and exposed and the stands and enclosures open to the elements, it is advisable to take the weather very much into account when planning the day's dress. Cold days can be Siberian and hot ones so boiling that even the soldiers have been known to faint. On wet days, it is acceptable to bring umbrellas, but spectators should resist putting them up until absolutely necessary.

ROYAL ASCOT

Royal Ascot remains one of the most important gatherings in the royal, racing and social calendar. A huge public gathering as well as a private royal party, it takes place every year in the third week of June and retains a very special atmosphere.

Entry to the Royal Enclosure is by approval only. Demand has increased so much over recent years that it is now quite difficult to get in. Only some of those who apply are successful. Admission lies within the unflinching jurisdiction of Her Majesty's Representative. The actual number of people who receive vouchers is not disclosed, and why those who are denied vouchers is never explained. The application procedure is strict. First-timers must plan early. Although the meeting is not until June, they must apply for their vouchers between January and March. After that no applications are considered. The Court & Social pages in *The Times* and the *Daily Telegraph* announce when the process can begin.

Applications must be addressed to: Her Majesty's Representative, The Ascot Office, St James's Palace, London, SW1A 1BP. They have to be in writing and in the third person, and should read:

> Sir Ernest Equine presents his compliments to Her Majesty's Representative and wishes to apply for vouchers to the Royal Enclosure. This is the first time he has applied.

Either spouse can apply, but each application can include only members of the applicant's immediate family. Friends must apply independently. It is important to make sure that all names of those requiring vouchers are included in the letter. This would thus read: 'Sir Ernest and Lady Equine and Miss Phillida Equine . . .' The applicant will then receive a sponsorship form, which requires details of name, name of father, address, profession and, in order of priority, the day for which vouchers are required. The day once allocated cannot be changed. Most important of all, the form has a section that has to be filled in by a proposer. This sponsor pledges to accept full responsibility for the applicant and has to say for how many years the applicant has been known personally to him/her. For his own part, the sponsor has to have been present in the Royal Ascot Enclosure for at least eight years and is debarred from signing more than two forms in any one year. Those applying for the first time should take care to choose a suitable sponsor, as it can make all the difference to the success of their application. People who have been successfully sponsored in the past and are on the Royal Enclosure list still have to reapply for their vouchers every year.

Those who have been approved receive vouchers in the post some time later. These are exchanged in due course for the actual badges, which are carefully inscribed with the name of the race-goer for whom they are intended. They can either be collected from St James's Palace up to a week before the meeting, sent by post, or collected at the race course. Badges are charged per day, but there is a saving to be made if you buy a weekly badge.

These badges must be worn at all times at Ascot, as the enclosure is closely guarded by fierce officials. Anyone not sporting the badge will not be let in. The now famous story of a badgeless Princess Royal being challenged at the gates of the Royal Enclosure illustrates this point.

At one time divorcees were not allowed in the Enclosure. This is quite understandably no longer the case. However, divorced women's partners must remember that they do have to apply separately and be sponsored if not already on the Royal Enclosure list. Junior vouchers are available to all those between the ages of sixteen and twenty-nine years, providing their dates of birth have been stated on the form. Foreign nationals apply for vouchers through their own embassy in London, where their ambassador can act as sponsor.

Dress
Rules on dress in the Royal Enclosure are as strictly enforced as the badge policy. Men have to wear morning dress, which can be either black or grey, but absolutely not any other colour. Black is currently considered smarter, although grey, which has developed somewhat unfortunate connotations, remains acceptable and indeed traditional for Ladies' Day. Waistcoats can be white, buff or grey, but garish patterns look vulgar and somehow clash with the often spectacularly attired women. A grey hat is worn with a grey coat, and a black with black, although it is acceptable to wear a grey hat with a black coat and even *vice versa*. Again, black is thought more distinguished, particularly if it is an old one in black silk plush. Service uniform is also acceptable.

However, it is to the women that Ascot belongs. One of their great dress-ups of the year, they are expected to wear very formal day dresses or suits. Hats are *de rigueur* and must have a crown. Colour is very much the order of the day, but headline-grabbing vulgarity, although part of the sense of occasion, is in poor taste. Overseas visitors may wear their national costume. The weather at Royal Ascot can range from the freezing to the boiling, and should be carefully considered when choosing what to wear. One very social and always beautifully dressed woman has two completely different outfits planned for all four of the days, so that she is elegantly turned out for all climatic eventualities. Such extravagance, although unnecessary, does illustrate the effort people put into their appearance for this most glamorous of race meetings.

THE ROYAL GARDEN PARTIES

These have become very much a part of the London summer, attended by throngs of people, who can be seen spilling out of the palace garden gates in the late afternoon sunshine. They are intended to allow the widest spectrum of subjects and guests to be entertained by The Queen. Guests are chosen from lists supplied by individuals and institutions such as the Government, the armed services and the Lord Lieutenants, as well as a host of other organisations and professions. Around eight thousand people attend each year.

Invitations, or rather commands, are sent on The Queen's behalf by the Lord Chamberlain, together with an admission card and details about parking. There is no need to reply; however, guests must remember to bring their admission cards on the day. Those who can't attend must return their cards, with the reason for not complying with a royal command. Again, only a good excuse for declining is acceptable.

Dress

Men wear morning dress, dark suits, service uniform, national dress or official dress (in the case of the clergy, etc.). Women wear smart day clothes, such as afternoon dresses, pretty suits or national dress. Hats, although no longer compulsory, are very much the order of the day but should not be quite as fanciful as those worn to Royal Ascot. Cameras are strictly forbidden and will be confiscated.

The Form

The garden parties last from four to six o'clock, although the gates open at 3.15. At four o'clock The Queen, accompanied by other members of the Royal Family, steps down from the palace into the garden, which in summer is a glorious Arcadian scene, complete with a lake, flamingos and white marquees. The National Anthem is then played by one of two bands, which will also provide jolly music throughout the afternoon. Firstly, some formal presentations are made, such as recently appointed Lord Lieutenants and chaplains. Then The Queen and sundry members of the Royal Family begin to circulate amongst the colourful throng. Guests are selected at random by those in attendance for presentation to Her Majesty and her party. Each chosen guest tells the relevant official his or her name, rank, title and a bit about themselves (jobs, interests and other achievements), so that there will be a conversational starting point. Do not attempt a potted CV; there is no time. If you have met The Queen on a previous occasion, it is polite to say so. You will then be presented. At around five the royal party disappear into their tent for tea with grander guests such as high commissioners, ambassadors and government ministers, while the rest of the guests are served in other tents. The remainder of the afternoon is devoted to walking around, looking at the flowers and eating chocolate cake. Shortly before six o'clock the Royal Family return to the Palace. The playing of the National Anthem signals the end of the festivities. Guests leave shortly afterwards. Although it is acceptable to leave a garden party before the royal party retires, few do so unless they have a seriously pressing engagement. Thank-you letters are not expected.

INVESTITURES

This is when most of the people who have been named in the twice-yearly honours lists are invited to Buckingham Palace to receive their orders, decorations and medals from The Queen. The ceremony takes place in the ballroom of Buckingham Palace and recipients are allowed to bring three guests drawn from their family or close friends.

The summons is sent out by the splendidly named Central Chancery of the Orders of Knighthood. Like all royal invitations they are tirelessly comprehensive about all relevant details, such as when to arrive, where to park and what to wear. Also, as ever, it is a command, and only the best reasons are sufficient grounds for refusal. There is a reply form to be completed.

Dress

Clothes are suitably formal. Men wear morning dress, lounge suits or service uniform. Women arrive in smart day clothes. Hats are now optional, but should not be monumental or of an overly fanciful nature, as such accessories can get in the way during the investing and, as in the theatre, block the views of others. The normally rigorous royal rule of prohibiting cameras is slightly relaxed on this occasion: although they are forbidden inside the Palace, they can be used outside in the quadrangle after the ceremony for photographs.

The Form

Investitures are morning affairs. Guests arrive between ten and ten thirty. As usual, the palace is well staffed to make sure no one gets lost in between the front door and the ballroom. Those being decorated are taken to an anteroom, where they are quickly rehearsed in the imminent procedure. Their guests are directed to the ballroom and shown to their seats. The Queen arrives at eleven o'clock and makes her way to her place on a dais, escorted by two Gurkha orderly officers. The assembly stands and the National Anthem is struck up by the orchestra. Her Majesty invites everyone to sit down. One by one, each recipient enters the ballroom and makes his or her way towards The Queen to the dulcet strains of the Household Division orchestra. It is most important not to rush this and give the impression you are trying to catch a train. The Lord Chamberlain, who stands on the Sovereign's right, announces each recipient's name and the achievement for which they are being given an award. The Queen takes the relevant decoration from a cushion held by a senior member of the Royal Household and pins it into place. Those being knighted kneel on the investiture stool to be dubbed with the investiture sword. A few words are exchanged and the newly honoured subject bows or curtseys and makes his or her way to seats at the back of the ballroom. Although every effort is made to keep things moving, the ceremony normally lasts for around an hour and ten minutes. The end is signalled by the playing of the National Anthem, after which The Queen leaves. Everyone else then makes their way out to the Palace quadrangle for smiles, congratulations and photographs.

THE PARTY FOR WINNERS OF THE QUEEN'S AWARD FOR INDUSTRY

This now happens every year in February or March. It takes the form of a drinks party given by The Queen at Buckingham Palace for companies who have won an award. There are normally three guests from each firm, drawn from all ranks of the organisation. Invitations come from the Master of the Royal Household with presentation cards enclosed, which obviously have to be brought along on the night. Dress is dark suits for men and cocktail dresses or smart day clothes for women. Members of the Royal Household present guests to The Queen, The Duke of Edinburgh and any other members of the Royal Family present. The party ends when The Queen withdraws.

LUNCHEON AT BUCKINGHAM PALACE

There has been a gradual move on the part of The Queen to introduce more informal modes of entertaining to supplement the great set pieces of state. Luncheon at Buckingham Palace is one of these initiatives. It normally includes two members of the Royal Household and eight guests drawn from different walks of life. It is important to remember that guests are invited singly, and thus husbands, wives and partners are not expected.

Informal though these events are, invitations to attend them remain royal commands. So, to avoid complications, it is usual for the relevant member of the Royal Household to telephone the prospective guest first to make sure whether the date of the lunch fits in with their arrangements. If so, then a formal invitation is sent in the post, with the usual information about when to arrive, parking, et al. As this invitation is very specific, it should be answered formally in writing (see p. 122 above) and returned to the private secretary or other member of the Household who sent it, not, obviously, directly to The Queen. It is also sensible to take the invitation along on the day as a form of identification.

The Form

This is very much like any luncheon party, with a little royal protocol thrown in. For instance, rather than being greeted by their hosts in the usual fashion, guests are assembled in a drawing room, introduced to each other, given a drink and then wait for The Queen and The Duke of Edinburgh to come in. Then each guest is presented. After this there is a little light chatting before The Queen leads the way into lunch. It is most important not to sit down until Her Majesty does. There then follows a very nice but plain lunch at which guests are expected to converse in a normal, but not very boisterous way. The Queen and The Duke of Edinburgh will obviously try and talk to everybody during the three courses, but anyone who has not been properly spoken to will be brought forward at coffee, which is served back in the drawing room. The party ends when The Queen and The Duke of Edinburgh say goodbye and disappear from whence they came. It is usual to write a thank-you letter, but unless the guests already know The Queen quite well, this should be addressed to the member of the Household, asking him to convey thanks to Her Majesty.

Entertaining Royalty

The Royal Family are entertained just as much as they entertain. The diaries of its more diligent members are almost black with carefully timed engagements, many of which are organised months in advance. Thus the early bird gets the worm, and those wishing to have royalty present must get their request in soonest, have a good reason for wanting one of the family there and be very organised and accommodating about arrangements.

Although technically any subject can petition the Sovereign, all overtures and invitations should go via the relevant regal conduits, unless you are a friend or regular associate of the Royal Family inviting them to a private gathering such as a family wedding. As a general rule of thumb, Private Secretaries are approached for national and metropolitan issues and local Lord Lieutenants for regional events, although there will be London occasions when its Lord Lieutenant will have to be consulted. The first step is to write to the relevant Private Secretary or Lord Lieutenant, explaining the exact nature of the occasion – whether it be a charity ball, launching a cross-channel rail link or laying the foundation stone for a new theatre – and asking him to explore the possibility of the royal attendance. This overture, although tentative, needs to be carefully written, as the Royal Family, who already have plenty of fixed commitments associated with their particular patronages and state functions, yearly receive a vast array of invitations, ranging quite literally from the theoretically sublime to the utterly ridiculous. If this initial enquiry is successful, the Private Secretary or Lord Lieutenant will then convey to the organisers the form, style and structure that would best suit their royal boss and what they would like to see and do. He will also invite them to send in a more formal and comprehensive letter of invitation, accompanied by a draft programme containing details about dates, timings and other practical matters. If, on the other hand, an initial overture is rebuffed, there is nothing to stop hopefuls approaching representatives of other members of the Royal Family. However, people should always think twice about making a nuisance of themselves.

THE PROCEDURE ONCE AN INVITATION IS ACCEPTED
Once an invitation is accepted, there follows a considerable amount of liaison with the Private Secretary or Lord Lieutenant, who will need to organise every aspect of the event down to the tiniest detail. It is only in this way that embarrassing problems and misunderstandings will be avoided. He will want to check the wording of any invitations that announce his principal as the guest of honour, and work out an exact programme of events, presentations and security arrangements. He or his office will invariably wish to make a reconnaissance trip for complicated events to go through the motions with the organiser and to ensure that everything will proceed smoothly. All locations, even the smallest art gallery, where there

is to be a brief royal appearance will need to be cased by a detective, who will check all security arrangements and plan a get-out should there be a problem. Once everything has been finalised, it is usual to circulate the programme on a strict 'need-to-know' basis. It is also absolutely vital to stick strictly to the agreed plan, and not be tempted to offer impromptu suggestions on the day in the hope that they might amuse Her Majesty. They won't. The Private Secretary or Lord Lieutenant will also be able to answer all questions about the visit.

GENERAL BEHAVIOUR

If the invitation is to contain any reference to the royal visitor, the Private Secretary will want to check the wording and pass the plate before it is printed. It is incorrect, inaccurate and rude ever to use the words 'invites' or 'requests the pleasure of your company' in conjunction with the royal name in the hope that by pretending the royal personage is in some way the host the party will seem even more appealing. The royal visitor is a guest like everyone else. The correct form is to use the phrase 'in the gracious presence of Her Majesty The Queen'.

At all public occasions when a member of the Royal Family is present, it is not polite in a line-up or informal presentation to hold up the proceedings by embarking on a long conversation while others wait. Every moment is precious. This is particularly true at film or theatre premières, when delays will mean keeping the rest of the audience waiting in the auditorium. Similarly, people, once presented, must make their way into the auditorium and not hang around in the foyer. In this way the royal party is the last to sit down.

At all royal events, well-mannered people do not follow a member of the Royal Family around like obsequious limpets and never march up to a member of the Royal Family directly and introduce themselves or others. The correct form, if there is still time on an official visit for more presentations, is to approach those in attendance – the Private Secretary, Lord Lieutenant, equerry, lady-in-waiting or protection officer – and ask: 'Do you think Her Majesty or His/Her Royal Highness would like to meet . . .?'

Although the Royal Household bans cameras inside the various palace precincts, it is less able to control people's photographic compulsions outside on very public appearances such as walk-abouts. On these occasions, onlookers must remember never, ever to thrust a camera in the face of a member of the Royal Family. Nor should those who are being spoken to expect their companions to do so. It is as distressing to a royal visitor as to anybody else to have relentless flashing and snapping in front of them. At

135

all royal gatherings, there is an official photographer, who is there to provide a pictorial record of events.

Talking to the Press

If you have conversed privately with a member of the Royal Family at a public occasion, you might be approached for details. Never give anything away. Remember that the most innocent comment made by the Royal Family can be misused mischievously and perniciously by duplicitous journalists, many of whom have their own very unsavoury agendas.

Furthermore, to peddle willingly personal communications, whether they be small confidences or more protracted stories, to the press is the worst possible manners, a betrayal not only of the person, but in the case of royalty of something much more important. Even seemingly harmless gossip is a breach of trust.

And finally, those who think that the royal machine behaves in a pompous way should remember that the Royal Family expect a certain level of behaviour, not merely out of self-importance, but out of respect for the generations of others who have held the position before them.

Departures

Rules about departure before The Queen are less stringent than at one time, when to stir before the Sovereign left was positively unforgivable. Nowadays, should there be good and sensible reason for going early, it is acceptable, if not good manners, to ask the household politely in advance.

DIPLOMATIC OCCASIONS

Diplomatic occasions, in line with their royal counterparts, have become much less formal, elaborate and lavish than in earlier times. However, like all traditional institutions with a rich history steeped in convention and precedence, diplomacy today still enjoys many social embellishments and customs that are no longer in general use but need to be understood by a good embassy guest.

Good manners are fundamental. Firstly, because they prevent you from upsetting others. Secondly, because they enable you to put people, often of very different nationalities, customs and creeds, at their ease. Thirdly, because they make a good impression in a *métier* where appearances matter. Therefore, at diplomatic occasions it is unwise to start discussions about contentious political, religious or racial issues. These topics easily offend and should be left to the experts. Thus it is not advisable to follow the lead of a well-known British businessman, who tried to bend the

Russian Ambassador's ear at a reception about the problems his companies and bankers were having with the horrendous corruption in Mother Russia. Although these are real problems, of interest not only to the said businessman but to other British corporations, they are out of place at a cocktail party.

Overt xenophobia is also obviously quite out of order. Automatic assumptions about a shared Eurocentric viewpoint – say on human rights – are also problematical and best not taken for granted once within an embassy's precincts. The same is true of simple codes of social behaviour. For instance, complimenting a woman's appearance is an established way in Britain to be friendly. This is not the case in other, particularly Arab, cultures, where you have to know people very well before comments of a personal nature are acceptable. Remember, if you do make an innocent remark that causes offence, let it drop by quickly moving on to another topic, rather than trying desperately to dig yourself out of the mess. Most well-mannered people present will recognise the problem and try and throw you a conversational lifeline. It should be grasped gratefully. Also, do not try to ape the host's social customs of greetings and language: Eskimo kisses have no place in SW1. Such attempts at international *bonhomie*, although usually well meaning, invariably appear condescending and inappropriate. Nearly all diplomats speak English; however, it is still considered very recherché for British people to be able to converse in French – the diplomatic language *par excellence*.

In Britain the diplomatic presence is headed up by the Commonwealth high commissioners and an army of ambassadors accredited to the Court of St James's. These officials are looked after by Her Majesty's Marshal of the Diplomatic Corps, whose duties range from the presentation of credentials and organising The Queen's Evening Reception to giving the Diplomatic Corps a good time in the Diplomatic Box at Royal Ascot. In terms of precedence high commissioners and ambassadors are very important, as they are the most senior representatives of their country. Thus even the most throwaway comment can easily be interpreted, if no longer quite as a national insult that will bring two great states to the brink of imminent war, as certainly deeply unproductive and rude.

Within their ranks, high commissioners and ambassadors have their own rigorous pecking order. They (and particularly their wives) can be wildly competitive and are easily offended at lapses in this protocol. Firstly, it is important to master the subtle semantic differences between the two. It is always High Commissioner *for* Never-Never Land but the Ambassador *of* Ruritania. The degree of precedence is splendidly democratic (and diplomatic) in a very British way, and is determined not by the size, wealth and power of the country concerned, but by how long its representative has been in the post. Thus the longest serving is the most senior and the most recently arrived the most junior. This system prevents the possibility of a representative of a foreign country feeling slighted by not being accorded the precedence he may feel his nation is due. There is even the rank of Doyen of the Diplomatic Corps, an honour bestowed on the longest-serving ambassador. He takes precedence over all the others. Those who need to know about ambassadorial precedence can consult the London Diplomatic list, which lists everybody first in alphabetical order and then in order of precedence. It is published by HMSO and updated every two months.

Spoken Forms of Address

Traditionally at a formal occasion a Commonwealth high commissioner or an ambassador should be addressed in the first instance as 'Your Excellency' and thereafter as 'Sir' or 'Madam', or by name if you know them. At a purely social event 'High Commissioner/Ambassador' is the usual form, addressing by name only if he or she is known to you.

In conversation, say for the purposes of introduction, a high commissioner is referred to as 'His/Her Excellency the High Commissioner for Canada' or 'His/Her Excellency the Canadian High Commissioner'. The form is similar for ambassadors, who are referred to as 'His/Her Excellency the Ambassador of Spain' or 'His/Her Excellency the Spanish Ambassador'. It is important to remember that there is no feminine adaptation of these roles. Thus the term 'Ambassadress' is purely a courtesy title used for wives of serving ambassadors. Wives of Commonwealth high commissioners and male spouses of ambassadors have no such embellishments, unless, of course, they are titled in their own right. Please note that in diplomatic circles 'the Netherlands' is used and never 'Holland'.

Written Forms of Address

Until relatively recently, letters to ambassadors were extremely formal – distinguished by the grand beginning of 'Your Excellency' and by extremely flowery endings such as 'I have the honour to be, with the highest consideration, Your Excellency's obedient servant'. Commonwealth high commissioners were treated to the similarly impressive sign-off: 'I have the honour to be Your Excellency's obedient servant'. Although these deferential flourishes are still technically correct, they are now thought old-fashioned and are rarely used.

Instead the social form is acceptable in almost all correspondence. Thus letters begin: 'Dear Ambassador/High Commissioner', or, if he is known to you: 'My dear Ambassador'. They can end quite simply with the everyday 'Yours sincerely', although it is more usual, and polite, to use the traditional 'Believe me, Yours sincerely'. One old diplomatic *politesse* endures and is much appreciated by ambassadors and high commissioners of the old school. This is to mention the words 'Your Excellency' in the opening paragraph and again in the closing one. In between just 'you' and 'your' are used.

When addressing envelopes 'His Excellency' should always be used and written in full. It should also precede all other titles (noble or military), which in turn are followed by the name. The suffix 'Esq.' is never used. Thus a typical example would be:

His Excellency General Achim von Schwartzundweiss the Ambassador of Austria/the Austrian Ambassador

The joint form of address for him and his wife would read:

His Excellency General Achim von Schwartzundweiss and Frau von Schwartzundweiss

Entertaining

Although foreign service budgets are not what they were, diplomats still do a lot of entertaining, ranging from the impressively grand to, occasionally, the embarrassingly frugal. These parties can take the form of lunches, dinners or, most usually, cocktail parties and other stand-up receptions. They are invariably given for a reason, such as to honour a visiting dignitary, promote a business interest, celebrate an important national day or entertain a visiting cultural organisation that is doing a tour. The reason is usually stated on the invitation. Many of the missions – such as the American, French and Italian – have particularly impressive embassies and residences, in which their ambassadors entertain most convivially. The style, splendour and formality of diplomatic party-giving varies considerably, and is immensely influenced by not just the nation and its regime, but the personal style of the current ambassador, or more usually his wife.

THE INVITATION

Diplomatic invitations should be replied to formally in writing and in the third person. If, however, a telephone number is given, this may be used instead, although the traditional form is still preferred. Faxed replies should be avoided, as they lack style. When attending any sort of diplomatic gathering it is sensible always to bring the invitation, as nowadays, particularly at dangerous times, security has to be very strict.

DRESS
The invitation will probably give some idea of what is expected sartorially. It is wise to pay attention to the signs. Nowadays most diplomatic gatherings require only dark suits for men and their equivalent for women. However, there are some that require dinner jackets and occasionally evening dress (white tie). If the word 'Decorations' appears on the invitations it means that the most formal style of evening dress is expected (see Chapter 17). This traditionally meant white tie, but nowadays black tie is quite often acceptable. Always ask if the invitation is not clear. As a general rule of thumb, a banquet still requires white tie, while dinners make do with black tie. Women's clothes, as always in these instances, take their cues from the men's. Thus black tie means a short or long dinner dress, and white tie a long evening dress. Trousers are not appropriate. Women also have to be aware that diplomatic dressing requires attention to the cultural notions of modesty of the host country. Thus it would be inconsiderate to arrive at a Muslim embassy with mounds of cleavage and/or arms on display. On the other hand, there is no need to make an embarrassing attempt at national costume, as is the wont of one public figure's wife.

CATERING
This also varies enormously, depending on the ambassadorial taste level and budget. In most cases it follows the food and drink trends elsewhere in society. Thus champagne and wine tend to be served more than spirits and mixed drinks: food is much more sensible, economical and health conscious than the ambassadorial amplitudes of yesteryear. Sometimes a choice of national cuisine is served, but this is usually not the case, as the food invariably needs to suit the preferences and dietary regulations of people from vastly differing cultures. If guests have specific dietary requirements, it is, as at all formal dinners, polite to let your hosts know in advance, rather than making a fuss on the night.

Sundry Diplomatic Courtesies
At one time there was always a huge amount of visiting card presenting, exchanging and passing around going on between diplomats and their guests. For instance, it was usual to leave a card with an ambassador after meeting him socially. Although this remains correct, and very useful, its observance is so infrequent that omitting to do so is no longer a diplomatic

solecism. Embassy visiting books do endure, and it is still customary to sign them when arriving or leaving. If you have not signed the book, it is customary to write a thank-you letter to your host or hostess.

Entertaining Diplomats

When inviting a major ambassador to attend a party or an official gathering, it is worth remembering that the big fish in the diplomatic pond – i.e. those representing major powers with extensive interests – are very important indeed. They are the direct representatives of their heads of state and are accorded suitable precedence. Their diaries are busy and fill up very quickly. The sensible hostess who has set her heart on a certain Excellency always rings up the embassy first to make sure that her quarry is free on the night she wants him. In this way, should he be already spoken for, she is able to change her proposed date without any loss of face. If the ambassador is available then a formal invitation is sent to him in the usual manner (see Chapter 8). Even minor ambassadors, who at one time seemed very free to go to anything, nowadays have much busier professional lives and thus need to be booked early.

It is also recommended, when feeding an ambassador and others not just from another country but another culture, to make enquiries at the embassy about dietary customs. Beef, pork and alcohol, although eaten with impunity and gusto here, are often off-limits elsewhere. It is wise too to be circumspect about the guest list and be careful about inviting people who are very amusing in most circumstances, but whose behaviour might offend someone from a very different cultural background. There was one dinner, attended by an important official from the Middle East, where the poor guest of honour spent most of his time looking at the floor in embarrassment, to avoid gawping at the barely clothed spectacular bosom next to him.

Further Information

The analogy of royalty and diplomacy also extends to the set-up that serves them. Most larger embassies have protocol sections, staffed by (usually) helpful people who will advise on all aspects of behaviour, food, clothes and customs. In addition to this service, the various attachés and secretaries should all be experts in their fields. If all else fails, there is the Protocol Department at our own Foreign and Commonwealth Office to consult.

OTHER FORMAL OCCASIONS

In addition to royal and diplomatic entertainment, there are a great many occasions staged by other proud and ancient institutions. Paramount are the gatherings given by the Lord Mayor and the Corporation of London, and the many City livery companies. These stage banquets, dinners, luncheons and receptions of a formality that often outdoes anything on offer at the royal palaces and grandest embassies. But they are not alone. The Inns of Court, the armed services and Oxbridge colleges all give grand gatherings graced by many arcane and vastly differing customs.

Space does not allow me to explain all these fascinating behavioural idiosyncrasies here, as they differ enormously not just from one *métier* to another, but also within specific spheres and organisations. However, there are several general points, which distinguish events of this kind from run-of-the-mill formal entertaining, and which the unsuspecting guest should know about.

High Tables

This custom comes down to us from the Middle Ages, when pecking orders and pageantry were as important at any banquet as the stuffed peacocks and boars' heads that graced the feast. Today such eye-catching culinary delights may have slipped from the menu, but the ritual practice of high table survives at many state, civic, university and legal banquets and dinners. The occupants of the high table are always the principal hosts and most important guests attending a banquet. They process to their table (normally a long rectangular raised one at the head of the room or chamber) after everybody else has assembled at their places. There are even some City livery companies whose traditions require their top table guests to go up before the hosts. As the top table party enters, the rest of the company stands and in many cases begins a slow hand-clap that accompanies its stately progress to, and later from, its prominent place. This practice may be offputting for overseas visitors, and so during reconnaissance visits to the City beforehand, those representing them are assured that the slow hand-clap is a traditional form of greeting rather than any comment on the timings of the principal guests' arrival. Thus any temptation to rush is to be avoided. Also, guests should be aware that this is not a universal custom, and so should not risk being the first, and maybe only, person to leap to their feet and start clapping. Such enthusiasm can be embarrassing, to say the least.

The Rose Bowl

The rite of the rose bowl is an ancient nicety that endures at livery, civic and college dinners. Made of anything from simple glass to priceless plate, these large bowls are filled with rose water, usually floating with petals, and are then passed around the company. Each guest delicately avails him- or herself of the contents either by dabbling their fingers in the water and drying them on a napkin or by dipping the corners of the napkin in the liquid and gently dabbing its moistened edge on to the temple or fingers. Which method is used is a personal matter, but the latter is rather more elegant, certainly more hygienic and more modern. Clumsy types must beware, and all people should remember that this act is merely symbolic and should not resemble a wash and brush-up in the bathroom.

Speeches

There are few formal dinners or banquets without speeches, which usually take place after the toasts and the end of the eating. However, some formal occasions nowadays provide for the speeches to be given before the dinner is served. This happened at the Guildhall luncheon in November 1992 to mark the fortieth anniversary of the accession of The Queen, and later again at the VE Day banquet there in 1995, when both speeches and toasts were given before the banquet. This procedure is increasingly popular because its format allows for a lengthier talk or speech to be given, while still ensuring that the evening concludes early enough for everybody to return home at a reasonable hour. This is particularly appreciated at livery dinners, as the modern City guest has to get up a lot earlier than his more languid predecessors.

There is also a trend to make speeches shorter, snappier and more entertaining. However, there are many tedious speakers, often overlubricated by good wine, still pontificating at length in historic halls across the realm. Ministers regurgitating Civil Service briefs are particular offenders. Whatever the *ennui*, guests must sit quietly during such speeches, laughing politely at attempts at jokes and avoiding whispering to their table mates and making catty asides. It is normal to clap politely at the beginning and the end.

Toasts

Toasts are invariably drunk at the end of formal luncheons, dinners and banquets. The form they take varies considerably and can be a nightmare for the *ingénue*, who can find himself standing up and raising his glass at completely the wrong time and in splendid, if toe-curling isolation.

The most usual is the Loyal Toast to the Sovereign, in which the simple words 'The Queen' are uttered without preamble. It is given after dinner, and after the second grace, if said. There is also sometimes a Second Loyal Toast. Since 1981 it has taken the form of 'Queen Elizabeth The Queen

Mother, The Prince Philip Duke of Edinburgh, The Prince (and at the time of writing Princess) of Wales and other members of the Royal Family'. Guests should look out for musicians, for if there are some present, they are likely to strike up the entire National Anthem for the Loyal Toast and the first six bars of it for the Second Loyal Toast. The procedure is as follows: the principal host rises and gives the toast. Everybody else stands up. If the National Anthem is to be played, glasses remain firmly on the table until the music has ended. When the band stops, glasses are raised and the toast is said and drunk. All sit.

However, toasts have many variations. Some are preceded by a short preamble or even a complete speech or address. Others have no preludes whatsoever. One vital rule is never, ever be the first to stand up, as some toasts are drunk sitting down. This is especially true of the navy (for obvious reasons of inclement seas and low-ceilinged mess decks), but also of some army regiments, who have some very odd procedures indeed.

Port

No formal dinner is complete without the passing of the port, despite the fact that today fewer people drink this historic beverage. Port is put on the table for guests to help themselves. It is always, always passed to the left. Port is never drunk before the Loyal Toast – in fact it often *is* the Loyal Toast. Should you miss the port on its relentless clockwise progress (as I once did when sitting next to an exceedingly bibulous man, who filled his glass before I had time to blink), then it is bad form to ask for the decanter to be returned to you, as is would mean – horror of horrors – that it would need to travel the wrong way. Instead, pass your empty glass to the left until it catches up with the decanter, where it is filled by the diner currently in possession of it.

The Loving Cup Ceremony

This is one that really bemuses the innocents. This ancient and somewhat paranoid little ritual is said to date back to Saxon times, when King Edward the Martyr, on the treacherous instigation of his stepmother, Queen Elfrida, was stabbed to death at Corfe Castle while he held a large drinking vessel to his face with both hands and was thus unable to defend himself. Since then, legend has it, no man has done this without making sure that an associate was there to protect him.

Today the continuation of this quaint rite is meant to symbolise that nobody present at a social gathering wishes ill of his fellow guests. It is usual for a cup containing spiced wine (sack) to pass in a clockwise direction, starting with the head of the table, although at very large dinners there might be two bowls moving simultaneously around the table to save time. When there is more than one cup moving around, it has been known for bets to be taken on which will reach the end of its journey first.

As space is often limited and people can be very clumsy, the Loving Cup ceremony requires concentration to avoid disaster. The procedure appears very complicated, but once mastered is relatively easy to execute, as everybody does the same. Rather like the tango, it takes two. Guest A accepts the cup from his neighbour. He/she then turns and faces the diner on his/her other side, whom we shall call Guest B. Guest B stands, and both A and B, facing each other, make a courteous bow or curtsey. Guest B then lifts the lid of the loving cup with his/her right (that is, dagger) hand and holds it aloft, to show to one and all that he is disarmed and has no mortal intent. Then Guest A lifts the cup to his lips and drinks a small symbolic sip as if taking communion. Nowadays it is acceptable for those who have a heavy cold, or who are concerned about the risk of infection from others using the cup, to take the cup to their lips but not actually drink from it. Guest A then delicately wipes the rim of the cup with the napkin encircling the cup. After this Guest B replaces the lid and both A and B make another little bow. Now Guest A passes the cup to Guest B and turns so that A and B are standing back-to-back. Guest B then turns to his neighbour (whom we shall call Guest C). Guest C rises and the whole ritual is re-enacted. Guest A does not sit down again until the cup is in the hands of Guest C. In this way there are always three people standing up: the guest who has drunk from the cup, the guest who is in the process of drinking from it and the guest who is about to partake of this arcane draught.

Smoking

This, as at all social gatherings today, is a vexed question that gets no easier. Traditionally it is beyond the pale to light up before the Loyal Toast. And though many people try to flout the custom, it remains crass bad manners to do so at any sort of formal banquet or dinner at which toasts are to be given. Some gatherings make a point of asking the toastmaster to announce: 'You may now smoke', but this habit always strikes me as being more suitable at a holiday camp than a grand livery company. Therefore, lighting up should be left until after the toast, and when coffee is served. As everywhere, it is polite to ask if the person beside you minds. As to the choice of smoke, cigars and cigarettes are acceptable; pipes are not. At state and some other banquets, coffee is served away from the table, and in these cases it is particularly unsuitable to smoke before this at the table.

Dress

The traditional dress is white tie for men and the corresponding long dresses for women. This attire is still expected at the Lord Mayor's and City state banquets, and at some livery company gatherings, although some of the smaller ones do now allow black tie. However, it is advisable to remember that the City of London adores a pageant and still expects a level of formality that today is rare elsewhere. Formal luncheons still require morning dress worn with a black waistcoat. Mobile telephones and bleepers are not acceptable accessories at these grand gatherings and should not be brought.

Food and Drink

Food at formal banquets is chosen to suit the tastes of as many people as possible. Thus there is unlikely to be anything too frightening on the menu. However, those who are vegetarian or have allergies or religious principles affecting food should let the organisers know when accepting the invitation. They will pass on the information so that the caterers can act accordingly. It is bad manners to make a fuss on the night, as such attention-seeking behaviour succeeds only in holding up an already complicated procedure. As food at formal banquets is brought round by staff, it is simplest not to take anything that you don't like. However, if presented with a culinary *fait accompli*, just toy with it a little with your knife and fork, but without eating it. Some people are expert at hiding food under bits of salad or garnish to make it look as if it has been eaten. On the other hand, self-sacrifice is not expected, even at the most august gatherings. There is no need to follow the example of one nervous woman who, faced with a first course that would have sent her straight to Bart's accident and emergency department, deftly tipped the offending nourishment into her rather too small evening bag, where it spent the entire evening.

Leaving the Table

This too can cause a certain amount of anguish, as it is popularly assumed that if The Queen ever goes to the lavatory, it is only *very* occasionally, and thus those attending a quasi-regal event must also resist the call of nature. This of course is nonsense. Those who need must. However, it is not clever to keep leaving the table during a banquet, no matter how discreetly. There is usually a gap of at least five minutes between the formal toasts and the speeches, while the coffee is being served, when guests may leave the table and return with the minimum of fuss. However, the best advice is to remember to go to the loo when you arrive and before entering the party. This avoids causing disruption during the banquet and the mad rush – and often, for women, interminable wait – at the end.

Leaving Early

One of the great social affections of today is feigning a lack of time. Therefore people who consider themselves busier than everyone else make a great thing about not staying too long or having to leave early. This behaviour has now extended from the business lunch (acceptable) to the formal banquet (frankly rude). However, there are times when guests have bona fide reasons for wanting to go before everybody else: an early flight, the last train to Watery Wallop or when recuperating from illness. In these cases, it is polite to let the organisers know beforehand, and also to have a word with the host. When the time comes, leave quietly at a natural interval in the proceedings. The five-minute gap in between the formal toasts and the speeches is an ideal juncture to depart prematurely without causing offence.

8

THE WRITTEN WORD

Despite the emergence of newer, faster and more sophisticated telecommu-
nications, the written word remains a powerful communicative and social
tool. It also retains an important place in modern-day etiquette. There has
been social change, however. For instance, where once a letter was the *only*
way to thank for a dinner party, now a promptly mailed postcard will do;
wedding invitations – their wording preserved unchanged for decades –
have adapted to accommodate the complexities of the modern fragmented
family; and increasing informality has meant that many old-fashioned
conventions have been abandoned in favour of a less stuffy approach.

In this chapter I will explain the current form concerning invitation
cards, stationery, letter and envelope style, and the Internet.

INVITATION CARDS
Written invitations (never refer to them as 'invites') remain the form for
many social occasions. As well as announcing a party and setting its tone,
they prevent any confusion about dates, timings, location, dress and the
hospitality provided. Nonetheless they can cause all manner of anxiety
amongst the socially nervous. A certain insecure hostess who repeatedly
changed the design, size and script of her invitation to a dance she was
giving for her son's twenty-first, found that the finished invitations went out
so late that many people were unable to accept. Whether this was due to
prior engagements or to the general opinion of the hostess, history does not
relate.

Most people run into difficulties when they make an uneasy compromise between tradition and innovation. If in doubt remember that, with the traditional approach, you can hardly go wrong. Attempts at originality, particularly those undertaken without style, can often end up looking uncouth.

This being said, many hosts, less hidebound than earlier generations, want to bring more individuality to their invitations, by perhaps opting for colour combinations other than the austere black on white or by incorporating an idiosyncratic visual device into designs. As a general rule of thumb, it is best to stick to the most traditional approach for such time-honoured rites of passage as birth announcements, twenty-first birthdays and weddings, and to reserve more individual designs for personal events such as a house-warming or Hallowe'en party. If you do choose to break the rules it must be done with confidence. Little looks less inspiring than a half-hearted break with tradition.

Over recent years the size of invitations has increased, as has the weight of paper used. Today the most frequent dimensions are five and a half inches by seven, and four and a half by six.

The Grand Style

The specially engraved 'stiffy' is – mainly due to its cost and the decrease in very grand entertaining – considerably less used than before. It is reserved for the most important and grand occasions, such as weddings, twenty-first dances and formal dinners and luncheons. A copper plate is specially engraved and the weight of card used is pretty substantial. However, those who wish to impress should remember that the type of card should be neither too monumental nor vulgar, unless the impression they wish to make is one of ostentation. The simplest treatment is always the most sophisticated.

An invitation should be on fairly thick card, around 600 grams, and should measure approximately five and a half inches by seven, depending on how much information it contains. The most usual script is copperplate. The most suitable colour combination remains black type on white or cream card. Square corners are smarter than rounded ones. Gold edges are best avoided, but, if used, should be discreetly bevelled and in a soft, never bright, gold.

The card must contain all the information the guest needs to know: who is giving the party, for whom, the occasion, the location, the date, the time and details about how to R.S.V.P. and what to wear. Traditionally invitations to formal luncheons and dinners are worded as follows:

149

Sir George and Lady Generous
request the pleasure of your company
at a dinner for their son, Lucky,
on Wednesday, 27th May
at
The Lavmakers Hall
London EC4

The R.S.V.P. details are engraved in the bottom left corner and the time and the dress in the bottom right. The old-fashioned custom of using 'honour' in place of 'pleasure' is still popular in the United States but is rarely used in Britain.

It is now usual, and more elegant, for the guest's name to be written by hand in the top left-hand corner, although some people and some grand organisations still retain the more old-fashioned style of engraving a dotted line below 'requests the pleasure of the company of' on which they fill in the name of the guest by hand. Those, nowadays rather few, individuals who entertain formally on a very regular basis also lay in a stock of invitation cards engraved with 'Lord and Lady Super-Generous request the pleasure of your company' and the R.S.V.P. address, with space left to write in all the other details by hand.

It is vital to make sure that the proof (all good stationers will offer a facsimile prior to engraving) is carefully checked. Mistakes are expensive and embarrassing.

The Use of 'at Home'

The use of 'at Home' has become increasingly popular because the 'requests the pleasure of your company' model has developed rather corporate overtones in recent years. It is also thought friendlier than its rather more starchy counterpart and is now widely used for dances, receptions, supper and dinners at which a certain amount of formality is expected. This being said, many people forget that it remains a solecism for 'at Home' cards to be engraved in anything other than the name of the hostess only, whether she be married or single. Men, although many choose to ignore the custom, should still use the more formal model of 'requests the pleasure of your company'. The same applies to invitations where both members of a married couple are the hosts. Companies ought never to be 'at Home' on an invitation. Although 'at Home' suggests a domestic gathering, it is acceptable to be 'at Home' in a hotel, restaurant or club.

The usual measurement for an 'at Home' invitation is four and a half by

Examples of commonly used 'at Home' cards

six inches, although cards of slightly larger dimensions are becoming more popular. Smaller cards, measuring three and a half inches by five and a half, engraved with only the hostess's name, 'at Home', R.S.V.P. and her address are suitable for most parties but never dances.

Traditionally 'at Home' invitations are composed of black copperplate engraved letters on white or cream card. If specially engraved for a specific occasion, they contain all relevant information and could read:

Lady Bountiful
at Home
Monday, 1st June

R.S.V.P.   Dancing
Liberty Hall   10.30 o'clock
Wimborne
Dorset

The smaller, multi-purpose 'at Home' card should carry only the following information:

Mrs Gloria Giving
at Home

R.S.V.P.
13 Lansdowne Lane
London W11

Everything else – the date, time and type of entertainment, 'drinks' or 'dinner' and the names of guests – is filled in by hand.

'At Home' cards that merely have 'at Home' and 'R.S.V.P.' engraved on them are widely available ready-engraved from good stationers and are the most economical option, but are unsuitable for a party that is in any way a special occasion. They usually measure four by six and a quarter inches and require the hostess to add by hand all other information, such as her name and address, the date, time, guest's name and other relevant details. Remember, though, that it is not done to write the year on 'at Home' cards.

'At Home' cards can also be used as a reminder after an invitation has been offered over the telephone. In this case, all details are filled in as if it were an invitation, except the R.S.V.P., which is scored out and 'to remind' written in by hand in its place. There is no need for this to be acknowledged by the guest.

The Styling of Hosts' and Hostesses' Names and Formal Invitations

The name of the host is generally engraved formally, although there are several stylistic variations. For instance, men are styled Mr John Jovial, never John Jovial Esq. Single women are shown as Miss Susan Smart, married ones as Mrs James Goodhost and divorcees as Mrs Helena Hearty. 'Ms' should never be used on a social invitation. Peers or peeresses are styled by their exact rank, although 'The' is omitted, for example Viscountess Grizzleton. Baronets always omit 'Bt.'. Prefixes such as 'The Right Honourable' are also left out, as are letters after the name, such as OBE. In the case of joint hosts or hostesses, the name of the person to whom the replies are to be sent is placed first.

The Contemporary Informal Variation

Many people, in tune with the reduced use of prefixes (Mr, Mrs, Lord and Lady) in modern life, eschew their use on formal invitations. For example:

Freddie Friendly and Charles Chummy
request the pleasure of your company
at their House-Warming Party
on 21 November

This is intended to create an egalitarian and more informal image. Although incorrect, it has become acceptable in many circumstances.

The Styling of Guests' Names on Formal Invitations

Guest's names are filled in by hand (with a fountain pen, never a ballpoint), in most cases in the top left-hand corner of the invitation card. The only exceptions are cards that are designed to include them in the centre of the card. The filling in of guests' names can also be tricky, as cards and envelopes require different treatment. Full prefixes, titles, ranks and decorations are used for envelopes but not on invitations. On these, the styling of guests' names normally mirrors the way the names of the hosts are presented.

Untitled people are styled simply as Mr, Mrs or Miss on the card. The same applies on the envelope, except in the case of men, when Esq. is used. A peer is treated to his full title on the envelope – for instance, 'The Viscount Grizzleton' – but is styled more informally on the card as Lord Grizzleton. The only exceptions are dukes and duchesses, who are referred to fully in all instances. A baronet is styled with 'Bt.' on the envelope, but not on the card. An honourable would read as The Hon. Annabel Tray on the envelope, but as Miss Annabel Tray on the card. Prefixes and letters after the name are expected on envelopes but not on cards. Both halves of a married couple are named on the card – i.e. Mr and Mrs David Plate – but the envelope would be addressed to Mrs David Plate alone, as convention assumes that only women organise social arrangements. In the case of unmarried couples or same-sex partnerships, the two names are used both on the invitation and the envelope – i.e. Mr Edward Spoon and Mr Rupert Fork-Lift on the card and Edward Spoon Esq. and Rupert Fork-Lift Esq. on the envelope. Grown-up children who live at home are sent separate invitations, and should not be styled 'and family' after their parents' names. However, it is quite acceptable to write 'and guest' after a singly invited guest who is allowed to bring someone.

JOINT FORMS OF ADDRESS
Complications can arise when husbands and wives are styled differently. This most often occurs when a woman retains a courtesy title because she is the daughter of a peer. In these cases the usual form is: 'Mr White and Lady Sarah White' (for the progeny of earls, marquesses and dukes); and 'Mr Black and the Hon. Mrs Black' (for the offspring of viscounts and barons). There can also be confusion with male courtesy titles. Whereas the younger son and daughter-in-law of a duke or marquess are simply called 'Lord and Lady Charles Scarlet', those of an earl, viscount or baron are styled either as 'The Hon. John and Mrs Pink' or, if the wife has her own courtesy title, as 'The Hon. Peter and Lady Emma Yellow'.

General Points

Although it used to be considered a solecism for guests to bring an invitation to a private party, increased gate-crashing has meant that, if necessary, it is permissible, but not stylish, to engrave 'Please bring this invitation with you' at the foot of the card. A more elegant alternative is to enclose a small card with this instruction printed on it. Required dress is expressed in various codes: 'white tie' means evening dress, 'black tie' means dinner jackets. The words 'lounge suits' should never appear on an invitation. 'Decorations' on a private invitation implies there may be royalty present. Unless there are words suggesting otherwise, a party is held at the R.S.V.P. address. Invitations to parties in out-of-the-way places are best accompanied by a map printed either on the back of the card or, more elegantly, on a separate sheet of paper.

Replying to Formal Invitations

A formal invitation requires a formal reply. This must be written by hand, in ink, on headed paper and in the third person:

> Lady Grizzleton thanks Mr Edward Spoon and Mr Rupert Fork-Lift for their kind invitation to dinner on Friday 21st April and has much pleasure in accepting.

or, alternatively:

> Lady Grizzleton thanks Mr Edward Spoon and Mr Rupert Fork-Lift for their kind invitation to dinner on Friday 21st April, but due to a previous engagement she regrets she is unable to accept.

When the invitation has included 'and Guest' after the invitee's name, then it is customary and polite that the reply should contain the name of the guest:

> Lady Grizzleton and her guest, Mrs Fatte, thank Mr Edward Spoon etc.

If the invitation gives a telephone number for replies (quite usual with less formal examples such as when no prefixes are used), then replies should be rung in. Should 'Regrets only' be used instead of R.S.V.P., then only those who can't come respond.

Wedding Invitations

The majority of wedding invitations remain in the traditional form they have enjoyed for decades. This is fitting because the marriage service itself, although often enthusiastically embraced by the most modern of couples, remains a ceremony of arcane and antique symbolism. Like other invitations, wedding ones have become larger and of a heavier weight over the years. Today the most usual dimensions are eight inches high by six across. Folded white or cream matt card is most commonly used, and black copperplate engraved script is the preferred typeface. Thermography – shiny black pseudo engraving (see p. 163 below) – is particularly depressing when used on wedding invitations and is not recommended.

Many otherwise educated and cultivated people seem to lose all grasp of grammar and common sense when composing the invitation. This, combined with the confusion of extended families, can result in awkward phrasing.

155

The choice of wording is, quite simply, governed by accepted custom and by the identity of the hosts of the wedding and their relationship with the bride.

The conventional approach, that of still married parents marrying their natural daughter, is the starting point for all other formulations and reads:

Brigadier and Mrs Basil Blimp
request the pleasure of your company
at the marriage of their daughter
Hermione
to
Mr Darren Arthur Smith
at St Anthony's Church, Knightsbridge,
on Wednesday, 14th March
at 2.30 o'clock
and afterwards at
The Boot and Bayonet Club

R.S.V.P.
Smellings Manor
Little Smelling
Loamshire

The variations on this theme are many and fascinating:

If Mrs Blimp is widowed, then, obviously, 'Mrs Basil Blimp' alone requests the pleasure (and vice versa). If Mrs Blimp is divorced from Brigadier Blimp, but not remarried to another, the wording is: 'Brigadier Basil Blimp and Mrs Elizabeth Blimp request the pleasure'. If Mrs Blimp has divorced and remarried and is now called Lady Charles Cove, and both she and Brigadier Blimp are briefly reuniting to host Hermione's nuptials, the card would read: 'Brigadier Basil Blimp and Lady Charles Cove request the pleasure'. If Mrs Blimp has remarried, is now Mrs Henry Buffer, and she and her new husband are giving the wedding, then the invitation would read: 'Mr and Mrs Henry Buffer request the pleasure of your company at the marriage of her daughter'. If sadly both Brigadier and Mrs Blimp have perished on the hunting field and their orphaned daughter's wedding is being given by her deceased mother's sister, then the invitation would read: 'Mr and Mrs Charles Codger-Brown request the pleasure of your company at the marriage of their niece, Hermione' (the same model applies if a bride's wedding is being hosted by her

Mr Nigel Bayliss Cox
and
Mrs Jennifer Stark
request the pleasure of your company
at the marriage of their daughter
Katherine Paula
to
Captain Jeremy Nicholas Standish
(The Blues and Royals)
on Saturday, 25th September
at 12.00 o'clock
at the Guards Chapel, Wellington Barracks
London, W.1.
and afterwards at
The Connaught

R.S.V.P
The Old Rectory
Lower Mills
Canterbury
Kent

Example of typical wedding invitation

godparents or guardians: in these cases 'godchildren' and 'ward' respectively would be used. If non-married relations such as siblings, brothers- or sisters-in-law or cousins are giving the wedding, their surnames should be repeated – 'Mr John Blimp and Mr Peter Blimp request the pleasure of your company at the marriage of their sister, Hermione'; the only exception is in the case of unmarried sisters: 'The Misses Blimp request the pleasure of your company at the marriage of their sister, Hermione'. Should the Blimps have separated acrimoniously and be unable to bear the sight of one another, then it may be sensible if only one of them gives the wedding; in this case the invitation should read: 'Brigadier Basil Blimp requests . . .' If Hermione's wedding is being hosted by her stepmother (for instance, in the case of both her natural parents being dead or unwilling), the invitation would be worded: 'Mrs Basil Blimp requests the pleasure of your company at the marriage of her step-daughter, Hermione'.

Should poor Hermione find her family arrangements too complicated to contemplate, then, of course, she could host her own wedding, although this would be most unusual on her first marriage. In this case the wording on the invitations would read:

Miss Hermione Blimp
requests the pleasure of your company
at her marriage
to
Mr Darren Arthur Smith
etc.

This format, as well as being ideal for young brides on a distant footing with their parents, is also appropriate for those who are marrying without parental approval. It is suitable too for what is diplomatically known as a 'late wedding' of mature partners, when there are no longer living parents or relations to give the bride away.

'Late weddings' and the nuptials of widows can also be hosted by the bride and groom together. A typical invitation would read:

Miss Gloria Good-Sort and Mr Charles Chappe
request the pleasure of your company at their marriage
etc.

Divorced couples barred from having a church wedding, but having a service of blessing, would send a card that could read:

158

Mrs Elfreda Egg and Mr David Duck
request the pleasure of your company
at a service of blessing following their marriage
etc.

The Styling of the Bride's Name

Except when a bride is hosting her own wedding, the accepted practice is for the first-time bride's name to appear without her surname; however, the often labyrinthine complexities of much-married families mean that, for reasons of clarity, the bride's own surname can be used where instructive. For instance, when a daughter is brought up by a stepfather and the girl's wedding is given by 'parents' who do not share her name because her mother has remarried and has a new identity. As with adaptations of style, this variation should be used only when absolutely necessary.

Brides celebrating second or subsequent marriages have slightly different conventions. A widow is still somewhat archaically described as 'Susan, widow of Mr Giles Goode-Fellow'. A divorcee is styled 'Mrs Susan Goode-Fellow'. A woman who has reverted to her maiden name uses her first name only. Brides hosting their own celebrations would be styled as Mrs Giles Goode-Fellow, Mrs Susan Goode-Fellow or Miss Susan Single, as applicable.

Invitations to Wedding Reception Only

As space is sometimes limited in churches and other places of worship, it is often necessary to produce a second invitation to invite guests to the wedding reception only. This could read:

Brigadier and Mrs Basil Blimp
request the pleasure of your company
at a reception following the marriage
of their daughter Hermione
to Mr Darren Arthur Smith
on Wednesday 14th March
at The Boot and Bayonet Club

R.S.V.P.   4.30 o'clock
Smellings Manor
Little Smelling
Loamshire

A similar format would also be used in the case of a dance given to celebrate a marriage. Remember, whereas it is accepted that a guest can be invited to the reception but not to the church, the reverse is a severe breach of etiquette.

Wedding invitations are often accompanied by other enclosures. Many hosts, exasperated by ill-mannered guests who fail to reply to invitations, enclose reply cards. These take the form of simple fill-in printed cards measuring three and a half inches by five and a half. Others, if the marriage is to take place at an inaccessible location, find it sensible to include a map. This should be printed on paper, not card, and should match the colour scheme of the invitation (normally white, cream or ivory with black lettering). There is one very rich family who enclosed air tickets to their distant festivities, prior to acceptance or refusal. This was intended to ensure a good turn-out, but, in fact, a mere mention of the availability of transport would have been more correct – and more economical! If transport of a modest manner – a bus to move guests from church to reception – is to be provided, this can also be announced on a small separate card. If a wedding is a vastly grand and complicated affair with several parts, then all relevant invitations and paperwork are sent in one go.

Postponements and Cancellations

Should a wedding be postponed or cancelled a card should be sent out announcing the fact. This would normally measure five and a half by three and a half inches and be printed, not engraved, on white or cream card. It could read:

> Owing to the illness of Mrs Basil Blimp, Brigadier and Mrs Blimp regret that they are obliged to postpone the invitations to the marriage of their daughter, Hermione, to Mr Darren Arthur Smith, which will now take place on Saturday 26th May at etc.

or:

> Owing to the sudden death of Brigadier Basil Blimp, Mrs Blimp regrets that she is obliged to cancel the invitations to the marriage of her daughter, Hermione, to Mr Darren Arthur Smith on etc.

In this case fresh invitations are sent out when the new date is arranged. At one time, in instances of family tragedy, it was usual for the second wedding to take place 'quietly'. Nowadays it is more usual to allow a decent gap and then proceed with the original style of wedding as planned. Notice, in the above instances, that it is the 'invitations' not the wedding that are cancelled. Weddings are cancelled only in the case of broken engagements. The card announcing this fact would read:

> Sir Basil and Lady Blimp announce that the marriage of their daughter, Hermione, to Mr Darren Arthur Smith, which was arranged for Wednesday 14th March will not take place.

Filling in Wedding Invitations and Writing Envelopes

The invitee's name is written by hand in ink with a fountain pen, preferably by the actual host or hostess, in the top left-hand corner of the invitation. There is no need to employ a calligrapher, although many do. Names are styled socially, e.g. Miss Alicia Apple, Mr Bernard Banana or Lord Kumquat. Prefixes and decorations such as 'The', 'His Excellency' or 'OBE' are not used on the card, but should be included on the envelope. Envelopes are written in full and in ink to match the card. Men without titles are referred to as Bernard Banana Esq., and those of title take their full social form – e.g. The Earl of Kumquat. Envelopes should be exactly the right size for the invitation and have diagonal, not straight, flaps.

Replying to Wedding Invitations

These, like all formal invitations, should be replied to in the third person and hand-written in ink. It is customary to write the date of the reply in the bottom left-hand corner. An acceptance would read:

> Miss Alicia Apple thanks Brigadier and Mrs Basil Blimp for the kind invitation to the marriage of their daughter, Hermione, to Mr Darren Arthur Smith at St Anthony's Church, Knightsbridge, on Wednesday, 14th March at 2.30 o'clock, and afterwards at The Boot and Bayonet Club, and is delighted to accept.

A refusal would read:

> Lord Kumquat thanks Brigadier and Mrs Basil Blimp for the kind invitation to the marriage of their daughter, Hermione, to Mr Darren Arthur Smith at St Anthony's Church, Knightsbridge, on Wednesday, 14th March at 2.30 o'clock, and afterwards at The Boot and Bayonet Club, but, due to a previous engagement, he regrets he is unable to attend.

161

STATIONERY

The choice of stationery is an important and telling one. It is your ambassador. It represents your values and aesthetics. Its selection depends on your personal taste, the image you wish the rest of the world to have of you and the amount of money you want to spend. However, there are conventions to be borne in mind, such as the form and placement of address and telephone numbers in a letterhead. Highly idiosyncratic designs may seem amusing at the time of ordering, but soon lose their entertainment value. The fun-loving woman who persuaded her stationers to reproduce her lipsticked lip print as a letterhead soon regretted it.

Writing Paper

Writing paper (still referred to as writing paper, not note or letter paper) should always be plain, never lined, and the best quality you can afford. Good-quality paper is distinguished by a watermark – an imprint of the manufacturer's name which becomes visible when held up to the light. Always choose a heavy weight of paper, which both looks and feels good and will allow you to write on both sides of the paper without fear of shadowing.

SIZE OF PAPER

Over the last couple of decades writing paper has gradually increased in size. Paper is available in a variety of dimensions. Small sizes can be elegant if occasionally impractical. Very large paper, such as A4, on the other hand, is not suitable for social letters and is best reserved for business correspondence. The best traditional size is eight inches by six and a quarter, not the more ordinary A5. The choice is largely determined by the size of your handwriting. Those who frequently write order two or sometimes three sizes of stationery to suit different lengths of correspondence.

WEIGHT OF PAPER

Writing papers are available in a variety of weights. Your choice is purely a matter of taste, but avoid buying paper that is too thin, as it can give a transparent, flimsy and somewhat cheap appearance. On the other hand, paper of a board-like stiffness can appear pretentious. The most normal weight of paper is between 100 and 160 grams.

COLOUR

White or ivory is the most formal, correct and classic colour for paper, although many people prefer shades of blue, grey or other more individual hues. The choice is entirely personal. Papers can be plain or with a coloured, but never gold, border around the edge. The choice of ink should enhance the colour of your writing paper, and vice versa.

HEADINGS

All smart stationery must carry a heading with the sender's address and telephone number, and any other information he considers relevant. Traditionally the style of these is always discreet. Ostentatious letterheads were always felt to be vulgar. However, there are all manner of imaginative uses of letterpress and typography, featuring the owner's name, crest or coronet, as well as depictions of his or her house. (One family has a delightful Lutyens cypher that encapsulates their address in a reed design.) Amusing and attractive as such treatments can be, remember that the traditional, more severe approach is the most elegant and correct.

Proper letterheads are engraved. These are made by first engraving copper plate with the owner's address, telephone number, etc., and then printing from this imprint. Although expensive, it provides the smartest and most stylish appearance and is generally perceived as important. The choice of typeface is purely a matter of preference; however, a Roman typeface looks better than an italic script, which is somehow reminiscent of a doctor's bill. The size should be in proportion with the paper as a whole. The colour you choose is also a matter of personal preference. Black characters on white is the most formal and classic combination and the most suitable for men, although many people find this monochrome approach somewhat austere. Dark blue on azure is also very conventional but slightly softer and thus more appropriate for women. Scarlet on cream is increasingly popular and smart. More individual hues such as violet or emerald can look good but have to be carefully chosen to work.

Although once the die or plate has been engraved repeat orders are relatively reasonable, engraving is expensive on the first order. People nowadays lead much more mobile lives than their parents and grandparents and may not welcome a repeated outlay on grandly engraved stationery every time they move. A choice of other finishes is now available. These have very differing degrees of acceptability.

Thermography

Sometimes known as 'poor man's engraving', thermography uses litho or letterpress printing, which is heated to 'raise' the ink. Although widely accepted for office and corporate use, it is not suitable for private stationery or invitations.

Flat Printing

Economical and simple, flat printing is always preferable to thermography for private use. Little stick-on labels printed with an address, although very economical, are to be avoided.

YOUR LETTERHEAD

How much information you include in your letterhead is entirely up to you. Traditionally less is more, with the shortest being the smartest: for example, Pemberley, Derbyshire. With the arrival of full postcodes, and unless you live in a truly grand, well-known house, such an approach can look quaintly pretentious.

The letterhead can either be centred or be arranged in the top left- and right-hand corners – the address goes on the right and the telephone/fax number on the left. How much information to include is again up to you. Traditionally all that was necessary was your address and telephone number. If you have more than one house you will need to commission stationery for each separate establishment. Some people like to include their name on the letterhead, but this is suitable for business stationery only. Those who work from home might like to follow the example of a woman who commissioned a plate engraved with both name and address, but ordered half to be printed with the name and half without, thus ending up with stationery for both business and social correspondence with minimal outlay.

Envelopes

For social correspondence, envelopes should have diamond (pointed) flaps – the deeper the better. Flat flaps are suitable for business letters only. Like writing paper, they should not be too flimsy: semi-translucent envelopes through which the script on the letter shows can look like what is known as 'junk mail'. Also, on a purely practical note, your letter has to survive the vicissitudes of the postal system. To overcome the problem of transparent envelopes, you can order them tissue-lined (blue-lined ones for yachts are particularly popular), although these are much more suitable for women than for men. Envelopes should be gummed, and not self-sealing. Brown envelopes are used for business purposes only.

Inks

Black remains the most correct and distinguished choice. Blue is very much in second place and is thought more suitable for women than for men. Blue-black is only appropriate for schoolboys. Coloured inks, although more acceptable than before, are still considered very suspect in traditional circles.

Correspondence Cards

Originally used only for notes to tradesmen, when they would bear a simple flat-printed name and address with a line beneath, in today's busy world correspondence cards have become acceptable for all manner of messages – thank-yous, travel instructions and informal invitations. Like all stationery they have mushroomed in size over the last couple of decades and are now often embellished with all sorts of elaborate engraving, monograms and flat-printed designs.

Informals

These are small, tent-shaped letters that fold along the top. They are usually available in two sizes: four inches by three, and three and a half by five and a half. Like correspondence cards they have become much more popular over recent years. They are ideal for short greetings or impromptu invitations, or as 'to remind' cards. Like tissue-lined envelopes they are more suitable for women than for men.

To Remind/Pour Memoire Cards

Once hardly seen, but hugely useful today in the age of the lazily mannered, 'to remind' cards are sent out as confirmations and reminders of telephone invitations. They are an alternative to the now established habit of writing 'to remind/*pour memoire*' on 'at Home' cards.

Change of Address Cards

These should be flat-printed, as engraving them would be unnecessarily extravagant and pretentious. The most usual size is four by six and a quarter inches. They can be done either before the event, when the wording would be:

CHANGE OF ADDRESS
As from Tuesday 4th March
Mr and Mrs Charles Newly-Moved
Flat 46, 3 Ennismuck Gardens,
London SW7 RB4. Tel: 0171-584 0000.

Or after, when it would read:

CHANGE OF ADDRESS
Mr and Mrs Charles Newly-Moved
are now living at Flat 46, 3 Ennismuck Gardens,
London SW7 RB4. Tel: 0171-584 0000.

165

Birth Announcements

Once a rarity, these beribboned missives positively proliferate, especially in circles where having a baby is treated as a momentous public achievement rather than merely a source of private happiness. To look good these should be simple. They consist of a small card measuring four inches by three and bearing an announcement from the parents which should read:

Mr and Mrs Peregrine Proud-Parent
are happy to announce
the birth of a . . .

To this a small card bearing the baby's first name, date of birth and sometimes weight is attached with a piece of ribbon. The most usual form is black engraved copperplate script on white card. The colour of the ribbon is normally pale blue for boys and pale pink for girls. However, I have seen yellow ribbon used by a rather politically correct couple determined to avoid gender-specific stereotyping.

Adoption Cards

Adoption, once something of a taboo subject, is now often announced as joyfully as a conventional birth with the issue of a card. Its form can follow that of a normal birth announcement, but would read:

Mr and Mrs Charles Happy wish to announce
the arrival of May Eloise in their lives

Christmas Cards

Christmas cards, once a simple exchange of seasonal goodwill between family and friends, are now used for all manner of personal and professional promotion: even the Royal Family now send out cards showing their beaming children. This being said, the more subtle and traditional approach remains the smartest, with some sort of religious or Old Master scene being the most usual image. Care however must be taken about forcing overtly Christian imagery on those of other faiths. The same applies to the greeting within. If in doubt go for the global 'Season's Greetings' that will offend no one. The most elegant cards are always small rather than large and should be sent in envelopes with (unsealed) diagonal flaps. Whereas it is fine to include a short letter to friends you rarely see, it is unacceptable to enclose a newsletter reporting the doings of you and your family over the past year.

Should you choose to have your cards specially printed with your name, remember that, in the case of married couples, the man's name comes first – e.g. Jeremy and Claire Hidebottom. When sending cards to close friends do not forget to cross out your surname. Those who do not wish to send cards should do just that and place an announcement in the press reading: 'Mr and Mrs Larry Lazy are not sending Christmas cards this year but wish all their friends and family . . .' People wishing to rationalise a burgeoning list should adopt some sort of selection criteria. One man who had endured an *annus horribilis* decided to restrict his list to only those who had shown particular kindness and help during his problems.

Visiting Cards

Mr. Peter J. Wilson

57ᵃ Harley Street
London, WIX 9PG.   071 251 9681

Anne-Marie Warwick

Flat 29
17 St. John's Wood Road
St. John's Wood
London NW8 7PX

Example of man's (*top*) and woman's (*bottom*) visiting cards

These are relics of a previous age when 'calling' was an everyday social activity. They are nevertheless still very useful for those with elegant and

167

busy social lives. Apart from their obvious function of being given to new people you would like to see again, they bring a personal touch to flower- and present-giving (it is usual to write a message by hand on the reverse), and are useful for attaching to enclosures in envelopes and for conveying short messages ranging from 'I love you' to 'Drinks, 4 Jan, 6.30 p.m.'.

The most chic visiting card is as spartan as possible: it bears only the owner's name, title and rank centred on the card, with his private and/or club addresses in the bottom left and right corners. It remains a solecism to include a telephone or fax number, which is always written in by hand on the reverse later, if desired.

Visiting cards should always be copperplate engraved. Thermography is out of the question. Black characters on white card is the classic combination. Although sizes have increased in recent years, the most elegant size for men is three by one and a half inches. If this is too small to cram long addresses on to, then three by one and three-quarters is suggested. Women's cards are traditionally larger than men's because, in the past, only 'fast' women carried small cards that could easily be disguised in the man's pile. Thus a woman's card usually measures two and an eighth by three and a half inches.

Business Cards

Whereas visiting cards have become very rare, their business equivalents have proliferated enormously. This is due to the increasing number of freelance and self-employed people in the workforce and the ever-increasing dominance of the corporate mentality on our national life. The normal size for a business card is three and a half by two inches. The name and professional title are centred in large characters, with the address, telephone, fax and e-mail numbers in smaller characters in the bottom left- and right-hand corners or ranged across the bottom of the card. The choice of typeface, colour of card, inclusion and design of a logo are entirely matters of personal taste, but should be in keeping with the style of business you operate. The grandest business cards are still engraved, but printed ones are now perfectly acceptable. Thermography, although passable in this business context, is not recommended.

Unlike a visiting card, a business card can show qualifications and appropriate suffixes after the name, such as FRCS. It is, however, not usual to prefix the name with any title or rank.

The inclusion of a home address should be avoided unless really necessary. It is not done in strict traditional circles, and is sometimes misguided: not everyone you meet in a professional capacity needs, or ought, to know your home address. The reverse of a business card often contains your professional details in different languages – Japanese and Arabic being the most usual.

Place Cards

These are used for writing guests' names on when laying out a *placement* for a dinner or lunch party. They can either be flat (for placing in a place-card holder) or folded tent-like to be free-standing. They are usually in white card and can have faint gold bevelled edges. The guest's name is always written by hand and in ink, never typed.

LETTER-WRITING

Lady Troubridge wrote in her definitive volume *The Book of Etiquette*: 'a letter, business or social, is simply to talk on paper'. This direction cannot be improved upon, other than offering a few stylistic tips. As in all creative writing, it is advisable never to use a long word when a short one will do, to avoid repetition of words and ideas, and to order your thoughts before putting pen to paper. A lively style is also recommended. 'As in everything connected with the social world, ease is absolutely essential to the correct letter: the style must not be stilted or forced,' opined Lady Troubridge. Remember also, when writing in passion and anger, the advice of an old man: 'Never put on paper what you would not care to see printed in a newspaper for all to read.' A proper letter should be in ink, never pencil, and preferably with a fountain pen and not a ballpoint or felt-tip. Good-quality paper is always milled to suit fountain pens and not the more liquid formulations of roller balls, etc.

When beginning a letter, the date is written out in full – i.e. Friday, 12th July. The abbreviated style of 30/12/99 is suitable really only for post- or correspondence cards, and is thought rather smart if one number (usually the middle one) or all are in Roman numerals. Do not emulate the rather affected man who came to classics late in life and started to use Ancient Greek numerals.

Starting a Letter

The universal opening to most letters is 'Dear . . .' with the exception of those to intimates, which can take the form of 'My dear' (rather stodgy but caring) or 'Darling' (seriously enamoured). How you style the recipient depends on how well you know him. If he is a friend then the first name is fine. If you don't know him personally, or he is older, then it is wise to use the formal 'Dear Mr Brown' or 'Dear Lord Purple'. The old, very formal style of 'Sir' when starting a letter to a peer you didn't know has virtually dropped out of use, although it is still employed when writing to the editor of a national newspaper. The entire name, such as 'Dear John Brown', sometimes finds its way on to business letters, but it is not suitable for social correspondence. 'Dear Sir' is reserved for business correspondence. It is usual to end the salutation with a comma.

The Body of the Letter

The body of a hand-written social letter begins below the comma at the end of the salutation. It is customary to get the main point of the letter into the first paragraph, but this is by no means essential. It is then usual to begin a new paragraph with each new idea. A good letter is attractively laid out, with margins on left and right and a slightly larger gap in between paragraphs than between lines. If replying to a letter, respond to the main points it contains, not slavishly to everything mentioned as if it were an examination paper. Remember Lady Troubridge's conversation analogy. The odd crossing-out is fine, particularly if you are a friend of the recipient. However, very scruffy and smudged letters are difficult to read as well as being unattractive, and are not recommended, particularly to those you are corresponding with for the first time. It is absolutely acceptable to write on both sides of the paper, except in the case of air mail paper.

Signing Off

How you have started a letter dictates how you should sign off. If you began a letter 'Dear First Name', then you sign off with your first name only; if you started 'Dear Mr Surname', then you sign off with your full name. The adverb you use with 'Yours' depends on the level of formality and familiarity. When closing a letter written to a name (i.e. not 'Dear Sir', etc.) 'Yours sincerely' is the most usual and formal: it is ideal on letters to people you don't know, but might need the addition of 'Best wishes' to warm it up in a letter to a friend. 'Yours truly' is more familiar but becoming obsolete. 'Yours ever' is very friendly (positively affectionate). 'Yours faithfully' is used to end letters which started with 'Dear Sir'. It is also possible to use merely 'Yours', but this can look somewhat abrupt and lazy. In addition there are several other sign-offs: 'Much love' and 'Best love', which suggest love of a platonic nature; 'Affectionately', which means just what it says; 'Kind regards', 'Best wishes' and 'Warmest regards', which can be used in conjunction with 'Yours sincerely' to narrow the distance implied by the latter. If in doubt about the familiarity, remember it is always better to err on the side of formality.

The use of PS (meaning *postscriptum*) for afterthoughts once you have signed off is fine for chatty letters to friends but not for more serious epistles. Remember that each separate point you write requires a new and ever-expanding PS: PS for note one, PPS for note two, PPPS for note three, etc. It is to be remembered that excessive uses of this gives a rather childish impression.

Postcard and Correspondence Card Style

Because these only have space for short messages, written frills are kept to a minimum. 'Dear So-and-so' is never used; neither is 'Yours sincerely' etc. The date is always written in abbreviated form – i.e. 28/5/99. On postcards the address is written on the right-hand side, with the message on the left. If sending a picture postcard as a thank-you, it is thoughtful to choose an image that is in some way relevant to the recipient or the reason for gratitude. An American millionaire tells of how impressed he was with a guest whom he had invited to a performance of Gounod's opera *Roméo et Juliette* and who had scoured the shops for a postcard bearing a picture of the ill-fated lovers. Correspondence cards can be totally covered in script, because they are sent in matching envelopes.

Hand-Writing versus Typing

Whereas business communications are invariably typed, personal correspondence should always be hand-written, preferably with a fountain pen and not a biro, pencil or felt-tip. The only exception is if the writer's handwriting is so inexorably illegible that it would be bad manners to inflict the tiresome scrawl on anybody other than a skilled student of ancient hieroglyphics. In this case it is permissible to type out a letter. However, to avoid too businesslike a look, it is important to choose (if using a WP) a font that does not appear too corporate, and, most important of all, to top and tail the letter by hand. The envelope can either be typed to match the letter, or hand-written to give a personal touch.

Examples of Commonly Used Letters

While it would be pointless and difficult to give stock examples of general letters, the following formulae for frequently used 'bread and butter' communications might be useful.

THANK-YOU LETTERS

The thank-you, although an endangered species, is one of the most delightful and effective of letters. It is required whenever thanks are due for a present, hospitality or a personal favour. When writing to a married couple, a thank-you letter is traditionally addressed to the wife only. Rather like a flower, it becomes less attractive the longer it is left. So remember, the most polite thank-you is a prompt one.

A letter of this kind should be short and to the point; however, any attempt to enliven the bread and butter formula is recommended. This can be done by alluding to a dish that was particularly well cooked, a shared joke or an observation about a gift. For example:

Dear Flo,

How kind of you to invite me to join your lunch party for Stephen's birthday. I thought it was a lovely gathering and was pleased to see that your guest of honour enjoyed himself as much as everyone else present did. Like me, he almost had to be forcibly restrained from consuming a third helping of your delicious pudding.

With many thanks,

Yours ever,

Harry Grateful

Finally, thank-you letters should always be personal, and not of the 'Round Robin' variety.

APOLOGY LETTERS

It is often easier to say sorry on paper than in person, and certainly a thoughtful letter is always a much more effective apology than an awkwardly mumbled verbal one. Its tone, which should be contrite but not obsequious, is obviously governed by the heinousness of the crime. However, in all cases an apology letter should be brief and should get immediately to the point in the first paragraph. Suggestions for restitution should be mentioned, but attempts to lighten things up with a little humour are risky and best avoided.

Dear Georgia,

I really am most awfully sorry for breaking your beautiful vase yesterday evening. You have the most lovely things in your house and to damage any of them causes me great sorrow. Please accept my apologies.

It was so kind of you to insist on taking it in to your porcelain restorers, but please could you ask them to send on the bill to me. It is the least that I can do.

Yours ever,

Christina Green

LETTERS OF CONDOLENCE

In our secular society death remains the final taboo that many people find difficult to discuss. However, it is important to take the time to write to the bereaved. An acquaintance of mine who suddenly lost a close friend always says that his grief was greatly tempered by the many kind letters he received. Condolence letters are generally sent to the next of kin, although one per family (such as to the widow) is now enough. When writing to relations of a recently deceased peer, it is the form to style their names in the titles they used while he lived, and not the new ones they acquired on his death. This applies until after the funeral.

> Dear Lady Bereaved
> I was so sad and shocked to hear of Sir John's recent death. He was always such a marvellous man and will be greatly missed by all who knew him. I remember how kind he was to my uncle when his marriage collapsed. Although the sympathy of friends is only of limited consolation at times such as these, if there is anything I can do to ease your grief, please let me know.
> Yours very sincerely,
> Robert Blue

ENVELOPES

These should match their contents. They should be in exactly the same weight, colour and type as the writing paper and should be the right size for the letter to fit in when folded once, or at most twice.

The address should be centred on the envelope and thus allow enough space for the stamp and for ample margins left and right. Whether you write out the name and address with a vertical or diagonal left margin is purely a matter of choice, but the latter is generally preferred.

How much information you include on an envelope is up to you, but it is good manners to style people formally and sensible to make the address as comprehensive as possible. When long postcodes came in, many of the old school refused to use them, considering them vulgar, but nowadays such attitudes seem pretentious. Social letters should always be addressed by hand and be fully punctuated. Many senders like to write their address on the reverse of the envelope, but this is really only done in the case of air mail. Letters sent by hand should have 'By Hand' written in place of the stamp in the top right-hand corner of the envelope. (Incidentally, letters which are sent by hand should by rights be folded closed and not sealed.) Personal letters sent to someone's place of work should be marked either

'Private' or 'Personal' on the top left-hand side: this should prevent the missive being opened by a secretary. If a letter is sent to someone while they are staying with a friend, then the wording on the envelope reads: 'John Browne Esq., c/o Charles Greene Esq., Mill Cottage, etc.' However, if the letter is mailed to an address only, without the name of the householder being mentioned, then the envelope would read: 'John Browne Esq., at Mill Cottage, etc.'

The choice of prefixes and suffixes has become somewhat blurred. The use of Esq. is just such a grey area. Traditionally Esq. (it is never written out in full) was used for all men above a certain level in society who did not possess a title. Those of the lower orders – i.e. tradespeople – were always known as 'Mr So-and-So'. Nowadays such obvious demarcations of class are viewed as insidious and redundant, and many people use Mr as an all-encompassing, democratic male prefix. That being said, 'Mr' lacks both style and distinction, and I would still recommend using Esq. in all social circumstances and most business ones. The ugly-sounding Ms is also problematic. Although many women have assumed this bland epithet, it remains incorrect to use it when addressing a social letter. Its role, if used at all, is confined to the business arena. Thus unmarried women are addressed as Miss, unmarried sisters as The Misses and married women as Mrs. Married and widowed women take either their husband's first name or his initial. Divorcees reinstate their own forename. If a woman is married but has a career in which she is known by her maiden name, then she is usually addressed on a professional level by her own name, and privately as her married self, unless she is known to have special views on the subject. One woman swears by her double identity, saying that to return home from her highly pressured job and revert to being a wife is an almost magical way to overcome the stress of the day. Unmarried couples, both heterosexual and homosexual, who live together are both styled on the envelope with the suitable prefixes and suffixes. Young boys are still correctly addressed as Master although this usage is gradually dying out, as it can upset some adolescents.

The styling of those with titles is more complicated. In social correspondence titles are written out thus: dukes are addressed as The Duke of Domby; marquesses, earls, viscounts and barons are addressed by their full title – i.e. The Marquess of Marvellous, The Earl of Euridice and The Viscount Valmouth; life peers also take the definite article. Formal prefixes such as Most Hon. are not used in social correspondence and are generally employed only on official envelopes and documents. A baronet is styled Sir Thomas Train, Bt. and a knight Sir Brian Shining. Wives of peers follow the male form, but obviously substitute the female version of the title.

Wives of baronets and knights are addressed as Lady Train and Lady Shining. 'The' is used when writing to honourables – i.e. The Hon. Fanny Rebel ('Honourable' is never written out in full, and the use of Hon$_{\text{ble}}$ is archaic). It has also been recently reinstated when addressing daughters of dukes, marquesses and earls, who were previously known just as Lady Mary Ping-Pong, but are now referred to as The Lady Mary Ping-Pong. (The same is also true of younger sons of dukes and marquesses. However, elder ones who possess a courtesy title, such as Viscount Verbena, never take the definite article.)

Stamps

A stamp should always be used on a private letter. Franking is for business correspondence only. The stamp is always stuck on the top right-hand corner of the envelope. If more than one is needed then they are placed side by side. Care ought to be taken to align stamps at right-angles with their envelope: stamps plonked randomly give a dotty impression.

NETIQUETTE

Just as there are right and wrong ways of writing letters, the sending of messages via the Internet is also governed by certain rules and customs. These rules, known as netiquette, are less rigid than those of the written medium, but people who fail to adhere to them will induce similar feelings of disapproval.

The essence of electronic mail – known as e-mail – is speed. There are over thirty million users of the Internet worldwide, any of whom can, if his or her address is known, be contacted at the touch of a button, though on crowded lines the message can take up to an hour to get through. The language of the Internet is similarly brief, and makes heavy use of abbreviations, symbols and acronyms, forms considered anathema by devotees of traditional, or 'snail', mail. E-mail is also less formal, though this should not be achieved at the expense of politeness. Introductory salutations such as 'Dear Siegfried' are omitted, and the sender's e-mail address and the date and time of sending usually appear automatically at the top of the message at the receiving end. A message should be given a suitable heading, indicating the subject matter, but otherwise it should begin with the main body copy. It is, however, important to sign off with your name, as your e-mail address may not be sufficient to inform the recipient of who you are.

Internet language becomes even less formal when you are corresponding on Usenet – that part of the Internet devoted to discussion groups, where several people who have never met can hold 'conversations' about anything from the politics of New Labour to the plots of Jane Austen novels. There are tens of thousands of discussion groups on Usenet covering as many topics. 'Newbies' – those new to the Internet – are advised to consult the lists of FAQS (Frequently Asked Questions) which are available in most newsletter groups along with answers to avoid the group being inundated with unnecessary e-mail. Before joining a discussion, you may like to emit a polite 'electronic cough', denoted by the letters PMFJI, which stand for 'pardon me for joining in'. What would Nancy Mitford have said?

When communicating, there are two things to avoid: SHOUTING, or the use of upper case letters to make a point; and 'spamming', the sending of junk e-mail to advertise some commercial venture. Spamming is known as the ultimate e-mail *faux pas*. Those who partake in it are likely to be 'flamed', whereby critical comments about them are displayed on the Internet for all to see.

Finally, it is perfectly acceptable to use symbols to brighten up your e-mail messages. Symbols are generally displayed on their sides, such as:

:-)	I'm happy
:-(	I'm sad
8-)	I wear glasses
%-/	I'm hungover
+-(:-)	I'm the Pope

9

THE SPOKEN WORD

How we speak to one another is one of the most obvious manifestations of manners – both good and bad. The well-mannered talker puts those around him at their ease, is as good a listener as he is a talker and has the ability to come up with easy and amusing chat. The ill-mannered speaker possesses none of these qualities.

Some people naturally seem to possess conversational accomplishments. The majority, however, have to learn these spoken social skills over time and with practice. As one sociologist said: 'We are all born shy. It's just that some of us are better at dealing with it.'

In this chapter I shall cover basic conversational skills and how to make introductions properly, as well as explaining the contemporary etiquette of the telephone, answering machines and mobile telephones.

CONVERSATION OPENERS

Opening gambits are amongst the most difficult to judge. The easiest one is to enquire how long the other person has known their hosts. This provides an instant common ground. If you have a little prior knowledge about the person you are being introduced to, such as a friend in common or a shared interest, this can also be a good starting point. Asking people what they do is not a suitable opener, as it can sound intrusive and judgemental in the case of those who don't work. Although such openers are clichés and can sound anodyne, they are intended merely as friendly conversational building blocks, from which more interesting topics will emerge.

177

IN CONVERSATION

The techniques of one-to-one conversation are different from those in a large group. When talking to one person, that individual receives your undivided attention. You listen to every word he says, acknowledge his jokes, even if they are not funny, and look him firmly in the eye and smile. 'Cocktail party eyes', i.e. glancing obviously over your companion's shoulder, to spy who else is at a party, are rude and hurtful. I have never forgotten the sadness of hearing an older woman friend, recently divorced, say: 'I have really come to the conclusion that after a certain age, women become invisible.'

When taking part in a group conversation, the form is more complex. Although some people are more suited to listening than talking, it's important that everybody gets a crack of the whip. It is therefore recommended to share the chat, and not allow either yourself or another to dominate the proceedings. For instance, if the topic is a current sex scandal, then it is important to bring a shy person into the conversation by saying: 'Well, what do you think about all this?' All but those who for some reason are keeping their own counsel will be only too delighted to venture an opinion. As more people are introduced into the group, and join in the conversation, it is polite to give them cues, such as: 'We were talking about the Smith/Brown scandal.' It is also a good idea to watch reactions in the group to make sure nobody is being offended by what is being said. If you sense danger signals, change the subject.

THE BRICK-DROPPER

Some people have a natural predisposition to tactlessness and tend to drop bricks wherever they go; some saintly souls never put a foot wrong; while most of us do commit the occasional *faux pas*. All cases demand some sort of conversational crisis management. Some circumstances need instant action; others should be allowed to die quietly before more damage is done. For instance, if you are listening to someone being uncharitable about another person, not present, but known to another member of the group, you must quickly chime in rather vaguely to that person: 'Don't you know Pinky?' The combatant will quickly pipe down. To avoid embarrassment, the more abrasive 'Perky is a friend of Pinky' should be used only when absolutely necessary. Humour can also be a clever tactic when a light touch is needed to diffuse tension. There is a story of a man declaring to a group that students of a certain university were either 'footballers or whores'. When a member of the group announced that his wife was a student at the said university, the raconteur, without a blink, responded: 'Oh really, what position does she play?'

On the other hand, it is sometimes a mistake to attempt to pick up a brick once you have dropped it. If you say something from which there is no recovery position, don't be tempted to dig yourself further into the hole, as one man did. He was busy regaling a small group about a fat woman he'd seen at a party squeezed into a very tight dress, who in his opinion had borne a 'striking resemblance to a truncated sausage', without realising that one of his audience was indeed an amply proportioned matron with just such a passing resemblance to a popular piece of *charcuterie*. Suddenly mortified, he then spent the next few minutes clumsily extolling the virtues of the Rubenesque figure and the silliness of diets, before his host came to his rescue. In cases where offence has obviously been caused, it is unwise to labour embarrassed apologies at the site of the crime and more sensible to have a quiet word in private later, or, in particularly sensitive situations, write a letter.

TABOO TOPICS

Although there are fewer taboo topics now, there are still guidelines to be borne in mind. Politics remains sticky ground with new acquaintances. Money, although an obsession with some, remains a private matter for many. It is not done to ask people how much they earn, what they paid for their house or how much their outfit cost. Discussion about ailments, allergies and alternative therapies has become acceptable, but can be very boring. Sex, like money, is a compulsive subject for some, but others are more reticent. Generally speaking, the older the company the less sexual and other personal topics are considered suitable. Making appreciative comments about food and décor, once thought very vulgar, is now almost encouraged. Excessive gossiping can make a negative first impression, and compulsive joke-telling needs to be kept carefully in check. Asking a woman her age remains forbidden.

THE USE OF COMPLIMENTS

Lady Troubridge once declared that making personal compliments in conversation was in bad taste. This is no longer the case. However, any compliment should be delicately given. Any attempts to be overly gushy can appear sycophantic and embarrassing to the recipient, and creepy to others. However, 'What a pretty dress' can be taken only as delightful, though personal platitudes such as: 'You look so well/so slim' are to be avoided, as these can be interpreted by the sensitive recipients as making pejorative observations about their previous state.

INTERRUPTING

Interrupting is the blight of modern-day conversation. Men tend to be greater culprits than women. Many people subliminally use other people's talk as a cue to launch into a related topic about themselves or their experiences. This is not only bad manners to the person who is already speaking, but extremely irritating to others who are following a conversation. In such cases the secret is to smile quickly at the interloper, but keep your eyes on the person already speaking and, if necessary, murmur: 'You were saying.'

NAME-DROPPING

This is done by the socially insecure in the mistaken belief that it impresses. As with many minor bad manners, it is best ignored, as little deflates the name-dropper more than discovering that his spoken showings-off have fallen on stony ground. The same applies to those irritating people who refer to famous figures by their first names alone, such as, 'Well, I was saying to Liz and Michelle . . .' (meaning Elizabeth Taylor and Michelle Pfeiffer), without any form of clarification. This again is invariably done to show off and is not to be encouraged. The best response is to repeatedly and pointedly ask: 'Liz who?' and murmur a vague 'Oh' on being told.

THE PREGNANT PAUSE

If conversation dries it is important to start it up again immediately. The conviviality of any social group can instantly evaporate if there is any length of gap. Social silence, rather like a 'dry' on the radio, can sound like an eternity. So do not wait for others to take on the mantle; plunge straight in with a new, preferably light remark, aimed at someone across the group or table and not next to you. Alternatively ask the group a question such as: 'What does everybody think about X?' In the unlikely event of no one responding, single out an individual who you feel sure does have an opinion by saying: 'George, you know about these things, what's your view?'

THE USE OF TITLES IN CONVERSATION

It remains a solecism to refer to peers in conversation, unless for the specific reason of clarification, by their descriptive title, such as the Earl of Wherever or the Marquess of Whatnot. They should be called Lord Wherever or Lord Whatnot. The only exceptions to this rule are dukes and duchesses, who are spoken to as the Duke or Duchess of Deciduous, and addressed as Duke and Duchess.

Royalty are usually referred to as Prince This and Princess That. The inclusion of 'The' before the names of the Queen's children – e.g. The Prince Edward – is nowadays not generally used in conversation. The only exceptions are The Princess Royal and royal dukes and duchesses. Queen Elizabeth The Queen Mother is spoken of as Queen Elizabeth. The Queen is simply The Queen.

THE USE OF FIRST NAMES

Although the use of instant first names grows more widespread, there are still many people who find it offensive. As a general rule of thumb, the older the person, the more likely it is they will expect to be called Mr, Mrs, Miss, Lord or Lady Whosoever. If in doubt the more formal appellation should be used.

BORES

Bores, although hardly a social asset, can be socially soothing, as they are usually so caught up with their own thoughts and words that others can switch off and momentarily rest their brains from conversation. This being said, bores are a social liability, and need to be dealt with lightly but conclusively. For instance, if a bore is prone to monologues and begins repeating a story that everybody has heard many times before, merely chime in: 'Is this the tale about your early life in Africa that you were telling me a couple of days ago?' The bore will soon shut up.

If you find yourself trapped at a party with a well-meaning but tedious person, the best-mannered tactic is the old-fashioned graceful one of saying: 'This is so interesting, but I do feel that I am monopolising you.' If this doesn't work, there is the more brutal but legitimate ploy of excusing yourself to find a drink or make a telephone call and not returning. Effective as this is, it is only suitable behaviour at largish gatherings, where you could easily be waylaid by your hostess or other guests.

INTRODUCTIONS

The making of verbal introductions is for many a nerve-racking experience. Common problems include worrying about interrupting conversations, the order of introduction, and, most mortifying of all, the sudden remarkable and frustrating disappearance of people's names from the brain.

Introductions are a necessity, because, in a curious way, until someone is introduced into a group, socially they only half exist. This is particularly true of the rather diffident souls who find it difficult to walk up to complete strangers and say: 'Hello, I'm Francesca Tree.'

181

As a general rule of thumb men are always introduced to women, and, in the case of people of the same sex, juniors are introduced to seniors. The most polite wording is: 'Serena, may I introduce Peter Beech', or merely, 'Serena Ash, this is Peter Beech.' Some hostesses say only: 'Peter Beech – Serena Ash', accompanied by strange hand gestures, which although acceptable is abrupt. Married couples are introduced individually, not as Peter and Betty Beech. However, certain women, particularly those with independent careers, now like to be known by their own name in the social as well as the business context. In this case it is sometimes helpful in conversation to make a reference to their married state, by saying: 'This is Betty Oak, Peter's wife', although the majority of married women are usually happy to be accorded their husband's surname in social situations. It is also useful, when introducing family members, to suggest the nature of the relationship: 'I don't believe you have met my cousin, Belinda Oak.' Children, regardless of sex, are always introduced to whoever, such as 'Mrs Poplar, I don't believe you have met my daughter, Clarissa.' Although more people now like to be known to children by their first name, many don't. It is thus recommended to present the adult formally, unless asked otherwise.

Introducing People With Titles

The introduction of titled people has become a difficult area for many, as increased informality has blurred the old rules. This situation is further complicated because significant numbers of those with titles are strangely selective about when and where they use them. As a general rule of thumb, it is always better to err on the formal rather than the familiar side. Many people with titles (young as well as old, new as well as ancient creations) take offence at over-familiarity. There is one young peeress who is often to be heard complaining that 'pushy people', after only one meeting, address her by not only her Christian name, but also her diminutive.

In this matter, as with many dilemmas of modern manners, the solution often lies in the ages of those concerned. The older generation tend to be more formal; the younger more egalitarian. One easy guide is to use Lord and Lady much in the same way as you would Mr and Mrs. Another one is to remember that it is quite useful to use someone's title when introducing them to strangers, as it prevents the possibility of the new people introducing them merely as Mr and Mrs X. Remember too that it is a solecism to speak of 'the Marquis of Sycamore' or 'the Viscountess Elder'. What is known as the 'distinctive' title is reserved for envelopes, mentions in newspapers, etc., and is never used in speech. Thus the Marquis of Sycamore would be referred to as 'Lord Sycamore'. It is then up to him to say: 'Please call me Jamie.'

When making verbal introductions it is important to speak clearly and not mumble names into your glass. It can be embarrassing for people to have to say to those they have just met: 'I'm terribly sorry, but I didn't catch your name.' It is also recommended to follow the example of the good diplomatic wives and add a little cue line to the introduction to give strangers a common ground on which to start their conversation. Examples of this might be: 'Christina has just come back from Budapest', or 'Annabel, may I introduce Valerian Larch. He has a house near your parents' in Devon.'

The Indirect Introduction

A largely lost art, the indirect introduction is a very useful social tool. This is used when you want to draw people into a conversation without having to do a formal introduction that might interrupt already convivial discussion. An example would be: 'William, Jeanie has been telling me about the new tenor, Vittorio Vibrato, have you heard him?' In this way William and Jeanie have been introduced to one another and have a conversational opening in one easy movement.

Introductions Outside the Social Setting

Writing before the war, Lady Troubridge declared that: 'Introductions on the street are bad form unless there is some special reason for them.' This is no longer the case. In fact, it is rude to be walking along the street with a friend, and to stop to talk to someone you know without effecting any introductions, thus making your companion feel like a spare part. The polite thing to do is to greet your acquaintance, introduce him quickly to whoever you are with and then have a brief conversation. The third person then has the option of joining in the conversation, merely listening or discreetly making himself scarce by stepping aside and looking in a shop window.

Being Introduced

Although it is important for the introducer to speak clearly, it behoves those being introduced to listen carefully to names. For most people this requires concentration, as the brain is less interested in a new individual's name than in other aspects of their make-up. Americans employ a useful model of repeating new names in conversation until they are ingrained on the mind, by saying: 'Have you always lived in London, John. John, I don't believe you have met Susan. John, I was saying to my wife, only yesterday . . .' This is somewhat trying to British ears and should not be overused. A certain clever woman always tries to visualise something when introduced to new people: if she meets a Mr Wood, she thinks about a group of trees.

She is never known to get a name wrong. If you are uncertain about a name, it is important to establish its accurate identity by saying: 'I'm so sorry, but it's so noisy in here that I couldn't make out whether you are called Dixon or Rixon.' It is much better to do this than to have a stab at guessing the name when the time comes to make an introduction.

The correct greeting on being introduced is 'How do you do.' If you find this a little stuffy, then the more casual 'Hello' will do at informal gatherings. Do not be tempted to say 'Pleased to meet you', which is still considered wrong. Also, 'How do you do' is a salutation and not a question, so do not reply 'Very well, thank you.' The correct response is just to say 'How do you do' back. It is also customary to shake hands. Convention dictates that women offer their hands first, but in an age when hand-shaking is no longer an automatic social reflex, it is both acceptable and advisable for both parties to proffer their hands immediately. A good handshake should be discreetly firm but never hearty. Very smart women are able to shake hands with an almost imperceptible little squeeze. As the hands are shaken it is also elegant to bow the head very slightly, smile and look the person in the eye. Any suggestion of looking away from their face or down at the floor can suggest shiftiness, although it is more often than not merely because of native shyness. If attending a party where no one is doing introductions, or if you spy a lonely soul skulking in the corner, it is now acceptable (at one time it was considered very bad form) to go up and introduce yourself by saying 'How do you do' and holding out your hand and speaking your name. Only the rudest of people will not respond.

Subsequent Meetings After Introduction

Once introductions have been made, it is hurtful not to acknowledge people should you run into them again. What is known as 'selective social memory' is a most unattractive and charmless trait. This does not mean you have to stop and talk to them, as you may not wish the acquaintance to progress any further. However, you must at least smile.

U AND NON-U REVISITED

Nancy Mitford would be intrigued and amused to know that almost half a century after she published the nuances of smart-speak in *Noblesse Oblige*, and despite a decrease in snobbery and an increase in internationalism, her lexicon of U and non-U words is still the accepted verbal *modus vivendi*. Only the other day a woman was overheard in a supermarket remarking about her son's fiancée: 'She's a nice girl, but I wish she wouldn't say "toilet".' Of all spoken solecisms, *toilet* remains the worst crime. *Lavatory* and *loo* are the acceptable alternatives. Second prize goes to *lounge*, which is always inappropriate. *Drawing room* or *sitting room* are preferred. In these rooms you might find *comfortable sofas* but not *comfy couches* or *settees*. At the table, *serviette*, *sweet* and *afters* are all still out, and should be substituted with *napkin* and *pudding*; *dessert* is applied to the fruit course only. At tea you still eat *jam* not *preserve*. You wear *scent* not *perfume* and go *riding* or *racing* and not *horse-riding* or *horse-racing*. Young people are called *children*, not *kiddies*; old ones might wear *false teeth*, but preferably not *dentures*. People *die*, and do not *pass away* or succumb to other life-ending euphemisms. Invalids are *ill* and are *sick* only when they are physically vomiting. Women become *pregnant*, but are never *expecting*. If you mishear, then you say *sorry* or even the rather abrupt *what*, never *pardon*. *Thank you* and *goodbye* are still preferable to *thanks* and *bye-bye*, but there is now very little in it. *Television* and *photographs* still have the edge on *TV* and *photos*. *Looking-glass*, as opposed to *mirror* (previously non-U), now sounds affected. The same is becoming true of *chimneypiece* versus *mantelpiece*, and *wireless* versus *radio*. To speak of the *phone* rather than the *telephone* is not quite the vocal solecism it once was, but to write it with an apostrophe – i.e. *'phone* – is still to be avoided. The quaint *ice* (previously U) has virtually disappeared, to be replaced by *ice cream* (previously non-U).

THE TELEPHONE

As mentioned above, it is important to remember that the telephone should be known by its full name, and not abbreviated to phone. When answering the telephone socially, it is today necessary only to say: 'Hello'. However, this hello must sound amenable, not the surly mutterings that often greet callers. You can, particularly if you work from home, also just say your name, although this is more suitable for answering a business line. You can also say your number, but many people, wary of nuisance calls, are rightly reluctant to give away too much information. If you do give your number, it is customary to say the last four digits only. But again this is really only for business. The pompous 'The de Marigold residence' is an affectation, invented in Hollywood and not to be used.

When making calls it is important to remember that you have no idea whether your call is coming at an inconvenient moment. Therefore, unless you are really close to the person you are calling, it is not advised to ring before 8.30 a.m. or after 10.30 p.m. Try and avoid ringing people at meal-times and be particularly careful when calling abroad to have worked out time zone differences accurately.

Also, should you be ringing up for a protracted chat, it is polite to ask: 'Can you talk now?' or 'Have you a few minutes?' This gives the recipient an opportunity to say: 'I'm so sorry, but I have people here. Can I call you back later?' Please note that the onus is on the person you have called, but is presently tied up, to ring you back. If ringing people at their office, remember they are not at home and are probably busy and may not have time to chat, so keep it brief.

If ringing a household where staff answer the telephone, unless you know it to be a super-egalitarian set-up, ask for Mrs Big or Lady Bigger, and not for Susan or Martine. There is one maid who grandly corrects anybody who calls asking for her mistress by her Christian name, by saying: 'I shall see if Madame X is in.' She doesn't stress the 'Madame'. She does not have to. Remember if leaving messages with foreign maids with limited English to keep it simple. It is also to be pointed out, regardless of the linguistic shortcomings of Spanish maids, that it is inconsiderate to leave hugely complicated messages with strangers. It is much better to say why you are ringing and leave a request to be called back. Remember always to leave your number. It is inconvenient for people to have to look it up.

When wishing to wind up a telephone call, it is rude to do it abruptly. Do not follow the example of a certain gruff and selfish man who was notorious for just suddenly exclaiming: 'Goodbye' while callers were in mid-sentence and then hanging up. Some people put his behaviour down to loose bowels. I say it was just bad manners. It is far better to say: 'I am so sorry, but it's already half past seven: I'm late for a date and must go.' Or, if you have made an arrangement, mention it during the conversation, and if the caller does not get the message, refer back to it when it is time to bring the conversation to a natural close.

Wrong Numbers

If you dial a wrong number, simply say: 'I'm so sorry but I have dialled the wrong number' and then gently hang up. Do not, as the ill bred are prone to do, sound so irritated that it implies the innocent recipient is at fault. Slamming the telephone down is even worse. If you are on the receiving end, try and sound gracious. While it can be helpful to find out what number the caller was trying to ring, do not be tempted to give yours away.

Answering Machines and Voice Mail

Houses without answering machines are increasingly rare, and busy people make jokes about their answering machines being in conference with each other. Some others leave them on the whole time, even when they are in, as a sort of mechanised secretarial screening device, and return their calls later. The old-fashioned snobbery of refusing to leave messages on answering machines is ridiculously outmoded and unhelpful, although to leave strings of messages in a row is not advised except in urgent circumstances.

People's recorded messages vary from the brief and functional to the floridly individual. The former is generally better, and any use of music and theatrical devices in the recording is to be avoided. The smartest messages always sound unstudied and insouciant. For security reasons it is better to have a message which contains the minimum information. The best one is: 'I'm sorry that we cannot come to the telephone at the moment, but if you would like to leave a message, then we will call you back. Thank you.' Implicit in this announcement is the information that the owner does not live alone, and is in but not near the telephone. Both tactics are said to deter burglars.

When leaving a message it is recommended that it should include your name, who you are calling for (if the household contains more than one person), the time of the call, and your number, which should be repeated. Remember always to talk slowly and clearly and to make the message as concise as possible.

A SMALL NOTE ON RETURNING CALLS
Telephone etiquette is rather like tennis: each player has alternate goes at the ball. It is rude to oblige someone to leave countless messages before deigning to call them back, and bad manners not to return calls as soon as possible, even if you don't want to speak to the person concerned or have to impart difficult words to them. It is also impolite, if taking a call for someone else who is not at home, to ask the caller to ring back later. The correct thing to do is to offer to take a message so that he or she, not the initial caller, can return the call.

Mobile Telephones

Of all recent everyday technological innovations, mobile telephones cause the greatest disapproval. Understandable as this is, there is no doubt that they are here to stay, as their convenience makes them an integral part of more and more people's business and social lives. Those of a more Luddite persuasion should remember that a similar reception greeted the advent of the telephone itself in the nineteenth century, when its arrival was feared by many to signal the end of conversation and of civilised life as it was then led.

This being said, mobile telephones can be very disruptive in restaurants and other public places, and their owners often show an inexcusable lack of consideration towards others around them. It is bad manners to engage in long and noisy conversations at a table or in a bar, bus or train, unless you want to be taken for an unsavoury character. It is equally undesirable, when having lunch or a drink with someone, to allow a mobile phone to ring constantly and to take calls while the other person sits there like a spare part. It is inexcusable to have them switched on in a church or at the theatre, opera or other places of public entertainment.

The polite approach is either to switch the apparatus off and have calls re-routed to an answering machine or service, or, rather elegantly, to leave it switched on at the reception desk of a restaurant or with the head waiter, or, in the case of a hotel, with the concierge. This highly civilised system means that if you receive a call, the staff will answer it, come and fetch you and thus enable you to take the call away from the table and in private. On the other hand, should you wish to make a call, the form is to leave the table, go to where the mobile telephone is being looked after and make the call there.

Bleepers

These, unless they are the sort that only vibrate silently against your body, should never be used in places of worship or public entertainment.

10

IN PRIVATE: THE CONDUCT OF PERSONAL RELATIONSHIPS

Personal relationships are an area where those with bad manners will be very quickly exposed. This is because private conduct relies on personal restraint rather than the regulating strictures of public opinion. Thus a man who appears a model of good manners and taste to his friends and colleagues sometimes believes that his standards of considerate behaviour may slip in private without it mattering. He is deluding only himself.

As there are, quite simply, the fewest hard and fast rules in the private domain, more effort and thought is expected of the individual. The first rule of the well-mannered private relationship is that it remains just that – a private matter for personal deliberation rather than a product for public consumption. Thus it is bad taste not only to boast of sexual conquests and passes that have been rebuffed, but also to indulge in the kind of crass psychotherapy that Judith Martin in *Miss Manner's Guide to Excruciating Correct Behaviour* cleverly describes as 'self-gossip – that is . . . making one's own activities so public as to force people who had been perfectly aware what was happening but essentially uninvolved to take stances of approval or disapproval'. In my opinion it is even worst taste to invade the public sphere with private secrets by 'washing your dirty linen in public'. The fact that several prominent people have harnessed the full force of the international media to do just that does not make it in any way acceptable, merely lamentable.

The Date

At one time there were as many stages in dating as there were in mourning. This is no longer the case. Nowadays the old-fashioned concept of dating has been superseded by the more vague concept of couples seeing each other. Thus many old dating manners have gone by the board, but nevertheless dilemmas of etiquette endure.

Starting a relationship is always tricky, as it establishes the roles of pursuer and pursued. Whereas one woman will appreciate a direct honest indication of interest, another might be offended. The secret has little to do with the snobbish considerations of correct behaviour, but with a lightness of touch that only the most churlish would take offence at.

At one time first dates were always instigated by men, and nice girls just had to wait until asked. This is no longer entirely the case. Traditionalists will always prefer the male initiative, but it is now often acceptable for women to invite men out for a date. However, what is easy for an assured woman may for a less confident or younger one seem an impossibility. For these women the more subtle approach can work, such as inviting a man to go out for drinks in a group or to join a dinner party. Neither of these actions would be considered pushy in the modern age.

Whoever instigates the first meeting has to take the responsibility for it. It is he/she who should suggest a date, time and place, rather than expecting the guest to come up with ideas. It is also preferred form to nominate the type of activity, such as, 'I wonder if you might like to have dinner with me sometime soon?' rather than the more pedestrian and more intrusive: 'I wonder if you are free on Friday 2nd December?' The former sounds more special and allows scope for the invitee to be subtly tantalising about availability.

Should the invitee refuse the invitation, he/she must make clear the underlying nature of the rebuttal. If he/she can't make it because of a genuine prior engagement, then the refusal must not seem like a rebuff. Words to the effect of: 'I would absolutely love to, but unfortunately I have an old friend staying with me. Could we make it another time?' usually do the trick. If on the other hand the invitee would rather walk barefoot to Beirut than spend an evening with a particular individual, then it is best to be politely but definitely discouraging. Do not use long fabrications that could be found out later and cause greater hurt, such as invented existing arrangements or impending trips out of the country. Those who know they don't want to see someone, but would like to let them down more gently, can accept the invitation but make it clear during the date that their affections and interest lie elsewhere.

The choice of date is entirely a matter of personal taste that promises to be mutually appealing and to provide a convivial time. Again *Miss Manners* gives excellent advice: 'There are three possible parts to a date, of which at least two must be offered: entertainment, food and affection. It is customary to begin a series of dates with a great deal of entertainment, a moderate amount of food, and the merest suggestion of affection. As the amount of affection increases, the entertainment can be reduced proportionately. When the affection is the entertainment, we no longer call it dating. Under no circumstance can the food be omitted.'

If it is to revolve around eating, it is worth bearing in mind that lunch and drinks are always more tentative and less of a commitment than dinner. Breakfasts are invariably unromantic for first dates and are better employed for business meetings. It is also best to avoid a restaurant that is either too noisy or too embarrassingly intimate. Both, for differing reasons, are unconducive to the success of first dates. Nor, perhaps, should they be too pompous, as such surroundings can make people feel tense. The object of the meeting is to relax in each other's company.

However, eating together can be quite a taxing one-to-one activity for two people who are virtually strangers. In these cases, the best advice is to invite a girl to something – an exhibition, play, film or club – where both parties will generally enjoy themselves and feel at home without the occasional awkwardness of dining *à deux*.

The person who instigates the date should expect to pay. The other party should accept gracefully and with thanks, except in situations where she or he has conceded to the invitation only out of politeness and really cannot envisage any further involvement, in which case an offer to go Dutch should be made. Most heterosexual men still like to pay. However, men who have been asked out by a woman should be understanding if she wishes to pick up the bill. On gay dates, although there can be some murmurs about splitting the bill, it is usual for the man or woman who proffered the invitation to pay. In all circumstances it is polite and thoughtful of the guest to make some sort of gesture at some stage of the evening, such as offering to stand a couple of glasses of champagne.

Allowing someone else to foot the bill may make the recipient feel obliged to grant admittance to the bedroom later. This is quite wrong, and no 'date' should feel in any way obliged to do anything they don't want to. That is the strumpet's lot. Certainly going Dutch on a bill in most cases brings down the sexual shutters in no uncertain terms, although in the case of those who share a radical outlook on social manners, and the very young, this is not always so. Also it should be remembered that lunch, tea or drinks is a much more chaste date than dinner, and ideal for those who want to take things slowly.

191

Thereafter who pays for the dates is up to the individual circumstances of the couple concerned. Men of traditional upbringing who are both well-off and generous will expect to fund all assignations. However, most modern men rarely possess these characteristics and thus expenses are now borne in a much more equal way, with couples alternating the guest/host roles. Women understand and appreciate a gesture and are often pleased to contribute in whatever way they can, as part of sharing the enjoyment of the date.

Going Home

Taxis, particularly the London black cabs, have always enjoyed a somewhat naughty reputation. This probably stems from an age when young people led much more supervised lives and taxis were one of the few places private enough for amorous encounters. It was during these more innocent times that the acronym NSIT (not safe in taxis) was coined by young girls about randy men, with whom a shared ride was an event. Today, taxis may have lost their illicit *frisson*, but the homeward-bound etiquette remains.

A man should always offer to drop a woman off after a first date, unless she lives in a completely different direction from him, in which case he should make sure that she is safely ensconced in a taxi before sorting out his own arrangements. If she takes her own taxi, he is under no obligation to pay her fare. If both parties share a taxi, careful and quick decisions have to be taken about whether one party merely drops the other off and carries on with his/her journey or is invited in. If a woman does not want a man to come in, then gentle but clear suggestions – such as: 'You tell the driver your address first, so that he can plan the journey properly' – should be put into the conversation. If a man is asked in, he must not assume that he has the green light for sex, although a woman who does this shouldn't be surprised if he does. It is still customary for a man to see a woman to her door before taking the taxi home. The woman should offer to contribute towards the fare, although, particularly on the first date, this offer should not be taken up.

Should a man drive a woman home and he is not to be invited in, it is usual for them to make their farewells in the car. He usually offers his cheek. He then, as with taxis, walks her to her door, says good night and returns to his car or waits until she has her key safely in the lock. It is bad manners for a man to try and inveigle his way into a woman's (or indeed another man's) flat or house if he is not wanted.

Thanking

Even if a man has paid for an entire evening it is still good manners for him to thank his guest for a lovely evening. This is not just old-fashioned gallantry, but also another opportunity to pay a compliment. The recipient should thank his/her host, even if he/she does not want to see them again. This should be either by telephone or by letter.

FLIRTING

Flirting is fun. It is also an art if done well. It is only dangerous (and ill-mannered) if it is used to undermine somebody else's relationship. However, many people, particularly the socially unconfident, may be disturbed by the flirt's quixotic charms. Thus the flirt with *savoir faire* must remember always to keep his or her technique light and know when there has been one deep glance or fleeting touch too many and it is time to back off.

At the same time the object of the flirt's attentions must not make the mistake of automatically assuming that he or she is getting the green light for sex. Flirtation is a very playful form of romantic activity, which is made all the more tantalising by its ambiguity. The flirt's art, if not a sex substitute, is a well-developed social skill to make life more entertaining.

MAKING A PASS

This is when flirting gets serious. It should never be undertaken lightly, for whereas flirting is merely sexual semaphore in the direction of someone else's territory, making a pass is a full-scale invasion. The elegant pass (as rare as a nightingale in Berkeley Square) is always expertly timed and perfectly gauged, and should be sexy without being offensive.

If a pass is rebuffed then it is bad manners to press attentions any further, even if you are convinced that he/she who said no means yes. However, recognition of an ambivalent response should be carefully thought through. Is she shy? Is she unwilling for fear of being thought 'easy' but genuinely interested, albeit on a more long-term basis only? Is she genuinely undecided because you don't know each other well enough? There is much bold male advice to the effect that men should seize the opportunity rather than being seen as weak and losing it. Good manners may not pay dividends in terms of immediate gratification, but can open the way to something much more rewarding in the longer term.

Those on the receiving end of unwanted attentions should deal with the situation promptly, succinctly but also lightly and kindly. The simplest way is just to ignore the advance, as there is little more deflating than instant invisibility. The other polite approach is to say quietly but firmly, 'Please don't do that.' However, these subtle responses are sometimes inadequate, if you are being relentlessly groped under the table by your neighbour at dinner. This happened to a certain spirited woman at an official dinner, who, weary of returning the offending paw to its owner, picked it up and pressed it firmly into a convenient bowl of mango sorbet, saying icily, 'I think you need to cool down.' Her assailant was so embarrassed that he left before coffee.

GOING OUT WITH SOMEONE MUCH RICHER THAN ONESELF

This invariably provides awkwardness for all but the most committed gold-digger. As in all relationships honesty is the recommended course of action. The less well-off partner has to make it subtly but abundantly clear that their financial status is somewhat different from their lover's. Very rich people often make the mistake of assuming that everybody they meet socially shares their spending power. There is one middle-ranking City executive who virtually bankrupted himself in the pursuit of expensive pleasures for his rich girlfriend, who in the end left him to marry a millionaire. On the other hand, the poorer partner must not assume that he or she should be paid for the whole time. While they may be unable to contribute to large expenses, they should make a point of paying what they can by buying small indulgences, such as programmes at the opera, thus preventing the richer one from starting to feel taken for granted. One young man, then an impecunious student, tells of the stunned and delighted reaction of a young heiress when he offered to buy her a drink. 'It is six months since anybody bought me a drink,' she said.

COMPLIMENTS AND PRESENTS

The giving and receiving of presents and compliments is an integral part of any happy relationship. Both sides need to know how to give and receive. Compliments should be regularly but carefully conceived to avoid sounding like platitudes. They should always be accepted gracefully, but never expected as a matter of course. Any compliment is wonderful, whether it is approving comments about a lover's appearance or full-blown declarations of delight and desire.

The giving of presents requires more circumspection. As a general rule of thumb, it is a mistake to start giving expensive items immediately in the early part of a relationship: only the most unabashed gold-digger will not feel some awkwardness about being bought. Therefore, when you first know somebody, stick to small but thoughtfully chosen offerings. More important things, such as jewellery, expensive holidays and cars, are fitting only if both parties wish to make a more lasting commitment or have an understanding of a more commercial nature.

Flowers make an ideal present at any stage of a relationship. They are the perfect no-strings overture – hence their popularity on Valentine's Day – and no matter how lavish can be joyfully accepted without embarrassment, because, as the ultimate perishable present, they have no long-term value. If men knew how potent flowers are in increasing a woman's feelings of attachment, they would give what they often think of as mere trifles more attention.

However, as with all presents, there needs to be care taken, particularly in an age when impersonal bouquets of flowers are routinely seen as thank-yous in business. Therefore it is no longer enough for the lover who wants to impress merely to ask his secretary to order something over the telephone on his credit card (unless his secretary is an ex-florist) and hope it will be up to scratch. Nowadays it is good manners to be seen to make an effort with a floral tribute. The first thing to remember is that florists are like restaurants or shops, with only a few establishments in fashion at any one time. Your bunch should be ordered from them and ought to tie in with your beloved's personal taste, domestic colour scheme or favourite blooms. In more out-of-the-way places, where senders are dependent on national floral delivery services, you should specify the sorts of blooms that are required.

If your loved one's taste in flowers is unknown, then go for early blooms of favourite varieties, such as the first sweet peas, newest hyacinths or earliest camellias or violets. Extra-special touches are particularly appreciated. One woman was sent two mysterious, anonymous bunches in quick succession. After much pondering, she realised that the flowers in the first bunch spelt her name and guessed, quite rightly, that the second held the identity of the sender.

Triangular massed arrangements full of lots of indifferent flowers (e.g. pink carnations, red roses and white gypsophila) that don't go together are really only for suburban crematoria. Also never, ever, send a red and white bouquet, as this, the colour of blood and bandages, has been unlucky since the Great War. Generally speaking, flowers are much more romantic than plants, although certain things – such as a pristine and fragrant gardenia or luscious orchid in a basket – make wonderful presents as the relationship matures. Senders should also, if possible, write their own card, rather than relying on the vagaries of an unknown shop assistant's hand. The most elegant card to use is, of course, a personal visiting card (see Chapter 8), with the endearment written on the back. If you do not have your own card, then use a perfectly plain white one, not your business card or a twee printed one that some florists supply. It is customary not to seal the small envelope, although there will be times when discretion is needed. It is now perfectly acceptable to send flowers to men, although those who work in severely macho environments should probably receive them at home. However, there is no need to follow the example of one woman, who sent the most masculine piece of vegetation you can find. Not wishing to embarrass her husband with pretty flowers, she sent him instead a cactus, which although rare bore an unhappy resemblance to a misshapen and very prickly phallus. This innocent present was well meaning but misjudged, as it was the subject of much ribbing from his colleagues.

INTRODUCTION OF LOVER INTO SOCIAL CIRCLE

This should never be rushed. People have all sorts of reasons for having sexual relationships, and they do not necessarily include whether an individual is good socially. Add to this the inescapable fact that modern relationships are becoming increasingly fragile and problematical, and you have plenty of justification for social reticence. Thus the pragmatist in personal matters rarely introduces a lover into his or her circle of friends until he or she feels established as a couple. And even then the introductions should be carefully limited.

Some people, for whom love seems all, misguidedly and often innocently start to drop their friends once in a relationship. This is a mistake, because whereas lovers invariably come and go, friends can always be there.

HOMOSEXUALITY

Britain, as a French ex-prime minister once pointed out, has always had a reputation for homosexuality. Certainly in recent years there seem to be record numbers of men coming out of the closet, particularly those who have previously been married. I know of one woman who suddenly finds herself living with a gay husband and a gay son. She is confused but bearing up remarkably well in the circumstances.

Homosexuality, like all sexual matters, remains a private thing. In modern sophisticated social settings, homosexual couples should be treated no differently from heterosexual ones. It is bad manners to ask somebody, 'Are you gay?' It is the worst taste to make homophobic remarks or to behave in a way that suggests you consider homosexuals in any way odd. I am reminded of an instance of a woman writing to the American doyenne of correct form, Miss Manners, to ask how she should greet a gay couple. The answer was quite simply, 'How do you do. How do you do.' Everybody should remember this simple model when dealing with gays and lesbians.

By the same token it is ill-mannered for gay people to be wildly outrageous and confrontational about their sexuality, particularly in front of those who might be embarrassed. The secret is to be utterly frank but totally unsensational. Most people get the message and few today are unsophisticated enough to disapprove.

TERMS FOR LOVERS

When people had just friends, fiancés and spouses, conversation was very straightforward. However, the range of contemporary relationships has brought about a number of sometimes confusing and usually cringe-making euphemisms such as *significant other*, and wet little terms such as *the person I live with*. The most innocuous, concise and popular term is *partner*, as it can cover a multitude of personal arrangements, but it is distinctly bland and lacks style. The old standbys *boyfriend* and *girlfriend* are still fine, but somehow remain better suited to younger rather than superannuated couples. It is over the top in a sort of passé, Swinging Sixties way to refer to or introduce someone in a social setting as one's *lover*, although it is curiously more acceptable to use it when referring to past affairs. The word *mistress* retains pejorative associations, particularly in the Anglo-Saxon world. The term *companion* is unnecessarily genteel. It is coy for a gay couple to hide behind *friend*, unless they have a reason for being discreet. They should use 'boy-/girlfriend', 'partner' or, if they must, 'the man I live with'.

DATING AGENCIES AND LONELY HEARTS COLUMNS

Rather curiously, as people have enjoyed ever greater sexual freedom and more chances of personal fulfilment, they seem to find it increasingly difficult to meet suitable partners. Thus a significant number of individuals, exasperated with the usual means of finding prospective companions, are joining dating agencies and either placing or answering advertisements for mates. Although it is difficult to work out the success rate of such transactions, it is obvious that no shortage of hopefuls has brought this once rather sad and shady practice almost into polite society. However, there are risks, and participants must be aware that they are making contact with strangers, who have not been subject to the usual filtering and screening process provided by family, friends and associates. Thus advertisements should never give away any useful data to the browsing psychopath such as name, address or telephone number. It is also important not to lie, and to exclude *bêtes noires* such as smoking. On the first date it is important to meet on neutral ground – preferably a busy hotel or bar for drinks or at most lunch, but never dinner – and to remember that the continued retention of a little anonymity is both alluring and circumspect. It is also advisable to prepare for defeat and disappointment and accept both gracefully.

WALKERS

One of the more curious side effects of the sexual revolution is that it has produced a species of companion with no sexual role. These can be divided into two categories: the traditional walker, and the super best friend. The former is usually, but not exclusively, male, and fulfils the social role of a spouse at events and activities. Traditionally they are the preserve of single, widowed or divorced women, but they increasingly accompany women whose interests are quite different from their husbands or whose husbands are too busy for a social life. Unlike a gigolo or agency escort they are utterly respectable because there are no sexual favours. They are also social equals, as they are not paid for their attentions, although it is completely accepted and even expected that if a man is walking a well-off woman, she picks up most, but not all, of the bills. The good-mannered walker always offers to make a small contribution, such as a couple of glasses of champagne before dinner or in the interval. He is also assiduous about thank-you letters. However, friends must not treat a woman and her walker as a couple. They should never be invited together to any event. She should be asked either singly, such as 'Mrs Lettice Lonely and Guest', or, if a married woman, with her husband. Remember that socially walkers, unlike husbands, are discretionary not mandatory.

The super best friend, on the other hand, is a kind of extra-special chum (usually of the opposite sex) with whom there is all the intimacy of a close relationship but no sexual contact to confuse matters. They are often trotted out when single or divorced women need an escort. Many women and some men have gay super best friends, but homosexuality is in no way a prerequisite to the role (the same is true of walkers). Super best friends tend to share everything – secrets, holidays and, in the case of one advanced pair, sexual partners too. However, all super best friends must remember that although they are extra-special individuals to their friends, should these friends fall in love, they have to be gracious enough to revert to the supporting rather than the principal role in the relationship. As with walkers, super best friends have no formal social connection, and should always be invited singly to formal gatherings.

ENDING A RELATIONSHIP

This is never easy, but it can be done elegantly. The secret of ending a relationship well is to leave the rejected party with his/her self-esteem in the best possible shape. Therefore, when breaking up a relationship it must be given its due importance. It should always be done face to face. The telephone call – or worse, the fax message – is quite inappropriate. The letter should be used only as a follow-up after the break-up meeting. It is in the worst taste for a girl- or boyfriend to find out that you are seeing another without hearing it first from your lips. If you expect the break-up to be a tearful occasion, it should not be done in public. In such circumstances the rejected one's home ground is best, because afterwards she (or even he!) can sob into her pillow in peace and ring her mother or best friend for consolation.

11

IN PUBLIC: MANNERS
OUT AND ABOUT

Complaints about bad manners in public are some of the most frequently heard moans of the modern age. Rudeness, lack of consideration for others and even danger in the public domain are all listed as signs of the unstoppable decline of civilised conduct. These, coupled with a rise in oafish, gauche and selfish behaviour in public places, would make it appear that basic civility has been totally suspended in favour of a crass populism. Happily, although manners might not be quite what they were, rumours about their death are greatly exaggerated. Although the pace and pressure of modern life have eroded many of the old-fashioned niceties of yesterday, the majority of people do exercise a remarkable amount of well-mannered behaviour towards their fellow citizens. Here, to reassure them, and to help others confused by the modern maelstrom, is a little guidance.

ON THE STREET
You might suppose that in a era when street crime has reached such frightening levels, manners have become somewhat redundant. Happily, you would be quite wrong. The majority of pedestrians still maintain an impressive amount of consideration about each other's space and thus respect one of the cardinal rules of public manners.

Generally speaking, it is bad manners to behave in a loud, disruptive or irritating way in public; this is the behavioural preserve of drunken louts leaving pubs at closing time. If part of a large group, it is inconsiderate to walk in a long horizontal line and thus block the way of others. It is more

200

polite to follow each other in small groups of two or three, although any attempt to adopt a school-like crocodile formation is to be avoided. It is still good manners for men to walk on the outside (i.e. roadside) edge of the pavement when accompanying women. This dates back to when men were needed to protect women from marauders and mud from dirty roads. It is also still polite for men to hold doors of shops and other public places open for women, and for juniors to do the same for their elders. By the same token, if a door is held open for you it is good manners to take it and say thank you. Little is more irritating than to be left holding a door for any length of time. Revolving doors have their own etiquette. Old-fashioned gallants maintain that the only polite way for two people to negotiate one is for the man to go in *before* the woman, push the contraption around and then emerge *after* her. This is too much of a palaver for today, when good manners only require the man to stand back and let the woman use the doors first.

Too blatant displays of affection look crass and out of place on the street. Other anti-social acts include carelessness with umbrellas – those who carry them must remember to adopt a civic approach to avoid inflicting nasty injuries on others; jay-walking, which is dangerous as well as inconsiderate; depositing litter anywhere other than a receptacle designed for the purpose; and eating, drinking and smoking, all of which look very unattractive on the street. Chewing gum is ugly and uncouth. Even less appealing on the pavement is the sight of dog dirt. Dog-owners must ensure that their pampered pets do their business either in the gutter or in a specially provided dog loo. Really good-mannered owners carry pooper-scoopers or plastic bags to remove any offending matter. Queuing, although not the great British institution it once was, is still part of the national psyche. Thus it remains bad manners to jump any queue, be it at a bus stop or in the collecting line for vouchers for the Royal Enclosure from St James's Palace on the Monday of Ascot week.

Shops

Shops are one of the key places where the ill mannered show themselves at their worst. This presumably is done in the mistaken belief that shop assistants don't matter and nobody notices anyway. Both suppositions are wrong. First, those who work in shops are like other human beings, and thus deserve to be treated with common courtesy. Second, bad behaviour in shops *is* observed. So remember that it is polite to say 'please' and 'thank you', and ill mannered to order shop staff around and give them a hard time because you are in a bad mood.

201

RESTAURANTS

Restaurants, even more than shops, are social arenas where behavioural discrepancies are all too obvious. Eating out, once a minor pastime in Britain, has become one of the most popular ways for people to spend their leisure time. And although restaurants range enormously in style, tone and levels of formality, the procedure remains remarkably similar in most establishments.

Making a Reservation

To avoid disappointment you should always make a reservation in all but the most casual of restaurants. Very popular places, of which there are usually a dozen on the go at any one time, will require reservations to be made up to two weeks in advance. Making a reservation also enables you to bag the table of your choice and discuss any special requirements. Reservations are made by telephone, for a specific time and in the name of the host.

Arriving at the Restaurant

It is sensible to arrive on time, unless you want to risk losing your table. It is rude to berate an establishment that has given away your table because you are forty minutes late. If you are the host it is very important to arrive punctually, as it is impolite to allow your guests to wait for any length of time. Being on time also gives you the opportunity to study the menu, so that you can give your guests your undivided attention when they arrive, as well as allowing you to make any special arrangements about paying the bill. However, life is such that hosts are often delayed. In this case it is now perfectly acceptable for the guests to go straight to the table, but totally unacceptable for them to start ordering drinks or, even worse, food before the host arrives. Remember, it is the host who is offering hospitality, not the restaurant. It is, however, quite done for guests to nibble on a piece of bread while they are waiting.

What you wear is a matter of personal choice, but should also take into consideration the style of the establishment. Although dress codes are much more relaxed than previously, many grand hotels and very smart restaurants will either turn away men not wearing a jacket and tie, or try to coax them into grisly garments kept for the use of underdressed guests. Women seem to enjoy a more lenient time, although it is worth remembering that dining usually requires more dressing up than lunching.

On entering the restaurant, you should first make yourself known to the restaurant manager or *maître d'hôtel*. He will show you to your table. Women follow first, with men bringing up the rear. If there are no staff to take you to the table, then a man leads the way. Men walking into restaurants with their hands in their pockets look like oiks. Those who proceed with folded arms look awkward. If a man is dining with a woman it is customary for her to sit facing into the restaurant. The same is true in any host/guest arrangement – the guest takes the seat with the view. In a large group it is usual to adopt the boy/girl and separated couples arrangements used for domestic dining.

Choosing and Ordering

Traditional restaurants divide their menus into two sections: the table d'hôte, which has details of dishes specially prepared that day and included in a set menu, and the à la carte, which offers a far greater choice of dishes that can be ordered separately. Many contemporary eateries supplement their à la carte menu with various dishes of the day rather than a complete fixed menu.

The set menu is always invariably cheaper than a selection made à la carte, and is always popular in times of recession. As a guest you are under no obligation to choose from the set menu. On the other hand, it is very bad form to choose the most expensive dishes from the à la carte section. If dining somewhere grandly traditional where the guest's menu is presented without prices, the guest should be particularly careful, although there is no need to follow the old-fashioned model that advised choosing grapefruit or chicken dishes because they would definitely be cheap. Hosts confronted with extravagant guests, although able to make suggestions, have no option but to indulge their demands.

Whether guests place their orders directly with the waiter or through their host has become a modern dining dilemma. Traditional good manners demand that the host orders everything on behalf of his guests (this is again because he or she is giving, not the restaurant – which is purely providing a service). I still adhere to this dictum, because it shows politeness. However, the practice of everybody ordering for himself is now so widespread – particularly at business lunches – that it has become almost acceptable. This being said, when enjoying the hospitality of someone from the old school it is strongly recommended to stick to the time-honoured model. Another idea is to adopt a hybrid form of ordering the dishes via the host, but discussing the details – such as how something is to be cooked and its accompaniments – with the staff.

It is customary to order the first two courses in one go, leaving pudding,

203

cheese or coffee to be sent for after the main course. The only exceptions tend to be in ethnic restaurants, where sometimes a repast is ordered in its entirety. If you are not very hungry, watching your weight, or on one of the fashionable fad diets, it is thoughtless to make a great song and dance about your dietary requirements, as such protestations of nutritional vulnerability can often be embarrassing for your host and deeply tedious for other guests. I have been to many business lunches where the true reason for the meeting has been obscured by protracted and tense discussions about whether the sauce includes wheat, or 'I simply can't drink that glass of mineral water because it's got a slice of lemon in it.' Similarly, if you have determined that your lunch is to be a calorie-free zone, then order a green salad as your first course, to avoid the awkward sight of an empty place setting. On the other hand, good manners do not require you to submit yourself to a ritual stuffing by an overzealous host. It is therefore perfectly acceptable not to drink or order pudding (most people don't). Sophisticated weight-watchers have long eaten lunches comprising two first courses alone. Remember when ordering dishes with hugely complicated names on the menu to ask for them simply. Therefore, if you have plumped for *Paupiettes de saumon avec petits turbans de concombres aux jus de l'oseille sauvage*, say to the waiter: 'I'd like the salmon, please.'

The Ordering of Wine

Whereas there is a certain amount of contemporary confusion about who orders the food, it is still the accepted custom for the host to sort out the wine. The only exception to this is if a woman is hosting a lunch, when she may ask the main male guest to choose the wine for her. This is, however, merely a chivalrous gesture, and more independent woman hosts tend to do the ordering themselves. Hosts can ask their guests whether they prefer white, red or rosé. If entertaining a large group it is customary to order two colours so that all dishes will have a suitable drink. In all but the most basic of establishments, wine is dealt with through a separate wine waiter or sommelier. Many of these are specialists in their area, and are happy to advise on the right choice. However, endless discussions on the merits of Beaune versus the Gevrey Chambertin, no matter how fascinating they are to you and the sommelier, are likely to make dreary listening for your guests. Do not feel obliged to order expensive wines, as house varieties are usually perfectly palatable. Some guests may not wish to drink wine, and would prefer merely to 'nurse' a glass of champagne. Others require only water, and should be given the choice between sparkling and still. Tap water from a jug is now drunk only by members of the older generation.

Once the wine choice is made, then the wine waiter will bring it to the table for the host to try. The waiter will first present the bottle to show that you are getting what was ordered. He will then pour a small amount into the host's glass for the host to taste. This is his opportunity to check if the wine is at the right temperature and drinkable. If it is not up to scratch you can send it back, but any complaints after this point are not really fair. Many men rush this little ritual, treating it as merely a formality. This is a shame, as the well-mannered host should always take time to guarantee his guests' comfort and the staff's interest and co-operation. Once the wine is passed, the waiter will then fill everybody's glass, starting with the women and ending with the host (providing he is a man).

It is worth pointing out at this time that if a woman is host, then she is accorded the same treatment as a man in the role, despite the endeavours of sexist Latin waiters. For instance, if a man is being given lunch by a woman, should the waiter show him the wine, then he must gesture towards his hostess (unless she designates him wine chooser or taster, as above). The same applies to the bill. However, the hostess's assumption of the traditional male role of host does not mean that she is no longer entitled to the courtesies long associated with her sex. Therefore, the male guest still stands every time she does, lights her cigarettes and helps her into her jacket.

Spotting Chums and Table-Hopping

It is quite usual to run into friends at restaurants, particularly in those where you are a regular customer. It is obviously fun and polite to acknowledge your friends, but rude to the company at your table to spend any length of time with them. Therefore the best course of action is to say hello quickly when you arrive, leave, or are *en route* for the loo. Do not sit down at your acquaintances' table, as this disrupts your friends' party and prolongs your absence from your group. It is perfectly acceptable to wave discreetly to people you know at neighbouring tables.

Dealing with Restaurant Staff

Well-trained waiters normally need little prompting. However, there are many badly run establishments where the staff are able to reduce their customers to a state of instant invisibility, as if blighted by an ancient mythological spell. Even in well-run places there will be times when you need to attract the waiter's attention. On no account should this be achieved by bellowing across the room, tapping your fingers on the table or, worst of all, clicking your fingers. It is much better to try and catch his eye more discreetly. Leaning back in one's chair and looking in his direction is very effective. A small hand gesture also works. Some people feel embarrassment about calling out, 'Waiter!': this is quite unnecessary, as such an appellation is both accurate and inoffensive. However, the use of 'miss' when addressing a waitress is vulgar. The same is true of the transatlantic 'sir' when calling a waiter. When speaking to restaurant staff it is important to be civil and say: 'Please may I have my bill now' and 'Thank you' when it arrives. This being said, excessive chumminess and relentless thanking is also to be avoided.

Complaining

Traditionally the British are held to be bad complainers: either they remain stoically silent in the face of inferior service or they assume a boorishly overbearing demeanour. Both approaches are ill advised and unproductive. If you are unhappy about a badly cooked dish, arrogant or sloppy service or grubby cutlery, say so. Most establishments worth their salt want to offer the best possible standard to their customers and thus need to know about any shortcomings. The secret is to put your complaint in a polite, non-aggressive, but firm way. If the shortcoming is a small one, such as a tepid dish that should be hot, then this simple problem can be dealt with by asking the waiter to change it. If, however, the problem is more fundamental, such as stroppy staff who would be much better suited to a job that does not involve dealing with the public, then a quiet word in private with the manager is preferable. On no account should the complainer lose his or her temper. In extreme and thankfully very rare cases, where it is impossible to get any satisfaction from the manager, a prompt, crisp and accurate letter the following day to a superior always produces remarkable results.

Smoking

Guidelines governing smoking in restaurants are confusing. Curiously, while smoking is increasingly seen as an anti-social habit, the social rules designed to restrict it have become more relaxed. This produces the bizarre sight that can often be witnessed in many restaurants of the smokers puffing away at every opportunity and the non-smokers turning up their noses. Neither group has right on their side, as restaurants are public places and thus require public toleration. Therefore, the smoker (unless sitting in one of the proliferating no-smoking sections) is perfectly entitled to smoke. He should, however, wait until after the main course, and check with his companions before he lights up that none of them minds. If his table is very near to other diners who are still eating, it is thoughtful to canvass their opinion too.

Doggie-Bagging and Mutual Eating

The American habit of asking for uneaten food to be wrapped up and taken away, presumably to be later fed to a canine companion, is not acceptable in Britain. Mutual eating – the increasing trend for diners to exchange morsels from each other's plates – is also an undesirable habit.

Paying the Bill

This can so often turn into a crisis, as money and cheques are handed around the table like a game of pass the parcel. Generally speaking, the host always pays the bill. However, the guest should invariably offer to make a contribution, by merely asking: 'May I . . .', although this gesture should not be pressed too strongly. The only exception is if a guest orders cigarettes, for which he should pay personally. If the guest wishes to contribute something, he or she can offer to leave a tip or to drop the host off after leaving the restaurant. Hosts who wish to avoid any discussion with guests about payment can slip off quietly towards the end of the proceedings to settle up with the head waiter. Another alternative, if the host is known to the restaurant, is to have the bill sent on.

When the bill arrives it is both sensible and acceptable to check it, although endless mathematical calculations should be avoided in front of friends. Also, should the host feel that he or she has been overcharged, any discussions ought to be had away from the table. If you wish to pay by credit card, it is worth checking whether the establishment accepts plastic – a surprising number don't. Any restaurant that does not should inform you at the time of accepting your reservation. Should you be paying cash and only have large notes, it is sometimes necessary to make it clear that you expect the change, and are not leaving an enormous tip. This being said, properly trained waiters will always return change unless told to do otherwise.

Splitting the Bill

If the bill is to be split and everybody is to pay his share, this should be implicit in the general conduct of the group. By this I mean that the seating plan and the choice and ordering of food and wine become collective activities rather than the responsibility of a single individual. When the bill arrives it is divided equally between all diners. It is churlish for those who chose merely to consume a green salad and mineral water to expect to make a smaller contribution than those who went for steak, chips and claret. On the other hand it is somewhat tacky for hearty eaters to feast on the most expensive items on the menu and expect everybody else to subsidise their extravagant tastes. If the bill has been split, the habit of one person taking the receipt for later claiming on company expenses is as unattractive as it is fraudulent. It is also the worst of manners to profit at your friends' expense.

TIPPING

Tipping remains a thorn in many people's social sides. They worry about when to tip, who to tip, how much to tip. There is really no reason for confusion. Tips are a gesture to express personal appreciation for a job well done. Although the catering industry is traditionally renowned for low pay, restaurant staff are remunerated by their employers to be there and serve you. Any tip is a bonus, not a right.

If the bill comes without a service charge included in the total, it is usual to leave between ten and fifteen per cent of the whole amount as a tip. Something around twelve per cent is about the mark, but how much you leave should be governed by how impressed you have been with the staff. You should feel no embarrassment about leaving a low, or even nonexistent tip, if their performance has been lacking. It is also worth pointing out that to overtip is as inappropriate as to undercompensate. The tip can either be added when you fill in the total on the credit card voucher, included in your cheque or left in cash – the last option ensures that your waiter actually gets it.

The tipping question becomes more vexed with the proliferation (and possible legislation) of service-included bills. These were introduced to prevent mean customers leaving without showing appreciation for the staff, but result in many people wondering whether they should leave any more on top. Technically there is no need to tip anything extra on a bill that has been calculated to include service. However, if you have been treated particularly impressively, it is thoughtful to leave a small extra sum in cash to show your appreciation.

Other Tipping Tips

Cloakroom attendants, with their supplicant saucers of change, expect to be tipped, and they should be. The amount varies according to the grandeur of the establishment. At the hairdresser's or barber's, the junior members of staff should be rewarded with a small gratuity, but not the manager or senior stylists. The same demarcation applies in hotels, where those who serve are tipped and those who manage are not (see p. 213 below). There is a curious discrepancy between sea and air travel. On board large ships such as ocean-going liners and cruisers (presumably because it is a more old-fashioned method of transportation than the airborne variety), it is customary to tip your cabin steward and others who have looked after you. The amount largely corresponds with dry land payments, but is obviously influenced by the length of the voyage and the comparative splendour of the ship. On smaller crafts such as yachts, it is often the form to leave an envelope with the captain to be distributed amongst the crew. Air travel is quite different. There is no tradition of tipping on commercial flights, although small gratuities are sometimes given in the case of chartered private jets. Taxi and mini-cab drivers receive tips (see p. 219 below).

Two Small Social Graces That Can Make a Big Difference

Although it is usual for staff to push in women's chairs and help them on with their coats, all men should learn to perform these little social graces themselves. Pushing in chairs properly is particularly important if disaster is to be avoided. I have seen more than one woman tipped on to the floor by well-meaning but unskilled hands. The main thing to remember is never to tilt the chair. As the woman bends her knees to sit down, take hold of the back of the chair with both hands and put your foot underneath. Next, gently push the chair forward using your hands and knees in unison. Under no circumstances should the chair be pulled further out before sliding it under the waiting posterior, as this only increases the risk of an embarrassing error. Helping women into their coats, unless done deftly, can turn into a bit of a wrestling match. The coat should be held midway between the collar and the shoulder seam. It is important to make sure that the sleeves are positioned for easy access. As soon as the woman has her hands in the correct sleeves, the coat should be firmly lifted on the shoulders. The secret is then to lift the coat again quickly to make sure it settles properly on to the clothes underneath.

THE THEATRE

The basis of good manners at the theatre is to remember that you are in a place of public entertainment, not at home. Your behaviour should be suitably public-spirited. You ought to be in your place before the curtain rises, refrain from talking (no matter how *sotto voce*), eating and drinking (except in the interval), canoodling or wearing so much scent that your neighbours start sneezing. Other anti-social distractions include jangling bracelets and big hairstyles. In essence, being an irritation to the audience around you and a distraction to the actors is the height of theatrical bad manners.

It is usual to book theatre tickets in advance, although for less popular shows it is often possible to buy them on the day from the box office.

Theatre agencies are really for large parties, but can sometimes be a last resort if the box office has already sold out. Prices vary considerably, depending on position, view and comfort. It is worth bearing in mind that making small economies can turn out to be very uncomfortable ones indeed. The most expensive places tend to be in the dress circle and the front of the stalls – seats decrease in price and quality the further up and back they go. What people wear usually mirrors the price of the seats, with those in the dress circle tending to be better turned out than those in the gallery. It is ill mannered to arrive at a theatre having made no sartorial effort.

Intervals at the theatre are always too short, so it is wise to order interval drinks before the performance begins. These will be waiting for you when you come out of the auditorium. It is also customary to tip the barman around twelve per cent of the bill.

THE OPERA AND THE BALLET

If good manners are important at the theatre, they are vital at the opera and ballet. At these cultural events, anti-social behaviour is deeply, and quite rightly, frowned on.

Punctuality is vital, as late-comers will not be allowed into the auditorium until a suitable break in the performance (normally the end of a scene or act), and thus are liable to miss much of the performance or to be relegated to watching it on a small television in the bar.

Tickets for the opera, and to a lesser extent the ballet, are expensive. This does not stop them – particularly those for the more accessible repertoire – being highly sought after. Therefore they will need to be booked up to three months in advance. This can be done by cheque in the post, over the telephone with a credit card, or in person at the box office. Those particularly keen to get tickets can either take out a subscription for several performances in a season, or become a 'friend' or 'private member' and thus get priority booking each season. Seat prices vary hugely, from stratospheric for the best seats on big nights with major stars, to nominal charges for obscure eyries in the gods on standard nights. For the opera I have long favoured boxes near the stage, because from them the sound is particularly rich; they also have a festive feel and are cosy vantage points for viewing the house. However, as their view of the stage is always restricted to some degree, they are not recommended for the ballet.

Thoughtful general conduct is very important. Any talking during the performance is unforgivable. One frequent *habitué* of Covent Garden regularly snarls conspicuous shushing noises to anybody who dares to open their mouth. The effect is instantaneous. Other anti-social acts include endless head movements, wearing noisy jewellery and the rustling of programmes. Eating is absolutely unforgivable. There is one story of a man who was so infuriated by the endless munching of two people behind him that at interval time he turned around and said: 'Would you kindly unwrap all the foodstuffs now you wish to consume during Act II.' The picnickers were suitably chastened. If you drop your programme or opera glasses it is preferable to leave picking them up until a suitable break in the performance. The question of when to applaud is also a complicated one. Technically you should clap only at the end of a scene or an act. However, if a singer has given a particularly good rendition of an aria, then it is acceptable to applaud. The important point to remember is not to start clapping until the music is quite finished. Should you enthusiastically decide to shout 'Bravo!' or give a standing ovation, you risk doing it alone. The bulk of applause and adulation is reserved for the end of the performance and the curtain calls. It is the height of rudeness and lack of consideration for the artists for members of the audience to get up and leave immediately the curtain has fallen, without even waiting a few moments to applaud those who have given their all to entertain them for the last few hours. It is ill mannered to arrive badly dressed at the opera or ballet. Shorts, jeans and anoraks (yes, anoraks!) are quite out of place. On the other hand, dinner jackets are over the top, except on gala nights, unless you are in Vienna, where dressing up is still usual. Finally, it is worth pointing out that contrary to common belief, one goes to *hear* an opera, not to see it.

COUNTRY HOUSE OPERA FESTIVALS

Opera performed in attractive arcadian surroundings with a leisurely interval to enjoy a delicious picnic supper are increasingly popular. The best-known British festivals are Glyndebourne and Garsington. Glyndebourne's festival started in the thirties. Today its season runs from May to August. The house boasts high musical standards and is best known for its excellent Mozart productions. However, its recent redevelopment, although undoubtably improving its technical acoustic qualities, has diminished this once wonderful place's special atmosphere. Garsington, on the other hand, is presenting itself as the pretender to Glyndebourne's lyric crown, although it has a very long way to go to achieve the latter's musical excellence. Particularly known for its staging of unknown Haydn operas, Garsington takes place under a canopy in a beautiful Oxfordshire garden designed earlier this century by Lady Ottoline Morrell.

The form for both places is very similar. Tickets are sought after and need to be applied for well in advance. However, those who ring up at the last minute for returns can be pleasantly surprised. Although dinner jackets for men and evening dresses for women are only 'recommended' rather than enforced, those who don't dress will find themselves in a very small and conspicuous minority.

It is usual to arrive in the late afternoon and to have some tea or take a stroll around the lovely gardens. Performances normally start around six and are punctuated by the long dinner interval. It is traditional to bring a rather grand, but not pretentious, picnic. However, it must be pointed out that this option can be problematical for the impractical and inexperienced. I have seen many people's evenings marred by tantrums over the Tupperware or slipped discs caused by heaving hampers packed with heavy silver and china, and, most upsetting of all, the bitten faces of one couple who settled themselves too near the lake at Garsington and thus acted unwittingly as supper for the midges. Picnickers should make sure that their spot is set up before the performance begins, with the food and champagne ready to be opened immediately the interval starts. One regular ensures a smooth-running evening under the stars by taking a butler to do all the dirty work. It is also important to remember, when working out what to wear, that even on the hottest summer days temperatures can plummet in the evening. Those who wish to take the easy – albeit not such fun – option can book a good dinner in Glyndebourne's Wallop dining rooms or the Barn at Garsington.

Behaviour at these festivals is much the same as at one of the metropolitan opera houses. This being said, there is a much more relaxed, convivial and courteous atmosphere that is quietly reminiscent of a civilised house party.

CONCERTS AND RECITALS

Good behaviour is also important at an orchestral concert, but absolutely vital for a small chamber concert or solo recital, where extraneous noise can not only disturb the audience but put the artist off his or her stride. Therefore you should remember not to talk, shuffle, fidget or cough noisily. If listening to *Lieder*, it is rude to turn the page of the translation while the vocalist is still singing. Also remember, when listening to a song cycle, that it is usual to clap at the end of the complete cycle and not after each single piece. The same applies to symphonies, concertos and sonatas, which are never applauded in between movements.

HOTELS

Hotels, particularly grand ones, can be difficult for the inexperienced. Some people claim to be intimidated by sumptuous rooms and serried rows of staff. This is a shame because good hotels are there to give service and pleasure.

It is generally sensible to book your hotel in advance and give some idea of your ETA (estimated time of arrival). It is usual to arrive in the afternoon to give the staff time to turn the room around. On arrival you check in at reception, where you also ask about the amenities the hotel offers and discuss any special requirements you might have. Then you will be shown to your room by a manager. He will explain to you how your room works and answer any questions. It is important to remember that he does not receive a tip. On the other hand, the porter who brings your bags up requires a small gratuity per piece of luggage. Your room should look as if you are the first person to use it. However, if it is not as pristine or as well appointed as you would like, complain politely. This can either be done over the internal telephone, or, more elegantly, by requesting the duty manager to come up and see you. Do not march angrily down in your bathrobe to berate the concierge.

A good relationship with the staff is vital to a propitious hotel stay. As in restaurants, they are there to help you, and most take a pride in doing so. They are not impressed by guests who throw their weight around or put on ridiculous airs and graces. So remember to say please and thank you, do not leave your room in a complete mess in the morning, and refrain from prancing around in the nude in front of room service. Also make yourself known to the concierge and restaurant manager, both of whom are there to improve the quality of your stay.

On the other hand, do not expect them to organise call girls or similar sexual diversions. Most reputable hotels will throw out guests who are obvious about using them for immoral purposes. However, most sophisticated hotels turn a blind eye to assignations of a non-commercial kind.

When it comes to tipping, remember that, as in a restaurant, the staff are paid to be there. Anything you give is a personal bonus. Therefore if you are staying for more than a few days, it is not necessary to tip the waiter each time he brings you something, or the chambermaid each time she makes up the bed. It is better to leave them a lump sum on your day of departure. If you can't find them, add ten per cent to your bill when checking out, and ask it to be distributed to the staff members in question.

Dress is less stringent than in the past. However, most grand hotels still expect men to don a jacket and tie for dining in their restaurants, although breakfast appears to have become an informal affair throughout the world. Remember that you are dressing for public delectation and that trainers, while acceptable in the Midwest, are not *comme il faut* at Claridges.

213

COCKTAIL BARS AND PUBS

In cocktail bars it is usual to sit down and to be served by a waiter. He will keep a running total of your bill (some places demand to hold a credit card for security) and then should be given a tip of around twelve per cent if service is not included in the total. It is not customary to offer to buy drinks for waiters or barmen in cocktail bars or hotels.

Pubs are quite different. Customers order their own drinks at the bar and either drink them there or carry them to nearby tables. It is usual to pay as you go. Bar staff are not tipped but are offered the occasional drink instead. Whether they actually buy the drink, or later pocket the value of it, is up to them. If a number of people are drinking together, it is expected that each of them buys a round. Pubs are by their nature sociable places and it is quite usual for strangers to strike up conversations and buy each other drinks. If a drink is accepted from a stranger it is an unwritten rule that the acceptee chats to his companion and then returns the favour. Pubs were once all-male domains, and until not so long ago used to be considered out of bounds for unaccompanied women, but this is no longer the case.

CHILDREN

Children, although utter delights to parents, can be extremely trying to others. Although only a few would welcome a return to the 'seen and not heard' model of earlier times, responsible parents must keep their offspring in order. These behavioural basics include discouraging children from dominating conversations, showing off, making huge amounts of noise and mess, being violent and anti-social to other children, showing rudeness to adults, and generally making life grim for those around them.

The easy availability of constant television and countless videos, and the advances of computer technology, have revolutionised the life of the modern child. Useful though they are at keeping children amused for long periods, they do nothing to develop social skills. Therefore, from the earliest possible age, children must become accustomed to the adult world. They should be taught to greet people properly and shake hands correctly. Curtseying and bowing, once *de rigueur*, are virtually never seen today. Once old enough to have a sensible view and credible conversation, children should be encouraged to discuss topics and enter grown-up discourses. This being said, precociousness, that traditional childhood sin, remains unappealing and should not be encouraged. Children should never interrupt adults when they are speaking, must

214

never shout other children down and ought not to address grown-ups by their first names unless invited to do so. They must never answer back to their parents, or, worse, other adults. Children should also be made to send thank-you letters as soon as they can write. Proper table manners should be insisted upon from the earliest age, as bad habits, once ingrained, are difficult to discourage. Children should always ask, 'Please may I get down?' before leaving the table. Nail-biting and other nervous habits should also be discouraged before such traits set in for life. Other errant acts that should not be tolerated include: making personal comments about others, pointing, using bad language (often picked up from parents) and throwing food around (hopefully not picked up from parents).

The role of children when parents entertain visitors also needs to be watched. If there are guests for drinks or dinner, whereas it is acceptable for children to be around and introduced in the early evening, there comes a point (around seven o'clock for small children) when their presence is *de trop* and they must be put to bed so that the adult world can continue unhindered. Lunch and tea are obviously quite different. They are today family events and are nowadays often used by parents to entertain other parents with children.

This book does not pretend to be a child-rearing manual, but it does recommend that any anti-social behaviour should be instantly dealt with. Whether this is done *negatively* – i.e. by punishment for a misdemeanour – or *positively* – i.e. a present promised for not repeating a crime – depends on which side of the contemporary child-rearing verities parents stand. What is important is that it is dealt with.

Whereas it is easy to discipline your own child, it is more difficult to sort out a misbehaving minor who belongs to someone else. As a general rule of thumb, unless a child is creating absolute havoc and you are *in loco parentis*, it should be left to the natural parent to sort out the problem. However, this does not mean that you have to grin and bear infantile indiscretions, and, should a doting parent appear unwilling to discipline a badly behaved progeny, then you are quite within your rights to complain.

EVERYDAY SOCIAL GREETINGS
Shaking Hands
Handshakes, originally intended to show that participants were unarmed, have for centuries been used as friendly greetings. To work they need to be done properly. Shaky (wet fish) handshakes always make bad impressions, while bone-clenching crunches are also undesirable. Gloves, if worn,

should always be taken off first. The right hand is always used in ordinary social settings. It is no longer necessary, except in the case of royalty or very grand older women, to wait to see if the other, more senior, person proffers his or her paw first. All handshakes should be firm enough to leave a brief impression of bodily contact. As a general rule of thumb, women, because they often wear rings set with potentially painful stones, are accorded gentler treatment than men. On no account should the other person's arm be shaken up and down, nor, except in the case of familiarity, must the left hand be placed on top of the right to double and lengthen the greeting. It is exceptionally bad manners deliberately to refuse a handshake. The *Handkuss* (when a man takes a woman's hand almost to his mouth), although accepted in grandly courteous Continental and Catholic circles, is precious and archaic elsewhere.

Social Kissing

Social kissing escalated to almost epidemic proportions as people sought a more relaxed alternative to the old-fashioned formal handshake, and is today an accepted social gesture. It is, however, not the same as shaking hands. For instance, whereas it is expected that you will shake hands with strangers, it is not done to kiss on first meetings. Also, while a handshake can be offered with impunity, if you are in any doubt about kissing someone socially, you should not do it. This is for two reasons: firstly, some people, particularly older ones, consider social kissing an intrusion from those who are other than close friends or relations; secondly, perhaps due to a contemporary obsession with health, the habit is becoming somewhat less usual.

Social kissing is quite unlike more intimate osculatory activities. It should consist of merely a fleeting and imperceptible contact with the skin. Some people – skilled practitioners of the air kiss – manage to do without any physical contact whatsoever, but by making stagey *mwah mwah* sounds signal social lift-off. Others gently bump cheeks like dainty dolphins. Under no circumstances should there be a suggestion of saliva. Unless you know somebody reasonably well, one kiss is usually enough. The double-pronged attack, although popular on the Continent, is still to be used sparingly. It is usual for men to kiss women on the right cheek. Lips are generally out of bounds in a formal public gesture.

Being on the receiving end of an unwanted social kiss can be difficult. Holding yourself quite upright will often deter the osculating intruder. If it doesn't, and whatever your feelings, it is rude and cruel to shy away or to show any signs of distaste. Social kissing between men, once utterly out of bounds in the Anglo-Saxon word, is becoming acceptable. Social kissing between women has always been, and remains, quite the norm.

THE GOOD PARTY GUEST
Parties

The well-mannered guest always replies promptly to invitations one way or the other. If he has accepted an invitation then he turns up; if he hasn't then he doesn't. His conduct is quite unlike the behaviour of a new breed of metropolitan party people, who have developed a recently isolated disease known as BI – Better Invitationitis. Sufferers from this irritating condition accept everything but turn up only to the best party on the day. They blatantly cancel existing invitations if something more amusing turns up. They also roll up at things that they have not replied to, or, even worse, were never invited to in the first place. Less insidious, but just as tedious, are those who do not bother to answer invitations at all – or at least not until the eleventh hour. This is exceptionally rude and thoughtless for hosts, who, unblissfully ignorant of the response to their party, are unable to plan accurately for numbers. If a guest finds out that he can no longer attend a party that he has accepted, then he must let his hosts know by telephone.

The properly timed arrival is also something the ill mannered get wrong. Although attitudes to punctuality are more relaxed than before, it remains rude to arrive late for a party. If attending a drinks party, then it is polite to arrive within half an hour of the start time, although there is no hard and fast rule about this. However, when invited to dinner there is little leeway. If invited for eight for eight thirty, then the best time to arrive is around 8.15. If invited to an unstructured all-evening party, then you can arrive at any time except when it is scheduled to end. This being said, it remains uncool to hang around for the entire duration of the party. It is always rude to arrive before the stated time.

The shortest amount of time that it is polite to spend at a party also causes problems. At a drinks party or other stand-up reception the absolute minimum is twenty minutes. This twenty minutes if best if it happens early on in the proceedings, as it gives you the opportunity to be seen and to talk to your hosts and anybody else whom it is important not to miss. The earliest point that you can leave a dinner party, unless there is a seriously pressing problem, is about three-quarters of an hour after everybody has finished eating. This allows enough time for people to have their coffee, let their dinners settle and feel the evening has reached a natural conclusion.

The good-mannered guest does not overstay his welcome. At a drinks party he should, in theory, make sure he has completed his farewells ten

217

minutes before the party's stated end. Being the last person to leave is not smart, particularly as other guests who are having dinner with the host need to wait until all the drinks-only guests have gone. At a dinner party, it is thoughtless to keep your hosts up, and any sign of fatigue on their part is to be taken as an important sign. Generally, during the week all dinner guests should have gone by midnight at the latest. At the weekend, it is possible – and often desirable – to stay later.

Good party behaviour is a breeze for the well-mannered guest. He arrives suitably dressed. He talks to everybody and does not monopolise favoured individuals for long periods. He does not glance over people's shoulders, or if he sees somebody more interesting suddenly drop the person he is talking to in favour of his new quarry. He does not get drunk, or stand permanently at the buffet hoovering up food. He does not clumsily bump into people while circulating (if he does, then he must apologise). He makes a particular point of seeking out his hosts and then finding them again before he leaves, to say thank you.

Dinner Parties

The good-mannered guest replies promptly to invitations to dinner parties and always arrives punctually. Contrary to popular belief, it is not necessary to take a present for the host or hostess. The habit of always bringing something is a relatively new innovation that was once frowned upon. Then it became acceptable to bring a small box of chocolates, but nothing else. Gradually, all manner of tributes, ranging from bottles of wine to bunches of flowers, became the norm. Today, although this sort of giving is endemic, it remains incorrect to bring a present to a formal dinner party, i.e. one at which dinner jackets are being worn. At other dinner parties, presents that will be welcomed by the host or hostess are acceptable. Flowers, although popular, are problematical, as they mean that the hostess, unless she has staff on duty, has to stop what she is doing to see to them. Far better, if wanting to make a floral tribute, is to follow the Continental habit of sending flowers the next day. Some guests even send them in advance, on the morning of the dinner party, saying how much they are looking forward to it. Bottles of wine are suitable in the case of very young or impecunious dinner party hosts.

MANNERS ON THE MOVE
Cars

The increased incidence of road rage proves the late Sir John Betjeman's point that people turn into fiends once they start hurtling around in their little metal boxes. Were he still alive today, I suspect the poet would conclude that they had become out-and-out devils. It is not my remit to point out that manners on the road have worsened (that is obvious to all), or to lay down the laws of motoring etiquette (the Highway Code does that admirably). However, I can suggest that a little chivalry goes a long way.

Well-mannered male motorists still open car doors for women on the kerb side, before walking around the car to let themselves in. If two couples (i.e. two men and two women) are travelling in one car, it is ill bred to put the women in the back and the men in the front. Instead, the sexes and couples should be evenly distributed. Well-brought-up girls still step out of cars (particularly sports cars) with their knees together. This deft movement prevents the embarrassing display of knickers.

Taxis

Taxis have a culture all of their own. They are generally flagged down on the street, rather than being ordered over the telephone. It is customary to state the destination through the front window before getting in. If a man is travelling with a woman, it remains good manners for him to hold the door for her and let her in first. She then sits in the far corner. He follows. On arrival at the destination he gets out first, leaves the door open for her, and then pays the cabby from the outside. If both passengers are sharing the fare, she gives the man her contribution while still in the car. If a group is travelling together, the most junior men should take the jump seats, unless they are prone to sickness when travelling backwards. It is expected to settle a taxi fare in cash. Those wishing to pay by cheque or credit card should clear it with the driver before starting their journey. It is usual to top up the fare by about ten per cent – a little more if the cabby has had to deal with luggage.

Mini-Cabs

It is usual for the passengers to sit on the back seat, unless there are more than two people travelling, in which case the youngest male should offer to sit in the front seat next to the driver. However, there is no firm rule about this, and as many grannies enjoy travelling up front, views from all concerned should be canvassed before setting off. As many mini-cab drivers do not bother to get out of their cars to open doors for passengers, the form for getting in remains the same as for private cars (see above). Payment procedures, unless you have an account, are the same as for black cabs.

219

Buses, Tube Trains and the Railway

The days have long gone when men were expected to give up their seats to women automatically. However, both sexes should offer their places to pregnant women, the elderly and the infirm. It is good manners to respect each other's space. This is not an easy task on a crowded tube train, as one woman relates with great amusement. She, a small individual, found herself spending her entire journey nestling in the cosy curve formed by an armpit belonging to a well-appointed female American tourist. The journey passed without comment, but before disembarking at her destination, the American beamed beatifically down at her travelling companion and said: 'Honey, I feel closer to you than I do to my own child.'

Aeroplanes

Manners are important on aeroplanes because you are spending time (often rather a lot of time) in confined conditions with strangers. Therefore, particularly if you are travelling economy class, it is very important not to trespass into your neighbour's space, either by spreading yourself or your belongings on to his or her seat or by constantly trying to strike up conversations. Once, on a transatlantic flight, I was subjected to an admittedly affable American's life story, starting from a childhood marred by parental abuse and concluding with his newly found happiness with a girl from Seattle. Although pleased for him, I could have screamed.

Other aeronautic activities that can cause problems include: eating peanuts, as this in such confined conditions can cause extreme discomfort or even be dangerous to a near neighbour who is allergic to them; smoking in the non-smoking seats; falling asleep on your neighbour's shoulder; and eating noisily or clumsily, which is very unattractive at close quarters. Wearing very strong scent is not kind, and laughing hysterically to oneself while listening to a comedy channel on headphones can be extremely unsettling to others. Further in-flight misdemeanours are heaving too much hand luggage into the cabin and being greedy with overhead storage; demanding more than your fair share of rations (quarter-bottles of champagne, etc.) and tipping them into your bag for later; and using mobile telephones (and laptops), which can interfere with navigational instruments. Owners of fractious children should also beware that their little darlings do not become everyone else's trial. One seasoned flyer recommends that parents take a small bag of new, cheap toys which can be produced one by one as children get bored.

OTHER PUBLIC PLACES
Clubs

Clubs come in many and varied forms, ranging from the old and crusty to the new and flashy. But it is the traditional St James's establishments around which much mystique and prestige are associated. At one time all men of any standing belonged to clubs. Different ones were associated with various walks of life: the Athenaeum with the Church; the Carlton Club with the Conservative Party; the Garrick with the stage; the Guards and Cavalry Club whose parish is obvious. There was also much snobbery attached to the subject, and certain establishments that were considered not up to scratch were awarded sneering nicknames. Men often belonged to more than one club, using them for different purposes. Sons followed fathers for generations, and women were rarely if ever admitted.

Now the picture is less rigid. Men prefer to spend more time with their families and lead more varied social lives, while women, once consigned to their own, all-female clubs, are increasingly free to visit and indeed join many of the old male bastions of St James's. There is also a new generation of more glittery establishments, trendy dives and set-ups aimed at the international businessman, where conventions are much less arcane and elitist than in clubs of the old school.

However, membership to the grandest clubs, such as White's, Brooks's and Boodle's, is still highly coveted and difficult to gain. Although actual procedures vary from one place to another, aspirants have to be 'put up' by two existing members. It used to be considered extremely bad form to ask a friend to nominate you. The rationale behind this was that it would be embarrassing, even damaging, to the reputation of the existing member if his acolyte was turned down. Far better, it was thought, was to be invited to apply. Today this old courtesy is not so widely observed, although the aspirant is advised to be subtle in his overtures.

It is usual for the prospective member to have a proposer and a seconder, and for his name to be put in a book where other existing members can add their name and thus support to his election. When there are enough names to support a new member, an election committee meets to decide whether the new man is to be admitted. In reality the most important quality for a candidate is that he is not going to be considered unsuitable or offensive by existing members. Those who fail this test are 'blackballed' and thus rejected. Although many potential members choose to ignore the old custom, it is not *comme il faut* for them to try and ingratiate themselves with existing members with lavish entertainments and blandishments such as slap-up dinners and the loan of Rolls-Royces for the races. The discreet and diplomatic approach remains the best option.

As in parliamentary life, committee members are influenced by others in the club, hence the often mysterious barring of ostensibly suitable people. Thus, only those who feel pretty confident about election to a particular club should embark on the process. By the same token, existing members should employ a certain amount of circumspection about who they put forward, unless they too wish to damage their standing in the club. They should also remember that unless a club needs to go on an aggressive recruitment campaign, it is considered bad form to nominate droves of hopefuls at any one time. Quality is definitely preferable to quantity. Waiting lists for the major clubs can be in excess of six years, and thus prospective members are advised to plan ahead and be patient. It is true to say, however, that a candidate with the correct credentials and the right sponsors can circumnavigate the process more easily than someone with the wrong associations.

You don't have to be a member of a club to visit one. Members constantly use their clubs for entertaining. There are, nevertheless, small codes of etiquette the guest needs to know. Firstly, it is important to remember that you are visiting a place that is to all intents and purposes your host's house, not a hotel or restaurant. Therefore it is rude to make yourself too much at home unless particularly encouraged to do so. It is also not done to ask the club servants to do things for you (communication should always be through your host), and under no circumstances should you tip the staff. On no account should you offer to go Dutch on a dinner bill at the club. If your friend would welcome a contribution, it should be tendered to him later, in private. If you are meeting someone at their club, you will be asked to wait in the hall for them. Do not start wandering into other rooms, the only exception to this being the lavatory.

Auctions

Auction etiquette is often mysterious to the uninitiated. If you are very rich you won't have to bother too much, as the big salerooms now have excessively obliging client service departments to handle things for you. However, others with less upholstered pockets need to know the basics. First, never go to an auction unless you really have money to spend. Second, remember that items from famous collections and enjoying a provenance (for which there is now a fetish) will fetch a greater price than more anonymous pieces. Third, although saleroom experts are sometimes better trained than before, there are still fakes around. Fourth, don't expect pieces picked up at auction to be in perfect condition.

On arrival at a sale, you will be expected to register at the front desk and, if you are new to the saleroom and do not have an account, supply proof of credit-worthiness. You then should be given a numbered paddle to bid with. On entering the saleroom you can stand or sit where you like, depending on how private or public you want to be. Many people bid from the back so that they can keep an eye on the proceedings. Others are so discreet that they make an arrangement with the auctioneer so that no one but him knows they are bidding, such as having their catalogue open when they are and closed when they are not. The catalogue lists all the lots and gives the estimated price. The reserve price is always at, or slightly below, the estimate (normally around 10%). If a lot does not make its reserve it is bought in and then either reoffered for sale or returned to its owner, although reasonable post-sale offers will be passed on to disappointed vendors.

The sale is conducted by an auctioneer, whose remit is to realise the best price for each lot. There are set increments in bidding, although the auctioneer can use his discretion. It is sensible in all cases for you to work out the maximum price you can pay. Although it is possible to bid below an increment, it is considered bad form and cheap behaviour to do so. If you can't attend an auction, or don't trust yourself not to get carried away, it is possible to leave your maximum price with the bids department, who will bid on your behalf. This method, although safe, is not very sporting and means that you can miss lots by narrow margins. It is also possible to bid by proxy or down the telephone.

Each lot obviously goes to the highest bidder. If that is you, prompt payment is preferred, unless you want to incur hefty storage charges. Once paid for, the lot can be taken away immediately, or delivered later, for which a charge is levied.

Gaming

Gambling is an ancient pastime, with a beguiling conduct that combines a certain ruthlessness with the most delicate of manners. Although regular gamblers know the intricacies of their games, the newcomer needs to be aware of a few basic conventions. First and foremost, you can afford to wager only what you can afford to lose, and much of the etiquette built into many of the rules of the games of chance are intended to safeguard against utter ruin. Whether you are in a public casino or a private gaming establishment it is recommended that you do not try to play games you are not very good at, as this will irritate the skilled hands. You should also avoid talking too loudly and animatedly (there is an excited hush peculiar to gaming rooms), and aim not to clutter up the gaming tables with glasses, handbags and other irrelevances. You should also be impassive in the face of both defeat and victory. If you lose it is unsporting to question the integrity of the croupiers, and if you win it is not cool to show too much delight. It goes without saying that you must pay your debts – not to do so is deeply dishonourable.

Gyms

Even if they rarely visit them, many people now belong to gyms and health clubs. Although these temples of health and fitness are concerned with rather basic aspects of the human condition, they have, nevertheless, developed an etiquette as distinct as other more elevated public places. The fundamental rule of gym etiquette is to remember that there are lots of shared facilities, and therefore thoughtful general conduct is the order of the day. Thus it is bad manners to hog equipment for long periods, to forget to wipe it down after use if you have made it sweaty, and not to put things away in the right place after use. It is also very unattractive to be disrespectful to those older and less fit than yourself, to behave rudely to the instructors and to appear to be irritatingly competitive on aerobic machines. Neanderthal displays of caveman bravado, such as excessive grunting, hissing and huffing when lifting weights, are also not appreciated and should be assiduously avoided.

Dress also needs thought. Although many of those who exercise regularly are, quite understandably, proud of their physiques, excessive bareness, such as men strutting around topless, is narcissistic and exhibitionist. Suitable support in tender places should also be worn. Women ought to wear a sports bra or similar garment. Men should sport a jockstrap or other support for reasons of both health and modesty. Training shoes should be clean. Gloves should be worn for weight lifting. Jewellery, other than a plastic watch, should never be seen in a gymnasium: it not only looks inappropriate but is potentially dangerous, as it can get caught in machinery. Eating is quite out of order in a gym, although exercisers should remember to drink plenty of water from disposable plastic cups to avoid dehydration.

High standards of personal hygiene are important both in the gym and in the changing rooms. Deodorants (there are now special formulations designed for the demands of sports activities) should always be applied. Sweaty kit should not be left to fester in lockers for long periods. In the steam room remember to sit on a towel and never to shave, cut your toe-nails, or, even worse, eat food. Always shower after exercise and before any body treatments or therapies. Do not leave used towels lying around.

Racing

Horse racing is always referred to as just racing – it is still considered ill bred to say 'horse racing'. It is divided into two types, each of which has its own season. The flat turf racing season runs approximately from the end of March to the beginning of November, with the first and last meetings normally held at Doncaster. National Hunt racing (that is, racing over obstacles) takes place throughout the winter and spring months, but lacks a definitive beginning or end to its seasons, as there are also jumping meetings during the summer months.

THE MAIN EVENTS

Of the thousands of races run throughout the country each year, there are several main meetings that remain the sport's glittering prizes. The five classics of the flat season are the 1,000 and the 2,000 Guineas Stakes at Newmarket in April/May, the Derby and the Oaks at Epsom in June, and the St Leger Stakes at Doncaster in September. These are the landmarks of the flat racing season. In addition, there are the three famous racing extravaganzas: Royal Ascot in June, the Goodwood July meeting, sometimes erroneously referred to as Glorious Goodwood, and The King George VI and The Queen Elizabeth Diamond Stakes. The highlights of the National Hunt season are the Grand National at Aintree and the Cheltenham National Hunt Festival (Gold Cup) in the spring.

Royal Ascot

This legendary meeting attracts people as much for its social appeal as for its racing. A more detailed description of the meeting and the procedure for application to the Royal Enclosure is explained on p.128. Royal Ascot takes place over four days, from Tuesday to Friday, and offers some of the best racing of the season. The Gold Cup is run on the Thursday, which is also known as Ladies' Day and is an occasion of high fashion (and high hats) as well as quality racing. There is also racing on the Saturday. This is known as Heath Day, but is not part of the royal meeting, and morning dress is not required for any enclosure on that day. Those who do not wish to enter, or are debarred from, the Royal Enclosure can buy tickets for the Grandstand directly from the racecourse. These also give access to the Paddock. Alternatively, it is great fun to take a box, which often comes complete with its own luncheon room and provides a very good base for the day.

The Other Meetings

After Royal Ascot, the Derby is the most celebrated racing occasion of the flat season. Traditionally held on the first Wednesday of June, when even the Stock Exchange was known to close and Parliament adjourned, it has now, as an experiment, been moved to the nearest Saturday. It is always a very happy meeting with a very special atmosphere. The race takes place on Epsom Downs around thirty miles south of London and is part of a three-day meeting. The smartest place to be is the Queen's Stand, which offers an excellent view of the proceedings. Tickets for the Queen's Stand at Epsom are reserved for annual members, although the racecourse does now offer a Classic Club Membership which offers a badge valid for all three days of the meeting and which allows holders entrance to the Queen's Stand on each day (providing they are correctly dressed). Dress at Epsom is different from Royal Ascot. Morning dress is required in the Queens Stand only for the actual Derby on Derby Day, with jacket and tie being worn for the other two days. Women wear formal daywear and a hat.

Later in the year is the Goodwood July meeting, which takes place high on the Sussex Downs. Traditionally it signified the end of the social Season (see p. 228 below). Goodwood is one of the most beautiful courses in the country and forms part of the estate of the Duke of Richmond and Gordon. Because it retains the atmosphere of a private party, it has a much more informal, garden party atmosphere that the other race meetings lack. If the weather is good, it can be an idyllic day; if bad, due to the course's proximity to the sea it can be bracing, to say the least. The best place to sit is in the Richmond Enclosure, which is restricted to Goodwood annual members and their guests. Dress is much less formal than for Royal Ascot. Morning dress is never worn, with men adopting pale lightweight suits which they sport with the ubiquitous Goodwood panama. Women wear summer dresses or light suits with straw hats.

BETTING

There are two main ways of betting at a racecourse. The first is with the bookmakers. They ply their trade in the betting ring beside the track, displaying their odds on boards. Bookmakers guarantee fixed odds: that is, if you bet £10 on a horse whose odds are 10–1 at the time of betting, you are guaranteed to get £100 back if it wins, plus your initial stake. It is advisable to get to the betting ring ten or more minutes before the race starts. It is an open market in the ring, and you are free to search out the bookmaker who is offering the best odds for your favourite horse. Always shop around.

The second method is the tote. This is short for totalisator, meaning pool betting. All the bets in a particular pool are added up and divided by the number of winning units to calculate the return a punter can expect on his stake. Thus you can never guarantee that the odds (known as dividends in a tote) shown when you place your bet will be the same as those at the end of the race – as the number of bets mounts up the balance of the pools changes, and so do the odds. Remember when betting to express your choice by the horse's number rather than name. You will be given a betting slip, which will need to be produced at the end of the race to collect your winnings. The tote is generally the most popular way of betting at a racecourse. Its outlets are always easy to find in the stands, but there are no fixed odds and you miss out on the excitement of the bookies' ring.

THE FORM AND READING A RACE CARD
To bet successfully it is important to know how to read a race card and to understand the form. The card gives details of the horse's name, draw in the race, owner, breeder, trainer and jockey, last season's form, parentage, colour, age and weight carried, the days since last raced, its sex and category (i.e. whether a colt, filly, stallion, mare or gelding) and past placings, such as whether it was a course winner or beaten favourite last time.

These facts and the form figures shown on the race card, which indicate where a horse has come in its previous few races, are useful guides to its current performance, but there are also other factors to be considered. For instance, the type of race: over what distance does the horse perform best, and on which courses? Does it run better when the going is soft or hard? How good is the jockey or trainer? How is the horse looking on the day in the paddock prior to running – does it appear tired, or keen? And so on. All these are worth considering before you gamble.

Spectators sit and stand in a variety of different stands and enclosures. The smartest, most expensive and most comfortable are the members' and Club enclosures such as the Royal Enclosure at Ascot, the Queen's Stand at the Derby, and the Richmond Enclosure at Goodwood, mentioned on p. 226 above. All require forward planning to get into. From their clearly demarcated precincts you will find easy access to the paddock (where the horses are paraded before each race), the winners' enclosure (for the presentation after each race) and the best view of the winning post. Attractive and social as these enclosures are, you can have a perfectly good day at the races in the other stands. Next in the usual pecking order is Tattersalls, where the bookmakers normally congregate. Last of all there is the Silver Ring, from which there is rarely any access to the paddock and only a distant view of the winning post.

227

THE SEASON

The Season, like many other distinctive aspects of British life, is difficult to define accurately. It derives its name from the days when, at certain times of the year, fashionable society gathered around its monarch to join in the royal amusements. These periods followed the end of the hunting and shooting season, which explains why the main part of the Season takes place in the summer months. It reached its apogee in the nineteenth century when young girls of good background (known as débutantes) were presented at Court and then did their 'Season'. This consisted of being introduced to what was then called 'society', attending masses of parties, entertainments and the great set events of the social calendar, and, hopefully, attracting the right sort of husband. The Queen ended Court presentations in the fifties, but the jolly time associated with the Season has continued, albeit in a much scaled-down form. Today most girls who do the season see it less as a marital market and more as a bridge between school and adult life, when they can meet like-minded people of their own age in relatively controlled circumstances. The scale of entertaining, too, has changed. Whereas in the past there were strings of private dances and other lavish forms of entertainment, nowadays there are more drinks parties and even barbecues. What is important is that all families participating make some sort of contribution.

As the scale of private hospitality has decreased, the public events that form the landmark of the social season have grown in significance. These include charity dances such as Queen Charlotte's Ball, now the highlight of the Season, and the string of jolly, largely sporting events such as Royal Ascot, Cowes Week and Henley. These events form the core of the modern Season and are patronised by all types of people intent on having a good time. Here I briefly outline the form of some of the major happenings, many of which are still attended by the Royal Family.

The Boat Race

The Oxford and Cambridge Boat Race is a prelude to the Season. As it takes place at the end of the March or the beginning of April it is invariably a chilly and bracing event. The four-and-a-quarter-mile course covers the Thames from Putney Bridge to Mortlake. There are two crews, one from Oxford University (the Dark Blues) and the other from Cambridge (the Light Blues). The race, although short (little more than twenty minutes), draws a large crowd of spectators along the course. However, the best places to watch are either from the rowing clubs along the river bank or from a launch following in the race's wake. From these vantage points the booze flows as liberally as the bonhomie; however, you will obviously need to be a member. Dress is very casual. Anybody who has attended Oxbridge tends to turn up loyally sporting varsity colours. At the winning ceremony it is usual for the trophy to be presented by a member of the Royal Family and for the losing crew to lead the cheers for the winners.

The Berkeley Dress Show

The Berkeley Dress Show happens in April. It is a major event of the Season, as it is where the year's fresh crop of débutantes make their first appearance, and is a fashion show in aid of the National Society for the Prevention of Cruelty to Children, previously held at the Berkeley Hotel but more recently at the Savoy. The debs undergo an intensive modelling course at Lucie Clayton (a school famous for teaching girls how to get out of a sports car while maintaining their dignity) and are subject to much good-natured scrutiny from the assembled throng of family, friends and ambitious mothers. The boys who sometimes accompany them also arouse interest. Tickets can be bought from the NSPCC.

Henley Royal Regatta

This five-day international rowing event takes place in July at the pretty riverside town from which it takes its name. It has become such a major (and crowded) happening of the Season that it has lost much of its former charm. Nevertheless, particularly if the weather is good, Henley remains a fun day out. The ideal place to be is the Stewards' Enclosure. Membership of this is largely limited to those connected with rowing and there is an extremely long waiting list. Members are, however, able to take guests, although the number of guest badges available over the weekend is limited. A very strict dress code is rigorously enforced in the Stewards' Enclosure. Men must wear: 'lounge suits, jackets with trousers and flannels and a tie or a cravat'. Boating blazers with ersatz stripes and boaters bristling with ribbons of dubious origin are to be avoided. The same is true of anything in pink, particularly Leander cerise, which is the prerogative of members of the famous Leander Club, who have their own enclosure. Women are forbidden to sport trousers or shorts and are required to wear a dress or suit that covers the knee. Most plump for pretty garden party dresses. Codes of dress and indeed behaviour are much less formal outside the Stewards' Enclosure, in the Regatta Enclosure, the stands and along the river bank.

Cowes Week

This takes place in August on the Isle of Wight. It is Britain's most famous regatta and traditionally signalled the flight of the fashionable world away from the London Season to more bracing pursuits. One of the most important events on the international sailing calendar, Cowes Week has long enjoyed royal patronage, and for the week the royal yacht *Britannia* (at the time of writing, cruelly consigned to Death Row) is moored there with Prince Philip at its figurative helm. The Cowes Combined Club, who run the regatta, include the very grand Royal Yacht Squadron, as well as the Royal Corinthian and Royal London. To enjoy Cowes to the full, it is preferable to be either a member or a guest of these various clubs. This is particularly so at night, when there are plenty of balls and drinks parties. The grandest invitation is, of course, to something on *Britannia*. The smartest dance ticket is one for the Royal Yacht Squadron Ball, which the Royal Family usually attend. On the Friday night there is an impressive fireworks display. Saturday sees the famous Bembridge Ball. Cowes has its own dress: the day requires the ultimate in 'casual smart' dressing, and ranges from really quite formal at the more starchy clubs to a sweater and chinos for lolling on the shore. Most clubs are now relaxed about women wearing trousers. A pair of rubber-soled deck shoes is a sartorial *sine qua non* for invitations on board. For balls, men's dress is either mess kit or black tie. Women can wear either long or short dresses but should remember that anything too tight in the skirt can look extremely embarrassing when clambering on and off ship. Shoes damaging to decks – such as stilettos – are to be avoided at all costs.

Wimbledon

The apex of the tennis year, Wimbledon is the only Grand Slam tournament played on grass. It is held at the All England Lawn Tennis and Croquet Club every year in June/July. Tickets are highly sought after and need to be applied for from the club between August and December of the preceding year. The dress code is generally very relaxed, although those invited into the Royal Box or the Members' Enclosure will need to be smartly turned out: men wear jackets and ties and women casually smart outfits. Smart hats (as for racing) are not worn. However, those who find themselves in the often blistering sunlight are strongly recommended to wear not too large sun hats and high-protection sunscreens if they are to avoid noses as red as the ubiquitous Wimbledon strawberries. There is an unwritten etiquette about applause at the tournament so that it ensures minimal distraction to the players. It is reserved for the end of a game, set or match. Do not applaud during rallies: most spectators are holding their breath. Nobody is admitted to the stands mid-game.

Lord's

Lord's Cricket Ground is the home of cricket and of the sport's illustrious governing body, the Marylebone Cricket Club (MCC). Here is where the annual Eton versus Harrow match, the NatWest Trophy final and the Benson & Hedges Cup final are played, in addition, of course, to Test Matches. The best place to be is the Pavilion, but with the waiting list for membership stretching towards two decades, you are best advised to be invited by existing members. Failing this, the private boxes (also highly coveted) are fun. The difference between conduct and dress in the ordinary stands and the Pavilion is indeed quite startling. In the former, spectators dress for comfort and behave in a 'village cricket' way – rather boisterously. However, within the inner sanctum of the Pavilion, no one is allowed to forget cricket's gentlemanly origins. There is a very strict dress code that insists men wear jackets and trousers, shirts, ties or cravats and proper shoes. Women, with the exception of the Queen, are not allowed in the pavilion during play, and clapping is slow, measured and redolent of more gentle times.

Polo

Over recent decades polo has enjoyed a great renaissance, and the big days are now firmly integrated into the social and corporate scenes. The sport's season runs from April to September and is played at leading clubs ranging from the Guards' Club at Smith's Lawn near Windsor, to Cirencester Park in Gloucestershire. Although the pace of the game is fast and furious, the atmosphere in the stands is relaxed, encouraged in no small amount by the good lunches provided by sponsors. At half-time, spectators are expected to walk the ground and 'tread in the divots' – small pieces of turf kicked up by the ponies' (never horses) hooves. Dress is smart-casual (many is the woman who has made an exhibition of herself by turning up dressed for Royal Ascot). Flat shoes are essential. Men sport grey suits, blazers and flannels, and a panama if the sun is shining.

Horse Trials

Horse trials go on up and down the country, but the best known and the most social are Badminton in May and Burghley in September. Badminton is the seat of the Duke of Beaufort, and has a larger, more impersonal air than the smaller, jollier Burghley. The trial consists of top-standard cross-country, show jumping and dressage. Tickets for the vast crowd are bought via the box office, although there are enclosures for members of the British Horse Society, and there is a drinks party hosted by the Duke in the house. Lady Victoria Leatham gives a lunch at Burghley. Both occasions also boast a vast range of trade stands offering an eye-boggling range of shopping. Dress is suitably rural but never grubby. Grand old women still wear a certain type of knee-length, slightly seated tweed skirt, although most now opt for Barbours and trousers. Remember to take a reasonably smart change should you be invited to any evening parties.

Chelsea Flower Show

The Chelsea Flower Show (colloquially known just as 'Chelsea'), despite the rise of the other important horticultural events, remains the apex of the horticultural year. Here, in the grounds of the Royal Hospital, plants and flowers of all kinds and all seasons are displayed for the delectation of vast crowds. Chelsea is in May and runs from Monday to Friday. On Monday there is a private view for The Queen, and in the evening a highly subscribed charity ball (apply early for tickets). Tuesday and Wednesday are for members of the Royal Horticultural Society (RHS), and Thursday and Friday are quite literally a free-for-all. Friday afternoon sees the marvellous sight, which always reminds me of Birnam Wood in *Macbeth*, of processions of people carrying flora of all shapes and sizes out of the show. Chelsea, probably due to the vast numbers attending, is an event when manners can be in inverse proportion to the amount of blooms on display; I once spotted a woman spectator actually picking the exhibits. However, on the private days, a charming garden party atmosphere still persists. Dress is casual but smart.

The Royal Academy Summer Exhibition

The Royal Academy Summer Exhibition at one time was thought to be the unofficial opening of the summer Season. Today this is not really the case, but certainly an invitation to the opening night party always symbolises that the Season is well under way. Artists of all kinds are invited to submit their work, and the huge resulting selection ranges from the accomplished to the deeply banal. The string of private views that follow the opening night party are social as well as artistic events and are patronised by a wide cross-section of people, who display all varieties of manners, both good and bad. At an exhibition, no matter how crowded, it is bad manners to walk in front of people who are viewing pictures, and inconsiderate to gather in gossiping gaggles too near the works and thus block the view of others. It is, however, not bad manners to cast aspersions on the work on display. That is part of the fun.

Queen Charlotte's Ball

Queen Charlotte's Ball is the highlight of the modern débutante Season. At one time it took place in May, but nowadays the ball happens in September, so as not to interfere with the girls' A levels. It is given in aid of the famous Queen Charlotte's Hospital in London. The centrepiece of the evening is the parade of the year's debs. All clad in white, as was the custom at Court presentations, they make their stately but sweet progress to a huge illuminated cake, escorted by fresh-faced boys of similar ages. To the side of the ceremonial confection stands a guest of honour who represents Queen Charlotte, and to whom each girl must curtsey. The ceremony concludes with the guest of honour cutting the cake, which will later be distributed on the wards of the hospital. After this, the débutantes and their partners take to the dance floor and lead the dancing with a Viennese waltz.

Private Dances

Once the staple of the Season, dances given in private houses are sadly much less frequent than before. At the time of writing, however, they did seem to be gathering momentum again, particularly in the country. Many families, to defray the huge cost of doing a dance properly, often combine three inter-generational celebrations, or they join forces with another family celebrating a similar event.

As a guest, it behoves you to reply to the invitation as soon as possible. This should be done in the third person (see Chapter 8). Dances and balls represent for the host a huge commitment, not just financially, but logistically. Thus it is disrespectful, ungrateful and rude not to let the hostess know if you are coming. One woman who was planning a dance to celebrate her son's twenty-first explained despairingly that even with the enclosing of easy-to-fill-in reply cards, she received only a twenty-five per cent response. It is also important to adhere to the dress requested on the card. This is easy nowadays, when most balls call only for dinner jackets for men and party frocks for women, not the white tie and ball dresses of yesteryear. On arrival you should be greeted by your host and hostess. If they prove elusive, it is up to you to seek them out immediately. It is not necessary to bring a present, but should the party be to celebrate a birthday, then a small present can be left with the staff on arrival. During the evening it is also the guests' responsibility to circulate and not remain in a small group, as is usual at public balls. It is also important in the course of the evening to talk and/or dance with the guest/guests of honour and with older family members. Men should always remember to ask all the women on their table and the hostess to dance, and it is also not good manners to monopolise one partner for the entire evening, no matter how fascinating. Also, if there is reeling, it is inadvisable – particularly for men – to join in unless you have some grasp of the steps. It is not good manners to get drunk, take drugs and generally behave badly, although many do so.

SUBSCRIPTION DANCES

These have largely taken the place of private dances, and are different because people pay for their tickets. However, many are run by such cliquey committees (particularly in the shires) that they end up feeling almost like a private dance, with the obvious difference that guests are paying for their fun. This does not stop a certain type of committee woman referring to the event as 'my dance'. Such affectations are to be frowned upon. Most of these dances are in aid of charity – in the politically correct nineties having a lavish time is OK providing it is, in theory, for a good cause. They range from massive affairs such as Queen Charlotte's Ball (described on p. 233 above) to more modest rural gatherings for local good causes.

It is usual for people to pay for their own tickets, although generous hosts often stump up for the whole table. If guests are confused about whether they are expected to pay, an offer of a contribution will put the record straight. Prices for tickets vary wildly, depending on the scale of the event, although drinks are rarely included. Unlike at private dances, the social emphasis is on your particular table. It is not good manners to disappear for hours to chat and dance with other tables, and it is extra important to make sure that no one on your table is left out of the fun. It is also churlish and ungrateful not to contribute generously to raffles and other fund-raising spots in the evening.

12

ENTERTAINING

The secret of a good party is proper organisation. Whether you decide to invite a few friends around for supper or throw a dance for a cast of thousands in the presence of a member of the Royal Family, there is no point in issuing a single invitation unless you are willing to devote the time and attention to making the event work properly. Even the most apparently spontaneous of hosts admits to always being in a ready-to-roll state – i.e. plenty of food, drink, etc., if not to hand then only a telephone call away. The second fundamental principle is never to overstretch yourself either financially or socially to create a pretentious event that will leave you feeling stressed and your guests less impressed than you would have liked. I have been to many parties which appear to have been conceived merely to make a show, rather than to ensure that people have a good time. The third principle is a little, but probably not too much, imagination.

In this chapter I shall deal with the major categories of parties. These include drinks, dinner, supper, lunch, children's parties, dances and house parties.

DRINKS PARTIES
Drinks parties are one of the most flexible and relatively economical ways to entertain a large number of people. They include pre-lunch drinks (now considered rather old-fashioned in London, but still prevalent in the country), early evening drinks, which lasts from approximately 6.30 to 8.30 (still the most popular), after-dinner drinks (rather less popular), and the

new extended mid-evening party, which normally runs from 7.30 to 9.30-ish (increasingly popular).

A good drinks party should be like the cocktails that originally inspired this form of hospitality – a varied mixture of elements that combine to make a delicious (if not intoxicating) whole. It should consist of enough people to make the room or rooms you are partying in feel full, but not hellishly overcrowded. The guest list should comprise a backbone of good friends (who you know will be on your side and will make an effort); people who have entertained you and to whom you would like to reciprocate (however, it is true to say that an invitation to a cocktail party is not taken as fair reciprocation for being asked to a dinner party); people who you are only acquainted with and would like to know better, but don't feel ready to invite to a dinner party; and a sprinkling of new people and friends of friends, who you feel might liven up the proceedings. The size can vary from a handful of close friends invited to meet a new arrival in a neighbourhood, to a vast annual bash to celebrate your birthday.

However, I offer a word of caution. Although variety is thought to be the spice of life, too much can be instant death to a drinks party. Remember, when composing your guest list, that it is unwise to invite people from vastly disparate groups if you want to be confident of the whole event gelling.

Invitations

The type of invitation you send out depends on the formality and scale of the party you intend throwing. A traditional specially engraved card (rare for drinks, more for receptions) implies a grand party, whereas a printed one suggests something much more casual but still large. The usual thing to do is for women to send out 'at Home' cards, filled in with the hostess's name, the guest's name, the date of the party and 'Drinks, 6.30 to 8.30' written on the right-hand side. Inveterate party-givers can order a supply of specially engraved 'at Home' cards with their name and address included in the design, but with spaces left for timings and dates.

Although increasing numbers of men use 'at Home' cards, it remains, by old custom, incorrect for them to do so. Men are expected to use a card bearing the more formal wording: 'requests the pleasure of your company'. The same rule applies when a couple entertains (see Chapter 8). Invitations should be sent out between three and four weeks in advance of the party.

It is recommended to invite more people than you actually want, to take account of any refusals. Envelopes should always be handwritten, not typed. Alternatively, and more formally, you could invite people by telephone (particularly if the gathering is small). However, it is always sensible to follow up any verbal invitation with a 'to remind' card shortly before your party (see Chapter 8), as even the nicest people can be vague.

Location

Your drinks party can take place either at your house or at an address specially rented for the occasion. It is vital to ensure proper ventilation, an abundance of large ashtrays and, unless numbers are very small, staff to help. Drinks parties are normally conducted standing up, but it is thoughtful to have some chairs here and there for more intimate conversations and the frail of limb. If you intend to spread the party across various rooms, ensure that the heart, i.e. the bulk, of the bash is based in the biggest room, with adjoining smaller spaces arranged as more serene social satellites.

What to Serve

As drinks parties are not intended as meals, you are not required to provide large amounts of food. However, you are obliged to serve copious quantities of drink. Although caterers typically allow approximately half a bottle of wine per guest, even with today's more circumspect attitudes to drink, increased consumption of soft drinks and fear of losing driving licences, this seems to be an underestimation. A certain girl who throws regular 'scrums' at her small flat maintains she never provides less than a bottle per person. So remember always to over- rather than under-order. Bottles and cases can be bought on a sale-or-return basis, so that you can take back unopened drink.

The quality of drink is as important as its quantity. Many people make the mistake of believing that all champagne is better than any other wine. This is quite wrong. Although champagne is the party drink *par excellence*, unless you can afford a decent one, you will do much better to serve a good wine. Generally white wine is more suitable than red, although it is recommended to offer a choice. Cocktails, after a long sojourn in social Siberia, are fashionable again. But it should be remembered that, as nowadays people are not used to drinking concentrated mixtures of spirits, you should be reasonably circumspect with your mixes – unless it is your intention to get everybody absolutely plastered. You should also offer non-alcoholic options, which, in addition to the ubiquitous mineral water and orange juice, should include something a little more tantalising, such as a Bentley's. Whatever you serve, do not feel you have to offer a huge choice. Your house is not a hotel. It is enough to provide around four or five alternatives, such as champagne, bellinis (champagne and peach juice), plenty of mineral water (both sparkling and still) and a more interesting non-alcoholic choice. Keep a few Coca-Colas and a bottle of whisky on the side for the truly intransigent. The drinks can either be served from a bar or, more elegantly, be circulated around the room on trays.

Food

As drinks parties are not generally given at times when meals are eaten, it is necessary to serve only small things to titillate the palate and line the stomach. The only exception to this is for the large mid-evening party, where nourishment should be a little more substantial. Nuts and olives are only suitable for very informal drinks for a handful of friends at home. Anything larger requires canapés, which can be either hot or cold or both. It is most important that they are small and easy to manoeuvre and eat. They are generally handed around the room on trays. Should they be served on toothpicks or skewers, the waiter/waitress must also carry a small plate or bowl for discarded sticks.

When Your Guests Arrive

The slow-starting drinks party can be agony for its host. Guests can be irritatingly unpunctual, so I always ask a few close and gregarious friends to arrive on time to get things going, talking to new arrivals and generally helping with introductions. On arrival guests' coats are put either in a spare bedroom (the old-fashioned custom of separate rooms for men's and women's clothes is much less common nowadays) or in a cloakroom if the party is in a rented location. It is then up to you to make sure they are immediately given a drink and introduced to other guests. In the early stages of the party it is easy to make sure that everybody has someone to talk to, but as it fills up you will have to watch out that no one is left out on a limb and that guests do not spend the entire evening conversing with people they already know. It is not usual for couples to stick together like limpets throughout an evening. A certain experienced hostess always begins her parties near the door to greet people when they arrive, then, as the party gets going, moves to a strategic position in the middle of the room, from where she can mount a radar-like operation, and finally ends her evening back by the door for fond farewells.

Introductions

Introductions need to be done speedily, accurately and politely. As already stated in Chapter 9, as a general rule of thumb: men are introduced to women and juniors to their elders. Married couples are always presented singly in their own right, such as: 'May I introduce Harry Happy. This is Sabrina Silly.' It is also useful, especially when introducing diffident types, to add a short prompt to the introduction, such as: 'Harry has just come back from Cuba.' If you are introducing a married woman who still uses her maiden name, then it is recommended to make some reference in the introduction, such as: 'This is Harry's wife, Serena Stoical.' When introducing someone to a member of your own family, it is important to make the nature of the relationship clear: 'I don't believe you have met my sister, Caroline Clever.' When introducing people to older distinguished people it is still gallant to employ the old-fashioned technique of bringing the *ingénue* up to the grandee and saying: 'May I introduce my old friend, Billy Bright.' Introducing people with titles can also be tricky. Nowadays most peers are happy to be introduced simply with their Christian name and title combined: 'I don't believe you have met John Yorkshire.' However, there are some, particularly older peers, who would take exception to this, and in this case it is wise to use the more formal model of: 'I don't believe you have met Lord Yorkshire.' Dukes are called 'Duke' socially, never 'Your Grace'. Newly created knights are usually particularly proud of their new handles. If in doubt, always err on the more formal side: it is never incorrect. However, remember it is a solecism to mention the full title in conversation, such as: 'I don't believe you have met John Dewsbury, Earl of Yorkshire.'

Bringing Your Party to a Close

Guests should not overstay their welcome. However, recent years have seen an increased laxity in social timings, with guests arriving late for parties and staying on accordingly. Thus actually getting rid of people has become problematic. As a host, it is your prerogative to decide the exact timings of your party. You need harbour no guilt or embarrassment about indicating when it is time to go. Only the rudest of guests will not respond. A friend of mine resorted to having a butler hold her front door open meaningfully until everyone had got the message. This approach strikes me as being somewhat draconian; I would suggest instead making sure that you, as host, have a dinner date to go to. Or, if you are still feeling sociable, propose that waifs and strays might like to go round the corner for a snack. If the latter is the case, remember that your obligation as host ceased when you left your drinks party, and everybody pays for their own supper. Alternatively you could recruit your friends who helped get the evening off to a good start to put the word about that it's time to go home. The other ploy is to stop serving drinks, but this is more usual at commercial gatherings than private ones. Never should lights be flashed on and off, pub-style.

DINNER PARTIES

Dinner parties, as well as being the most unbeatable way to give hospitality, are often the most demanding. Unless you are employing professional help either to cook and serve the food or to prepare it up to a ready-to-go state, it is advisable to keep the menu as straightforward as possible. Nowadays many hostesses invite one to 'suppers' rather than dinners, which denotes that simple dishes, such as fish pie, will be served. Remember, your guests come primarily to see you and to enjoy the company of other people at the gathering. The food, although an important component of the evening, is not the star turn. You are. It is very disconcerting for guests to witness a host in great anxiety as he or she tries to orchestrate complicated menus as well as entertain visitors. I have been to many dinner parties where my hosts have reduced themselves to little more than skivvies. By the same token, I have been to many others where the hosts have been so laid back – or, dare I say it, disorganised – that my dinner has appeared only after hours spent getting drunk and depressed on the sofa.

Invitations

The type of invitation issued is often determined by the degree of formality of your dinner. For instance, a specially engraved card for a particular event suggests the greatest formality, and should be sent around one month in advance to ensure that everybody you wish to be there will be able to attend. (It is also a good idea to keep a back-up list of substitutions should people be unable to attend. Most hostesses have their cache of spare men for such occasions.) On the other hand, the much more usual informal invitation by telephone implies a more relaxed gathering and can often be issued at shorter notice. It is always worth following up a verbal invitation with a 'to remind' or '*pour memoire*' card, as even the most well-meaning people can be remarkably forgetful.

The usual method is now to send out 'at Home' cards with 'Dinner, 8 for 8.30' written by hand: this suggests a formality but not grandeur. Alternatively, people who give regular rather grand formal dinner parties can invest in a stock of cards engraved with all constant details, such as name, address and the nature of the entertainment, with space for the date and time of each dinner party to be added by hand.

The type of invitation also gives guests an indication of what they should wear. A grand invitation suggests smart dress; a less formal one something more casual. Despite this, there is huge confusion about dressing for dinner. I have been to many parties where the men's clothes have ranged from sweaters to dark suits, with the corresponding uncomfortable diversity in the attire of the women present (see Chapter 17). It is therefore up to the host or hostess to offer discreet but clear guidelines. If dinner jackets are to be worn for a Saturday night dinner, as they still often are in the country, the hostess must either say so or put it in writing on the card. If, on the other hand, a hostess says, 'Come as you are', she must be prepared for just that. I remember once being asked to dress 'casually' for a dinner, but was dismayed to find on arrival that most of our small party were wearing jacket and tie, because they had earlier gone to a smartish drinks party nearby.

The Menu

The composition of a dinner party menu is for many a modern-day marathon. Virtually everybody aspires to a fashionable food allergy or intolerance, is losing weight or has recently given up something. Choosing a menu that all will like is extremely difficult. On the plus side, this obsession with health (and economy) means that the hugely complicated, calorific and expensive multi-course extravaganzas of yesteryear are all but extinct. The modern-day dinner party, unless a hugely elaborate affair, need consist of no more than three or four courses: a first, main, pudding and/or cheese. The accompanying drinks are equally simple: champagne (aperitif), white, red and sometimes a pudding wine, as well as still and sparkling mineral water. Port, brandy and other digestifs are less popular, although I recently attended a delightfully old-fashioned dinner party at which the hostess produced whisky sodas for the men and cordial for the women, to 'send them on their way'.

When choosing a menu, it should be balanced. Courses should be alternately light and sustaining, rich and refreshing, strongly flavoured and subtle. Ingredients should be seasonal and of the best quality. Remember, it is much better to serve delicious omelettes made from fresh, free-range eggs than a cheap steak of dubious, and possibly dangerous, provenance. Unless you have properly trained domestic help on the night, do not attempt over-elaborate menus that require extensive last-minute preparations and prolonged absences in the kitchen away from your guests. The same simplicity applies to the presentation of the food, which should be attractive but not pretentious – your guests have come to see you, not to judge an examination for HND *Cuisine Artistique.*

Vegetarians, Vegans, Diabetics and Those with Other Dietary Considerations

Vegetarianism, once considered a maverick activity, is now quite mainstream. Ever-increasing awareness of lighter, healthier eating means that it is now acceptable to serve a dinner party that consists of a salad-based first course and fish or chicken with innovative vegetable dishes as the main

241

one. Therefore, clever hostesses with vegetarians on their guest lists are quite able to construct a menu that will suit all present. Vegans – those who will not eat any animal product whatsoever – are more of a problem. In these cases, as it is unfair to oblige other guests to conform to a vegan regimen, special dishes have to be prepared for the vegan guest. Most diabetics are expert at managing their condition, but it is dangerous for them to go for long periods without sustenance. It is therefore important to dine directly when diabetics are present.

Wines

The choice of wine depends on the food you are serving. Although the 'I drink what I like with everything' attitude has gained ground over recent years, there is simply no doubt that certain wines complement specific foods in the most delightful way. For example, a good Chablis is the perfect way to wash down a piece of grilled fish. As a general rule of thumb, most fish and shellfish is eaten with dry white wine, and most meat with red wine (traditionally, highly seasoned roasts and game were eaten with burgundy and lighter dishes with claret, although today this distinction is fading and the choice of which red is largely a matter of taste); most pudding is washed down with sweet wine or champagne, and most cheese with a full-bodied red or port. There are, however, exceptions. For instance, certain salmon dishes lend themselves well to a white burgundy or even a rosé. Red wines (with a few exceptions, such as Beaujolais, which is drunk chilled) should be served at room temperature (the cork eased some hours prior to drinking), although when serving an ancient red wine that has been languishing in a cellar for a long time and may well be past its best, it is recommended to open it only a few minutes before it is to be drunk. White wines and champagne should be thoroughly but not too arctically chilled. Three hours in a refrigerator should be enough to chill champagne to the correct serving temperature of 5–6°C. Mineral water should be similarly cold but not freezing. Certain wines, particularly aged and distinguished reds, develop sediment and 'bottle stink' and will need to be decanted, via a wine-strainer, into a glass decanter. When decanting, remember to pour wine very gently through the sieve to avoid disturbing the sediment, and to stop the process while there are still a couple of inches of wine remaining in the bottle.

The Table

Attention to detail is important. This applies as much to an informal supper for a few friends as it does to a formal dinner for two hundred. The table should be as immaculately and even artistically laid as possible, for it will provide the focal point of the evening. Table linen and napkins (*never* paper for a dinner party) need to be freshly laundered, candles should be new (candles are *de rigueur* at a dinner party but never used at a lunch party) and there must always be fresh, seasonal flowers on the table. Silverware needs to be polished, and glasses absolutely gleaming. Guests should never be offered chipped china. You ought also to have a supply of extra glasses and silver at hand, should any clumsy or absent-minded guests drop their fork on the floor, leaving the serving spoon floundering in the mashed potato or knock over their glass.

When laying the table, remember that while it is perfectly acceptable to cram the maximum number of people around a table for an informal supper, a grander, more formal dinner requires space in between guests to allow room for more elaborate table settings, to make it easier for any help to wait on guests, and to provide a more elegant arrangement for conversation. Even numbers are always easier to accommodate than odd. Thirteen diners is thought particularly unlucky. There is no optimum number for a good dinner party, although eight, ten and fourteen always seem very pleasing.

Most people make the mistake of laying the table before arranging the chairs. In fact the seating must be done first. The best arrangement allows guests to sit directly opposite one another. This is easy with rectangular and square tables but needs to be carefully thought out when laying a round or oval table. Chairs generally should be around a foot and a half away from the table.

SEATING

This is commonly called *placement*, but is more correctly known as *place à table*. At one time there were extremely strict forms of precedence that dictated how people were seated. The highest-ranking man always sat on the hostess's right, with the next most prominent woman on his right and so on. Different levels of the peerage, the Church and the diplomatic corps all had their place in the pecking order. Nowadays, unless there is a specific guest/guests of honour, seating plans at a social, rather than an official, dinner are more relaxed and normally arranged to make the most of the different personalities of the guests. However, it is as well to remember that certain guests of the older generation might take umbrage about being placed in an inferior position. Therefore, it is still important for the host to sit at the head of the table, with his leading female guest on his right, and for the hostess to be at the foot of the table with the most important male guest on her right. The spouses of the principal guests occupy the second positions, i.e. on the left of the host and hostess. Couples are always split up

– with the exception of engaged couples, and, by tradition, couples in their first year of marriage, who are seated side by side. Gay couples are treated as other ordinary married couples and should be separated. Unless it is a single-sex dinner, guests should be arranged in a boy, girl, boy, girl sequence, although nowadays a balanced number is no longer the social imperative that it once was. The practice, popular for a while, of rearranging people after the pudding, by perhaps getting the men to move two spaces along, is not a social innovation to be encouraged. However, there are occasions – the visit of a distinguished visitor from overseas, for example, when many have been invited to meet the guest of honour – when changing places may be welcomed. Known gropers should be seated next to the plainest of the company.

PLACE CARDS
Place cards are particularly useful when there are more than about half a dozen guests. They can be placed either directly on the table or in special holders, which often come in very amusing designs. They should always be handwritten in fountain pen, and never typed. How you style the name on the card depends on the level of formality of your party. The most formal way will use the guest's full prefix, i.e. 'Mr Johnnie Derwentwater'. Titled guests are styled socially: the Earl of Kensington would be 'Lord Kensington'.

LAYING THE TABLE
There are generally two types of table surface. The first is hard: table mats on wood (other materials include glass or marble); the second soft: a tablecloth. The former gives a particularly masculine impression, and is an excellent way of showing off a beautiful table and silverware polished to perfection. The latter, however, is very useful if your table boasts a less-than-perfect surface, but remember, use an undercloth of baize to prevent hot dishes damaging the table underneath. Classic white (double) damask is the most distinguished choice, although coloured cloths are acceptable. Remember always to make sure that the cloth is square on the table, with the centre crease directly in the middle and an equal and generous amount of overhang all around.

Next arrange your centrepiece. This can range from elaborate silver epergnes bristling with fruit, flowers and sweetmeats to a simple bowl of the first spring blooms. Whether large or small, the centrepiece needs to be low enough to allow conversation with those opposite you. I remember attending an official dinner which boasted a central flower decoration of such impregnable hedge-like proportions that the guests directly opposite me remained a mystery until coffee. Flowers, as well as being short-stemmed, should not be too fragrant, as they can interfere with the aroma of the cooking, and should be in a colour scheme that is harmonious with the rest of the table and its setting. The old-fashioned idea that flowers should match the dress of the hostess is probably too precious for modern tastes. Fruit should be washed thoroughly, polished and arranged in such a way that the small, squash varieties are at the top of the display, supported by larger, heavier ones underneath.

LIGHTING

Although I have attended a dinner party in an ultra-modern high-tech flat, where individual ceiling halogen lights beamed down the most wonderfully warm light on to each guest, candles are still essential at most dinner parties to create the right mood and look. Their soft light makes even the most raddled guest appear attractive. Candlesticks are usually put on either side of the centrepiece. The quantity of candlesticks depends on the number of guests, but the old rule of thumb was that two were enough for two diners, four for six, six for eight, and anything bigger required candelabra. Should you be attempting something seriously grand with more than one candelabrum, the biggest one should always be in the centre of the table. White, or off-white, candles remain the most formal choice, and generally speaking the shorter the candlestick, the longer the candle. If you do not have enough candle power you will have to supplement it with electric light to prevent the evening becoming too Stygian, but this should not be so bright that it kills the glow of the candlelight.

CONDIMENTS

Salt cellars, pepper-shakers and mustard pots (if served) are placed at regular intervals between the centrepiece and the place settings. At very grand dinners, there may be as many as one set per two diners. Pepper mills, particular the large sort favoured by Italian *trattorias*, are out of place at a formal dinner, but have become acceptable at less grand affairs. Generally speaking, the salt and pepper are placed parallel with each other, with the mustard in front of them. If only salt and pepper pots are used, then the salt is placed in front of the pepper. Salt, pepper and mustard pots must always be removed after the main course and before the pudding. If using a commercially produced relish, such as chutney for curry, it must be served in sauce boats or small dishes and never, ever in the bottle in which it was bought. Salt and pepper 'cruets' have always been and still are 'genteel', and are thus banned.

LAYING THE PLACE SETTING

With the increased wish to lead a simpler, less cluttered life, the trend has been to use much less silverware than the battalions of knives, forks and spoons that were once thought indispensable to civilised eating. However, if you are entertaining properly, it is wise not to take this too far. It is very disruptive to the flow of events if implements have to be supplemented throughout the evening. And although many people make a point of behaving as if they were abroad by asking guests to use the same knife and fork throughout, this looks somewhat pretentious, and stingy, this side of the Channel. It is also quite out of the question at a formal dinner party.

A proper place setting should always look balanced and be equidistant from its neighbours and in line with the centrepiece. Old-fashioned butlers and the grander regiments still measure their tables for accurate spacing and a pleasing composition. If using table mats, they should be placed parallel to, and about an inch away from, the edge of the table: their design – if figurative – should be facing the diner. The right silverware is then arranged on either side of the mat. It is put out in the order in which it will be used, with the implements for the first course on the outermost edge. Forks are always placed on the left and knives and spoons on the right. Knives sit with their blades facing inwards and forks with their prongs pointing upwards. The habit of placing the bread knife on the side plate is sometimes done if space is tight, but is incorrect. Fish knives and forks, despite their dubious reputation, are acceptable as well as being practical and often very beautiful. At one time when people served elaborate meals of numerous courses, it was usual to lay the table only as far as the main course (the implements for succeeding courses being brought in as necessary), but now that dinner parties rarely add up to more than three or four courses, it is customary to put everything out at the beginning. The habit of placing the pudding spoon and fork and/or cheese knife above the place mat is known as 'nursery', and is quite incorrect at a dinner party. This place is rightly the preserve of the (now slightly old-fashioned) crescent-shaped salad plate.

CHINA

As with silverware, it is no longer necessary to have mountains of china of different shapes and dimensions that were once vital for grand entertaining. Nor is it necessary to have an entirely matching dinner service. In fact, many houses have special dessert plates and some of the smartest hostesses make a point of mixing china into a colour or style theme. Another innovation is the base plate, a very large flat plate, which has long been popular in America. This goes between the table/mat and the first and main course plates and is, in time, used to eat salad from.

The traditional dinner service would include the following: a dinner plate between ten and ten and three quarter inches across; a lunch and supper plate, around nine inches across, for the first course; a soup dish with an underplate; an eight-inch plate for pudding and cheese; and a six-inch side plate. Some hostesses consider side plates redundant at dinner. If used, they should be removed after the main course. In addition, you will need a selection of serving dishes, tureens and sauce and gravy boats, which can be of china, glass or silver.

NAPKINS

Napkins can be laid either in the space where the dinner plate will go, or on the side plate, but never in a glass. The best ones are made from either plain linen or linen double damask. They usually measure two feet square; anything smaller is not suitable for a dinner party. They can either be left flat or folded into simple shapes. Very elaborately folded napkins, although no doubt a tribute to the origamist's art, can look overdone and somewhat overhandled to modern eyes – accustomed as they are to simplicity and hygiene. Paper napkins have no place at a dinner party.

GLASSES

Lay glasses last to avoid knocking them over. They are placed on the right-hand side of the setting, just above the dinner knife, and are arranged from front to back in the order in which they will be used, or in little clusters. The water glass is placed slightly behind and on the left of the wine glasses. Remember to lay a glass for each drink you are serving and to pick them up by the stem only, to avoid leaving ugly and unappetising fingerprints.

Although it is possible to invest in a different type of glass for every conceivable drink, it is not necessary to do so. It is also not essential that all glasses should entirely match: particularly if you own random sets of lovely old glass. White wine is generally served in narrower glasses than red, for which a more rounded goblet shape is appropriate. Wine glasses should be neither too big nor too small. Small glasses are right for sherry, port and liqueurs, and large ones for water, beer and soft drinks. Champagne is served in fluted glasses and not in 'boats', which are downmarket, impractical and associated with elderly starlets. By the same token sherry 'schooners' and the ubiquitous 'paris goblet' are for pub use only. Coasters (genteel small mats for glasses) are never placed on an elegant table, no matter how precious the wood.

Sideboards

These are marvellously useful at dinner parties, particularly if you do not have staff. On them you can put extra silver, glasses and serving spoons. Add to this future courses, such as salad, pudding, cheese and chocolates, as well as hot dishes, which can be kept warm on a hot plate. They will also accommodate wines in the absence of *cellarets* (cabinets with compartments for holding wine bottles). They are also an ideal place to leave used dishes until you are able to get to the kitchen, and salt cellars and pepper pots after the main course.

The Arrival of Your Guests

Well-mannered guests will arrive slightly, but only a few minutes, later than the appointed time. By then, you should have changed, be looking your best and appearing totally relaxed. It is extremely off-putting to a newly arrived guest to be greeted by a stressed host or hostess. Such a beginning gets any evening off to a very awkward start. If you do not have someone to take the coats, it is acceptable to ask people to put their own in a nearby bedroom, although it is much more polite to remove and store each guest's coat yourself. On arrival, each guest is offered a drink: champagne, white wine or the recently revived cocktail. Old-style aperitifs such as sherry and gin and tonic, although still popular in the country, are rarely served in more metropolitan circles. Remember also to have non-alcoholic drinks at hand too: many people with an eye on healthier living and drink-driving penalties often defer drinking wine until they are at table.

Guests are immediately introduced to the assembled company. Even with quite large dinner parties, it is recommended to try to introduce everybody on arrival. As it is inadvisable to allow people to drink for any length of time on an empty stomach, you may also want to hand round small things that line the stomach without spoiling the appetite for the forthcoming meal. These can range from simple cocktail biscuits to exotic Japanese crackers and elaborate canapés. Keeping on the ball is vital to this early part of the evening. It is important to spend time with all your guests, while maintaining a watchful eye on the kitchen and the clock. It is usual to go into dinner after about half an hour, and certainly within one hour of the first arrivals. Polite guests must not be penalised because of others arriving late. If, after an unacceptable time, certain guests have not arrived, the dinner must proceed without them.

Dinner is normally served between eight and nine o'clock, although the fashionable trend to eat later and later means that it is usual to sit down as late as 9.30. Ten o'clock takes digestive forbearance too far! It should be remembered that many people are obliged to relieve baby-sitters or get up early the following morning and might not welcome an extended party – no matter how entertaining – into the early hours. Late arrivals should be offered a drink on arrival, although the good-mannered guest will always refuse.

Going in to Dinner
When going in to dinner, the hostess will lead the way and direct her guests to their places. If there are no place cards it is perfectly fine for her to read her placement from a diagram or list on a piece of paper. She, and other female guests, should also sit straight away to allow the men to do the same and thus avoid delays and the food getting cold.

Order of Service
Now begins the theatre of the dinner party. After the overture over drinks, each course should follow another as smoothly as acts in a play. As in an entertainment, success depends on host, hostess and any staff on duty knowing what they have to do and when. If you are lucky enough to have well-schooled staff to serve, there is probably little you need to do other than supervise the proceedings, which should appear the model of synchronised simplicity. There is one well-known City financier who always stations one liveried footman per two guests to ensure that his splendid entertainments run smoothly.

Food is *always* served from the left and drink from the right. The principal element of the course – i.e. meat or fish – is served first, followed by the relevant accompaniments. Gravies and sauces are served last. Even vegetables have their own order of precedence. Traditionally the most seasonal were served first – e.g. asparagus in May – followed by everything else; potatoes are always served last. Serving spoons and forks are placed so that they are most convenient for the guest – on the left-hand side of the tureen, with the spoon on the right-hand side of the fork. Wine should be poured gently, with the bottle held firmly in the right hand. The forefinger is pressed against the shoulder of the bottle, the thumb around an inch below and the second finger on the other side of the bottle exactly opposite the thumb. A decanter is held firmly around the neck. Champagne should always be opened quietly by gently easing the cork while holding the bottle at a slight angle above the horizontal and turning it. Large festive pops and spillages are in the worst taste. It is vulgar to slosh wine noisily and messily into the glass and to fill a glass more than two thirds full. At grand dinners with staff, bottles do not appear on the table. Plates, unless the food to be served on them is cold, must be heated, as there is little less appealing than watching delicious hot food quickly congealing on cold plates. They are also placed from the left. Bowls, for food such as soup, should be placed on a plate (not a saucer), and the two put down and taken away together. Every course at a formal dinner, including salad and cheese, needs a new plate, although at informal gatherings it is acceptable to use your main course plate for salad and your side plate for cheese.

Traditionally the order of service begins with the most important woman guest and then proceeds in a clockwise direction, with the host being served second. If you are throwing a big dinner with more than one servant, then a second staff member starts simultaneously with the hostess and moves clockwise until he ends up where number one began. If you are giving a banquet with an army of help, the table is subdivided in the same way.

Nowadays, you are more likely to have to be cook, footman and host rolled into one. Food is again served from the left and drink from the right, starting with the most important woman. Remember to keep moving and not engage in conversation, oblivious to food congealing on plates. Never be tempted to place a napkin on your wrist – this is acceptable in restaurants, but never done at home.

Alternatively, and more usually, you might want to pass the food around and allow the guests to serve themselves. If this is the case, dishes are passed anti-clockwise, so that each guest can serve him or herself from the left. Wine should be served by the host. It is important to make sure that wine is served immediately guests sit down; that glasses are constantly refilled, empty bottles assiduously removed and, if different wines are served with successive courses, that half-filled bottles of a preceding course are not left behind, unless particularly requested by a guest.

No plates are removed from the table until everybody has finished – including those who have eaten second or even third helpings. They are generally taken away in pairs, and not in huge stacks. The relevant accompaniments are also removed at this time. Salt and pepper pots, as well as other condiments, are always taken away before the pudding.

Gaps in between courses are problematical. Too short, and your evening appears hurried and anxious; too long and it loses cohesion. Generally speaking, there should be an interval of no more than a few minutes, although it is acceptable to allow a longer break before pudding.

Although cold first courses are often put in place before the guests sit down at public functions, at home it is more appealing to bring food freshly to the table.

If you decide to offer buffet service in which guests help themselves, it is best to restrict this method to one, at most two courses, unless you want an extremely disrupted evening. I remember going to a party at which guests had to help themselves to everything, including coffee. The result was an evening reminiscent of a self-service café. This being said, buffets offer a friendly, informal way to entertain. Items are arranged from left to right, in the order in which they will be needed: plates first, followed by main dishes, accompaniments and sauces. The host will normally stand near the buffet to explain the dishes and keep things moving. He serves himself last.

Should you be entertaining very informally in the kitchen, it is acceptable for you to serve each guest yourself, checking likes, dislikes and quantities as you go, and passing the fully assembled plate along the table. Again you serve yourself last. Remember that penetrating smells and dishes which cause huge amounts of steam can upset your guests and pervade their clothes unpleasantly.

Etiquette at the End of Dinner

This has become far more relaxed in recent years. Port was always drunk at table, then the sexes separated, with the women departing to the drawing room for 'girl-talk' and the men remaining at table for brandies, cigars and conversation other than that which was totally suitable in the company of women. Today these customs endure in only the most traditional houses. Pudding wine rivals port as the end-of-dinner drink, and most women resent being dismissed from the dining table. It also can be a shame to interrupt the conviviality and discourse of a good dinner party.

Nevertheless, this time-honoured pageant is still part of the classic formal dinner party. Port is generally brought in with the cheese. It is drunk in small, stemmed glasses. The usual procedure is for the host to serve the guest on his right, then himself, and then pass the decanter to his *left*. Although it may appear Batemanesque in the extreme, it is absolutely vital to remember that port is always passed this way, *never, ever* to the right. Getting the port wrong is considered by some, particularly those serving in the grander regiments, a social *faux pas* without equal. The decanter is thereafter gently circulated, everybody helping themselves, until all have had their fill.

When it is time for the women to retire, the hostess slowly rises from her seat while catching the eye of the principal female guest, who, in turn, gradually also stands up, so that the remaining women can get the message

251

and rise too. The men then stand politely and the one nearest the door, in the absence of staff, holds it open for the women to leave. The principal woman guest leads the way, with the hostess bringing up the rear.

Coffee is traditionally served away from the table in the drawing room, although many hosts, again in the interest of conversational continuity, serve it at table. That being said, taking coffee in a different setting does allow people who have been unable to talk to each other earlier in the evening to have a chat. Instant coffee should never be seen at a dinner party, and it is important to have decaffeinated coffee and herb teas as alternatives for those for whom caffeine in the evening would mean a sleepless night. It is usual to serve chocolate with coffee: truffles and other assorted unusual delicacies are considered much more sophisticated than the now ubiquitous and somehow slightly discredited after-dinner mint. You should also have brandy and/or liqueurs available, although nowadays more people request a thirst-quenching glass of water than an intoxicating digestif.

If men remain at table, it is recommended not to lose track of the time. Around twenty minutes is enough. As a very young man, I remember staying with some extremely dull hosts, who kept us so long at table discussing nothing in particular in a cloud of tobacco smoke that by the time we went through to the drawing room, the women had long departed to bed. Lucky them.

Drunken Guests

It is not unusual for guests to drink too much in the course of a long and jolly dinner party. In these circumstances the host has an obligation to make sure that the drunkard is not making a nuisance of himself to other guests and to prevent him from driving home if he is in a unfit state. The host must either order a taxi for his guest or, in exceptional cases, drive him home himself. Alternatively a bed for the night should be offered.

Smoking

At one time, when attitudes to smoking were more relaxed and the habit was widespread, a host provided cigarettes for his guests. This, although generous, is no longer expected. It is nevertheless still correct to offer cigars at a formal dinner.

Should you have friends who are asthmatic or who have a serious aversion to smoking, it is recommended not to invite them to dinner parties at which committed smokers will be present. If you as the host hate the habit, you can quite legitimately never invite smokers to your table. However, it is not appropriate to forbid a guest to smoke in your house once he or she is there. It is also churlish to say things like: 'I'll go and find you something to use as an ashtray' to express your disapproval. It is polite to grin and bear the smoke and quietly open a window. On the other hand, only the most insensitive of smokers will puff away relentlessly when he knows his habit is not popular with his host and fellow guests. Whatever the host's attitude is to smoking, it is vital that ashtrays should be plentiful and constantly emptied.

After-Dinner Entertainment

After-dinner entertainment is very popular again, particularly at the end of celebratory dinner parties. These attractions can take the form of a cabaret or a conjuror, both of which are currently in vogue. Alternatively you could offer the more traditional and delightful attractions of a musical performer/performers, or a little dancing for the guests. In these cases, it is useful to follow the old-established custom of writing 'music' or 'dancing' on the bottom right-hand corner of your invitation, so that guests can prepare themselves for a long evening.

THE LUNCH PARTY

The lunch party (the word luncheon is rarely used today for a private occasion except for very grand midday repasts) is a delightful way to entertain. Nowadays quite often restricted to the weekend, it is less formal than a dinner party, requires a simpler, lighter menu and is usually, but certainly not always, less alcoholic. Traditionally guests were asked for around one o'clock, but nowadays it is perfectly acceptable (at the weekend) to start it later to allow it to linger into the afternoon.

Old-style etiquette suggested that invitations to lunch parties were sent out less far in advance than those for a dinner. This is no longer the case, as people are today likely to be as busy in the middle of the day as in the evening. Invitations can be issued either over the telephone or in rare cases by a short informal letter. It is not usual to send a specially engraved card for a lunch party, although an 'at Home' card is fine. An elegant solution is to invite over the telephone and follow up with a *'pour memoire'* in the post.

When laying the table it is suggested that you use prettier or more informal china than you might for a dinner party. Glass must glisten and silver must be polished, as any smeary tarnishing that might go unnoticed in candlelight will be very obvious in broad daylight. It is important to remember not to lay candlesticks. This might sound obvious – after all, who needs extra light in the middle of the day? – but it is surprising how many people, presumably to make a show, do put them out. On the other hand, flowers are essential to decorate the lunch table.

The food served can be much simpler than would be suitable for a dinner party. As a teenager, I remember attending a small lunch at which the menu consisted of only a cheese soufflé followed by ripe peaches, washed down with a couple of glasses of Puligny Montrachet, and thinking it the most delicious, chic meal I had ever eaten. The maximum number of courses should not exceed three. By the same token it is not necessary to serve lots of different wines. It is no longer a social solecism to serve soup at lunchtimes, although it does remain incorrect to provide a first course before a traditional roast Sunday lunch.

Lunch parties can be more family-related affairs at which children are present. Little darlings can often be the ruin of a lunch party. At one time, children, unless of a civilised age and disposition, never joined an adult lunch table. Today, parental fashions and foreign influences mean that children of all ages and temperaments are now very much part of the main table. Lax parenting has also produced boisterous, ill-mannered and noisy children. Therefore, when planning a lunch party at which children will be present, it may be best to lay dispensable china and glass so that it will not be a tragedy if any gets broken. Serve an easy-to-eat menu and do not invite people (and there are many) who find the under-twelves trying.

Some guests will also insist on bringing their pets, usually dogs. This always strikes me as being exceptionally thoughtless, as there may be guests who are allergic to animals, or have phobias. As host, you can suggest that the animal is put outside and later walked by the owner. Remember that although you are expected to offer sustenance to all human guests, you are under no obligation to their animals. It is up to the dog's owner to feed its charge.

THE ALFRESCO LUNCH
Always a risk in Britain, but a delight when it works, the alfresco lunch should consist of the simplest – largely cold and picnic-like – menu. Remember to put the table in a sheltered spot away from wind and strong sunlight, and be prepared to lend sweaters and cardigans to those who have come under-dressed.

THE BARBECUE
Very popular, but often a disaster, a successful barbecue is the result of practice. If you have near neighbours it may be an antisocial way to entertain your friends, as it can pollute the air with clouds of pungent smoke. Should you decide to go ahead, offer fare that is within your range.

Avoid complex barbecuing unless you have the relevant expertise. Dress is always casual.

THE TEA PARTY

Now a very rare occurrence indeed. This is a shame, because a tea party is an ideal way to entertain a number of people informally and economically. Guests are normally invited over the telephone and asked for around 4.30. It is necessary to serve both China and Indian tea (made from loose tea, not teabags) and to offer both milk and slices of lemon as accompaniments. Proper china is essential. Contemporary concern for health and slimness means that the food does not have to be of gargantuan proportions, but it is important to serve something, even if it is just a slice of chocolate cake, a scone or a toasted muffin or crumpet. Sandwiches too are delicious. They must be made properly, from finely sliced white or brown bread, lightly spread with butter, never margarine. Crusts *must* be cut off. Traditional fillings such as ham, tomato, salmon, egg and, best of all, cucumber are still the most popular and delicious. More lurid concoctions such as peanut butter and jelly are for children's parties.

CHILDREN'S PARTIES

Children's parties are not for the faint-hearted. They need to be organised with the precision and courage of a military campaign. They are normally given to celebrate a child's birthday and are usually glorified tea parties with entertainments and presents attached.

The guest list should consist of children within a fairly narrow age band, as the pre-pubescent are notoriously ageist. There should also be a good balance of boys and girls, for it is generally agreed that the earlier you can get children accustomed to the opposite sex, the easier relationships will be later. Also, unless you are feeling incredibly brave, do not allow your child to invite armies of tinies. I know of a mother of a super-social six-year-old who discovered she was to entertain an entire school. Regardless of numbers, you will need support in the form of other parents, nannies or helpers.

The best invitations to children's parties are written by the child itself. The choice of invitation is purely a matter of taste, but it should be fun and colourful and not formal or pompous. If the party is to celebrate a birthday it must say so. The invitations should be sent at least three weeks in advance.

Children's parties are normally held between three and six o'clock. During this time the children will enjoy various games, a massive tea and most important of all an entertainer, such as a conjuror, juggler or puppet show (Punch and Judy, in these politically correct days, is now thought to be a little too full of domestic violence). It has also become popular to have a particular theme for a party, such as a favourite film or TV programme: dinosaur parties were rife at the time of the launch of *Jurassic Park*. The table setting should be fun and inexpensive. The children's party is the only party where it is good manners to use paper plates, tumblers and napkins – in copious quantities.

Although many parents try to encourage their offspring to eat a healthier diet, children still adore the jellies, crisps, sausages on sticks and soft drinks that, although they may be anathema to the modern nutritionist, are the standard fare for a truly jolly children's party. The centrepiece of the spread must be an elaborate and amusing cake.

Your child must greet all his or her guests personally on their arrival, and thank them for any presents they have brought. It is customary to provide a little going-home present for each guest, though not essential.

ENTERTAINING ON THE GRAND SCALE

Big parties – private dinner dances and balls – are the most demanding but also the most thrilling way to entertain. A splendid party is remembered fondly for years by both host and guest. Nowadays these increasingly rare events tend to be restricted to celebrations of twenty-first birthdays or very significant wedding anniversaries. Coming-out dances for young girls, once regulars of the Season, are rare indeed, having been replaced by drinks parties and other more modest entertainments.

First of all, should you decide to go for the ultimate party plunge, it is important to allow a significant budget (a dance with band, dinner, flowers, etc. will cost a great deal of money). It is therefore quite usual for different age groups to join forces to defray the cost, by celebrating landmark occasions across the generations – such as the wedding anniversary of one generation, a significant birthday in the second, and a coming-of-age in the third.

Second, allow yourself plenty of planning time. A good party will take months to organise. It will require specially engraved cards sent well in advance, vanloads of flowers, a constant flow of champagne for up to twelve hours, dinner, breakfast and sometimes a little supper in between, lots of fun guests, an army of staff, a band and/or a discothèque, a dance floor, magnificently decorated rooms and or/marquees. If you live in the country, you may have to organise house parties at nearby houses for guests (less common now), or failing this suggest hotels (more usual today).

Third, unless you are used to entertaining on the grand scale, it is strongly recommended that you hire a party planner to help with the event. If you choose the right one, they are worth every penny of their substantial fee and can even save you money in the long term. They know all the short cuts, the pitfalls, the importance of having plenty of space and lots of lavatories, the smart bands, the fashionable florists, the most substantial marquee supplier, the most innovative lighting engineer and, if you want it, a gossip columnist too. They will also help draw up and supervise the guest list, organise engraving and printing of cards and chase up R.S.V.P.s. Good planners will also be able to sort out the labyrinthine and hugely time-consuming complexities of *placement*: one celebrated organiser always puts the bores together; others dot them like dark holes in the social firmament. Planners, rather sadly, can even supply amusing guests for desperate hostesses. I have been to several parties over the years at which the guest lists have comprised varying degrees of rent-a-crowd, and to one not very memorable but vastly extravagant dinner dance with fireworks at which the poor, bemused hostess did not seem to know who anybody was.

Generally guests are invited at around eight o'clock. Dinner should follow within the hour. It is most unfair to keep people standing around for ages. When assigning guests their tables it is much more elegant to give them a tiny envelope containing a card bearing their table number than to make them crowd around lists pinned to boards. Dancing will start around 10 to 10.30. The choice of music can be vexing, as it is difficult to please everybody. Some schools of thought recommend keeping it all middle-of-the-road, while one well-known and experienced party-giver suggests exhausting the old with their music first and then, with a dramatic change of lighting and music, start up the rave for the young. Others provide different types of music in separate locations, although this can cause a party to fragment. Also remember that sustained very loud music can kill conversation – and thus sometimes the party – stone dead. Whatever type of music you choose, remember never to be tempted to start up the band again once it has stopped for the evening. Social momentum, once broken, is difficult to start up again.

Transportation also needs to be thought out. Hosts who live within an hour of London now often run a shuttle bus service to the party. Others offer valet parking. If neither of these is possible, do ensure that your car park is adequately lit and thus avoid the indignity of inebriated matrons slipping into ditches. Fireworks, although popular with guests, are less so with nearby livestock and elderly residents. If held in a private house, a dance can carry on until dawn, when breakfast is traditionally served. However, with fewer grand houses in private hands, and with worries about security, damage and expensive insurance, increasing numbers of private dances are held in hired public places such as hotels and novel locations. These normally end earlier and often without breakfast.

ENTERTAINING ROYALTY

The royal guest is always the guest of honour. No matter how informal and jolly the circumstances, you and your other guests must remember that all members of the Royal Family are perfectly aware of who they are and expect others to acknowledge their status. This does not mean behaving in a stiff and sycophantic way, but by affording simple courtesies such as a small bow or curtsey on first meeting. Also, by the same token, although the well-mannered royal guest will always make others feel comfortable, it is polite and practical to warn other guests if there will be royalty present at a party.

The Invitation

When inviting royalty it is important first to decide, as with any guest, whether you are on close enough terms to proffer an invitation, and second to remember that there is a very distinct pecking order, with The Queen and Queen Elizabeth The Queen Mother (never referred to as just 'The Queen Mother') at the apex of the pinnacle, followed by descending degrees of precedence.

Regardless of the rank of your royal guest, unless you are a friend, social as well as official invitations should be offered via a member of his or her household, such as the Private Secretary or a lady-in-waiting, or alternatively the local Lord Lieutenant. It should be in writing, although tentative hostesses sometimes ring the member of the household to ascertain the prospective guest's probable amenability and availability to an invitation. The intermediary will act as a conduit, indicating whether the royal guest is able to accept the invitation and answering any questions. They may also ask for details of other proposed guests, to which it is considered polite to accede. Particularly in the case of senior members of the family, the household will want to have some idea of the degree of security risk.

When writing, remember the convention of using capital letters liberally, even mid-sentence, when referring to the member of the Royal Family. Address the envelope to 'The Private Secretary to Her Majesty The Queen', or 'The Private Secretary to His Royal Highness The Prince of Wales'. In the letter refer to your royal guest in the third person, in the first instance as Her Majesty and thereafter as The Queen, or His Royal Highness followed by The Prince of Wales.

Members of the Royal Family are refreshingly punctual. It remains important for all other guests to be present and correct before the royal guest arrives. On arrival, the host should be standing outside his front door to meet the guest, who is greeted with a small bow or curtsey: large court curtseys are out of place in a social setting. The Queen and Queen Elizabeth The Queen Mother are addressed firstly as 'Your Majesty' and thereafter as 'Ma'am', which is pronounced to rhyme with 'jam', never 'smarm'. Everybody else is first addressed as 'Your Royal Highness' and thereafter as 'Sir' or 'Ma'am'. This being said, there is no need to lard the conversation with lots of 'Sirs' and 'Ma'ams' unless you wish to appear obsequious.

The other guests wait standing in the room where the party is to take place. It is usual with smaller groups for guests to assemble in a semicircle, so that the royal visitor can say hello to everyone at the same time. To avoid a pregnant pause at the end of the ellipse, it is clever to have someone who has already been introduced at hand so that conversation can continue directly. When introducing your other guests to the royal one, it takes the form of a presentation. For instance, you would say, 'Ma'am, may I present Henry Holland.' If you are introducing a member of your family, you should qualify this in the introduction: 'Sir, may I present my son, Billy.' Everybody bobs or bows on being presented.

To handle royalty well socially, you have to master the age-old courtly skill of combining deference and familiarity. Generally speaking, as would be expected, the senior members are more rigid about form than the younger ones. With them it is wise for the inexperienced to remember that the old solecisms – not waiting to be spoken to, asking direct questions, and changing the subject – although lesser gaffes than before, have not disappeared. On the other hand, the Royal Family enjoy conversation, can be very funny and like to have as good a time as anybody else. At table it is usual for the royal visitor to be seated in the guest-of-honour position, next to the host or hostess, or, alternatively, at right angles to the host halfway down the table.

Conventions about sitting in and leaving the royal presence are also now more relaxed. For instance, whereas it remains very rude for a young man to sit in the same room in which a member of the Royal Family is standing, it is acceptable for an old person with a bad back to be seated. Similarly, although it would be quite wrong to leave a dinner party before the royal guest has departed, it is now acceptable, although not the best manners, to ask your hostess to allow you to slip away quietly from a larger party if you have a pressing engagement.

As host of a party which includes royalty, you will have to make sure that other guests are behaving neither with a rigidity and reserve that makes socialising impossible, nor, on the other hand, with an embarrassing degree of familiarity. Over-boisterous behaviour, swearing and physical contact are all quite beyond the pale. No one present will ever forget the occasion of an informal party where a senior female member of the Royal Family was the principal guest and a particularly pushy and perhaps slightly drunk man crossed the invisible line between friendliness and intrusiveness. The royal reaction was akin to witnessing a spell in a fairy tale when an entire kingdom is cast into winter.

You will also have to look after the personal protection officer. All members of the Royal Family have them. Before your party he will want to view your property to make sure it is secure. On the night he will accompany his charge, and although he will not expect to be part of the party, he will need to be nearby, and provided with food and drink (non-alcoholic, of course).

HOUSE PARTIES

House parties were conceived at a time when an abundant supply of cheap and willing domestic help made them as much a joy for the hostess as for her guests. In these servant-depleted days, they are a test of any hostess's stamina, forbearance, generosity and skills of organisation.

The first step is careful forward planning. Your guest list should be chosen with care, bearing in mind that those staying in your house are going to spend a lot of time at close quarters. So be sure that nobody is likely to come to blows over the weekend. Do not be too influenced by the 'variety is the spice of life' school and be seduced into inviting people who have very little in common. After all, as the host you don't want to be constantly on duty making things run smoothly. You need a group who will be happy to do things together. The deeply tired or lazy should not be included; if sleep is so important to them they should do it at home.

Secondly, give plenty of notice. You may have to book busy and popular people months in advance to ensure your chosen guest list. Nowadays both men and women have to work longer hours than their predecessors and will thus have much less time available to spend on rustic retreats or Arcadian idylls. Invitations can be issued either over the telephone or in writing.

Thirdly, remember that you will need lots of stamina, the tact of the top diplomat and the practical skills of the staff of a five-star hotel. I am constantly amazed at the Jekyll and Hyde capabilities of house guests who manage to transform themselves from normal individuals into passive sloths who expect to be waited on hand and foot. It is also worth remembering that weekending can be somewhat terrifying to the timid, who can find two and a half days spent in a strange house with unfamiliar people incredibly daunting. These tender types will need special attention.

When planning the weekend, it is important to strike a happy balance between relaxation and entertainment. Little is more depressing for guests than to spend disconsolate hours at a loose end. On the other hand, it is exhausting to be subjected to a punishing timetable more suited to an Outward Bound trip. Organise a main social focus, such as a black-tie dinner party on the Saturday night, a visit to local racing, or a drinks party at a neighbour's on Sunday morning, supplemented by such optional activities as an excursion to look at a noteworthy house or beauty spot. Sporting activities such as riding, tennis, fishing and shooting are also much appreciated, if they are in your gift. If you own a swimming pool, remember to make this clear so that people can bring their bathing things. It is not the host's responsibility to be constantly at the beck and call of his house guests, and only the most insensitive of guests will not make themselves scarce at certain times.

Wise hosts give detailed instructions to first-time guests on how to get there, particularly if they are planning for arrivals to be in time for a particular meal. I recall driving down to Hampshire with a friend on a journey that should have taken only one hour. Despite directions from the kind hostess, we managed to travel for two hours, before finally giving up, confused and frustrated, and having to be rescued by our host. If guests don't drive it is perfectly acceptable to ask other guests who are coming from the same direction and have spare seats to give them lifts. Failing this, it is helpful if you can advise on train connections and times. The now archaic custom of engraving 'nearest station . . .' on your writing paper these days looks pretentious. It is customary and polite either to meet your guests' trains or to arrange to have them picked up and not expect them to get a taxi to the house.

As with any sort of entertaining, it is up to you to decide when you want your guests to arrive and leave. The old Edwardian weekend that stretched languorously from Thursday to Monday is long past. Nowadays most run from Friday evening to after lunch on Sunday, although some guests will drive down on Saturday morning. You should also give guidelines about dress and indicate whether you will be dressing for dinner or remaining totally casual throughout, mentioning any sporting activities for which special clothes will be needed. Most guests know to bring gum boots for walking. However, it is wise to keep a few pairs in stock in different sizes for those who don't.

Bedrooms

Assigning bedrooms can be a sensitive aspect of planning a house party. In theory, couples tend to be put in double rooms and singles in single ones.

However, there are subtle considerations. If you invite a married couple who you know to be having difficulties with their relationship or to be leading separate lives, it is tactful to put them in a double room containing two single beds rather than one double, or perhaps interconnecting rooms. Do not, however, be tempted to install them in separate bedrooms, as this makes a public expression of a private matter. Similarly, if you are aware of any discreet assignations that are taking place between your guests, it is worth bearing this in mind when organising the sleeping arrangements. There is one hostess who has what she calls her 'naughty tower' (actually a small but secluded turret), where many affairs have taken place in a series of interconnecting rooms. The arrangements for unmarried couples can also be awkward. Long-established partnerships should be treated as *de facto* marriages. Newer relationships sometimes require a little research. If you are in a dilemma about whether a couple wish to share a room, it is still customary to ask the woman. Few engaged couples maintain a pretence of chastity, and thus most expect a double room or interconnecting chambers. The same is true of single-sex relationships, who should be offered the choice of shared or separate quarters.

For the sake of privacy, you may wish to separate your guests' sleeping arrangements from your own. One particular woman lives in what she modestly calls a 'cottage' in the home counties – actually a rambling dwelling consisting of cottages with extensions, providing separate wings, one of which she occupies with her husband. A second is for her children, and a third for guests. Generally the most important or older guests are given the best rooms, with the young occupying the less choice quarters. If you are entertaining a large group and space is limited, you may ask young single men or women to share with others of the same sex. (One well-known party planner creates actual junior dormitories for really massive house parties.)

A certain amount of effort must be put into making guest accommodation comfortable. One thoughtful hostess spends one night a year in each of her many guest rooms to make sure that they are up to scratch. Rooms must be aired – it is grim for guests to have to crawl into a damp bed that has not been used for a long time. There must be clean linen on the bed, plenty of clean towels in the bathroom, fresh flowers, plenty of hangers in the wardrobe, extra heaters and bedding if the weather is cold and the central heating is either inadequate or nonexistent, a good-sized looking-glass, a box of biscuits and carafes of water by each bed. There should also be a good supply of writing paper. This has several useful and surprising functions. The first is for which it was intended. Many people who never normally write a letter become amazingly epistolary as guests, especially when they are staying somewhere grand. Second, encouraging letter-writing in their rooms will give you some well-earned time off. Third, 'I'm just going to my room to write a few letters' is a marvellously useful social euphemism which can cover a host of private activities, ranging from an innocent snooze after lunch to more active post-prandial antics. There should also be plenty of books provided. One of the joys of weekending is being given access to a small captive library of books you thought you had forgotten, volumes long out of print and enticing new titles. Considerate hosts pick suitable volumes for bedside tables. The bathrooms should be equipped with pristine soaps, shampoos, disposable razors, toothpaste, spare toothbrushes and combs, aspirins, sanitary towels, tissues, cotton wool buds and any other personal items that guests might have forgotten and could feel embarrassed about requesting.

When Your Guests Arrive

When your guests arrive it is important to appear genuinely pleased to see them and to accept any present, no matter how unattractive, with pleasure. If your weekend begins on Friday evening, it is often best to offer a relaxed and casual start, as guests may well be exhausted from their week's labours and delayed through heavy traffic, without time to change when they arrive. Therefore a light supper or even some sort of buffet arrangement is ideal. It is at this meal that you as host must lay down the ground rules for the weekend. Remember that while it is the host's role to look after his guests as royally as possible, by the same token guests are obliged to fit in with your domestic routines and foibles. Thus, you must outline any events and outings planned, give suggestions on how they can amuse themselves at other times, point out any idiosyncrasies of the house, from eccentric plumbing to persistent poltergeists, and explain how your family lives, including arrangements for bathrooms and mealtimes. This is particularly important on the vexed question of breakfast, which can cause any amount of nervous speculation from guests. If you intend to serve breakfast at a specific hour, you must say so. If it is your custom for women to be brought breakfast in their room while men come down, then explain. Likewise, if arrangements are more bohemian and guests are expected to fend for themselves, this should be pointed out. Modern tastes for a light breakfast mean that many hosts serve breakfast on a tray in guests' rooms. This means that the guests can have a slow start, at their leisure, and that you as host are spared being on top social form at an early hour.

As host you are expected to provide comprehensive hospitality throughout the stay. This means breakfast, lunch, tea and dinner every day, as well as pre-lunch and pre- and post-dinner drinks. Although thoughtful guests might offer to take you out for one meal to give you a rest, don't bank on it. Unless you keep adequate staff, it is also recommended that you get in a bit of extra domestic help. The practical and physical strain of wining, dining and amusing a group, no matter how small, is considerable, and if you are to enjoy yourself it is useful to have someone there to cope with the mountains of clearing and washing-up and the cooking and serving of meals. Domestic agencies and caterers can be brought in to do the whole thing, including the shopping. When planning meals, it is fun to invite local people for specific meals or drinks to meet your guests. This serves the dual purpose of preventing your guests from becoming bored with one another's company and providing your neighbours with a little diversion from their usual, perhaps limited, circle. It is also recommended that you make a note of guests' dietary peculiarities for future reference.

During the Weekend
Throughout their stay you must make sure that your guests are happily amused, and that nobody feels particularly left out. If one party finds themselves constantly out on a limb, it is thoughtful to ask another guest to try and include them more. If this is not possible, then you, as host, might like to devote special attention by taking them on a walk to show them local attractions, or by including them in any small activity to make them feel special. While a good host always lays on plenty of activities to amuse his guests, he must, however, not force people to do things from which they would rather abstain. As to accepting offers of help from your guests, whereas it is fine to expect them maybe to help occasionally with the clearing up or gathering logs for the fire, it is quite unacceptable to put them to work. There is a certain amusing woman who, without any malice aforethought, expects visiting couples to assume the dual roles of guests and live-in help. The men are expected to bring in logs and keep the fires constantly burning, serve endless streams of local guests with drinks and help walk the dogs. The women's duties have included preparing every vegetable eaten throughout the weekend, stuffing a goose and doing most of the washing-up. Few of these put-upon people return for more punishment. That said, if you run an unservanted household, you should expect your guests to make their own beds, tidy their rooms and scour their baths.

Coping with Problems
Weekending by its complex nature is fraught with pitfalls for both hosts and guests. The stories of house party contretemps are legion. Some are

probably apocryphal. A favourite one is that of a nervous young man who, invited to a well-known and grand house, found that he needed to go to the lavatory during the night. In the struggle to find a bedside light he knocked over what he presumed to be a glass of water. The hapless man then proceeded to feel his way through the darkness across the wall until he found a light switch by the door. On turning on the light, to his horror he discovered that the presumed glass of water was no less than an inkwell brimming with jet-black ink, which he had palm-printed right across the exquisite silk-lined walls of his chambers. Crushed with embarrassment, he stole out of the house at dawn and never returned.

Animals too can cause problems. Thought by most people to be indispensable to country life, animals can at best worry those not used to them and at worst cause severe health problems to those with allergies. If you have pets and are entertaining people who you know to have problems with animals, it is up to you to keep the two apart as much as possible. Remember, just because you find your pampered pet the most fascinating creature in creation, it does not mean that this view is shared by others.

Another area of confusion is over staff tips. If you keep staff, whether it be a live-in complement or just a daily, everyone who has contributed to your guests' comfort deserves a tip, and you are quite within your rights to mention it to guests who obviously and habitually renege on leaving a token. House guests might be confused as how much to leave: it is up to you to have worked out a going rate. One young peeress blatantly tells her guests on arrival a fixed and slightly exorbitant rate for each couple staying per member of staff, as well as another sporting charge for the keeper calculated on the number of birds shot. This brash approach is not recommended. Subtler tactics are much better, such as those of a chatelaine of a small stately home who makes up any shortcomings on a stingy guest's behalf and says: 'I do hope you don't mind, but I noticed you hadn't left anything for Mrs So-and-So, so I gave her ten pounds on your behalf.' This method is foolproof, and guests are always embarrassed into settling up and never missing a tip again. Some guests are also embarrassed about actually doing the distributing to staff members. In these cases you should offer to do it for them.

Drugs, Drunkenness and Bad Behaviour
Your house is your domain. And although it is up to you to make sure that your guests feel at home as much as possible, it is not part of your remit to put up with behaviour you find distasteful. Although drugs appear to be widely available, the possession or use of hard and soft drugs remains a

criminal offence, and the behaviour they induce can be disturbing and irritating to others. If you don't want drugs around, say so. Should your guest choose to ignore your wishes, you are perfectly within your rights to ask him or her to leave. After all, who needs friends who do not respect the sensibilities of their host? Drunkenness is more widespread. Although occasional inebriation is acceptable, even amusing, people who overtly display a drink problem and who are routinely 'tired and emotional' are probably best not included in a house party.

Closing Your House Party

Ill-mannered people, unless they have pressing engagements at home or elsewhere, are often reluctant to leave a convivial house party. A forbearing women tells a story of how one guest, a slightly morose young man, began to complain of a cold when it was time to go, and asked if he could stay on a couple of days while he recovered. No illness materialised, but he was still there ten days later. The long-suffering hostess finally had to ask him to leave. Far better had she explained, as experienced hostesses do, the duration of the stay proposed when she originally offered the invitation. This is less important for weekends, when most people know to make themselves scarce if not after Sunday lunch then immediately after tea, but is essential if your house party is to run, say, during Ascot or Cowes week. In this case you should say or write: 'We do hope you will be able to come to stay with us from June 16 to 21.' In this way there can be no misunderstandings. On departure day hints about suitable trains and favourable road conditions and offers of lifts should also speed events to a suitable close.

ENTERTAINING IN A RESTAURANT OR CLUB

Long prevalent abroad, this habit has become increasingly popular in Britain over recent years, as living spaces have become more cramped and restaurants better and more varied. One young man who until recently lived in a minute studio in St James's encapsulated this new *modus vivendi* succinctly when he told me: 'Home is my bedroom and Brooks's my dining and drawing room.' Entertaining in a public place also has the added advantage of taking the strain entirely out of running the evening smoothly, as the arrangements are handled by professionals. It is also an ideal way to entertain business acquaintances whom you might not wish to bring to your house. However, entertaining away from home can have drawbacks. The first is expense, which can be crippling if you do not control the level of hospitality and your friends overindulge in à la carte excesses. It is far more economical for you to work out a set menu, as you would in your own home, serving specific aperitifs, wines and digestifs of your choice. This will not only save your pocket; it will also give the event a personal touch. Another way to personalise entertaining away from home is to do it in the same place with regular staff. In this way a public place will become an extension of your private domain, where everybody knows your likes and dislikes. Entertaining in a private room of a restaurant can seem more personal than in its public areas and is ideal if you wish to say a few words should you be celebrating a special occasion. If entertaining a group, remember, as each guest leaves, to stand up and escort him or her to the door.

TAKEAWAYS

The use of pre-prepared food from outside has achieved a far wider social acceptability. The euphemism of 'Lady Sieff is in the kitchen tonight', meaning: 'I haven't had time to cook/I don't know how to cook and thus have bought everything from Marks & Spencer', is an increasingly frequent cry from metropolitan singles. The more sophisticated are more likely to have something ordered from somewhere grander, but the result is similar. Although this form of entertaining is now just about acceptable when supping with a few close friends, it is, unless used in limited quantities – i.e. just for a first course or a pudding – insulting at a proper dinner party, when a more personal effort is expected.

13

THE COUNTRY WEEKEND

At its best the country weekend probably represents a peak of Anglo-Saxon culture. At its worst it can be torture beyond compare for all concerned. Country house disaster stories are legion and only go to illustrate what social minefields they are for the unsuspecting *ingénue*, unprepared for the idiosyncrasies, eccentricities and arcane customs of British domestic life.

The first thing to remember is that you always go 'down' to the country, never 'up', regardless of geographical considerations. The second is that people are at their strangest in their own homes and thus it is provident to prepare yourself for levels of behaviour that might be considered unusual elsewhere. Third, do not let ghastly good taste get in the way of your enjoyment. For instance, if you don't understand something, such as the terpsichorean idiosyncrasies of a particularly complex eightsome reel, say so before you get on to the dance floor, making a fool of yourself and irritating others. Or if you do something embarrassing, own up, just as a certain woman did while staying with a well-known marchioness of the old school. The guest inadvertently tipped the contents of an ashtray into the elderly peeress's bucket-shaped bag, mistakenly thinking it was the waste-paper basket. The culprit, rather than being caught with her hands in her hostess's bag, digging out the fag ends, reported her misdemeanour immediately. The marchioness, in the circumstances, was most gracious.

Guest lists for such weekends are usually carefully constructed. Invitations are proffered (in person, by telephone or by letter) well in advance, particularly if there is to be shooting or other sporting activities. It is therefore good manners to respond to the invitation directly, and if you accept, not to drop out at the last minute, unless there is very good reason. If the host says there will be tennis or swimming, or: 'We tend to dress in the evening', this is a subtle message for you to bring the right clothes. He should also give you some idea of time of arrival, but if he appears vague then you should ask at what time he would like to see you. Nowadays, most country weekends are short affairs, starting on Friday evening or Saturday morning and ending after lunch on a Sunday. Sometimes a hostess will say: 'I do hope you will stay to tea,' by which she means she expects you to leave immediately afterwards. It is rude both to turn up early for a weekend and to overstay your welcome. If you are driving and it is your first visit to a particular house, it is sensible to ask for detailed directions. You may also be asked to give a lift to a carless fellow guest. Should you be taking the train, your host should make sure you are picked up at the station. Very rich people might offer to fly you down in a helicopter.

Although life in even the grandest of piles is a lot more informal than it was, it is necessary to pack the right clothes and not rely on hosts and other guests to make up for sartorial shortcomings. These include gear for any sporting activities you will be participating in, whether it be a tweed shooting suit, riding clothes or tennis kit; for day a tweed jacket, corduroys and lots of jerseys; footwear which should include stout walking shoes and boots; very cosy nightwear if the house is cold; a change for the evening, which at traditional houses still means dinner jackets and smoking jackets for men and the equivalent for women; a waterproof such as a Barbour; and, if there is racing or church, a country suit. Remember always to dress in the style of the house you are visiting: a very grand one will require an impressive wardrobe, a simple one will need only a few casual clothes. Always look as if you have made an effort with your appearance without looking overdressed: it is a compliment to your hosts. It is worth bearing in mind, particularly when staying at very grown-up houses, that your suit-case might be unpacked by someone else.

It is thoughtful to arrive punctually, as hosts become fretful about missing guests. The question of present-giving (or, as the Americans say, 'hostess gifts') is a vexed one. At one time, if invited to stay with the rich and grand, it was a solecism to arrive with a present. I remember the consternation at a dinner party given by one of France's most sumptuous families, the owners of famous vineyards, as one well-meaning *ingénue* arrived with a bottle of wine. This is changing, and even the grandest hostesses now enjoy and expect a small token such as a box of chocolates, a book, or something that could not be viewed in any way as practical. Hosts of more moderate means will appreciate a side of smoked salmon or a favourite something from town that is unavailable locally. Hard-up hosts welcome all contributions. If staying with friends for any length of time, it is also thoughtful to offer to take them out to dinner or lunch at some point. This both expresses thanks for their hospitality and gives them a rest from the food factory.

THE ROLE OF GUESTS

Guests have to sing for their supper. To work well, a house party requires almost as much effort from the guests as from the hosts. Therefore it is good manners to be both sociable and enthusiastic, as well as being independent enough not to be under the host's feet all the time. It is bad manners to languish in bed all morning, unless the host has expressly given the go-ahead for a seriously late start. In smart houses breakfast can be brought to your room when wanted, or is more likely to be served downstairs at an appointed hour, where it is the custom to serve yourself even in a house bristling with staff. In unstaffed houses it is usual for you to keep your own room tidy, make your bed and offer to help with the preparation of meals and gathering of wood, etc. At very grand staffed houses, such offers are redundant and embarrassing. At all times guests, although behaving as if they are at home, must fit in with the domestic arrangements of the house and not treat the place as if it were a hotel. It is rude to be late for meal times, sports and outings. It is inconsiderate to use masses of water if the plumbing is prehistoric or to spend hours in the bathroom if you are sharing facilities with other guests.

The telephone can also be a source of irritation. It is rude to make countless protracted calls and have strings of people ringing in as if you were at home. Technically you should always ask to use the telephone, but in large houses this is somewhat impractical. Also, if you are expecting a call it is courteous to inform the host by saying: 'I do hope you don't mind, but I'm expecting a call from my boyfriend this afternoon.' As far as paying for calls is concerned, it is polite to leave something if you have made more than a couple of local calls, unless the host is so rich that such a contribution seems ludicrous. Television has its own particular etiquette. There is nowadays more television, video and cable watching than was the case in country houses of yore, when televisions were rarely seen in main rooms. Nevertheless, it is rude to spend hours looking at the box (after all, you can do that at home), unless it is late at night and in your own room. It remains bad manners, if your host is present, to change channels without asking him first, and impolite to ask to view your favourite series, unless he intends to do the same.

Smokers need to be thoughtful. People in the country are on the whole less difficult about smoking (they tend to be more old-fashioned and live in bigger houses) than metropolitan types. This being said, it is unwise to light up before gaining the sanction of the hostess, and very inadvisable to smoke in bed, particularly if it is a four-poster festooned with ancient and desiccated hangings, as more than one person has learnt to their cost.

THE STAFF

Fully staffed houses have become such a rarity that the unaccustomed claim to be uncomfortable when confronted with serried ranks of servants. This attitude is a shame and pointless. It is enormous fun to stay in a properly run grand house that hums quietly and distantly with domestic activity, and where guests do not have to worry about anything other than enjoying themselves.

A fully staffed house is likely to have a butler, who traditionally is the senior male servant, and whose duties include answering the door and the telephone, overseeing the other male staff, looking after the wine cellar, serving drinks and organising luggage. Nowadays he will probably perform other tasks, previously the province of more junior functionaries such as chauffeurs and footmen, and thus can be seen driving the cars and polishing the silver. His female equivalent is the housekeeper, whose job description is in her title, and who traditionally is in charge of maids and cleaners, although these days she probably has to do the beds herself. In addition there will be a cook and, if there are children, a nanny. Many houses, even seriously grand ones, make do with a couple, who split household duties between them and are sometimes aided by a mini-squadron of dailies who come in twice a week. Hardly any houses keep old-style footmen, valets and ladies' maids, although a surprising number, particularly of tycoons, do run full-time chauffeurs. Outside there will be a gardener, possibly grooms, and, if it is a sporting estate, a gamekeeper.

It is important to be polite and friendly to staff at all times, and to remember that they are professionals in their sphere. Those unused to servants sometimes behave in a way that causes embarrassment all round: too haughtily, too chummily or too apologetically.

On the other hand, taking advantage of servants is equally bad. Although it is fine for a woman to ask a maid to help her with a difficult zipper in a dress or a fiddly clasp on the family sparklers, or for a man to expect a little help with his studs, it is bad form to ask other people's servants to perform little personal tasks and run errands. Remember that they work for your hosts not for you, and already have more than enough to do. It is also in the worst taste to discuss with them your hosts (their bosses) and other house guests, to wheedle information out of them, to complain as if you were in a hotel, and to do anything that might embarrass them.

Although today all domestic staff (with the exception of certain scandalously exploited individuals from the Third World) are much better paid than their predecessors, they are still due tips from house guests. All staff who have helped you should be tipped. The only exception is the nanny, who, if she has taken charge of your children, might expect a small present. The daily, who you no doubt won't have seen, but who has obviously contributed to your comfort, should be left a little something in an envelope. Certain tips can be left in bedrooms, although it is kinder to distribute them in envelope in person before you leave, but without making too much of a song and dance about it. It is extremely gauche to appear embarrassed or awkward about this little ceremony. Sums vary, and a quick word with your host or hostess will clarify the going rate.

ANIMALS

Animals, although a *sine qua non* of country life, and highly esteemed members of many families, can cause problems. It is bad manners to allow your dogs to bark, or worse snarl at visitors, and to press them on to non-animal-loving visitors. By the same token, guests who own pets and would like to bring them along to join the house party should always ask permission first. Once there, owners must ensure that their animals do not make a nuisance of themselves with other guests. Guests' animals who patently don't get on with the host's need to be removed as soon as possible.

People with allergies to animals are particularly vulnerable to having their weekends ruined. Those who suffer very badly probably do best not to accept invitations from riding households crawling with gun dogs, family cats and other fauna. On the other hand, people with less severe conditions should always tell their hostess of their problems in advance, so that she can try and keep the offending parties apart as much as possible. Although the grandest people do it, it is bad manners and unhygienic to feed animals from the table.

Dogs attacking guests is deeply embarrassing. What can be thought of as high spirits by the owner of a pampered pet will often be interpreted as out-and-out savagery by the hapless victim. A certain woman, the proud possessor of a boisterous labrador called Millie, tells the story of her hound biting a hole in a nervous bridge guest's *haute couture* trousers. 'I mopped her [the guest] in Dettol and offered to organise invisible mending,' she says. In the circumstances it was the least that good manners demanded.

COUNTRY SPORTS

These are often the main focus of the country weekend, particularly in the winter months. Traditionally they include field sports such as hunting (fox and stag), shooting and fishing, but can also include stalking, coursing and beagling. Although the ultimate aim of field sports is to cull game and quarry species, the well-mannered sportsman goes to great lengths to give the quarry the greatest possible chance of survival. Hence the palaver that the hunting of foxes involves, and the great speed and altitude that pheasants are driven to on the best shoots.

Shooting

Shooting is more popular than ever, and is attracting many newcomers to the sport. Traditionally boys learnt the skills from their fathers, other seniors and gamekeepers, often walking with an empty gun. They were frequently given their début on a Boys' Shoot on Boxing Day. The new breed of shot will have enrolled at one of the shooting schools, where even many practised shots will take lessons to keep their technique up.

In Britain there are many schools of this kind, the best often run by the top gunsmiths. Here people learn not only the basic skills of shooting, but all the carefully conceived safely rules and the finer points of shooting etiquette. It is the combination of all three of these sporting facets that makes a good shot.

Shooting is a highly skilled and dangerous sport, and no one should ever accept an invitation to shoot without the right experience. It is also an activity where manners and safety procedures have been carefully developed to provide maximum sport and enjoyment with minimum danger to the participants. Being dangerous is considered frightfully rude. Offenders are quite simply sent home.

However, accidents do happen. Shooting manners expect the guilty gun to leave the party immediately (to save embarrassment to the others), and if the mishap is a tragic one, unwritten rules of etiquette expect him never to shoot again. Shooting form also expects the other guns to be deeply discreet about the incident.

HANDLING A GUN

The first step to avoiding a tragedy is to learn to handle a gun properly. First, when loaded, it should never be pointed anywhere but up in the air or to the ground, and always away from other guns and beaters. Second, it needs to be carried carefully, by holding it under your arm broken, or over a bent arm with

273

the muzzle pointing earthwards. Third, after loading, close it by bringing the stock up to meet the barrels. In this way the gun is pointing to the ground and not towards a hapless individual. It is considered very bad form to carry a closed gun, because others cannot know if it is loaded or not.

There is thus an entirely sensible convention of carrying a gun 'broken', that is, opened and without cartridges, so that it is obvious to one and all that there is no possible danger. By the same token, always assume that a closed gun is never safe. The gun is also always broken before it is handed from one man to another, when crossing fences and ditches, and during walk-up shoots. On driven shoots all firearms are unloaded in between drives and put into canvas or leather gun sleeves or slips. It is very bad manners to shoot after a drive has finished (this is normally signalled by a whistle or a horn), and in the worst taste to march off like a vindictive schoolboy administering the *coup de grâce* to wounded game. Nowadays, environmentally conscious hosts insist that all spent cartridges are picked up at the end of drives. You are also expected to mark for the pickers-up and their dogs, as it is bad form to leave dead birds to rot. Portable telephones are quite out of place on a shoot, and if brought, should be resolutely switched off. One peer fines his guests if theirs ring.

THE GAME SEASONS
These are strictly adhered to, and all aspiring shots must learn the dates. Grouse, ptarmigan and snipe are the earliest: they start on 12 August (the Glorious Twelfth) and finish in December. Partridges run from the beginning of September to the end of January; pheasants from the beginning of October to the beginning of February; capercaillie from the start of October to the end of January; wild duck and geese from the beginning of September until towards the end of February; woodcock from the opening of October to the close of January. The dates are only a basic guide, and 'the bag in season', or what is to be shot and what isn't, varies considerably from one shoot to another. For instance, some pheasant shoots begin the season by shooting cock (male) pheasants only. Others work on a cock:hen ratio, which means you can pot a hen only after hitting a cock. Some shoots leave pheasants (more robust birds than partridges) alone until after Christmas. Others never touch pigeons or ground game (rabbits and hares). The position of foxes, too, is a vexed one. Rather grand shots will consider it in the worst taste to shoot foxes (after all, that's what hunting is for), while others, particularly if running a rough shoot, will be only too pleased for foxes (along with other vermin such as jays and squirrels) to be killed. It is usual for hosts to explain the form before setting out. However, many forget

because they take their own rules for granted. Thus it is a good idea to ask what guests are allowed to shoot.

THE SHOOTING DAY

The days when every self-respecting country estate (no matter how small) boasted shooting parties throughout the season to which friends and family were constantly invited are long gone. Nowadays even the grandest families let their shoots for long stretches of the seasons to make them pay, and even operate syndicates at which participants (even family members) pay for a day's sport. When invitations are offered it is invariably with an ulterior motive of sporting reciprocation that season, and few shots can expect to be invited more than once a season. Also, the number of invitations is commensurate with a gun's technique. Word soon goes around about astonishingly good shots, who quickly find their diaries filling up during the winter months. Bad shots are treated to exactly the opposite response.

SHOOTING TERMS

Like all ancient and evolved British customs, shooting has a lingo of its very own. The most important semantic fundamental is that a *gun* does not refer just to the firearm, but to the man shooting it too. The *drive* is each sweep undertaken during a day's shooting. The *stand* or *peg* is where guns are stationed on all shoots other than grouse ones, when they are positioned at *butts*, or in *hides* for duck. *Beaters* (sometimes known as *drivers*) flush out the game. *Loaders* do what their name suggests, particularly when guns are *shooting double* (with two guns – increasingly rare). The *hill* is how a moor is referred to in Scotland. A *piece* is a packed shooting lunch north of the border. A *covert* (the 't' is never sounded) is a wood. A *covey* is a group of grouse or partridge. A *bouquet* is for some a group of pheasants. A *wisp* is a delightful term for a group of snipe. *All Out!* is what beaters call at the end of a drive. The *bag* is game killed in a day. A *brace* means two birds (one male and one female) and is used for grouse, partridges and usually pheasants. Wild ducks are counted by the *couple*.

SHOOTING KIT

Traditionally the only acceptable gun on a British shoot was a double-barrelled side-by-side model. This is still the preferred weapon, but the prejudice against over-and-under-guns is receding. Needless to say, automatic or pump guns are so beyond the pale that they don't figure. The most popular guns are .12, but .16 or .20 calibre is acceptable, providing you

275

equip yourself with enough cartridges. Add to this a cartridge bag, gun sleeve, and hip flask, which should be generously handed around.

SHOOTING CLOTHES

The classic three-piece shooting suit with plus-fours or breeks, no matter how archaic its appearance, remains the most practical and stylish dress for shooting. It should be made of very hearty tweed in colours that blend into the landscape. There is a fashion for increasingly colourful garters, but these may raise eyebrows in serious shooting circles. Combat camouflage gear will cause laughter, and ersatz shooting clothes bristling with toggles and patches send out dubious messages.

On smart shoots it is necessary to wear a collar and tie. Rollnecks are suitable only for more informal forays. Hats are *de rigueur* and can be either trilbys or caps. A good waterproof (such as a Barbour) and green studded boots are also advised, although the sturdiest of Scottish shots may scoff at any man who needs more than tweeds and brogues to protect him from the elements. Boots that come over the ankles are recommended for very wet conditions.

Most guns, especially if the weather is clear, like an early start. It is important to arrive on time, for shooting is one area of our national life where punctuality is still greatly valued. Late-comers should not be surprised if the party has moved off without them.

On a properly organised driven shoot, the guns stand in a firing line at positions marked by a number on a stick and which have been drawn earlier in the day. A team of beaters drive the game over the guns by walking in a line towards them. The number of guns can range from a handful to around ten: more than this is difficult to manage properly and safely. As the middle of the line usually gets the best sport, it is customary for guns to swap their positions as the day goes on, so that all have a share of the best birds.

GENERAL BEHAVIOUR

A shoot is not the place for flamboyance. It is important to keep as quiet, still and out of sight as possible so as not to frighten the game off. The expression 'shoot at sky' is often given as a code for a day's shooting: this means if you can't see sky behind the birds, don't shoot. It is bad manners and dangerous to swing the gun grandly along the shooting line, or to shoot ahead of you (i.e. towards the beaters) or anywhere that could be remotely interpreted as in the direction of the other guns. Do not be surprised if you are asked to leave the field for such transgressions. By the same token, if you see another shot behaving badly, tell either him or your host immediately. It is important to keep a record of your hits and to mark them so that they can be retrieved afterwards. However, it is in bad taste to be boastful about your score: it is not unusual for guns to shoot the same bird simultaneously, but it is bad form to 'poach' another's bird, that is, one that is coming towards him and is obviously his quarry. On the other hand, if he misses or merely wounds it, it's fair game for one and all. Winged birds should be promptly finished off. It is better manners to use both barrels on one bird in order to dispatch it properly than to attempt a right and a left without being certain that the first bird is dead. On a plentiful day it is sporting to pick out only the more difficult high-flying birds. It is deeply unsporting in any circumstances to blow a pheasant to pieces at short range. This was a sad phenomenon of the eighties shooting boom, when pheasants were bulk-bred with little attention to quality, and huge, overfed birds could be seen sluggishly heaving themselves towards low-altitude annihilation. Luckily the more austere nineties have restored quality to the breeding pens. A white pheasant should never, ever be shot.

DOGS AND OTHER COMPANIONS
On a properly run shoot, where there are plenty of picker-uppers to retrieve shot game, your dog may be not appreciated. This being said, many guns see it as their right to have their dog with them if they wish. In such cases the beast must not run in before the end of the drive (except to pick a winged – wounded – bird, or 'runner'), as this is irritating for other guns and is also dangerous. Certainly on smaller shoots properly trained gun dogs may well be welcome. Always ask first. However, on no account should an ordinary pet (i.e. a non-gun dog) ever be taken.

Companions of the human species can also be more trouble than they are worth, and can greatly lessen a gun's chances of being asked back. Always ask first if friends are acceptable. It is never a good idea to bring along a chum who has no idea of the finer, or not so fine, aspects of shooting conduct, and a compete solecism to attempt to 'share' your gun with him or her. It is you, not your friend, who has been invited to go shooting. It is therefore advisable for any companions to be as unobtrusive as possible. They should, however, dress as if they are shooting and not out for a day's sightseeing, avoid inane chattering, particularly at the firing line, and generally keep out of the way. Non-shooters can, however, be helpful for reloading guns, keeping gun dogs under control and marking the position of fallen birds.

GROUSE

Considered by its *aficionados* as the ultimate shooting experience, and certainly by me as the most delectable game for the table, grouse shooting has its own way of doing things. For a start it takes place on open moorland rather than woodland, the preserve of the pheasants. Thus the guns have little natural cover and are normally stationed in a line of stone- or turf-built butts, rather than at numbered pegs. The sport is exacting and provides a *frisson* not apparent in the safer pursuit of pheasants. Grouse fly quickly and low, tracing the contours of the moor, and often appear for only a few tantalising moments. Thus guns have to be quick, agile and able to shoot low without imperilling those around them. Not for beginners.

THE SHOOTING LUNCH

This can range from a few sandwiches brought by the participants, to grand sit-down affairs on the moor or back at the house. It is normally eaten in the middle of the day, but if light is limited, such as in the depths of the winter, or for practical reasons, guns sometimes shoot through until the light begins to fade, with only a swig of hot soup or Scotch for sustenance. Guns and beaters never lunch together, and neither side would have it any other way.

THE BAG

This is the haul of game shot. At the end of the day it is usually divided into a brace of birds for everybody, and the rest are sold off to game dealers to help pay for the beaters and other costs. It is the greatest compliment to shoot a lot of game for your host, as the quantity of game shot on an estate will indirectly add to the value of his property. On a grouse moor there is a tradition of giving each gun two brace – one old and one new.

A properly organised shoot is labour intensive, and the result of considerable planning on the keeper's part. It is thus customary to tip him, and any loaders and beaters, at the end of the day, when sharing out the bag. Around £20 for a good day is an acceptable minimum, although some estates have very exact indices calculated against the quantity of game shot. Some estates don't tip. Again, ask your host the form.

THANKING

A thank-you letter should always be written after an invitation to shoot. Quite often, if staying at the host's house, a present is also appropriate.

THE GAME BOOK
This is where guns keep a careful tally of all game shot or caught. The late Douglas Sutherland tells, in *The English Gentleman*, of one man in whom that habit was so ingrained that 'when he decided to take his own life he was careful first to enter himself in the game book under "various" before pressing the trigger'.

Hunting

Hunting, never fox-hunting, is the most exhilarating of country sports. It can also be extremely dangerous for the inexperienced: many are the broken limbs (and worse) at the end of the season. Its etiquette is the social manifestation of the sport's rules, conventions and safety procedures, and needs to be mastered by the novice.

In recent years the sport has been put under increasing pressures. The best known of these are the disruptive attentions of the sabs (saboteurs), whose methods are far from well mannered. Farmers are, quite understandably, more and more sensitive to economic damage. And unfriendly parliamentary murmuring threatens the very existence of the sport. Despite these problems, hunting has never been more popular: there are more people hunting than ever before, and record numbers are coming to the sport for the first time.

The hunting season begins in November, but is preceded by a cub-hunting season (now often known in our more squeamish times as pre-season hunting), which starts once the harvest is in. Cub-hunting, a dummy run for the main season, is when new hounds are initiated and the pack is coached into working as a team. It is by invitation of the Master and usually happens in the very early morning.

Beginners can find it difficult to get a day's hunting, and need to be invited by an existing member. It is sensible for the newcomer to make his first appearance on New Day (a special day for newcomers), and in the company of his mentor. It is not sensible for newcomers to hunt on Boxing Day or other big days, because the field will be very full. First-timers should aim to go out midweek, when numbers will be much smaller. If new to a pack, it is also sensible to ask the hunt secretary if he might introduce you to someone who could act as your pilot and look after you on the day.

When out for the first time, the best course of action is always to keep your head down, to avoid uncontrollable behaviour, to respect the countryside and the position of farmers and other landowners over whose land the hunt thunders, and, most importantly, to remember that houndwork – that is, the skill of the Master and his huntsmen in controlling the pack – is the *sine qua non* of a successful day's sport, and thus needs to be respected.

279

All these criteria will be considered should you wish to join the hunt, which like all clubs admits only new members who respect its rules, have a knowledge of the sport and share an *esprit de corps*.

THE MFH

The MFH, or Master of Foxhounds, has long been an important figure in country life. He has supreme control over his hunt and can send anybody home whom he considers to be behaving badly. It is his decision to blow for home when he thinks it appropriate at the end of a day's hunting. On correspondence it is polite always to use the initials MFH after his (or her) name. All members of the hunt must address the Master as such on the hunting field.

Many hunts have two or more masters, known as Joint Masters (the most senior being the longest serving). Very often, when one of the Joint Masters hunts hounds (this is known as carrying the horn), his junior member will act as Field Master. He will also be assisted by professional or amateur huntsmen.

OTHER SPECIALIST TERMS

The hounds are always known as *hounds*, without the definite article. It is the greatest hunting solecism to refer to them as 'dogs'. They come in *packs*, and their tails are known as *sterns* but pronounced 'starns'. Hounds never bark, instead they *give tongue* or are *speaking*, and their noise is called *music*, maybe because hearing it is indeed music to the ears, as it lets the hunter know the pack is on the track. Hounds are counted in *couples*, are said to be *running* when hunting, and their direction, i.e. the scent of the fox, is called the *line*. Like all canines they live in *kennels*, but are divided into the *dog* and the *bitch* packs, and, although traditionally hunted on different days, many hunts are now mixed. A male fox is known as a *dog* and a female as a *vixen*. A fox's tail is called a *brush*. The *field* refers to the horsemen taking part, but not the master or the hunt servants.

DRESS

Hunting clothes are madly dashing, but their sartorial conventions need to be properly understood, as they indicate the wearer's role on the field. They should not be put together in too arty a way, as preciousness has no place on the hunting field.

The Master and Hunt Servants

These wear a hunting cap; a hunt coat that is cut with a wider skirt and higher collar than that which members wear and which is pink (scarlet) or in the hunt's specific colours; a hunting shirt with a stock, a waistcoat, white breeches, top boots (i.e. those with unpolished mahogany-brown tops) with spurs, gloves and a crop.

Members and Guests
The correct and most dashing headgear for men is a silk top hat (specially made to a greater thickness and strength than ordinary ones), which is also an excellent defence against brambles. Nowadays there are models with built-in skull caps to make them more secure. However, on some hunts nowadays it can be thought of as being too swanky (particularly if worn by those who are coming to the sport for the first time). Instead many men wear velvet riding caps, which are more practical. In the interests of safety, many of the army regiments insist on their men wearing crash helmets. Chin straps are also now acceptable. In some hunts, particularly in the New Forest and the north, men wear bowler hats, but in most cases this headgear is usually sported by farmers. Even jockey caps are seen on some hunts, but, it must be said, not on smart ones. The rest of the outfit consists of a black coat, buff – preferably buckskin – breeches, a hunting tie with a plain pin, yellow or white gloves and plain black hunting boots.

Women wear similar outfits to men. They generally sport bowler hats or black riding caps. Those who ride side-saddle – increasingly popular and much less precarious than it looks – dress in a riding habit and wear either a bowler or a top hat with a veil. Both sexes wear the hunt button, once awarded. Children traditionally wear bowler hats, although in some countries (this is how a hunt's area is defined) they often wear riding caps with chin straps.

Although there is no firm rule, 'Hunting Pink' is the usual way to refer to the distinctive red or scarlet hunting jacket. One custom is, however, written in stone: it is sported *only* by the Master of a hunt and by other men at his invitation. The only exceptions are hunts that have their own colours, such as the Beaufort, where a very handsome blue and buff is the order of the day. The Master can also wear his own hunt colours when hunting with another pack. The hunting tie is supposed to protect the neck from whiplash caused by endless fast jumping, as well as making an instant bandage, sling or tourniquet in emergencies. It must always be tied firmly and secured with a plain gold pin, which is fixed horizontally for safety reasons. Spurs are an essential part of hunt dress, and if you do not possess your own they can be hired at a local livery stable. 'Rat-catcher' is nothing to do with roaming rodents, but is an outfit that consists of a long tweed jacket, buff breeches or jodhpurs, black or brown boots and a speckled stock or tie. It is worn by male and female members and guests for cub-hunting. It is also how children are dressed throughout the season. Waxed jackets are very frowned upon, particularly on the smarter hunts.

HUNTING'S FUNDAMENTAL RULE

The most fundamental rule of hunting is that it is not the member personally who is hunting the fox, but a pack of hounds under the skilled direction of the MFH and his huntsmen. They are totally responsible for the hounds and are aided by two or three whippers-in. Thus it is vital neither to get in the way, nor to cross the line so as to let your horse kick the hounds – remember always to turn your mount to face hounds as they pass close by. The greatest of hunting solecisms is to overtake or ride in front of the Master, unless specifically asked to do so. It is also bad form to follow the pack like a galloping limpet, although there is usually a line for the field to follow, led by the Field Master. Neither is it done to ask the Master about his plans for the hunt. And finally, it is the ultimate sin to sleep with the Master's wife, no matter how hot-blooded the chase makes you.

A TYPICAL HUNTING DAY

Most hunts start very promptly at quarter to eleven or eleven o'clock in the morning, with the meet. This is a glorious sight. Being late is an insult to the Master and the hunt. It is usual for those who live nearby to hack there, while those who come any distance have to box it and must remember to park with all four wheels off the road. It is essential to say good morning to the Master and Field Master. Everybody has to pay a cap fee. This is never given to the Master or his staff, but to the hunt secretary or his deputy. It is always given in cash: one parvenu who was heard to enquire 'Do you take Amex?' was nearly sent home. The cap fee must always be settled before moving off. Never wait to be asked.

When coming to a meet, it is important to be immaculately turned out. Also allow plenty of time to avoid the horse being in a sweat because it has had to race to get there. If at a lawn meet, always thank the hosts for any hospitality.

The proceedings then begin with hounds being taken to a covert (pronounced 'cover') to flush out a fox, with the rest of the field following, keeping a sensible and silent distance so as not to distract the hounds. When the fox breaks cover, a short ('gone away') blast is signalled by the horn, and the hunt is on and continues until the fox is killed, lost or goes to ground. The fox, of course, often disappears during a day's sport, and much skill and scent are employed trying to find it. If you see the fox again before the Master, it is best not to start hollering, but to try to indicate its presence to the huntsmen (perhaps by touching your hat, lifting it and gesturing it in the direction the fox has run, then pointing your mount towards the quarry), so as not to distract hounds and have lots of unseemly shouting on the field. At the kill remember to keep your horse away from hounds and expect to look after a hunt servant's horse while the final rite is being carried out. Always bid goodbye to the MFH when leaving the hunting field.

GENERAL HUNTING MANNERS
Respect for the Countryside
A large hunt can create a huge amount of mayhem on farming land. Thus it behoves those hunting not to be selfish in the pursuit of their sport and to try to maintain a good relationship between the hunt and farmers. This means never riding into fields being grazed by livestock, trying to avoid fields planted with crops, and not trampling down market gardens. Remember that much of your subscription goes to repairing damage to the country and that care in hunting will prevent your payments increasing, as well as improving your hunt's standing in the locality.

Highway Code
It is very important not to obstruct roads and country lanes. Always pull to the side to allow cars to pass, and remember not to linger on roads in between runs, as the majority of hunting accidents involve collisions with cars.

Kicking
If your horse is a kicker, make sure that it sports a red ribbon on its tail, and keep your distance from other riders as much as possible. It is thoughtful to stay at the back of the field. To avoid kicking hounds, make sure that your mount faces them when they pass. Should this precaution fail and a hound gets the hoof, then the honourable thing to do is to report it to the hunt staff and write a quick apology letter to the Master after the meet.

Jumping
Jumps add enormously to a good day's hunting, and good manners make sure that everyone gets a slice of the action and avoids accidents. Always

283

try to allow other riders enough room to get a proper run at a jump, never cut in front of another who is about to leap, and, very important, do not go for a jump until the preceding rider is safely over. Any damage to gates and fences should be reported.

Gates

As always in country life, gates must be securely closed after use. However, during runs it is enough for each rider to push the gate open with his whip, move through, then hold it ajar for the following rider to move through and take the gate with his whip. The last one through should close it properly. Remember, as the VIPs of the day, the Master and his staff should have all gates swiftly opened for them. If someone dismounts to open a gate for you, it is polite not only to say thank you, but to wait for him to get on again before you ride off.

Barbed Wire

Often horribly dangerous, barbed wire is a hunting hazard and all riders should be warned if you see it. The traditional cry is 'Ware [pronounced 'wor'] wire!' Some riders carry cutters.

Chivalry on the Field

It would be ridiculous to consider the mostly fearsome females who hunt as the 'weaker' sex. Thus, most of the everyday courtesies that regulate civilised life are suspended on the hunting field, with one exception: if there is a choice between a man or a woman dismounting, for whatever reason – such as opening a gate – then it is expected that he rather than she gets down. Also, should a woman fall, it would be cruel not to go to her aid. One man who went to help a famous hunting peeress, who had managed to slip while riding side-saddle with the Belvoir, was greeted by the sight of the woman spread-eagled in a thicket. 'Can I do anything for you?' he enquired politely. 'Yes, kiss me!' came the reply. History does not relate his reaction.

SABOTEURS

Hunt saboteurs, also known as sabs, or antis, are the bane of the sport, and if you hunt, there is a good chance that you will have to deal with them. The approved manner is to treat them like any other normal member of the public. This is not easy, as their behaviour, which includes such anti-social acts as spitting, hurling abuse, kicking the horse, grabbing its reins, throwing stones at riders, blowing horns to confuse the hounds and spraying citronella to ruin scents, can hardly be described as in any way normal. The simplest and best approach is to ignore them completely and get on with the business of hunting the fox. Alternatively, you can just politely say: 'Good morning.' Should such disarming tactics fail, as sadly they often do, turn the other cheek and do not allow yourself to be drawn into playing their game. Altercations, or worse, physical retaliations, are to be assiduously avoided.

The smarter hunts tend to get a better class of anti, and the police are generally better informed about their movements. Although the majority of the police do a splendid job of keeping the sabs at bay, it is a mistake to assume that they are always on the side of the hunt – sometimes their sympathies are with the sabs. This being said, the new Criminal Justice Act, which contains legislation specifically to help the police control New Age travellers and hunt saboteurs, has proved such an effective weapon against the antis that a quieter time is being had across the country. It should also be said that silent, non-militant protest that does not try to disrupt the hunt has the most impact.

THE HUNT BALL

Once the focal point of the county social scene, hunt balls are not quite what they were. Indeed, many diehards would question that they should be described as balls at all. 'A ball is really when everybody dines in house parties before and then comes on, rather than the modern version, which are really just dinner-dances,' laments one old hunting hand. Traditionally hunt balls were always given at the local big house. These days they are quite often likely to take place in a hotel or other hired place. They are in effect like any other subscription dance, with people buying their tickets, and the proceeds going to the hunt funds. They are organised by committees and the guest lists are largely made up of all a hunt's subscribers, all farmers on whose land it hunts and people who have been coming for years. Breakfast is usually served. At the smarter ones, white tie with pink evening coat is still the order of the day (men who do not hunt wear ordinary white tie or Highland dress, where applicable), although many hunt balls are now just black tie.

Fishing

By fishing, country hosts invariable mean fly fishing for game fish such as salmon, trout, grayling and sea trout, not the more down-market coarse fishing popular with anglers along river banks up and down the land. The open season for trout runs approximately from March to the end of

September, but there are regional variations. Seasons for salmon and sea trout differ from river to river.

Many estates have their own fishing, which provides good income and, when not let, an agreeable and gentle sport for guests. As with all these specialist sports, it is bad manners for the novice to pretend to possess skill and experience he does not have. Quite understandably, noise is not appreciated.

Traditional rules on keeping fish are, however, changing. It used to be the rule that you kept everything you caught, for, like grouse, the value of the stretch depended on the annual catch. Nowadays, particularly in Scottish salmon rivers, the emphasis is on preserving ever more depleted stocks, as fewer salmon are returning. Thus, over the last ten years, a more conservationist spirit has informed the actions of fishing hosts, and it is now sensible to ask whether you are expected to put your sport back after landing it. After all, the whole point of this highest form of fishing is not so much the catch as the skill and sensitivity of the sport that precedes it.

Salmon fishing is sometimes referred to as the champagne of the sport and has the most developed etiquette. Most salmon rivers consist of pools of smooth-running water separated by rapids. Fishing takes place in these pools, and there should generally be no more than three fishermen, always known as 'rods', to each pool. When arriving at a particular pool you must never start downstream of someone already fishing there, as this is considered extremely bad form. Always start above them, and leave a good hundred yards between you and the next rod. If a neighbouring rod hooks a fish it is polite to reel in your own line to avoid tangling with his.

It is acceptable to cast your line as far across the water as you like – within an inch of the opposite bank if necessary, even though it may belong to a different owner. However, when wading or fishing from a boat you should not venture further than halfway across the water, unless both banks are owned by your hosts.

Having caught a fish and played it to the bank, you can either beach it on the shore or enlist the help of a fellow fisherman or ghillie. Established fishing etiquette expects people to help fellow fishermen land their catch. The old method of gaffing, when the fish is dragged in on the end of a spike, although not illegal is deeply frowned upon. This is not least because it spoils the delicious flesh of the fish.

On some rivers there are restrictions on the number of fish each rod may catch. For instance, on the Dee in Aberdeenshire, only one salmon per week is permitted during the spring. This is to counteract a recent scarcity of salmon making the spring run on some rivers. Such preservation orders are not law, but should be respected at all times. Your host will tell you if they apply on his river.

Finally, discarded pieces of fishing line should always be cut up into small pieces to eliminate the risk of birds and animals ensnaring themselves.

Stalking

Stalking, or deer-shooting, is a highly skilled sport that involves the stalking of red, fallow and roe deer through rough upland country until they are near enough to shoot. The usual firearm is a single-shot rifle. Seasons vary according to the location and the species being hunted.

CLOTHING AND ETIQUETTE

Correct clothes for stalking are necessary as much for camouflage and comfort as for etiquette. Tweed is preferred, in the form of a matching jacket and plus-fours or breeches. Waistcoats are optional. The cloth needs to be thick and tough to survive the rigours of a moor or hill, as a day's stalking may entail much crawling across rocks and boggy marshes in pursuit of the quarry.

Thick tweed is also a very good protection against rain and wind, and will additionally, and most importantly, help the stalker to blend into his surroundings. Red deer have highly developed senses of sight, sound and smell, and a garishly clad stalker will clear a hill of deer in minutes. Light browns and greens and heathery hues are the best camouflage; a novice turning up in red socks and a blue shirt will be made to go home and change. It is also important that clothes do not rustle: for this reason, brand-new Barbours and, worse still, modern wind-proof cagouls are frowned on by some hosts. A tweed cap or deerstalker should be worn, and suitable walking boots. Some stalkers like to wear gaiters over their socks or tied around their trousers for extra protection against wet and gorse. There are no rules here. Comfort is the key: a day's stalking could involve up to twenty miles' gruelling walking. It is also advisable to wear layers of clothing that can easily be peeled off and packed in a bag, as you can get very hot with all the upland exertions. Also remember to take some sustenance, such as a bar of chocolate and something to drink, as well as a pair of binoculars or a telescope, and a thumb-stick, which is essential when walking over hilly, uneven and sloping terrain.

Stalking also requires its participants to be fit. A host will be deeply unimpressed with a guest who has to stop every five minutes for a rest, and no one on the point of expiry is likely to manage to shoot a rifle properly. There are, however, sometimes exceptions to this fitness rule. A certain distinguished businessman used to be flown to the top of his hill in a helicopter. Whether this approach is sporting is debatable, but as he was over eighty and a fabulous shot, he was forgiven.

A host will generally organise his guests into one or two parties of up to four or five people. Groups larger than this make stalking impractical. Each group will be accompanied by a professional stalker, who will lead the sportsmen and guide them towards the deer. When the moment of shooting arrives, it is the stalker who decides which deer to shoot and when. He has the final word.

When a man shoots his first deer, it is still customary for the stalker or the host to blood the hunter by wiping a smear of the still warm animal's blood across his face. It is the worst form to appear anything other than utterly delighted to be on the receiving end of this ancient rite. Convention also suggests that the face should not be washed until the next morning at the earliest. Some stalkers also observe the old tradition of placing a bunch of heather from the hill in the mouth of the dead deer.

True sportsmen carry their rifles up the hills and through the forest, but a stalker will, if required, carry a guest's rifle for him. One host on the west coast of Scotland recalls how on one occasion all four of his guests insisted on using their own rifles and on obliging his stalker to carry all four guns on his back. The guests at least had the grace to offer him a hefty tip.

Finally, it is most important to be quiet on a stalk. Guests should follow the stalker in single file, and must not talk except in whispers. A stalker will probably be far too tactful to tell a guest to keep his voice down, but a loudmouth will ruin the day's sport for everyone.

14

THE NEW RELATIONSHIP
WITH DOMESTIC STAFF

The relationship with domestic staff has changed considerably over recent years. The days when people went into domestic service for ever are long gone, and with them many of the good and bad paternalistic attitudes of the past. Today's domestic servants are more likely to view their roles as part of their career path and not a way of life: hence the army of jolly Antipodeans who crop up nannying and cooking and also work in what is now euphemistically known as the 'hospitality business'. Modern servants are also likely to enjoy a more – but never totally – equal relationship with their employers. Added to this, today good help is extremely difficult not only to find but to keep, so modern servants are increasingly more highly valued than their predecessors and thus have a keener appreciation of their own worth.

However, there are still many abuses, particularly by people who, often as the first generation of their families to keep staff, don't understand that civility is the right of all citizens, regardless of their station in life. It is often the *nouveaux riches* who, as the proud possessors of the requisite inclination and funds, find themselves the custodians of the seriously grand manner.

The nature of employment has also changed. Whereas in the past staff were employed on a somewhat informal cash-oriented basis, stricter government controls on National Insurance and employers' liability for PAYE have meant greater responsibilities being placed on those who employ domestic staff. Added to this, increasingly rigorous asylum and immigration law is quickly tightening up many loopholes in the domestic help market. Those thinking about employing foreign nationals are strongly advised to check individual passports before making a decision.

Increased legislation has had two effects. The first is a growing tendency towards treating a domestic job as any other in the labour market. The modern servant now often has a proper contract of employment, in which terms about pay, holiday and notice are clearly spelt out.

The second effect, as in other areas of the economy, is the proliferation of freelance contracts and arrangements. Just as businesses save on cost and maximise choice by contracting out to specialists as and when they need them, private houses are now doing the same. Maids, cooks and drivers may work for more than one household on a self-employed basis. I know two art dealers who share a butler, who splits his week between the twin set-ups. There are rarely any problems unless both men decide to entertain on the same night. There is also a proliferation of agencies which come in to do basic services such as cleaning. As well as this, specific tasks – such as clothes care, dry-cleaning, laundry and mending, once the province of the ladies' maid and the gentleman's gentleman – are now often sent out to specialists.

The other major change is the blurring of traditional servant roles. In the old-style fully staffed houses, butlers, housekeepers, footmen, cooks, maids, chauffeurs and grooms existed in a very distinct pecking order and had very specific roles and duties. All this has changed. Jobs have overlapped to such an extent that the modern-day butler will probably find himself doing everything from opening the door to bringing in the wood.

Forms of address have also changed. Ever-increasing informality in the domestic sphere has had its effect on that most fundamental semiotic between master and servant – the way they address each other. Generally, when speaking to staff, first names are the order of the day. The old use of surnames only without any prefix is now so outdated that it is almost offensive and endures only in the most superannuated of set-ups. However, older members of staff, such as housekeepers over forty, may still be referred to as Mrs Homebody.

When it comes to how staff address their employers, the rule is still largely formal. Thus 'Sir' and 'Madam', 'Mr' and 'Mrs' (followed by employer's name) and 'My Lord' and 'My Lady' or 'Your Lordship' and 'Your Ladyship' are very much the order of the day. Dukes and duchesses are still usually addressed as 'Your Grace'. The use of 'Master' for young male members of a family is increasingly rare. In very trendy households, there is a fashion for employers to invite staff to call them by their first names. This, although well-meaning and egalitarian, can cause problems. In these matters there is always an invisible line that both parties cross at their peril, for by doing so there can be a confusion of relative roles, a gradual eroding of authority and unnecessary awkwardness at difficult times. None of this is productive.

Regardless of changing fashion, though, the fundamental tenets of a successful master/servant relationship remain the same: those of mutual respect and trust. As it is such a personal arrangement, the good manners of consideration, courtesy and kindness are even more important than in other aspects of everyday life. It is also vital for employers to sketch out the goal posts of the relationship and thus set the barriers that neither side will cross. This applies to privacy, confidences and modes of address. At all times it must be remembered that too relaxed and open an approach can lead to difficulties if there is a problem in the future, while too supercilious a demeanour will win you no friends below stairs.

FINDING THE RIGHT STAFF

The best way to find the right domestic staff is always by personal recommendation. Failing this, a reputable agency should be consulted, which will make a charge for its services. It is important to be absolutely clear about the type of person you are looking for and the terms offered. From this information an agency should send you suitable applicants. It is worth bearing in mind that the Royal Household is one of the best training grounds for domestic staff.

The interview should be conducted in a very businesslike manner. Many people, new to the wonderful world of proper domestic help, display either nervous awkwardness or overt chumminess at these meetings. Both approaches are inappropriate and unproductive. The most important thing is to be absolutely clear about the nature of the work expected. This is more essential today than ever, as the traditional roles of servants have over-lapped considerably. It is also vital to stick to that job description once they start: a good member of staff is a professional, not just a general *ad hoc* dogsbody.

References

References have always been important. In the modern world they are essential. Whereas in the past written references from a great house or other reputable source were taken at face value, now only a fool would rely on these alone. Thus it is vital to check all references, either by letter or by speaking on the telephone. The introduction of the fax has also meant that it is easy to substantiate references from all corners of the globe.

The same thoroughly professional approach should be used when giving references. It is important and considerate to any possible future employers to be utterly frank but fair about an individual's capabilities. It is very bad form, and culpable and dangerous, to recommend anybody whom you would shrink from re-employing.

The Contract of Employment

It is also now very important to draw up a proper contract of employment for the successful candidate. This will include not only all the usual terms of employment, but also an accurate description of the nature of the job and all its duties. In this way both sides know where they stand and there are likely to be fewer disputes if things go wrong.

THE FULLY STAFFED HOUSE

As recently as the sixties, fully staffed houses were quite usual. A mother of a friend tells of engaging a nanny in 1961, only to have her very quickly hand in her notice because her new position did not provide a footman to serve her dinner. Nowadays such grandeur is positively laughable. Only a handful of houses, mainly in the country, have the sufficient funds and inclination to run a fully staffed establishment. However, there are still many houses that employ some or all of the following.

The Butler

Although the butler remains the head of a household, he is now less likely to be the rather special being of before. His duties vary considerably from house to house. Traditionally he looks after the wine cellar, opens the door, hands round drinks, carves and serves at meals and generally makes sure that everything is done properly. In the absence of footmen, valets and chauffeurs he can also adopt the role of general factotum. However, he would generally not be responsible for the care of children or for very domestic tasks such as cleaning or bed-making.

There is also, in the case of the very rich, a new breed of super-butler who, in many ways, has replaced the lady of the house when it comes to domestic arrangements. Now wives often have their own businesses and interests and do not want to spend their mornings going through menus and paying tradespeople. In these cases the butler will actually be given a budget to buy supplies and services for his master. In really sumptous houses the super-butler wields sums as substantial as those of a small business, and uses computer technology to run his accounts, keep a record of guests and their likes and dislikes, and order the private jet down the modem.

Footmen

These 'baby butlers', often be-liveried, are now extremely rare, but are still to be found in households where seriously lavish entertaining persists, and are extremely useful. Their job is to help the butler hand round drinks, serve diners and clear plates, and to perform more menial tasks such as cleaning the silver, etc.

The Housekeeper

Just as traditionally the butler was the senior male servant, the housekeeper was his female equivalent. Today's housekeepers tend to be less Mrs Danvers and more Mrs Mop, but they are vital, particularly for large families who enjoy having house guests. The housekeeper is in charge of basic domestic necessities such as cleaning, bed-making, shopping and sometimes cooking. In very large and grand houses she may have a team working for her, but in most cases she will probably have to perform these duties with the help of a daily. It is not usual for the housekeeper to be expected to look after babies and children. In the old days housekeepers always lived in, but today there is an increasing tendency for them to come and go on a daily basis.

Cooks and Chefs

Culinary expectations have increased enormously in the last few years. Thus the residential 'good plain' cook of the past is likely to be somewhat out of her depth with the sophisticated, health-conscious palate of today. Therefore in her wake has come a new breed of peripatetic cooks who can rustle up anything from a Thai lunch party to a sushi supper. There is also a fashion for those with gourmet tastes and deep pockets actually to employ a proper chef, who will whip up dinners of the highest professional standards. These people are stars in their spheres and their duties revolve around the kitchen and no further. Some of these super-chefs become so well known that they leave to open restaurants.

The Chauffeur

The chauffeur, often now referred to as a driver, is one category of staff that is still very much in evidence. Often linked to – and paid for – by business, he is usually responsible for driving just the head of the household around and is not necessarily meant to be at the beck and call of all family members and house guests, although I do know of one clan that employs no fewer than three chauffeurs for the benefit of its highly social members. The chauffeur is also responsible for the upkeep and cleaning of the car/cars. With certain high-profile families, he might also be expected to combine the skills of security officer and bodyguard.

Maids

This today covers a multitude of female domestic roles, ranging from a simple daily to a female factotum. However, the old-fashioned parlour maid, whose role was equivalent to the footman, has gone the way of the Ealing comedy.

Valets and Ladies' Maids

Now little more than a memory for most people, these are private functionaries, whose duties include personal needs such as pressing, cleaning, laying out and looking after clothes, polishing shoes, dressing, waking up, running baths and accompanying on trips. I know of one woman whose maid not only dresses (and undresses) her each day, but even dries her after her bath. These instances are very rare. The valet or lady's maid's duties are now more likely to be absorbed into other domestic functions or contracted out to specialists.

The Personal Assistant

This new form of domestic staff is a combination of modern PA and traditional servant. Like the secretary who runs the office, the personal assistant is the amanuensis of the house. His or her duties encompass everything to do with the employer's private life, including shopping, organising laundry and dry-cleaning, entertaining, travel arrangements, some driving, serving and other services associated with the traditional butler and valet, as well as supervising other domestic staff such as dailies, cooks and caterers. As the traditional distinction between home and work life has become blurred, the home PA will spend a great deal of time liaising with the office staff. In many cases his costs are put through the business. The relationship between employer and personal assistant is likely to be more informal than with the old school of domestic and be similar to that enjoyed between a corporate boss and his secretary. Thus this role ideally suits current egalitarian attitudes.

The Nanny

The nanny has always enjoyed a very special place in British domestic life. In recent years, however, the form she takes has changed considerably. A more fluid society and modern attitudes to child-rearing have all but completely seen off the starched matron of yesteryear, both beloved and reviled by the older generation. These women not only subsumed any intention of producing their own children, but actually took on the surname of the family that they worked for, with Nanny Yorkshire considering herself far grander than Nanny Smith. They tended to work for the same family indefinitely, often rearing two generations before being retired to a distant eyrie, where they spent their dotage knitting, mending and reminiscing. Neither family nor staff, but both at the same time, they occupied a closely guarded social no man's land.

This world, for better or worse, has gone. Today's nanny is more likely to be a young girl (or now very occasionally a boy), who may not see nannying as a vocation for life, but more as a good and fulfilling way of earning a living, seeing another country, travelling and meeting people. She is also likely to be a lot more expensive than dear old Nanny Brown, and expect perks ranging from all her personal items such as toothpaste being included in the family shop to her own car. She, also unlike her chaste forebears, may have followers – in many cases rather a lot of them.

Of all domestic staff, the nanny is the most important, for she looks after people, not plate. Unlike other categories, demand for really good nannies greatly outstrips supply. It is thus vital to be extremely careful about who you choose. Always go for a properly trained nanny. She will have completed two or more years' training in child care and education at either one of the top residential colleges, such as Norland or Princess Christian, or within the state sector. The traditional qualifications have been superseded by the Diploma in Nursery Nursing awarded by the Council for Awards in Children's Care and Education (CACHE). However, it is important to remember that training varies considerably, and although the inputs are often the same, the outputs are often very different, and not all girls will be *au fait* with the care of the very young and the newborn. Always check relevant training and experience very carefully.

The applicant must come from one of the reputable agencies or schools or by direct recommendation from a close friend, although remember that a nanny who has been an excellent employee for one family may not be the appropriate choice for another. Rigorous scrutiny of her references is essential. Always read them carefully and then check the facts yourself verbally with the referees. Also ask the referees frank questions, such as the positive and negative qualities of the applicant, whether they would re-employ her, and even if they consider her suitable for the prospective charge/charges. Interpret any reticence as a red light.

It is then vital to conduct interviews on your ground to make sure that she will fit in. Remember, however, that although the interview is ostensibly for the family to interview the prospective nanny, she/he will also be making judgements, particularly when it comes to a residential post. The interview is also the time to be utterly clear about the terms of employment, the nature of the work and house rules. Most professional nannies are usually seeking employment that involves only nursery duties, and are not prepared to take on the light housework, secretarial or other chores that ill-mannered employers often try to fob off on to them. These ancillary functions are for an au pair or mother's help, not a professional, qualified and experienced nanny, who would feel insulted to be treated as a domestic.

Nowadays it is expected to have a second interview or more informal meeting with the children concerned so that an employer can make sure the chemistry works. (Norland College insists on an overnight stay.) This is usually done in the presence of the parents, but in some cases the prospective nanny can be left alone with her new charges. Do not employ a nanny if the children really dislike her, but remember that children have a natural caution if they are losing a nanny they are fond of, and will need a period of readjustment.

The successful applicant should then be provided with and later asked to sign a written contract outlining details of hours, pay, holidays, conditions offered and duties required. It is in everybody's interest to have a written contract. This piece of paper is priceless, as it sets in stone the relative positions of both parties and avoids the all too often sudden departure of a new but dissatisfied nanny after a few weeks.

The ideal relationship between a nanny and her employer has also changed. Today she is much more likely to be a co-parent than a surrogate one. Modern hands-on mothers want to have the last word and to control how their children are brought up, and are not willing to cede control to old-fashioned-style nannies who were notorious for wanting everything their own way in the nursery. Generally speaking there are two types of post, the formal and the informal. The contemporary nanny, except in very grand houses, is likely to be treated much more like a member of the family. It is in these informal posts that the qualities of mutual trust come into their own.

The role of nanny also differs from that of other domestic help by the very intimate nature of the work. Thus, when employing a residential nanny, it is important to make sure that she has her own privacy and space to relax in after work. Her free time should be respected and not exploited. If she is expected to baby-sit, this needs to be stated in the contract and included in her package. Live-in nannies can expect the use of the telephone, but how much needs to be clarified to avoid endless expensive long-distance calls. Some houses give their nannies their own line for this reason. The employer also needs to be very clear about regulations concerning visitors, and particularly boyfriends, coming into the house. Whereas it is fine for a nanny to have some callers, a stream of visitors – especially nocturnal ones – is quite unacceptable.

The Maternity Nurse

Now extremely fashionable, the maternity nurse looks after a new baby for around the first six weeks of its life. She is sometimes a nanny of the old school who fancies a quick stint with a baby rather than becoming involved on a longer-term basis. Often maternity nurses are some of the best child-care professionals around, as they have the energy and flexibility that makes them very sought-after. The services of a maternity nurse are sometimes given as a present by a mother to a daughter, and are ideal for getting mother and baby into a routine. Her duties consist of around-the-clock care of the baby, and do not extend to anything else. She also helps the mother during a period when she is feeling absolutely exhausted and possibly, if it is a first baby, scared about being on her own with the demanding bundle.

The Mother's Help

This is a kind of poor woman's nanny. The main part of her job revolves around assisting the mother with the care of infant and children, but she is also expected to muck in with household duties such as cleaning, ironing and shopping.

Au Pairs

A staple of British bourgeois life, the au pair occupies a special role in home life. She is normally an unmarried girl, sometimes a single boy, between the ages of seventeen and twenty-seven who comes to Britain to live with an English-speaking family for a maximum of two years to learn the language. Non-EC nationals need to register with the Home Office, or at the local police station if living outside London.

The au pair is not a servant. Her (or his) role is to help the family with light housework, some laundry and ironing, looking after small children, picking them up from school, and so on. She is, however, not a professional nanny, and should not be expected to take sole charge of children for long periods. Neither is she a cleaner, laundress or odd-job person. Cleaning the windows or the car, ironing an entire household's laundry, digging the garden or shampooing the poodle are not appropriate chores for an au pair. Under Home Office guidelines, an au pair works for up to five hours a day, five days a week, and possibly Saturday mornings. She can also be expected to do two or three nights' baby-sitting. It is usual for the au pair to work part time in the morning and afternoon/evening, leaving her free to go to language classes during the day. In return for her domestic duties, she receives free board and lodging, as well as a small allowance in excess of £35 a week. Most families also buy her a travel pass. She is responsible for paying for her return fare to England and for her language tuition. As au pairs come to a country primarily to learn its language, it is bad form to use her sojourn as an opportunity to brush up on your French, Polish, Swahili or whatever her native tongue is. Families should encourage her to study and speak English with the family. In general, an au pair eats with the children/ family during the day and has supper either with the children early in the evening or later on her own. As national customs vary enormously, it is both useful and courteous to explain house rules as soon as an au pair arrives. Non-smoking or vegetarian households are best advised to employ kindred spirits. As with nannies, au pairs are entitled to their own room with a desk and preferably their own television, but not to a rampant sex life on the premises.

The Daily

The daily is today the mainstay of many houses' domestic routines. Even great piles that once boasted a rich and varied indoor staff that today could run Claridge's are kept up by a team of doughty dailies from local villages. London houses too are kept in order by an often unseen army of Philippinos, Eastern European, Spanish and other women (occasionally men) from around the globe. All have their national idiosyncrasies. All, if they are any good, need to be treasured, as good dailies are hard to find. The main function of the daily is to keep the house clean. She, or he, may additionally be able to do ironing, mending and a spot of gardening. Advanced, super-diversified dailies can also be asked to do a little simple cooking and serving at parties, but it must be remembered that these skills are optional extras and usually reflected in a greater fees. Dailies are paid by the hour, although those who do ironing often charge by the piece. Households unable to find an individual daily can enlist the services of one of the increasing number of cleaning agencies, who take on contract cleaning which is also charged on an hourly basis or by the job.

The Couple

This was seen as the answer to the servant problem, but often does not live up to expectations. The ideal couple are mature but not doddery. He does the traditional male duties such as buttling, gardening and driving, while she looks after housekeeping and cooking. Such couples are hard to find, tend to be expensive and will usually require pretty impressive accommodation, such as their own cottage. However, when the arrangement works, it makes a splendid back-up. One family employed a very camp gay couple, who so relished their roles (which they performed excellently) that they left to set up a guest house locally.

Temporary Staff

This sector of the domestic help market is now huge. It is ideal for the many modern houses that exist only with the support of dailies and nannies, and that enlist the help of specialists only when necessary. These include professional caterers, cooks, butlers, florists and waiters, as well as young students or aspiring actors supplementing their incomes. Many individuals develop a private coterie of households for whom they work regularly; others offer their services through agencies and party planners.

As with all domestic staff it is vitally important to go through a reliable employment agency. There are many dubious people about, and you do not want them walking around serving drinks at your party. There is one man, reluctant to pay agency prices, who assembled a motley crew of waiters to work at his birthday party. Only he was surprised to discover that half his silver had mysteriously disappeared by the end of the evening.

Agency staff can be paid directly, with the agency's commission charged separately; alternatively the whole thing can be invoiced at a later date. The fees for waiters, bartenders and cleaners are usually counted by the hour, whereas cooks assess their charges by the number of people they will be catering for. Tips are optional and can attract tax.

When employing a temporary cook it is most important to brief her/him properly beforehand. One young cook tells the story of being packed off to a distant corner of Scotland for a four-week stint cooking for an eccentric family during the grouse season. Expecting merely to rustle up roast birds with all the trimmings for hungry guns, she was mortified to discover that she also had to provide a full catering service for the family's collection of teddy bears!

A temporary cook needs to know in advance the number of guests, the nature and level of formality of the party, weekend or holiday, and whether there will be other staff to serve and wash up. She is responsible for all the shopping, preparation and cooking of food and will often supply extra cooking equipment if a house is lacking in the necessary *batterie de cuisine*.

Good temporary butlers are worth their weight in gold. They will completely run your party, open the door, take coats, organise the waiters, or hand round drinks and canapés at drinks parties and serve at dinner parties. Like temporary cooks they need as much information as possible beforehand to do their job properly. As well as the usual butler preparations, such as laying the table and decanting wine, they can often supply drinks, glasses and other equipment from their professional contacts. If hiring a butler on an individual basis rather than via an agency, ask him to supply you with an invoice.

Temporary waiting staff can range from hardy professionals to less experienced part-timers. Whereas the former can be safely left to get on with their job, the latter will need directions from either the host or his butler. Temporary bartenders must be properly trained.

BABY-SITTERS
Baby-sitters are recruited either from specialist agencies or, more usually, by private recommendation. They are paid by the hour and should always be given emergency numbers. It is usual also to leave them supper, and polite to ring if you expect to be later than arranged. It is also proper to offer them a taxi home or, as is increasingly the case, a bed for the night.

CATERERS
Catering firms are necessary for any large-scale entertainments beyond a household's usual domestic resources. They are ideal for weddings, dances and other large gatherings. They provide not only the staff, but everything you need for a particular party, including tables, chairs, linen, lighting, silverware and flowers. If employing a caterer for the first time, always ask for a tasting from the menu to avoid disappointment on the night.

CLOTHES FOR STAFF
These too have changed. At one time domestic staff sported very distinct uniforms. Now this is no longer the case. Many servants, if not quite wearing their own clothes, are seen in much more neutral outfits than before. In the case of women this is perhaps just a black skirt and white blouse. Butlers, except in TV dramas, rarely sport the tails and stiff collars of yesteryear; these have been replaced by a short box jacket worn with striped trousers, or just a dark suit. The same is true of footmen, who today are more like junior butlers and are sadly rarely seen in their splendid livery of the past. Traditional nannies of the Norland College variety still wear

uniforms, but for the majority – particularly the new breed of child-carer – jeans and sweaters seem almost endemic. Housekeepers, dailies and cleaners usually wear suitable clothes for housework. Au pairs wear their own clothes. Chauffeurs wear either proper uniforms with peaked caps, or dark suits.

SALARIES, ACCOMMODATION AND PERKS

Increased expectations on both sides have seen considerable improvements in staff conditions. Salaries are far more generous than before and are likely to include provisions for pensions and private health care. Accommodation has come a long way since the freezing semi-dormitories of the past. Today residential staff will expect at least a comfortable room and their own bathroom, if not a flat or cottage. Many staff, particularly those who have to do a lot of running around, are also given a car. When it comes to time off and holidays, there needs to be a certain amount of give and take. As servants often travel with their employers and, in the case of very rich people with several houses, have long periods to themselves, holidays are often restricted to two or three weeks a year. Time off also depends on circumstances, but as a general rule of thumb one and a half days a week is a guide. If, however, a staff member has worked flat out – say through a couple of weeks of solid shooting – then it is thoughtful to give them the weekend off. Staff will always expect tips from weekend guests, who should leave their gratuities in little envelopes with the name of the servant written on the outside. All domestic staff receive Christmas boxes, which are always given in cash as a type of bonus. Clever staff also give Christmas presents to their employers.

DISCIPLINE

It goes without saying that employers who provide a high level of salary and conditions are due a similarly impressive standard of work from their staff. However, problems, ranging from simple laziness manifesting itself as unpunctuality, to more heinous crimes such as pilfering, do occur. In these cases it is important to deal with difficulties immediately. In the first instance, a quiet word in private is recommended: staff should never be ticked off in public. If this goes unheeded, two written warnings (always keep copies) should be sent. If all this fails, then the sack is in order. All criminal activities must be reported to the police.

A similarly hands-on approach is also recommended when there is inter-servant squabbling between staff about who does what and who is senior to whom. This problem happens usually only in houses where there are several staff members and in establishments where employers have been woolly about responsibilities, territory and lines of command. In these cases it behoves the employer to sort things out tactfully but firmly by perhaps giving written job descriptions. Troublemakers should be weeded out, as they can be a very disruptive influence on other staff members.

FOLLOWERS

At one time a rigid morality forbade 'followers' to such an extent that it was a miracle that those in service ever managed to reproduce. Things today are obviously more permissive. However, particularly if the house is small and there are children in a family, it is not acceptable for residential staff to entertain at home. They should expect to play away from their place of employment. In larger establishments, where staff may occupy flats and cottages away from the family, a more relaxed regime may prevail. In these cases the employee must always ask permission from his or her employer to have visitors.

15

BUSINESS MANNERS

Business manners, although obviously stemming from the same roots as social manners, have developed their own codes and protocols. They are also, in a business climate that has become less gentlemanly and more competitive, insecure and ruthless, increasingly difficult to sustain with any amount of conviction. However, many behavioural patterns endure, and good manners remain a useful and much appreciated tool and weapon, both within the corporate environment and in the world of business outside.

How companies organise themselves varies enormously, depending on the type of industry they operate in. Law firms remain formal, while the media world becomes increasingly casual. The new emphasis on freelance and flexible working contracts has also affected the old certainties – and thus manners – that previously prevailed in large paternalistic and corporatist companies. Nevertheless, certain truths are as real as ever. First, regardless of how a company or department is structured, people remain fiercely territorial about their patch: this is a fundamental fact that governs all office courtesies. Second, nobody likes dealing with rude, abrasive or obstreperous colleagues.

APPLYING FOR A JOB
The best way to apply for a job remains by word of mouth, head-hunter or personal recommendation. The possession of one or more of these weapons will put you at an immediate advantage over the competitors who have

merely applied from an advertisement. This being said, all candidates are subject to the same selection procedures.

The Curriculum Vitae

Most people make the mistake of making a CV too long, and cramming too much – often irrelevant – information into it. Good CVs are short, rarely more than one page, and must be clearly, neatly and simply typed out. Any attempt at wild or winsome originality is to be avoided. I once received a CV in the form of a hologram, that my office and I found impossible to read.

The CV should have your full name, date of birth, address, schools, universities and colleges with relevant academic achievements, and details of your current and past jobs. Previously it was the form to list events in chronological order, but now the job history begins with the current employment and goes back in time. The giving of references at the end has become less important, as references are followed up after an interview. However, if you do specify referees, there is no need to enclose copies of the references with the CV. Such eager anticipation smacks of desperation.

The CV should be accompanied by a short covering letter. It is vital that this should be neat, grammatical and properly spelt and that the addressee's full name, title and address is absolutely correct. Anything less is the first breach of business manners. The use of 'Dear Sir or Madam' is such a solecism that most missives that begin thus are immediately slipped into the waste-paper basket. The phrase 'please find enclosed' is best not used. Opinions differ as to whether a job application letter should be hand-written or typed, as some employers set considerable store by applicants' handwriting. Personally I think it should be typed, with the salutation and sign-off put on by hand. After all, those with graphological criteria presumably can tell enough from this. A good covering letter could read thus:

Dear Miss Opportunity,

I understand that Robert Reference has spoken of me to you, and of my wish to discuss working within your organisation. I have long admired your company from the competition benches, and now feel that I have much to offer your firm. Here, as promised, is my curriculum vitae.

I look forward to hearing from you.

Yours sincerely,
Johnnie Hopeful

As you can see, the letter is concise and quietly tempting. Remember that finding the right job is about making a mutually beneficial partnership and that an initial application is merely to introduce the applicant.

Interviews

Interviews are like school examinations. Some people are good at them and others are not: both groups can easily give a false impression of themselves. Is said that we form most of our opinions about people in the first few minutes that we meet them. It is therefore essential that you are feeling and looking your best. You should also be punctual and have genned up on the organisation you are being interviewed for. Your demeanour should be enthusiastic but never pushy, friendly but not sycophantic, focused but not aggressive, and keen but never desperate. Always shake hands. Do not smoke unless offered a cigarette. You will be asked about your experience to date, and told what the role you are applying for will entail. It is polite to wait to ask your questions until after the interviewer has asked his. It is important to remember that, in addition to your qualifications, drive and ideas, an interviewer will be looking for someone who is going to fit in. It is therefore advisable to empathise immediately with him/her or them (if you are being seen by a selection panel) and remember that a little charm can go a long way. Smarm, even in small doses, is to be ruthlessly avoided.

By the same token you must bear in mind that the right job is one that not only offers the salary, challenges and prospects you seek, but that you will enjoy doing day after day. If being interviewed informally, say over lunch or a drink, remember that the interviewer will be observing how you react not only to him, but to the world at large.

References

These are normally from past employers, or from individuals who know you. Either you will be asked to hand them over at the interview, or the new company will ask for names, addresses and telephone numbers so they can approach them directly. The old rule of one professional and one character reference still holds good. It is rude to offer someone as a referee before seeking their permission first.

The Follow-up Letter

A short but not obsequious letter after the interview is both polite and expedient. It should thank the interviewer for his time, define any grey areas that remained after the meeting, restress salient points and finish by emphasising how much you would enjoy working for the organisation and how much you feel you have to offer.

The successful applicant will be told the good news either by telephone or by letter, and will receive a contract, which he or she should read carefully. Many companies are rather more tardy about getting in touch with those who have been rejected. This in itself is not good manners, and it is therefore perfectly acceptable to ring up if you hear nothing.

MANNERS IN THE OFFICE

Although once in the early part of my career I was criticised for treating the office as if it were a sedentary cocktail party, I still believe that manners are as important at work as they are in a social setting. Thus the simple courtesies of saying 'please' and 'thank you' apply. The basic tenet of good manners – that nothing should be said or done that might cause embarrassment or offence – should also be borne in mind at all times, although as there are many occasions when difficult actions need to be taken and harsh things said, its application becomes problematic.

This being said, things should be done with grace. In everyday office life it is important to cultivate an amicable (this does not mean over-friendly) relationship with everybody, and to assume, unless proven otherwise, that colleagues are good at their job and are generally worthwhile human beings. There is no place for aggressiveness or distrust.

Loyalty

Despite the often appalling cavalier attitude many companies display towards their employees, loyalty to one's boss and company remains a fundamental behavioural necessity in the office. This does not mean that you should not question policy, nor work doggedly for the same outfit all your career. But it does mean that as long as you stay in a company's employ you should remain, at least in public, totally loyal to it.

Punctuality

Although the greater laxity in social timings has influenced business punctuality, it is bad manners to be late for work, meetings and conferences, etc. It is particularly rude to be late for outside appointments. If you are delayed, always ring *en route* and apologise on arrival.

Hierarchy and Pecking Orders

Despite the arrival of trendy modern management methods, companies big and small remain deeply territorial organisations. Those with good manners

306

respect other colleagues' professional space. In well-run offices the pecking order and line of command are usually pretty well defined. In others a little research might be needed to avoid treading on toes.

As a general rule of thumb, offices are much more casual than previously, with first names being increasingly universal in all but the most old-school establishments. However, this does not mean that there is any excuse for overfamiliarity, as many have discovered to their cost. Superiors, by the very nature of their position, need to be deferred to. This does not mean that they cannot be disagreed with, but it does mean they are not to be disobeyed. They should never be sucked up to: sycophancy is in the worst taste.

Professional equals need also to be treated as colleagues and not rivals. It is generally bad manners to summon a colleague to your office, unless it is to meet someone who is visiting the organisation. When the colleague arrives it is important to stand up and introduce them to the visitor and offer them a seat. It is also extremely bad form to palm off your own work on to another, to use their space and desk as a dumping ground and constantly to borrow their computer, staplers and other office supplies.

It is in the treatment of subordinates that the bad mannered show themselves at their worst. Everybody in a company, regardless of their position, deserves to be treated with respect. Not to do this is a serious breach of business etiquette. Therefore juniors should never be ordered around, patronised or humiliated in public. Their bosses should remember that juniors expect them to structure their working patterns, give them a little encouragement and let them have a life outside the office. One well-known businesswoman is renowned for under-using her secretary in the day, only to present her with some massive task at around 5.20. It is also bad manners to ask your secretary to do things that are not his or her responsibility: this ranges from acting as a messenger of awkward tidings to colleagues, to expecting him or her to organise your social life as well as your business one, which is very bad form indeed. Those who share a secretary should set the ground rules on how his or her time is to be partitioned, and not leave it up to the junior to make embarrassing choices.

The secret is to look on any relationship with a subordinate as a partnership, and to delegate as many tasks as you feel the junior can cope with. After all, the more you empower others, the more new responsibilities you are free to take on for yourself.

Difficult Conversations

In most cases it is unattractive and unnecessary for managers to throw their weight around with subordinates. Most people know their place in the food chain and are aware of who in the end calls the shots and has the last vote. Any awkward or potentially embarrassing conversations, such as criticising a colleague's standard of work, must always be done in private. It is the height of bad manners to cause a scene in public. Discussions about pay increases are often thorny, and can be very awkward when bosses of large public companies who receive vast salaries appear mean with the smaller fish in their pond. This being said, salaries are invariably the biggest outlay on a company's books, and directors are always at pains to keep costs under control. In such circumstances it is clever policy and good manners to have all relevant facts at your fingertips, such as comparisons with salaries paid in other similar companies, past increases and actual present performance.

The most difficult conversation of all, that of firing somebody, is particularly onerous. This should always be done in person, never through a third party, or worse, by letter, memo or fax. In cases of a serious misdemeanour, such as stealing, embezzling or other fraud, there is no need to feel anything more than regret. At other times, when circumstances within a firm have changed, when reduced performance requires redundancy, or when people's roles have become obsolete and there is nowhere else for them to go, the dismissal must be done in a way that preserves the greatest dignity for the recipient. Some people maintain you should always fire people in the morning. All would recommend that it is good manners and practical to stress the more positive aspects of redundancy, such as generous payments and glowing references. All parties should aim to be as frank and amicable as humanly possible, as the same people have a habit of reappearing again and again in any industry.

Office Courtesies

Old-fashioned chivalry has a limited role in the modern office. For instance, it is not necessary for men to stand up every time a woman comes into a meeting, and whereas in social life men are always introduced to women, in the corporate environment it is silly to present the chairman to the junior secretary. Lifts, however, are different. It is still good manners for men to let women in first, regardless of their place in the office hierarchy. Also, smart corporate bosses maintain that it is polite, when receiving visitors at work, for the secretary to meet them at the lift, but for the boss to return them to it after the meeting. Social kissing has no place in an office except when someone is about to disappear off on a three-week holiday. In general terms, bodily contact must be kept to a minimum in the office. Good managers should make sure they know the names and jobs of all their employees, except in exceptional circumstances, such as vast manufacturing companies, when such knowledge would be impossible. One publishing magnate commissions a corporate video each year of his staff so that he can mug up on their names and roles. When travelling for business with colleagues, it is neither good manners, nor clever management, for the top people to fly club and the more junior ones economy. All the party should travel together to promote team spirit and to allow time to discuss strategy.

Dress

Dress codes today vary enormously, from the most sombre suits in the traditional City institutions to Lycra cycling shorts and T-shirts in the case of certain inner London local authorities. Any employee has to strike the balance between conformity and individuality. However, one thing is certain: to arrive at the office looking grubby and down at heel is not only bad manners, but bad strategy.

BUSINESS STATIONERY AND CORRESPONDENCE

Business stationery differs from its social sibling in several ways. Although, like social stationery, it should be of the best affordable quality, as cheap paper with an unattractive letterhead can make only a bad impression, business writing paper is generally larger than social – A4 size being the most usual dimensions, although a supply of A5 is also useful for very short missives. Letterheads tend to be printed rather than engraved. Thermography, although anathema on the social scene, is sometimes acceptable in a business context (e.g. for invitations), although I must confess to finding it universally grisly.

Stationery design and graphics should obviously reflect the character and business of the company concerned. It should include the firm's logo (if appropriate), its address, telephone, fax, e-mail and other numbers, such as Internet site. It can also encompass the registered address (if different from the trading one), the company registration number and sometimes the list of directors. Unlike social paper it can also show the name of the sender. In the case of freelances and sole traders this would be centred on the top of the paper. In the instance of an employee in a corporation, his name, followed by his professional title, would go on the left-hand side of the paper under the main information of the letterhead. Business stationery should also include the ever-useful correspondence cards, compliments slips, possibly stick-on labels for large envelopes, fax sheets (unless WP-generated) and envelopes, which, unlike in social life, can have straight flaps.

The secret to business correspondence is to keep it to a minimum. This is particularly pertinent in the age of junk mail, when every office is inundated by unwanted rubbish. Therefore a letter or fax should be written only when a telephone call will not do, such as when specifying a contractual arrangement, making an unusual request, presenting new ideas that need to be mulled over, or making points that need recording. They are also useful when expressing professional (not personal) thanks, condolences or congratulations, and replying to formal invitations.

The business letter is, however, a great weapon. If you have had a disagreement, it is an expedient way of laying out your argument while simultaneously patching things up and promoting a reasonable response. It will clarify any misunderstandings after an inconclusive meeting or telephone call. It can also be used to charm. The fundamental points of a good business letter include the following: first, it should be neatly and professionally typed, although to avoid the mass-produced word-processed-looking letter, many of the more sophisticated captains of industry and commerce always top and tail by hand. The other exception to the typed rule is a quick note on a correspondence card to a business acquaintance, thanking him for lunch, etc. Second, all names and titles should be a hundred per cent accurate. Third, its contents should be expressed as clearly and succinctly as possible. Even more than in social correspondence, new paragraphs should be started for each fresh idea. Jokes are best not cracked in a business letter, unless you are a friend of the recipient.

Nowadays a business letter should be laid out in a fully blocked style, with no punctuation outside the body of the letter. Old-fashioned establishments may like to retain the traditional fully punctuated and indented style. However, a hybrid that combines aspects of both ancient and modern is to be avoided.

Letters that open with 'Dear Mr Clark' should end 'Yours sincerely', and those that begin with 'Dear Sir' close with 'Yours faithfully'. It is always recommended to write to a specific person rather than an anonymous Sir or Madam, which should be used only when it is impossible to address a specific individual. The use of 'Yours truly' is virtually obsolete. Letters, particularly to people you already know, can be personalised, by adding 'With best wishes' or 'Kind regards' at the end, or by topping and tailing letters by hand.

The Use of Ms

The use of Ms is a convenient female equivalent of Mr and is widely used – and accepted – in business. However, it remains more correct and altogether smarter to find out exactly how a woman prefers to be styled, whether it be Miss, Mrs or Ms.

The choice of a woman's surname, once she has married, can also present problems. Many women, for convenience's sake, continue to work under their maiden name. Others, particularly those with traditional views on marriage, go through the often convoluted process of professional conversion to their husband's name (women who do this are strongly urged to initiate their new identity immediately they return to work after their marriage). Others compromise by taking their husband's surname, but retaining their own first name, as divorcees have traditionally done. So instead of being known as Mrs John Married, a married woman would call herself Mrs Jane Married at work. Increasing, although still small, numbers of women are adopting the American habit of creating a double-barrelled hybrid of both spouse's names. For instance, a woman who was previously just Stephanie Single becomes Stephanie Single-Smith on her marriage to Mr Smith. All forms are correct.

Company paper should be used only when communicating company business. Therefore it ought not to be used for totally personal letters (i.e. when the message has nothing to do with the professional self), missives that express personal rather than corporate opinions, freelance activities that have nothing to do with the job, applications for positions in other firms, or letters making complaints to department stores or requesting loans from banks.

Business Cards

Whereas personal cards are an increasing rarity, business cards proliferate like wire hangers in a wardrobe. While social cards should always be classically understated, the business variety can be more assertive. Their style should obviously mirror the nature of your operation. The size varies depending on how much information needs to be contained, but smaller is always preferable to larger. The name is centred with any professional qualification and role. Traditionally the address goes either on the bottom left-hand side with the telephone, fax and e-mail numbers on the right, or is arranged in one long line at the bottom of the card, although there is increasing scope for other design solutions. The company name can go either above or below the employee's name. Logos are generally placed above. Prefixes such as Mr, Mrs and Miss are generally not used.

The Business Telephone

When answering a business line it is recommended to sound reasonably pleased to hear from the caller. Bored or irritated responses reflect badly not only on the individual but on the organisation too. It is unprofessional just to say 'hello', as is usual at home. It is important to announce your name or department – both if necessary. When picking up a colleague's telephone it is useful to refer to that person by saying: 'John Brown's office', 'John Brown's desk' or, more informally, 'John's line'. If JB is taking another call, then tell the caller and ask whether they would like to hold. If JB's conversation seems as if it is to be a protracted one, then it is polite to take a number, possible message, and say that you will ask JB to return the call. Good message-taking is a fundamental office courtesy. It is vital, in addition to writing down fully and legibly the caller's name, to take his telephone number as well (even if he says your colleague already has it). The date and time of the call is also useful. Avoid writing messages on corners of documents, backs of envelopes and sundry pieces of errant paper where they could easily be overlooked or lost. It is exceptionally rude and disconcerting to leave a caller holding on to a silent line for long periods, wondering whether they have been cut off, forgotten, or, even worse, ignored. Really courteous people always refer to the caller's name, once they know it, by saying: 'Mr White, I'm afraid that Mr Brown is still on the other line.' If at any stage the line goes dead, then it is up to the caller to ring back. Once a message has been left, it is then the obligation of the recipient to return the call. It is rude to ignore messages and to force the caller to ring back, as it is for those who take messages for absent colleagues or bosses to ask callers to call again later.

The telephone, as well as being a medium of communication, is also an instrument of protection. Difficult, unwanted or merely inconvenient and ill-timed calls can be dealt with in several ways, none of which should involve rudeness. Very trying, time-wasting and pointless ones need to be terminated as quickly as possible, by saying honestly: 'I'm sorry, there is really nothing we can do to help' and maybe suggesting a genuine alternative. On no account should the buck be passed to an unsuspecting colleague, just because you cannot be bothered, or are frightened to deal with an unpalatable task; and under no circumstances – no matter how abusive the caller becomes – should you lose your temper. Ill-timed calls need a subtler treatment. 'I'm sorry, Mr Brown is busy' is ill mannered because it implies that he is involved with matters of much greater magnitude than anything the caller might wish to discuss. 'I'm sorry, he is out of the office' should be used only if that is indeed the case, as it is easy to be rumbled. 'I'm afraid he is in a meeting', although it has developed overtones of the brush-off, is fine, but somewhat distant. 'He is away from his desk' or 'with someone' is better, because it suggests only a very temporary absence. 'He has been in meetings all day' should be used only when absolutely necessary. 'He has been in meetings all week' means that all pretence at civility is at an end. If you take a call that requires a response you are unprepared for, it is expedient to say: 'I'm so sorry, but I'm already late for a meeting. Could I call you back later?'

Useful though these little dodges are, they are not to be relied upon to any great extent, for like all shields they weaken with overuse. All calls, no matter how awkward, need to be dealt with and returned sooner rather than later. It is invidious to expect subordinates to act as a buffer. It is also inadvisable to pretend to be your own secretary when fielding your calls. This little ruse is not unknown but is invariably found out and suggests a certain duplicity as well as cowardice. The same is true of hiding behind answering machines.

However, as people are expected to be busy at work, business calls should be short and to the point. It is good manners to have all relevant paperwork assembled prior to placing a call, rather than rudely causing breaks in the conversation while you shuffle bits of paper around. Also, if the call is to be in any way long or complicated, then it is thoughtful to enquire if it is a good time to talk. When making such calls, I sometimes find it useful to start off with a brief resumé along the lines of: 'I've rung you to discuss three things – A, B and C'; this sets the parameters of the conversation, and also gives the other person time to order their thoughts.

Personal calls remain a grey area in the office. Although theoretically companies discourage private telephoning, and some actually monitor calls to ascertain who is spending their working days ringing their friends, personal calls have become an integral part of office life. The secret is not to make them a dominating factor. It is distracting for colleagues to work to an intrusive accompaniment of somebody else's social arrangements and personal dramas, and irritating for them to take endless non-professional messages. A friend of mine works with such a person, and now feels she is so *au fait* with her life that she could begin the official biography – not that she feels the reading public would be particularly fascinated.

The Business Answering Machine

Once a rarity, answering machines are fast becoming integral components of secretary-depleted offices and essential to those who work from home. The recorded message should therefore be cheerful and businesslike. Attempts at idiosyncratic whimsy are best reserved (if used at all – I would recommend not) for machines that serve a solely domestic or social purpose. Unlike on private lines, the announcement should include the number and the name of the person, persons or department the machine serves and should give an indication of whether they can be reached another way, such as on a mobile number. The message left should be equally professional, and should include the caller's name, the nature of the call (unless confidentiality is required), the time and sometimes the date of the call. All information should be as brief as possible. Some indication of the urgency of the call is also recommended. Answering machine owners should remember that it behoves them to check their messages regularly, return calls soonest and not expect those who have left a message to ring again.

Facsimile Machines

These have so improved office communication that we all wonder how on earth we coped before. However, like all good things they are open to abuse. It is irritating to ask people to fax you something that can be easily discussed over the telephone – this is a ploy used by the slow-witted to give themselves time to try and understand things, and is not appreciated by busy people of normal intelligence. Unless the recipient is in possession of a private number, faxing is not recommended for anything that might be considered remotely personal, contentious or embarrassing. Faxes are also not suitable media for invitations or thank-you letters.

Faxes should always be sent with a covering page that gives details of the sender and recipient and the number of pages contained in the document. Because much of their attraction is connected with speed and convenience, they should be as short as possible; there is still something dispiriting about receiving reams of paper reminiscent of a television advertisement for lavatory paper.

BUSINESS ENTERTAINING

Business entertaining, although superficially very similar to everyday socialising, is actually quite different. It is also divided into two distinct types: external, i.e. the entertaining of clients; and internal, i.e. office parties.

The Business Lunch

This today is the most frequent form of external business entertaining. Although the basic tenets of social entertaining apply, there are several business-only aspects of etiquette to be borne in mind. The first is that, although any business lunch should be a convivial and relaxed event, it must be conceived for a reason more than just the purely social, such as selling an idea, getting to know a contact better or thanking for services rendered. At the same time, it is also important to point out that a business lunch should never be intended or taken as a bribe. Second, unlike a purely social affair, guests and hosts are expected to talk shop at some stage of the proceedings. Some very direct types get down to business straight away, thus leaving the rest of the time for fun and gossip. I find this approach somewhat unsubtle, and would recommend introducing the main topic early in the second course. Third, the placement has nothing to do with social conventions. People are placed where it is most expedient for business. It is usual for the selling parties, regardless of sex or social precedence, to sit as much as possible facing the buying parties, thus avoiding distracting turns of the head. Fourth, time is of greater consideration, with the epicurean epics of earlier times appearing old-fashioned and unprofessional nowadays. Although it is rude to rush a business lunch, there are little time-saving devices, such as arriving punctually, going straight to the table for an aperitif rather than spending time in the bar, and rarely ordering pudding.

THE CHOICE OF RESTAURANT

The perfect business restaurant is somewhat different from the ideal social one. First, it should not be too noisy or too crowded, unless it is your aim to make considered thought and discussion impossible. Second, it should be reasonably formal and well run, so that you can get on with your job and the restaurant's staff theirs. Third, the tables should be reasonably spacious, to allow room for notebooks or other relevant papers (although it must be said that to clutter the table with bumph is inappropriate in a restaurant and should be kept for the meeting room). Fourth, there should be adequate space between tables to ensure confidentiality. Fifth, it helps if you choose a restaurant where you are a regular. Alternatively, you could consider eschewing restaurants completely, in favour of entertaining in your own boardroom or other presentable space. This is an increasingly popular, cost-effective and more personal and private way to entertain.

Lunch or Dinner?

Some individuals, particularly workaholics, appear to make little distinction between the business lunch and dinner. Most people, although happy to attend a short business cocktail after work, still prefer to spend the rest of their evenings off duty with their partners, family or friends. The exceptions to the lunch-only guideline are when foreign clients and contacts are in town and need entertaining, or large official dinners such as professional award ceremonies or congratulatory get-togethers.

Corporate Entertaining

This can mean anything from sponsoring a polo tournament, or inviting hundreds of your closest friends, clients and allies to a cocktail party to launch a new product, to merely taking a few business associates to the opera. The aim is the same in each case: to present the company in the best possible light, so that it appears successful, stylish and accessible. The tone should be the soft rather than the hard sell, and thus any direct business negotiation is out of place at such gatherings.

Invitations for corporate entertaining vary depending on the scale of the event. An invitation to the opera or a box at Ascot can be made informally over the telephone and then confirmed in a short letter afterwards. For a cocktail party or lunch a printed or engraved (thermographed if you must) card needs to be sent no less than two weeks, preferably one month, in advance, perhaps accompanied by a short letter or press release if extra explanation is necessary. A major event will need an invitation card, a reply card, perhaps an itinerary, travel instructions, and any badges, passes or car park stickers, and need to be sent out no less than a month in advance. The stationery should of course be of the best quality and taste that budgets allow.

All invitations need to be comprehensive in the information they offer. This includes what the event is, who is giving it, its timings, its location, the food and drink that will be served – e.g. 'Champagne' or 'Luncheon', etc. – and perhaps some idea of dress – e.g. 'black tie', etc. Most importantly, it must include an easy R.S.V.P. Except with the most formal of invitations, it is now usual to write a name and number for replies. Alternatively enclose a reply card. Guests must reply immediately so that hosts can ascertain numbers for caterers. It is deplorable manners to emulate certain ill-bred types, who store up unanswered invitations and turn up on the day if the fancy takes them. It is also an affront to etiquette to accept invitations to sit-down breakfasts or lunches and then not bother to show up without ringing first to offer apologies. When a guest receives an invitation that asks him or her along with a guest, it is sensible to nominate someone who knows the subtle differences between corporate entertainment and a private party and will easily integrate in a quasi-professional environment. I invariably take business friends to whom I wish to reciprocate hospitality or thank for a favour, and who understand that corporate entertaining is as much to do with work as it is with play.

316

The practicalities of organising a corporate party and a private one are very similar (see Chapter 12). However, there is one small but crucial difference. Whereas people can be accommodating about a private celebration that is not entirely up to scratch, they are much less forgiving of a business occasion that is anything less than immaculate. Thus it is vital to ensure that all corporate entertaining is professionally and stylishly organised. This means engaging the right caterer (or party planner if it is a major event), composing a well thought-out invitation list and making sure that members of staff behave in an exemplary fashion at all times. Plastic name tags, although often worn at down-market conferences, have no place at a smart corporate party.

The Office Party

This is the domestic face – and in many cases the down side – of corporate entertaining. It can be a staff-only event, generally taking place at Christmas, when long-standing employees leave, and at sundry times when a little bureaucratic bonhomie is thought in order. For such informal gatherings it is not usual to have a specially printed invitation. Memos, e-mail and telephone calls are all suitable conduits. Alternatively it can take the form of a large annual party, such as the much-maligned and rather less popular annual dinner and dance, when employees bring a partner. Here an appropriate invitation would be produced.

The major behavioural pitfalls of such events are drunkenness and indiscretions, both sexual and professional. All are inadvisable and most are bad manners. Etiquette (and kindness) demands that no one within the department/company should be left out of the invitation list and that guests should circulate and not stick to their usual cronies. If there is dancing, the same applies, and the plain, the unpopular and the unimportant should not be made to feel like wallflowers. It is bad manners and pushy to monopolise the boss, who will want to circulate. On the other hand it is rude not to talk to him or her – albeit briefly. If there are spouses present, then the old idea of the first and last dances being theirs still holds. Couples, no matter what the state of their relationship, must present a united front in the office. It is not expected to write a thank-you letter after an informal office party. However, if it has been a formal, expensive bash, then it is polite to pen a few words of appreciation afterwards.

MEMOS AND MEETINGS

Memos are to be treated with respect both by those who send and by those who receive them. They are used when it is necessary to express thoughts, information and directions that require a permanence that a spoken communication would not give. These include documents that need to be kept on file, agreements, announcements, minutes from meetings, outlines for new projects and amendments to old ones. They should not be used for very personal communications such as complaints, or indeed praise, about job performance, when a letter is more appropriate. Senders should use memos when they feel comfortable about there being a permanent record of their message. The written style of a memo, as with all business correspondence, should be short and simple, but not curt or pompous. There is no salutation or sign-off. Memos are always typed and dated. The words 'Private and Confidential' should be typed across all those that require discretion. Copies should be sent to all relevant parties as well as the direct recipient.

Meetings form an integral part of office life, but should not be an overriding factor, as time spent in conference is time away from other tasks. Clever managers announce not only the time a meeting will start, but also when it should close. Meetings should take place only when there is a good reason, and should consist of only those who are directly relevant. They ought to happen in a congenial place conducive to constructive discussion, and should have a clearly defined agenda, which, if possible, should be known to the participants beforehand, to enable a little preparation. Everybody attending should arrive punctually. Meetings can range from a small informal chat between colleagues to a full-blown conference or board meeting, where it will be necessary to nominate a chairperson to make sure the proceedings are efficiently and fairly run. This chairperson can either be elected by his or her peers, or will, more likely, be the most senior person present. It is he who should ensure that everybody gets a fair crack of the whip, without descending to mud-slinging abuse or time-wasting monologues; and at more formal convenings he declares the meeting open, manages the agenda, takes the vote and closes down the proceedings. At important meetings it is usual to have a secretary to take minutes (notes), which are circulated to all present afterwards. It is bad manners not to turn up at a meeting where your presence has been requested, to appear uninterested or bored once you are there, to monopolise AOB (any other business) at the end with personal and probably irrelevant hobby-horses, to dominate the meeting, to interrupt others, to allow personal animosity to govern your demeanour to anyone present, to mutter asides to the person seated next to you, to air opinions afterwards to selected colleagues that you were too cowardly to bring into open discussion, and, worst of all, to storm out of a meeting in a huff.

PRIVATE LIVES IN PUBLIC PLACES – THE OFFICE AFFAIR

Although the old dictum, 'Keep your pen out of the company ink,' is by far the best advice, it does not prevent vast numbers of people from embarking on affairs with those they work with. Once colleagues become couples, they have generally crossed the relationship Rubicon and things will never be the same again within the office. Therefore the well-mannered and sensible approach is discretion, decency and decorum at all times. If two people are conducting an illicit liaison that they wish (invariably vainly) to remain a secret, then they must not be seen arriving or leaving together, enjoying cosy lunches *à deux* or canoodling in the car park. If the affair is to become public knowledge, it is good manners to tell the head of department or managing director first. Once official, an office affair, and its repercussions, is heavily scrutinised, and shrewd lovers will aim to leave their love at home. It is bad manners to bring private life into the public arena of the office. Thus PDAs (public displays of affection) are to be discouraged. By the same token, private squabbles have no place at work. I once worked in an office where two people conducted a volatile and blatant relationship that regularly descended to abusive altercations and once actual physical violence. The effect was distracting, embarrassing and ultimately so divisive that the junior member of the relationship was obliged to leave. Favouritism, often a by-product of a special relationship, is also insidious and has to be carefully watched.

Should a couple decide to marry, they must inform management at once. Company policies on this vary enormously, from disapproval so outright in some old-fashioned firms that one partner is expected to leave, to altogether more liberal reactions, in which congratulations and a small office party to celebrate are in order.

SEXUAL HARASSMENT

Sexual harassment is so much in the news that no modern office seems to be complete without it. However, a genuine charge of sexual harassment carries with it strict penalties and should never be made lightly. This being said, to press unsolicited sexual attentions – either verbal or physical – on a colleague remains perhaps the worst office manners, and victims of such abuse, no matter how junior their position, should not in any way feel forced to endure them or suffer in silence. In the first instance, most cases of unwanted advances should be dismissed firmly but good-naturedly. If they continue, it may be necessary to ask a superior to intercede on your behalf. In these circumstances the embarrassment to the perpetrator is normally so crushing that libidinous overtures cease immediately.

OFFICE POLITICS

Good manners and office politics, although uneasy bedfellows, are not mutually exclusive. There are certain simple procedures that can ease tension, aid communication and lessen feelings of isolation and victimisation. For instance, it is bad manners to spread rumours, to gossip incessantly about others, to form divisive cliques, to sneak on a work-mate, and to malign colleagues and the firm. It is not good office politics to seem stressed, overworked, irritable, resentful if others receive promotion or praise, and conceited and bumptious if you do. It is not clever to grease up to the managing director but be rude to the messenger boy. It is politic and good manners to be polite and positive with everybody at all times, unless special circumstances require otherwise. The canny employee, no matter how Machiavellian his tendencies, resists the temptation to enter the political arena unless absolutely necessary. Office politics, rather like salt, can in small quantities improve any dish, but used in excess will lead to an attack of biliousness.

Resigning

All good things, and sometime bad ones, come to an end. In virtually all cases it is inadvisable to leave an employer on acrimonious terms, whatever the actual circumstances. Therefore, unhappy employees should resist the temptation of having an embarrassing showdown and storming out. It is customary to write a letter of resignation to a department head or managing director, which again should be devoid of bitterness and mud-slinging. If, however, the employee feels irredeemably disgruntled about his situation, a verbal face-to-face is invariably better than a written one, as such epistles can be interpreted as libellous in a court of law.

Those who find themselves in the grim position of being sacked, whatever their inner feelings, should never lose their temper, as very little can be gained by such a display. The same can be said of pleading for clemency and another chance, unless you want to lose your dignity along with your job. The maintenance of manners, no matter how superfluous they may seem, will enable you coolly to negotiate any settlements that are due to you and to live through the purgatory of your remaining time in the company, whether it be half an hour to clear your desk or a more protracted period of notice.

Office Collections

When someone leaves an office, unless the circumstances are irredeemably acrimonious, it is usual to hold a small farewell drinks party at the end of the person concerned's last day. The drink can either be paid for from office funds or from a whip-round. Either way, it is also usual for there to be a collection for a goodbye present and card. Etiquette expects all members of an office (with the possible exception of temps) to contribute, no matter what their private opinion of the leaving individual might be. It is also customary for those who put in money to sign the card. It is not done for those who refused to contribute to include their monicker.

16

TABLE MANNERS

Table manners are rather like accents: easy to learn, but difficult to get right. Many people make the mistake of over-gentrifying the way they eat and end up looking affected in a way that was once called 'genteel' and today just looks ridiculous. Recently, I recall seeing a rather spherical woman daintily trying to dissect a kumquat with a tiny knife and fork: the effect was both impractical and comical, and suggested the nineties equivalent of the twenties housewife drinking her tea with her 'pinkie' in the air.

The best table manners are the most unobtrusive ones: manners that imperceptibly oil the prandial proceedings and get the food eaten as elegantly as possible. A well-mannered diner is attentive to others around him, both socially – by talking to other guests – and in a practical way – by making sure that, in the absence of staff, dishes, condiments and wine are passed around to all who need them. The best-mannered dinner companion is one who puts others' needs before his or her own.

To understand the mechanics of elegant eating, we need to look at the tools of the trade. The knife remains the principal eating implement. Pre-dating the fork by several centuries, it is held in the right hand, its handle lying in the palm while being secured by the thumb on the side and the index finger on the top of the handle. On no account must it be held like a pencil: resting on the side of the hand between the base of the thumb and the index finger. It is also recommended to try to hold the knife as high as possible and not let the index finger creep on to the top of the blade, where it might pick up deeply unappetising particles of food. Eating from a knife is excessively bad manners.

If the knife was a symbol of our primitive eating habits, then the fork can be seen as a sign of our ever-developing civilisation. Introduced into general use during the seventeenth century, it is used in conjunction with the knife and spoon, as well as on its own. When used with a knife or spoon, the fork should be held in the palm of the left hand with the prongs pointing downwards. If used on its own, e.g. for a first course, it is held in the right hand, resting on the third finger and held steady by the thumb and index finger.

The spoon is held by the right hand, supported by the third finger and secured by the thumb and index. Remember, always, whether consuming soup or pudding, eat from the side of the spoon and never torpedo-like from the end of the implement.

Napkins

These are another vital aspect of civilised eating. Never called serviettes, they should be spread on the knees immediately on sitting down but not tucked into clothing. They are used for dabbing not scraping the lips, and by some people for wiping the edge of a glass between sips of wine. At the end of meals, they are left scrunched up by the side of the place setting. The old British, and grubby, idea of folding up your napkin for future use has largely been abandoned.

Finger Bowls

Stories of unsuspecting guests drinking from finger bowls (and even of polite hosts doing the same so as not to embarrass their guests) are legion. Finger bowls are purely for delicate ablutions at the table and are served whenever foods are to be eaten by hand. They are generally made from silver and filled with tepid water. In restaurants, but not at home, they are sometimes livened up by a floating slice of lemon or lime, or, by the artistically inclined, by a flower petal. The form is to dip your fingers gently into the water and then pat, not rub, them dry with a napkin.

Drinking Wine

It is bad manners to refill your glass without offering to do the same for your neighbours beforehand. Never fill a glass more than two thirds full. Hold it by the stem when drinking and do not gulp it down as if you have been in the desert for several hours. Also avoid letting your glass look over-fingered and smeared with unappetising food particles.

GENERAL PROCEDURE

Although much depends on the formality of the dinner or lunch party you are attending, several basic tenets of civilised behaviour apply under most circumstances.

Men should not sit down until all women are seated. It is rude to sit cross-legged or to swing on your chair, and elbows on tables are still not appreciated, particularly at formal dinners. It is absolutely repellent to talk with your mouth full, and unappealing to eat noisily and messily.

If you are in a restaurant you will be served by a waiter. If you are dining in a private house with staff, you will be offered the food by a servant, but it is up to you to help yourself, using the implements provided. This is called 'butler service'. In the absence of staff, your host or hostess might bring the food round themselves, although this can be very disruptive to the sociability of an evening. Alternatively they may serve the main part of a course seated at their place and pass a plate to each guest: it is then up to the company to help themselves to vegetables and other accompaniments, and generally to keep the proceedings moving. Or guests might be asked to help themselves from a sideboard or side table, where plates and the entire course is provided. This is a fun, informal but traditional way to serve food and is particularly suitable for Sunday lunches in the country. Guests must remember not to spend time chatting at the sideboard and holding up the queue. Some hosts will bring an entire course fully 'plated' to the table. This method became very popular in the eighties, when presentation was thought very important, but is less popular now. Nowadays you are more likely to be treated to the increasingly informal 'kitchen' supper, where guests eat in that most homely of rooms and dishes are generally just plonked on the table for people to help themselves. This form of entertaining is popular because it enables busy hosts to prepare a party with the minimum of fuss and in the presence of their guests.

However you are served, it is not done to appear too greedy and to pile up your plate with heaps of food. It is also bad manners to use your own cutlery to serve yourself from platters and tureens: use the serving implements instead. Eating directly from communal serving dishes is a revolting habit and should never be done, even when everybody has been served. Picking chicken flesh from a carcass is equally unattractive. If you are hungry it is quite acceptable to take a second helping.

When to begin eating is a source of much tentative angst for guests. I have been to many parties where delicious food congeals on plates as nervous guests wait for everybody to be served. It is perfectly correct to start eating as soon as you are served, although the sophisticated guest will always hover a few moments before tucking in. Condiments should be used sparingly. Salt is always placed on the side of the plate and never sprinkled directly on to food.

When eating, it is bad manners to hoover up your food. Take a little at a time and place your knife and fork across each other like swords to indicate you have not finished. The rest of the time you should be conversing with other guests. The form is to take your cue from your hostess and usually means women devoting the first course to the person on their left, the second to whoever is sitting on their right, and then to play it by ear after that. It is bad manners to monopolise one person, no matter how fascinating, and to ignore another because they are boring. Also, when talking in groups larger than one to one, it is rude and thoughtless to spend any length of time discussing somebody who is unknown to the other parties, unless the conversation can be made relevant to all listening. It is also not generally appreciated, if a gathering is having a general discussion, for two people suddenly to start engaging in their own separate private conversation.

It used to be vulgar to discuss the food. Nowadays it is quite acceptable to make appreciative remarks, particularly as the host will probably have cooked it himself. Other traditionally taboo topics – such as politics, religion, illness, servants and sex – are nowadays increasingly acceptable and have become positive conversational staples of the modern dinner party. However, it would be a mistake to believe they have not been replaced by new taboos. This includes the ever-burgeoning 'isms', such as racism and sexism, many of which are now deeply offensive to others. It also remains true that although conversation is an art, attempts to turn the dining table into a debating society are unwelcome, and thus very contentious topics are best avoided in most company.

When you have finished eating, place your knife, fork or spoon in a six-thirty position on the plate.

REFUSING FOOD

Refusing food offered to you was always considered rude unless there was a concrete medical reason for doing so (such as diabetes or allergy). However, nowadays the position is less clear. We live in an age of fashionable food intolerance, bizarre diets and generally rather depressing all-pervading guilt about nourishment. Thus hosts have learned to be sanguine about guests' nutritional requirements and will try to be accommodating. Nevertheless, it is up to the guest to let the host know before the date of the party if they are vegetarian, allergic to certain foods or simply cannot deviate from a special diet for even one evening. Most busy hostesses today keep notes of people's food idiosyncrasies, but many of them admit to excising guests who are too much trouble. I remember going to a small dinner party given by a charming woman, who always serves really delicious food. One guest, a well-known figure in the magazine world, had arrived with her own entire alternative dinner, ranging from her aperitif (a particular brand of carrot juice newly imported from Eastern Europe) to strange seeds normally reserved for parrots which she munched noisily as a chocolate substitute. The guest in question spent so much time in the kitchen organising her food that we all agreed there was little point in her attending the dinner party at all.

Offers of help in a servantless household, however well meant, are best not pressed too strongly, unless your host or hostess has particularly communal leanings. Few party-givers wish to see their party disintegrate, as guests busy themselves with clearing, fetching and carrying. After all, the guest's main duty is to amuse and entertain, not slave and serve.

How to Eat Specific Foods

People often get themselves worked up about eating unfamiliar foods. This dinner table anguish is really unnecessary, as the old advice still applies: if in doubt simply wait until other members of the party start eating and copy them. In the meantime here are the basics.

Soup

Soup is eaten with a special round soup spoon, although some very old-fashioned rural houses still use a serving spoon. When eating soup (note that soup is always eaten and never drunk), the spoon is pushed away from you and then tipped not sucked into the mouth. It is perfectly acceptable to tip the soup bowl forwards to scoop up the last few drops. It is, however, unacceptable to turn the dish towards you. The exception to this is in the case of consommé (a clear soup that goes in and out of fashion, and is currently rather 'in'), which is usually served in a special dish with handles and can be drunk directly from the dish.

Bread Rolls

Bread rolls are eaten with the left hand, and are always broken into bite-sized pieces and eaten individually. It is vulgar to bite into bread. If butter is used, a small pat is taken from a butter dish and placed on the edge of a side plate, and each piece is buttered individually.

First Courses

The first course – the word 'starter' is somewhat vulgar – is generally eaten with the fork alone, unless it comprises awkwardly sized things such as large prawns or giant oak-leaf lettuce leaves. Thoughtful hosts and restaurateurs avoid offering dishes that are gastronomical obstacle courses.

Eggs

Quails' – and more rarely gulls' and plovers' – eggs are served hard-boiled, often in their shells. Peel each egg with your hands and roll it in the condiment provided, usually celery salt, then eat singly with the left hand.

Salads

These are generally eaten with a fork alone and not cut with a knife. This custom dates back to early times, when poison was sometimes injected into the veins of lettuce, and to cut into your leaves would have suggested that you harboured sinister suspicions about your host.

Caviar

True aficionados eat caviar from the small pad of flesh between the thumb and forefinger on the outside of their left hands, although this will look most pretentious in a social setting. Opt instead for spooning a small amount on to your plate and eating it with just a scrap of toast. Simplicity is all when consuming caviar, and accompaniments such as chopped egg, onions and even a squeeze of lemon juice should be avoided.

Oysters

These are luxury foods, around which much mystique has evolved. They are eaten in the months which contain the letter R, and their season begins in September. Oysters are served raw in their shells with lemon segments which you squeeze into your shell. They can be eaten by holding the shell in the left hand and spearing the contents with a fork (there is a special oyster fork designed for this purpose, although an ordinary one will do), then drinking the remaining juice from the shell; or by tipping the entire contents directly into the mouth from the shell.

Lobster

Lobster is generally served in its shell cut in half, either boiled or grilled, hot or cold and with a sauce or mayonnaise. Eat the easy bits first – the white meat in the tail and the coral – with a knife and fork. Then attack the claws, which contain pink meat and are more difficult to negotiate. These should have already been cracked for you, but if not, you will need to use special lobster crackers, which will have been provided for this purpose. The remaining meat on a lobster is delicious but very inaccessible and needs special tools and a certain amount of time and determination to extricate it. A similar technique applies to eating crab and crayfish.

Mussels

Although the authentic way to eat mussels is to use an empty shell as a spoon, the polite method is to hold each shell in your left hand and use a fork to loosen and consume the mollusc within. Place the empty shells either on the side of your plate, or on a separate debris plate if provided.

Other Shellfish

Potted brown shrimps are served in solidified butter and are eaten on hot toast. Larger prawns are served whole and need to be topped and tailed and peeled. This can be done by hand or with a knife and fork if provided.

Pâtés and Terrines

As a general rule, pâté is eaten by spreading a small amount of the stuff on bite-sized pieces of toast, in the case of finer pâtés such as foie gras, while bread is used for more rustic varieties. Each piece is prepared and eaten singly. You never spread a whole slice of bread with pâté as you would for school sandwiches. Terrines can be difficult to eat on bread and are usually best consumed with a fork.

Globe Artichokes

These are fiddly but delicious to eat, and are ideal for slimmers who need something to occupy themselves with at the table without consuming very much at all. Eaten hot or cold, each leaf is torn off individually and its flesh base dipped into a dressing or sauce and then scraped off by the lower teeth. The discarded leaf is then left tidily on the side of the plate. When all the leaves have been dealt with, the delicious choke is revealed, which is eaten with knife and fork. However, it is vital to remove the choke's inedible hairy stamens first to avoid tragedy at the dinner table.

Asparagus

Asparagus, unless an ingredient in a salad or vegetable course, is always eaten with the left hand and never with a knife and fork. Its tips are dipped into an accompanying sauce or dressing and then eaten down to about an inch and a half from the end, or until the spears become tough. It is a solecism to guzzle up these stumps and leave nothing on your plate.

Fish

At one time fish was correctly eaten with two forks. Now knives and forks are the accepted implements. Fish can be eaten either off or on the bone. The former is unlikely to cause any problems, while the latter reduces the inept to a considerable amount of messy spluttering. When eating fish on the bone, it is smarter to fillet it as you go, by cutting along the backbone and lifting each mouthful individually from the bone. The top side, starting at the head end, is eaten first, then flesh from underneath the skeleton. On no account must the backbone, or indeed the fish, be turned over. Stray fishbones are spat discreetly into the left fist and placed on the side of your plate, and not, except in a life-threatening emergency, extricated with the fingers.

Main Courses

These are eaten with a knife and fork. The knife is held in the right hand and used to cut up the food and push a small selection on to the fork for eating. The fork is held in the left hand with prongs down. On some occasions, for instance when eating nursery food such as shepherd's, cottage or fish pie, the fork is used alone. It is quite wrong in Britain to adopt the American method of first cutting up the food with a knife and then eating it with a fork alone. The use of the hands to pick up small bones to eat inaccessible bits of chops and game birds is theoretically acceptable, but is best avoided in public. When eating game you might also discover an errant piece of shot lurking in the flesh. This is removed by spitting it out into a cupped left hand and depositing it on the side of the plate.

Sorbet

Sorbet is usually served in a small chilled glass to cleanse the palate between courses. Eat it with a small spoon.

Pasta

Is eaten with a fork alone; not with a spoon and never with a knife. Spaghetti, although messy to eat, is easy to deal with once the basic technique is mastered. Place the fork vertically on the plate and twizzle around a small quantity of pasta, pulling it towards the side of the plate, and perfect bite-sized bundles will form.

Peas

Peas, such simple little things, cause all manner of problems. The most correct way to consume them remains to squash them on to the top of the fork, although more people appear to be adopting the American custom of turning the fork over and pushing a quantity of peas on to the inside of the fork with the knife. However, I find this looks clumsy and requires a not very friendly pointing of the elbow to anyone sitting on the left hand of the eater.

Pudding

Pudding, never 'sweet', 'afters' or 'dessert' (except when describing a fruit course), is always eaten with a spoon and fork, with the exception of ices and sorbets, which are consumed with a small spoon alone.

Cheese

When helping yourself to cheese, it is important to remember that a cheese must be left as near as possible to the state you found it in, as it has to serve everybody. Remember with a round cheese to cut out a segment, and when attacking a triangular piece to cut a lengthwise slice, not across the edge or tip. A whole Stilton is different and is scooped out with a spoon or wedged. The accompanying crackers or biscuits must be eaten as bread rolls, i.e. small pieces are broken off and buttered individually before being consumed with a morsel of cheese. Whether you eat the rind is purely a matter of taste.

Fruit

The eating of fruit, or 'dessert', can be a social minefield for the uninitiated. Those of a clumsy disposition ought to practise at home, although it must be admitted that conventions are not as stringent as in the past. For instance, the skinning of larger fruit such as apples and pears was once *de rigueur*, but with the increased emphasis on a high-fibre healthy diet this is now optional.

APPLES

These can be eaten by first holding in the left hand and with the right using a knife to skin them by scraping off a long strip of peel, around half an inch wide. Remember it is smartest to start at the top of the apple and to cut the peel in one long, unbroken length. The skinned apple is then placed on the peel, quartered, cored and eaten with the hand. Alternatively you can first quarter the apple and then peel each segment individually.

PEARS
Although the grandest way to skin a pear is said to be with a teaspoon, they are generally eaten like apples, although some people like to use a knife and fork.

ORANGES
Probably the messiest fruits to eat at table, oranges are peeled either in a circular motion, as described above under 'Apples', or sometimes in quarters. It is important to remove all the white pith. Individual segments are generally eaten by hand, although again a knife and fork can be used.

OTHER CITRUS FRUITS
Clementines, tangerines, mineolas and satsumas are all peeled by hand and their segments eaten by hand.

KUMQUATS
Are eaten whole and by hand, although it is usual to cut the top end off first.

GRAPES
It is extremely bad manners to help yourself to individual grapes from the fruit bowl. Instead use grape scissors, if provided, or your hands to detach a small bunch, and eat each grape by hand.

BANANAS
Another tricky one, bananas must never be eaten monkey-style at the table. Firstly, peel with a knife, pulling off the skin in vertical strips. Cut off around one third of an inch at each end, and then cut small discs of fruit and eat either with the fingers or with a fork if provided.

SOFT FRUIT WITH STONES
Peaches, nectarines, apricots and plums are quartered and their stones left on the side of the plate.

CHERRIES
Help yourself to a small handful of fruit and eat whole. The stones are spat into the cupped left hand and deposited on the side of the plate.

LYCHEES
These are peeled by hand, *à la* hard-boiled egg, eaten whole and the stone removed in the same way as cherries.

FIGS

Figs are eaten by first cutting the fruit downward into four sections. Turn down the quarters to form a flower. Cut each 'petal' loose, bring to the mouth with both hands and eat the delicious pink flesh. Discarded skins are left neatly on the side of the plate. Alternatively you can use a knife and fork, if provided.

PINEAPPLE

It is rare that you will have to cope with a whole uncut pineapple at the table. Should the occasion arise, cut yourself a *horizontal* slice. Remove the skin and woody centre, and eat with a knife and fork.

MANGOES

Very tricky. Mangoes require the dexterity of a small-time conjuror to eat elegantly from scratch. Firstly, slice off an oval-shaped chunk/thick slice of fruit with skin. Secondly, slice down the cut piece in a grid pattern. Thirdly, turn back the skin on itself. This forces the flesh to push up into easy-to-eat cubes. Use either a knife or fork and spoon to eat the flesh. Repeat procedure until only the stone remains.

PAPAYAS

Also called paw-paws, these are sliced in half lengthways and eaten like an avocado with a spoon and fork.

Other Tricky Things

CORN ON THE COB

Surely one of the messiest of dishes, corn on the cob is held either with special prongs or by the hands at each end and then brought to the mouth and the corn gradually chewed off. Beware: stray bits of corn will probably become stuck in the teeth and will need to be discreetly removed.

SNAILS

These are eaten directly from their shells, which are secured by the left hand with tongs while the right hand extracts the snail with a special implement.

CHOPSTICKS

Japanese, Chinese and other Oriental food is now so popular that you are just as likely to be confronted with chopsticks in a private house as in a restaurant. Rest one chopstick on the side of the right hand between the thumb and third finger. Lay the second chopstick parallel with the first, and gripping it with thumb and forefinger use a pincer-type movement to lift food from plate to mouth. The process can be reversed for left-handers. When not being used, chopsticks are placed by the right-hand side of the plate, usually on special rests. When eating sushi, remember that they are usually eaten by hand, not with chopsticks, and that the fish part alone (not the rice) is dipped into the soy sauce.

OTHER NON-EUROPEAN STYLES

There has also been a huge increase in the popularity of Islamic and Indian cuisine, which often requires food to be eaten with bread or lettuce leaves – or even the fingers. In these cases the food is scooped up and brought to the mouth. One word of warning: always use the right hand, not the left. The left hand should never touch food or mouth directly.

TEA AND COFFEE

When serving tea or coffee, the main beverage is always served first, with any accompaniment – milk, cream, lemon or sugar – being added *after- wards*. Remember, when drinking from a tea or coffee cup, to hold it between your fingers and thumb; do not allow fingers to curl around the handle. Never drink with the little finger in the air. Do not make slurping noises.

17

DRESS

Indecision about what to wear is one of the most visible manifestations of contemporary social confusion and insecurity. The elevation of comfort above all other considerations, the flawed belief that informality equals conviviality, and downright laziness have resulted in a contradictory and illogical dress sense that would stump the most *mondaine* of time travellers beaming into a modern dinner party as he observed the crazy cocktail of sartorial semiotics around the table.

However, the tide – at least outside the shellsuit-wearing brigade – is turning. This is because of two fundamental human instincts that have been overlooked by the slobs. One is the ancient need of people to decorate themselves, which started long before the first murmuring of civilisation and continues today. The other is our very natural wish to please others, be admired by our peers and attract a mate. Add to this the security that a few unwritten rules can bring, and the enduring need for dressing up becomes clear.

The first step is to forget the old British adage that it is ill bred to be overdressed. This guideline has outlived its shelf life, as it was conceived in a period when it was the accepted norm to dress up for any activity more than gardening. At this time overdressing meant being got up in a flashy, overly elaborate or embarrassing way and took no account of the modern invasion of sports-inspired clothes that has enslaved whole swathes of the nation into sweats and trainers.

Now it is advisable and good manners to err on the over- rather than the underdressed when invited to a party. This is because by being seen to make an effort you are paying your host or hostess a great compliment, as well as making yourself look your most attractive. After all, the short time required for getting yourself dressed is negligible compared with the hours the hostess might have put in preparing the party. This does not mean wearing a tiara to a Sunday lunch party, but merely that both sexes should turn up looking as though they have changed and are doing more than merely walking the dog.

But by the same token, it behoves hosts and hostesses to give a little direction about what they expect their guests to wear. Clarity is all here. No one wants to be in the embarrassing, if highly amusing, position of one unfortunate man who was invited to stay at a castle in Ireland. On asking his host what the dress would be, he was told: 'Just the usual fancy dress' (meaning black tie). Being a simple soul, he followed his host's words implicitly, and on Saturday night duly strode into the drawing room in a full suit of armour, only to find his fellow guests unremarkably attired in black tie. Mortified, he clanked up to his host and hissed: 'You bastard!' They never spoke again. Therefore, hosts, if inviting for a dinner party, should say: 'It's only suits' or: 'We are just in the kitchen, come as you are.' Once these instructions are given, it behoves hosts to stick to their sartorial guns, and not, having said 'Come as you are', on the night slip into their glad rags and thus embarrass their guests who turn up in sweaters.

The other tip is a fashion chestnut, but cannot be over-emphasised or repeated too often. Both men and women should always buy the best-quality clothes they can afford. These are truly investments because they look better and last longer. One good dinner jacket or top-notch dinner dress is worth more than a dozen cheaper items. Cost per wear theory means that they soon pay for the initial outlay.

Also, unless you have an unlimited budget that allows wardrobes to be updated every season, it is always advisable to aim for a more classic approach to dressing, rather than being tempted by the drop-dead trendy. This approach is particularly relevant to special occasion clothes. A classically elegant evening dress can effortlessly attend endless parties, while its more flashy fashionable sister looks tired after only a couple of outings.

Finally, remember that logically and aesthetically couples should vaguely look as if they are associated with each other, should complement each other sartorially and should give the impression that they are going to the same party. This may seem obvious, but in recent years a marked dichotomy has emerged between the sexes in which, say, for a standard dinner party the women dress up and the men do not. One authority feels that this is because men spend all week dressed up at the office and fancy a change, and for women, many of whom might be at home looking after children, the reverse is the case. Whatever the reason, it is obviously silly for a man not to wear a suit when his spouse has made an effort, and equally odd for a woman to put on a party dress for a barbecue at which the men will be in shirtsleeves.

In the following pages, I shall explain the current acceptable dress for the most commonly occurring occasions. As traditionally women's clothes take their cue from the dress code expected from men, it is easiest to split the sections into the well-known male categories.

EVENING DRESS/WHITE TIE

This is rarely worn today, but when it is, it means that the very grandest, formal and immaculate appearance is expected. Men wear black evening tail coat, teamed with matching trousers with two lines of braid, stiff boiled shirt, detachable stick-up or wing collar, white bow tie (usually marcella), white evening waistcoat (again usually marcella), black 'whole-cut' patent shoes with black ribbon laces, and black silk socks. The outfit is completed by decorative, largely white and preferably antique studs, cufflinks and waistcoat buttons. Decorations (see p. 337 below) are often worn.

Women wear long, formal evening dresses. Short frocks, no matter how glamorous, are not acceptable and trousers should not even be considered. These rules are particularly strictly adhered to in Scotland. I know of one girl who was forced to wear a hideous long white dress over her skimpy little number before she was allowed into a ball. Traditionally long evening dresses can expose a generous expanse of *décolletage*. However, if the evening is to include vigorous dancing, such as reeling, strapless and very precarious boned dresses are best avoided, as it is not unknown during particularly energetic turns for the wearer to launch herself in one direction and the dress to move resolutely in the other. While this is an eagerly awaited treat for lecherous old buffers, it is deeply embarrassing for the girl concerned. One deeply practical girl always recommends that all women, when trying on evening dresses in shops, should engage in a few gentle gymnastics and do a certain amount of jumping about to test the safety factor. She also cautions against wearing big jewellery which might either bounce off and break or alternatively knock out your partner, or worse, your hostess. Long hair too should be restrained, as it can be pretty distressing at high speed. Shoes should be comfortable.

Long evening gloves remain the correct accessory, although their observance is much less rigorously followed, particularly by girls under twenty-five. A thoughtful débutante also suggests that young girls remember their age, particularly when attending royal or super-grand gatherings, where there will automatically be a significant contingent of wrinklies who might take exception to slips of girls turning up looking like empresses.

Decorations

Decorations are sometimes worn on formal occasions by members of the various orders of chivalry and those who have been awarded medals. Gatherings when decorations are worn are basically divided into two types. The first is when The Queen, Queen Elizabeth The Queen Mother or other members of the Royal Family are present and it is deemed fit that decorations should be worn; the second is when a host decides that the nature or importance of a particular gathering makes the wearing of them appropriate. Invitations always indicate whether decorations are to be worn. Otherwise they should definitely not appear. The sporting of decorations is, however, at the discretion of the holder, although not to do so strikes me as very ungracious, particularly in the presence of royalty.

On full evening dress or white tie occasions, such as state banquets and city livery dinners, the invitation should state 'Evening Dress – Decorations'. Knights and dames wear the most senior chivalric orders to which they belong. They can wear a maximum of four stars (Garter, Thistle, etc.) which are displayed on the left side of the evening coat or dress. Knights Grand Cross also wear a broad sash (riband) with a badge. One neck badge suspended on a miniature (half-size) ribbon of an order may be worn just below the bow tie. Any miniature (half-size) orders and decorations are worn on a metal bar. When the dress is only dinner jackets (black tie) the invitation will state 'Dinner Jacket – Decorations'. On these occasions the main players are miniatures, which are worn on the left breast of a jacket. One star and one neck badge on a miniature ribbon can also be worn.

Decorations are today rarely worn with morning dress and are largely restricted to special official public functions, religious services connected with the orders of chivalry or grand memorial services. In these cases whoever is organising the event should indicate whether decorations are appropriate. Full-sized orders, decorations and medals are worn, and up to four stars, although broad sash ribands are quite inappropriate and should not be put on. Dark suits and overcoats also occasionally take decorations, most notably at Remembrance Sunday services and regimental gatherings. In these cases full-sized medals are worn on the left of the jacket or coat. A neck badge may also be worn, although stars and ribands do not appear.

In all cases British decorations take precedence over foreign ones, except on occasions at the relevant embassy, when the foreign head of state is present, and on occasions associated with the country concerned. The word 'decorations' on an invitation also gives directions as to what women should wear. As well as wearing appropriate orders, decorations and medals they can also sport their most important jewellery, including tiaras. It should be remembered, however, that tiaras are a suitable adornment for married women only. Single ones must wait until their wedding. Collars of the orders of knighthood are worn by knights at appropriate ceremonies when notification has been given, and on collar days. They are never worn after sunset.

DINNER JACKETS/BLACK TIE

Black tie, once a very specific sartorial category, is today an amorphous description for clothes suitable for occasions ranging from the annual office party to dinner at Admiralty House. Men have it easier than women. When the invitation says black tie, he wears a black wool barathea dinner jacket, which can either be single- or double-breasted, and should have ribbed silk lapels, preferably not satin, no vents and covered buttons. The old basket-weave jackets are particularly distinguished but virtually impossible to find now. Trousers should taper, be cut for braces and sport one row of braid. The evening shirt, in cotton or silk, has either a marcella or a pleated front. It must have a soft turn-down collar, not the stiff winged variety (that is the province of white tie alone). Predominantly black studs with matching cuff links are the usual fastening, although more decorative options are also acceptable. The tie should be black (colours are somewhat common) silk barathea or faille. Cummerbunds can be worn, but evening waistcoats remain much more *comme il faut*. Shoes can be either patent pumps or lace-ups, the latter being infinitely preferable if there is to be dancing. An evening watch is an elegant accessory. Velvet smoking jackets, once worn only in the privacy of one's own house, are now perfectly acceptable outside and particularly popular in the country. These are traditionally worn with dinner jackets/trousers.

For women 'black tie' today is infinitely more complicated, as its presence on a card can signify any level of dress, ranging from a little lycra number to just sub-white-tie levels of splendour. The old clearly defined distinctions between dinner and dance dresses have largely disappeared and their place has been taken merely by confusion. Thus it is important to ascertain from the hostess what dress she is expecting. Good hostesses could follow the lead of a well-known duchess, who sends a written invitation to friends that includes a few short lines dispelling any dress confusion: 'Saturday night is black tie, but palazzo pants will be absolutely fine.'

The invitation itself will also give clues. A simple drinks party from 6.30 to 8.30 will require only a little black dress, while a more lavish affair to celebrate someone's twenty-first, which consists of drinks, dinner and dancing, needs a much grander dress. As an inveterate party-going friend says: 'The greater the effort of the hostess, the greater the level of formality expected of the guest.'

The choice of long or short dress can also be vexing. Traditionally long is more formal than short, but these distinctions are fast disappearing. At one recent party – which was probably one of the most chic events of the autumn – there was an equal preponderance of long and short: neither category had the upper hand. The choice today is largely based on what suits the wearer, her legs and her relative age. Long is the preferred comfortable option of older women, while young girls invariably feel more suited to short. However, a long dress or skirt remains the safest option for all, as it is always special, and appropriate to any black tie event grander than a cocktail party. Best jewels, with plenty of sparklers, can be worn, but obviously tiaras are inappropriate.

Town v. Country

It is to be remembered that a distinct dichotomy in dressing has evolved between town and country style. While London is the place of innovative chic and even the flash dresser, the country still clings more resolutely to traditional, formal and understated ways of dressing *au soir*. Furthermore, with the typical British perverseness that always floors foreigners, the plain – if not frumpy – rustic style is still considered infinitely grander than the most glamorous metropolitan kit. This applies not only in its natural county habitat, but often in town too – hence the reason why at subscription dances in London, dumpy county women in ancient taffeta still sometimes manage to have the edge on the couture-clad bejewelled wives of plutocrats.

Thus beyond the M25 it is advisable to err on the side of caution if you do not want to risk offending a hostess for whom the more arresting pages of *Vogue* can be as distant as the snows of Antarctica. Certain items, such as women's dinner jackets, which remain *sans pareil* in town, are still *de trop* in the country. The skimpy little number which might appear sexy in SW3 will be dismissed as merely slutty in Somerset. The perforated crocheted shirt, although almost a uniform in Trustafarian Notting Hill, will imperil your social life as well as your health in the Highlands. It is quite literally horses for courses.

TROUSERS OR SKIRT?

Trousers, once unseen after six, are increasingly acceptable. However, only certain varieties can be worn, and only at specific types of parties. As a general rule of thumb, trousers are a risk at any gathering where there is to be dancing, where the skirt still reigns supreme. They are, however, now not just acceptable but very elegant at a cocktail party or a London dinner party. This being said, they must be very obviously evening trousers and not have any daytime overtones about them. However, it is worth bearing in mind that certain country-dwelling wrinklies still consider 'slacks' suitable only for walking the dog, gardening, or sailing.

FANCY DRESS

For a race that is widely held to be so diffident, the British have always enjoyed a marked empathy with dressing-up. This enthusiasm has many manifestations, ranging from the pomp and pageantry that surrounds our Crown and state via the fairy-tale ensembles sported by brides and their attendants across the land, to the ever-increasing precocity of adolescent boys donning dinner jackets for the first time and the annual parade of millinery marvels at Royal Ascot.

However, it is in the institution of the fancy dress party that our latent sartorial theatricality finds both its finest and its worst hour. Some people love it; others dread the whole thing with such a passion that they pretend to be out of the country on the night of their best friend's *bal masqué*. This is a shame, because fancy dress is really just a more fanciful and theatrical extension of everyday dressing. Its basic criteria are the same: it must suit the occasion and the person. Thus, if given a theme, stick to it, and more importantly, choose an outfit that suits your looks and physiognomy. For instance, hearty blondes make good Valkyries and slender young men ideal macaronies. Only the naturally alluring should attempt seriously sexy outfits. Nobody should wear impractical outfits that make dancing, eating and other basic functions impossible, as a friend who once masqueraded as a tomato found to his cost. Cross-dressing is very popular in England, rather curiously particularly with military types, but again participants should display a relative attempt at an aesthetic approach. Men not used to wearing high heels should practise walking at home to avoid accidents on the dance floor.

UNCHANGED

This used to mean come as you are, but in a day when men were probably wearing suits and women the equivalent. Therefore, no one should be fooled that today it means literally what it says and turn up in jeans. Nowadays the term, unless the hosts say differently, means not black tie. Thus men should turn up in suits or jackets and trousers with a formal shirt, cuff links and a tie. Women wear presentable day clothes.

SMART DAY/FORMAL DAY DRESS

This is a type of dressing at which the British excel. It includes clothes for weddings, smart race meetings and all formal day events. Men's clothes range from morning coats for the most important occasions, such as Royal Ascot and traditional weddings, to dark suits. Morning dress consists of a curve-fronted body coat. Black is currently considered much smarter than grey, which has acquired slight wide-boy connotations, although it is still traditional to wear it on Ladies' Day (Thursday) at Ascot. At weddings, although grey coats are occasionally sported by the groom and his best man, black ones have the upper hand sartorially. The choice of waistcoat depends on the event. White, grey or buff is best for racing. Fancy or coloured ones are to be treated with care and are best reserved for young weddings. Black is (now rarely) worn for grand memorial services, at the Cenotaph and for certain daytime City functions. Trousers can be striped or checked and should carry one pleat. They must be cut for braces, as little is more unappealing than an expanse of shirt (particularly girding a corpulent midriff) appearing between the bottom of the waistcoat and belted trousers. Although fewer men bother to make the effort, the shirt should, to be correct, be worn with a stiff white turned-down detachable collar. The tie can be heavy woven silk, but never a foulard. Shoes must be formal lace-ups: Gucci loafers simply will not do. Morning dress also traditionally calls for a top hat. It must be worn in the Royal Enclosure at Ascot but has become optional at weddings. If worn, however, the type of top hat is important. Again black is smarter than grey. The most elegant style is an old bell-shaped hat in a silk plush that is no longer made. The modern ones are but pale imitations. Gloves can be carried at weddings, but are a nuisance at the races. Grey is traditional with a grey coat, yellow with a black one. A watch and chain can also look distinguished with such a formal outfit.

Women's clothes for smart day wear should be formal but colourful. Suits, dresses worn with jackets, and hats with everything are the usual choices. As a general rule of thumb neither white nor black are recommended for weddings. The former is the prerogative of the bride and the latter, unless it is broken up with colour or just used for accessories, is too sombre for such a happy day. Brighter plumage is altogether more suitable.

The same is true of smart race meetings, which traditionally give many British women one of their few opportunities to show off and dress really fashionably. However, fashionably does not mean vulgarly. Sartorial stipulations to enter the Royal Enclosure are strict: hats without crowns and trousers are not allowed. White gloves, although sometimes worn, are now considered outmoded. Thus orange spandex outfits worn with naff headgear are to be left at home. Accessories need to be well chosen and in top condition. Many English women totally ruin the effect of expensive designer clothes by wearing them with their everyday handbag and scuffed suede shoes better suited to walking the dog. Very high heels are also a mistake, both stylistically and practically, as they are uncomfortable for standing for long periods, sink into the turf and end up with grassy beards for the day. They also look tarty, and – as with all come-hither garments – should be worn only by those who mean it.

Hats

These are pivotal to the woman's smart day wardrobe. They are *de rigueur* at weddings, Royal Ascot and other smart races. They are preferable but no longer essential at royal garden parties, christenings and other church services. Unlike their grandmothers, most women today are unused to wearing hats (particularly large ones) and are thus prone to spatial misapprehensions and clumsy collisions when meeting and greeting. A very social friend recommends practising with a new hat at home to avoid embarrassment on the day. She also cautions about wearing millinery that is too small and points out that, whereas it is easy to make a hat smaller, the reverse is almost impossible. Veils, too, for all their allure, need practice, particularly by smokers and messy eaters.

Men and Hats

Men who wear hats must be aware that the sporting of headwear is an ancient and evolved custom that still retains its own idiosyncratic etiquette. This is because hats cover the most important part of the anatomy and thus have a greater sartorial significance than other pieces of clothing: hence the age-old iconic importance of the royal crown, the bishop's mitre, and so on. Therefore, how hats are used has a great impact, and the old conventions should be observed in the modern world.

Hats should always be removed in the presence of royalty and the dead (for instance, when a funeral cortège passes), and always in a private house. Taking them off in public buildings such as shops and offices is optional, although it is usual to remove them in lifts. Christian churches call for men to be bare-headed, while Jewish synagogues expect men's heads to be covered.

The hat is also used for greetings. When meeting somebody or passing them on the street it is traditional for men to touch the brim of their hats. If meeting a woman a man can also raise his hat gently and maybe remove it if talking to her for any length of time. Well-mannered equestrians often touch their hat briefly with their whip. These gestures should always be small and fleeting, never exaggerated or clumsy.

SMART/CASUAL

This is a difficult but important category, as it is widely worn today at many events. It has to look presentable, but not too formal. The pivotal garment for men is a blazer or other sports jacket. It is adaptable and versatile and can be worn with flannels, shirt and tie at one end of the spectrum, or in the more relaxed idiom of cotton trousers, polo shirt and sweater. With it a man would wear brown shoes. Casual-looking linen or cotton suits can also look good. Panama hats make ideal accessories on hot days. Trainers do not.

The smart/casual woman's wardrobe is also based around a blazer-type jacket. It can be worn with either a pretty dress or a long skirt/smart trousers, shirt or blouse and flat shoes. Casual does not mean leggings, sweatshirt and gym shoes – all of which should be left at home. Distinctly formal and overdressed touches – such as big important hats, high heels, lots of jewellery and strident colour schemes – are equally out of place. The smart/casual wardrobe has to have an understated, sporty but appropriate look about it in order to succeed.

COME AS YOU ARE

This instruction has to be handled with care. Basically it is a social synonym for 'dress casually' and should not be interpreted as a licence to turn up in a dirty shirt and shredded jeans. For men it means cords and a sweater in winter, and cotton trousers or Bermuda shorts (in the day), casual shirt and deck shoes during the summer months. Women wear similar clothes: shorts and shirts in the summer, sweaters and trousers or skirts in the winter.

GROOMING

In very recent times the social misapprehension has developed that it is grand to be grubby. This is quite untrue. Lack of personal hygiene has little to do with class, more with laziness, low self-esteem and lack of social awareness. Only a fool underestimates the power of personal hygiene. Both men and women should keep their hair, nails and all other places scrupulously clean. Women should avoid wearing too much make-up, particularly in the country, where the painted doll look is not appreciated. A beautiful friend of mine always goes by the guide, 'If you think you might have put too much make-up on, you have.' As she says, it is always easier to add more later than try to rub it off. Scent too should be worn judiciously and not at all before six o'clock in the country. Arresting hairstyles are also out of place away from London. Overmanicured nails – particularly of the Chinese empress kind – can also look dodgy. Coloured nail vanish tends to look common on young girls, who should wear clear. Men's nails should always be clipped as short and as squarely as possible. Varnish for men is utterly unacceptable. Their shoes should always be polished.

OFFICE STYLE

The secret here for both sexes is to dress as they would like to be treated. Men who look dishevelled run the risk of appearing the same in their work. Women should eschew tarty high-heeled shoes, unless that is how they wish to be known about the office. On the other hand there is no need for them to wear aggressively masculine suits, with no hint of femininity.

COUNTRY CLOTHES

These are intended to blend and not make a fashion statement. Men should wear a lot of tweed in earthy, grassy and heathery hues, teamed with corduroys, flannels, and sweaters. Those who shoot, hunt or fish should invest in the right clothes (see Chapter 13), which are also practical but look appropriate. Sharp City suits look wrong too and should be substituted with a nice thorn-proof country number. A good supply of sturdy outerwear is also a necessity and should include some stout boots, a Barbour or other waterproof, and a hat, gloves and scarf.

Women's attire is roughly the same and should include a good tweed jacket, a selection of casual trousers, a practical skirt, a thick sweater for outdoors and a thin one for inside, and walking shoes/Wellington boots. It is important to make sure that boots are not too large and floppy and thus difficult to walk in, tiring and hugely attractive to mud. Add to this a selection of warmers including scarves, gloves and a practical and undressy hat in either elderly tweed or waterproof cloth. Any woman who shoots seriously should invest in a girl's version of the traditional man's shooting suit, which will not only look splendid but be very useful too. A couple of thermal vests and leggings are also highly recommended, as is generally wearing lots of layers for outdoor activities that can be removed or replaced at will as body temperatures soar and plummet. Country changes should be much simpler than in town: for lunch it could be a little cashmere sweater worn with flannels and flat shoes, while dinner could be simple evening dress or a velvet skirt and blouse. Jewellery should be discreet. Hair should be tidy, make-up soft and natural.

APPENDIX: CORRECT
FORMS OF ADDRESS

Name	Envelope	Opening of Letter	Verbal Address	Place Card
The Royal Family				
Her Majesty The Queen	The Private Secretary to Her Majesty The Queen*	Dear Sir (or Madam if applicable) on first correspond-ence, and thereafter by name.	Your Majesty, Ma'am	HM The Queen
His Royal Highness The Duke of Edinburgh	as above	as above	Your Royal Highness, Sir	HRH The Duke of Edinburgh
Her Majesty Queen Elizabeth The Queen Mother	as above	as above	Your Majesty, Ma'am	HM Queen Elizabeth The Queen Mother
His Royal Highness The Prince of Wales	as above	as above	Your Royal Highness, Sir	HRH The Prince of Wales
*Letters can be sent direct (see *Debrett's Correct Form*) but it is simpler and more practical to correspond through a Private Secretary.				

His Royal Highness The Duke of York	as above	as above	Your Royal Highness, Sir	HRH The Duke of York
His Royal Highness The Prince Edward	as above	as above	Your Royal Highness, Sir	HRH The Prince Edward
Her Royal Highness The Princess Royal	as above	as above	Your Royal Highness, Ma'am	HRH The Princess Royal
Her Royal Highness The Princess Margaret, Countess of Snowdon	as above	as above	Your Royal Highness, Ma'am	HRH The Princess Margaret, Countess of Snowdon
Her Royal Highness Princess Alice, Duchess of Gloucester	as above	as above	Your Royal Highness, Ma'am	HRH Princess Alice, Duchess of Gloucester
His Royal Highness The Duke of Gloucester	as above	as above	Your Royal Highness, Sir	HRH The Duke of Gloucester
His Royal Highness The Duke of Kent	as above	as above	Your Royal Highness, Sir	HRH The Duke of Kent
His Royal Highness Prince Michael of Kent	as above	as above	Your Royal Highness, Sir	HRH Prince Michael of Kent
Her Royal Highness Princess Alexandra, the Hon. Lady Ogilvy	as above	as above	Your Royal Highness, Ma'am	HRH Princess Alexandra, the Hon. Lady Ogilvy
Peers, Baronets and Knights				
Duke	The Duke of Dumfound	Dear Duke/Dear Duke of Dumfound	Duke	Duke of Dumfound

Duchess	The Duchess of Dumfound	Dear Duchess/Dear Duchess of Dumfound	Duchess	Duchess of Dumfound
Eldest son of duke (usually takes his father's second title as a courtesy title)	Marquess of Masquerade	Dear Lord Masquerade	Lord Masquerade	Lord Masquerade
Younger son of a duke	The Lord James Family-Name	Dear Lord James	Lord James	Lord James Family-Name
Wife of younger son of a duke	The Lady James Family-Name	Dear Lady James	Lady James	Lady James Family-Name
Daughter of a duke	The Lady Jemima Family-Name	Dear Lady Jemima	Lady Jemima	Lady Jemima Family-Name
Marquess	The Marquess of Malaprop	Dear Lord Malaprop	Lord Malaprop	Lord Malaprop
Marchioness	The Marchioness of Malaprop	Dear Lady Malaprop	Lady Malaprop	Lady Malaprop
Eldest son of marquess (usually takes his father's second title as a courtesy title)	Viscount Valmouth	Dear Lord Valmouth	Lord Valmouth	Lord Valmouth
Younger son/daughter of marquess	Same form as younger son/daughter of duke			
Earl	The Earl of Everso	Dear Lord Everso	Lord Everso	Lord Everso
Countess	The Countess of Everso	Dear Lady Everso	Lady Everso	Lady Everso
Eldest son of earl (usually takes his father's second title as a courtesy title)	Viscount Verynice	Dear Lord Verynice	Lord Verynice	Lord Verynice

Younger son of earl	The Hon. Frederick Family-Name	Dear Mr Family-Name	Mr Family-Name	Mr Frederick Family-Name
Wife of younger son of earl	The Hon. Mrs Frederick Family-Name	Dear Mrs Family-Name	Mrs Family-Name	Mrs Frederick Family-Name
Daughter of earl	The Lady Frederika Family-Name	Dear Lady Frederika	Lady Frederika	Lady Frederika Family-Name
Viscount	The Viscount Vittle	Dear Lord Vittle	Lord Vittle	Lord Vittle
Viscountess	The Viscountess Vittle	Dear Lady Vittle	Lady Vittle	Lady Vittle
Son of a viscount	The Hon. Victor Family-Name	Dear Mr Family-Name	Mr Family-Name	Mr Victor Family-Name
Wife of a viscount's son	The Hon. Mrs Victor Family-Name	Dear Mrs Family-Name	Mrs Family-Name	Mrs Victor Family-Name
Daughter of a viscount	The Hon. Annabel Family-Name	Dear Miss Family-Name	Miss Family-Name	Miss Annabel Family-Name
Baron	The Lord Tickle	Dear Lord Tickle	Lord Tickle	Lord Tickle
Baron's wife	The Lady Tickle	Dear Lady Tickle	Lady Tickle	Lady Tickle
Children of baron	Same form as children of viscounts			
Baronet	Sir Brinsley Boob, Bt.	Dear Sir Brinsley	Sir Brinsley	Sir Brinsley Boob
Wife of baronet	Laby Boob	Dear Lady Boob	Lady Boob	Lady Boob
Children of baronet	These have no titles			
Life peer	The Lord Widget of Wantage	Dear Lord Widget	Lord Widget	Lord Widget
Wife of life peer	The Lady Widget of Wantage	Dear Lady Widget	Lady Widget	Lady Widget
Children of life peer	The Hon. John/Jane Family-Name	Dear Mr/Miss Family-Name	Mr/Miss Family Name	Mr/Miss John/Jane Family-Name
Knight	Sir John Organ*	Dear Sir John	Sir John	Sir John Organ

*Knights other than Knights Bachelor, i.e. Knights of the various Orders of Chivalry, also take post nominal letters after the name on the envelope, e.g. GCB and KCVO.

Knight's wife	Lady Organ	Dear Lady Organ	Lady Organ	Lady Organ
Women's Titles				
Hereditary peeress in her own right	The Countess of Cabbage	Dear Lady Cabbage	Lady Cabbage	Lady Cabbage
Widow of hereditary peer	The Dowager Marchioness of Malpractice* Some widowed peeresses now prefer to be styled with their own first names, e.g. Dorothea, Duchess of Deceit	Dear Lady Malpractice	Lady Malpractice	Lady Malpractice
Former wife of hereditary peer	Elvira, Countess of Euridice	Dear Lady Euridice	Lady Euridice	Lady Euridice
Life peeress	The Baroness Blott of Balham	Dear Lady Blott	Lady Blott	Lady Blott
Dame	Dame Daphne Dogood	Dear Dame Daphne	Dame Daphne	Dame Daphne Dogood
Widow of baronet	Dowager Lady Organ	Dear Lady Organ	Lady Organ	Dowager Lady Organ
Special Scottish and Irish Titles				
Eldest son of Scottish peer (or peeress in her own right)	The Master of Ben Nevis/Lord Ben Nevis	Dear Master of Ben Nevis/Dear Lord Ben Nevis	Master/Lord Ben Nevis	Master of Ben Nevis/Lord Ben Nevis
Irish hereditary knight	The Knight of Shamrock	Dear Knight	Knight	Knight of Shamrock
Wife of Irish hereditary knight	Madam Shamrock	Dear Madam Shamrock	Madam Shamrock	Madam Shamrock

* The title Dowager is today a tricky one. Officially a peer's widow is styled Dowager, unless there is already a dowager still living in the family. In this situation the junior widow is styled with her first name, i.e. Victoria, Viscountess Veneering. However, in reality, many official dowagers also prefer to be styled with their first names. It is sensible to check individual circumstances. Also remember that when the present peer is unmarried, it is customary for the widow of the late peer to continue styling herself as during her marriage. Only on the present peer's marriage would she become either The Dowager Viscountess Veneering, or Veruka, Viscountess Veneering.

Scottish chief or chieftain	The MacScottie of MacScottie	Dear MacScottie of MacScottie	MacScottie of MacScottie	The MacScottie of MacScottie
Woman chief	Madam/Mrs MacScottie of MacScottie	Dear Madam/ Mrs MacScottie of MacScottie	Madam/Mrs MacScottie of MacScottie	Madam/Mrs MacScottie of MacScottie
Wife of Scottish chief	Madam/Mrs MacScottie of MacScottie	Dear Madam/Mrs MacScottie of MacScottie	Madam/Mrs MacScottie of MacScottie	Madam/Mrs MacScottie of MacScottie
Eldest son of chief	Hamish MacScottie of MacScottie, yr	Dear MacScottie of MacScottie, yr	MacScottie of MacScottie, yr	MacScottie of MacScottie, yr
Wife of eldest son of chief	Mrs Hamish MacScottie of MacScottie, yr	Dear Mrs MacScottie of MacScottie, yr	Mrs MacScottie of MacScottie, yr	Mrs MacScottie of MacScottie, yr
Other children of chief	Sons are addressed without any title, e.g. John MacScottie Esq. Daughters, however, would be Miss MacScottie of MacScottie (eldest daughter) or Miss Flora MacScottie of MacScottie (others)			
Irish chieftains	The O'Dooley of the Blarney	Dear O'Dooley	O'Dooley	The O'Dooley of the Blarney
Wife of Irish chieftain	Madam O'Dooley of the Blarney	Dear Madam O'Dooley	Madam O'Dooley	Madam O'Dooley of the Blarney
Children of Irish chieftains	Have no special titles			
Untitled People				
Men	John Smith Esq.	Dear Mr Smith	Mr Smith	Mr John Smith
Married women	Mrs John Smith	Dear Mrs Smith	Mrs Smith	Mrs John Smith

351

Unmarried women	Miss Jane Smith (more senior spinsters would be known as just Miss Smith)	Dear Miss Smith	Miss Smith	Miss Jane Smith
Widows	Mrs John Smith	Dear Mrs Smith	Mrs Smith	Mrs John Smith
Divorcees	Mrs Janet Smith	Dear Mrs Smith	Mrs Smith	Mrs Janet Smith
Government and Parliament				
The Prime Minister	The Rt. Hon. Brian Beige MP, The Prime Minister	Dear Prime Minister	Prime Minister	Prime Minister
The Deputy Prime Minister	The Rt. Hon. Victor Vaseline, The Deputy Prime Minister	Dear Deputy Prime Minister	Deputy Prime Minister	Deputy Prime Minister
The Chancellor of the Exchequer	The Rt. Hon. Kendrick Ledger, The Chancellor of the Exchequer	Dear Chancellor	Chancellor	Chancellor of the Exchequer
Lord Privy Seal	The Rt. Hon. The Earl of Adhesive, The Lord Privy Seal	Dear Lord Privy Seal	Lord Privy Seal	Lord Privy Seal
The President of the Board of Trade	The Rt. Hon. The President of the Board of Trade	Dear President	President	President of the Board of Trade
Minister	The Rt. Hon. Sir Henry Hopeless KBE MP, Secretary of State for Lost Causes	Dear Minister	Minister	Sir Henry Hopeless, Secretary of State for Lost Causes
Backbencher	Percy Party-Hack Esq. MP	Dear Mr Party-Hack	Mr Party-Hack	Mr Percy Party-Hack
The Law				
The Lord Chancellor	The Rt. Hon. The Lord Chancellor	Dear Lord Chancellor	Lord Chancellor	Lord Chancellor
The Lord Chief Justice of England	The Rt. Hon. The Lord Chief Justice of England	Dear Lord Chief Justice	Lord Chief Justice	Lord Chief Justice
Master of the Rolls	The Rt. Hon. The Master of the Rolls	Dear Master of the Rolls/Dear Name	By title/name	The Master of the Rolls

The President of the Family Division	The Rt. Hon. The President of the Family Division	Dear President/ Dear Name	By title/name	By title/name
Lords of Appeal (in Ordinary)	The Rt. Hon. The Lord Wigge	Dear Lord Wigge	Lord Wigge	Lord Wigge
Lord Justice of the Court of Appeal	The Rt. Hon. Lord Justice Fair	Dear Lord Justice	Lord Justice	Lord Justice Fair
High-court judge	The Hon. Mr Justice Scribe	Dear Judge	Mr Scribe	Mr Simon Scribe
Woman high-court judge	The Hon. Mrs Justice Brief DBE	Dear Judge/Dear Dame Brenda	Dame Brenda	Mrs Justice Brief
Circuit judge	His Honour Judge Round/His Honour Sir Rupert Round (if he or she was a Queen's Counsel when at the Bar, then QC should follow name)	Dear Judge	Judge	Judge Round
Queen's Counsel	Orlando Oath Esq. QC	Dear Mr Oath	Mr Oath	Mr Orlando Oath
The Armed Services	Although the rank of an officer and his decorations should be written in full on the envelope for official use, the Armed Services now, for security reasons, discourage this practice in the case of mail sent to a private address. Thus Commander Edward Ensign CBE, Royal Navy, becomes Edward Ensign Esq CBE.			
Royal Navy				
Admiral of the Fleet	Admiral of the Fleet, the Earl of Dreadnought GCB KBE	Dear Lord Dreadnought	Lord Dreadnought	Admiral of the Fleet Lord Dreadnought

353

Admiral	Admiral Sir David Destroyer GCB	Dear Sir David/Dear Admiral Destroyer (if not a knight)	Sir David/ Admiral Destroyer (if not knight)	Admiral Sir David Destroyer/ Admiral Destroyer (if not knight)
Commodore	Commodore Francis Frigate CBE, Royal Navy (or RN)	Dear Commodore Frigate	Commodore	Commodore Frigate
Captain, Commander, Lieutenant Commander, Lieutenant, Sub Lieutenant	Same as for Commodore, but with appropriate title			
Midshipman, Officer Cadet	Midshipman (Mid)/Officer Cadet (O/C) David Dinghy, Royal Navy	Dear Mr Dinghy	Mr Dinghy	Midshipman/ Officer Cadet Dinghy
	All officers below the rank of Rear Admiral are entitled to the words 'Royal Navy' after their name and any decorations, etc. This may be abbreviated to 'RN', but only when the abbreviated form of the rank is used			
Royal Marine	The rank of Lieutenant Colonel and below takes 'Royal Marines' or 'RM' after any decorations			
The Army				
Officers from Field Marshal to Captain	These follow the same form as naval ranks, e.g. Major General Terence Tank CB CBE	Dear General (or Dear Sir Terence)/Dear General Tank (if not a knight)	Sir Terence Tank/General Tank (if not a knight)	General Sir Terence Tank/General Tank (if not a knight)
Lieutenant and lower ranks	Bernard Bearskin Esq., Gulfstream Guards	Dear Mr Bearskin	Mr Bearskin	Mr Bearskin

Royal Air Force	The form is the same as for the other two services. Envelopes for official use carry the rank, title and decorations. The letters 'RAF' also follow for serving officers. Flying Officers and Pilot Officers are addressed as Esq. on the envelope and Mr in correspondence			
Air Marshal	Air Marshal Sir William Wings KCB CBE RAF	Dear Sir William/Dear Air Marshal Wings (if not a knight)	Sir William/Air Marshal Wings (if not a knight)	Air Marshal Sir William Wings
The Clergy				
The Church of England				
Archbishop	The Most Reverend and Right Honourable the Lord Archbishop of York	Dear Archbishop/ by name	Archbishop	Archbishop of York
Bishop	The Right Reverend the Bishop of Barchester	Dear Bishop	Bishop	Bishop of Barchester
Bishop of London (always a Privy Councillor)	The Right Reverend and Right Honourable the Lord Bishop of London	Dear Bishop	Bishop	Bishop of London
Diocesan bishop	The Right Reverend the Lord Bishop of Barchestershire	Dear Lord Bishop	Lord Bishop	Lord Bishop of Barchester- shire
Dean and provost	The Very Reverend the Dean of Midchester	Dear Dean	Dean	Dean of Midchester
Archdeacon	The Venerable Archdeacon of Amplitude	Dear Archdeacon	Archdeacon	Archdeacon of Amplitude
Canon	The Reverend Canon Charles Cassock	Dear Canon/ Dear Canon Cassock	Canon	Canon Charles Cassock

Other clergy	The Reverend Jane Trendy	Dear Miss Trendy	Miss Trendy/Vicar or Rector (if the cleric so addressed is the incumbent of the parish where you live or worship)	Miss Trendy
	The use of abbreviations: Reverend is now often abbreviated to Revd or Rev., Right Reverend to Rt. Revd or Rt. Rev., Father to Fr, Prebendary to Preb. and Venerable to Ven., although there are still clergy who prefer the full forms given here. Reverend, Right Reverend and Venerable, whether abbreviated or not, should always be preceded by the definite article. The form 'Reverend Smith' should never be used this side of the Atlantic. If the Christian names or initials are not known then the correct form is The Reverend Mr/Mrs/Miss Smith			
Roman Catholic Church				
The Pope	His Holiness The Pope	Your Holiness/Most Holy Father	Your Holiness	His Holiness The Pope
Apostolic Nuncio	His Excellency Archbishop Victorio Vaticana, the Apostolic Nuncio	Your Excellency	Your Excellency	HE The Apostolic Nuncio

Cardinal	His Eminence the Cardinal Archbishop of Eastminster/His Eminence James Smith, Cardinal Archbishop of Eastminster/His Eminence Charles Crimson (if not an archbishop)	Your Eminence/ Dear Cardinal Crimson	Your Eminence/ Cardinal Crimson	HE Cardinal Crimson
Archbishop	His Grace the Archbishop of Amethyst	Your Grace/Dear Archbishop	Your Grace/ Archbishop	Archbishop of Amethyst
Bishop	The Right Reverend Peter Purple, Bishop of Bingchester	My Lord Bishop/Dear Bishop	My Lord/Bishop Purple	Bishop Purple
Monsignor	The Right Reverend/The Very Reverend (if canon) Monsignor Mauve	Dear Monsignor Mauve	Monsignor Mauve	Monsignor Mauve
Other priests	The Reverend Father Flame	Dear Father Flame	Father	Father Flame
Abbot	The Right Reverend the Abbot of Azure (followed by the initials of his order)	Dear Father Abbot/Dear Abbot Azure	Father Abbot	Abbot Azure
Jewish				
The Chief Rabbi	The Chief Rabbi	Dear Chief Rabbi	Chief Rabbi	Chief Rabbi
Rabbi	Rabbi Raymond Rubenstein/Rabbi Dr Rubenstein (if a doctor)	Dear Rabbi Rubenstein/ Dear Dr Rubenstein (if a doctor)	Rabbi Rubenstein/Dr Rubenstein	Rabbi Rubenstein/Dr Rubenstein
Ministers	The Reverend Jacob Horovitz/The Reverend Dr Jacob Horovitz	Dear Mr Horovitz/Dear Dr Horovitz	Mr Horovitz/Dr Horovitz	Mr Jacob Horovitz/Dr Jacob Horovitz

357

Local Government				
Lord (and Lady) Mayor	The Right Honourable Lord Mayor of Lilliput (NB Some lord mayors are styled The Right Worshipful instead of The Right Honourable. Always check individual circumstances.)	Dear Lord Mayor	My Lord Mayor/Lord Mayor	Lord Mayor
Lady Mayoress (i.e. wife of mayor)	The Lady Mayoress of Lilliput	Dear Lady Mayoress	Lady Mayoress	Lady Mayoress
Consort of lady mayor is called The Lord Mayor's Consort, but is addressed by his name	Maurice Municipal Esq.	Dear Mr Municipal	Mr Municipal	Mr Maurice Municipal
Mayor	This is a complex issue. As a general rule of thumb, mayors of cities and certain historic towns are known as: The Right Worshipful the Mayor of Midchester. Other town mayors are usually addressed as: The Worshipful Mayor of Cranford. However, this is only part of the picture and further reference should be made to *Debrett's Correct Form*	Dear Mr Mayor	Mr Mayor	Mayor of Midchester
Alderman (applicable only for Corporation of London)	Mr Alderman Appy/ Alderman Sir Anthony Appier/Alderman the Rt. Hon. The Lord Appiest/ Major and Alderman Henry Appy. (The form is the same in the case of women.)	Dear Alderman/ Dear Name	Alderman Appy	Alderman Appy

City, borough or district councillor	Councillor Clever	Dear Councillor	Councillor	Councillor Clever
Medical				
Doctor	Dr Peregrine Pill MD FCRP/Sir Peregrine Pill MD FRCP (if a knight)	Dear Dr Pill/Dear Sir Peregrine (if a knight)	Dr Pill/Sir Peregrine (if a knight)	Dr Peregrine Pill/Sir Peregrine Pill (if a knight)
Surgeon	Stanley Scalpel Esq. MS FRCS/Sir Stanley Scalpel MS FRCS (if a knight)	Dear Mr Scalpel/Dear Sir Stanley (if a knight)	Mr Scalpel/Sir Stanley (if a knight)	Mr Stanley Scalpel/Sir Stanley Scalpel (if a knight)
Dentist	Dentists are correctly addressed as surgeons, i.e. Mr, unless extra qualifications allow them to be known as Dr. However, a recent pronouncement by the General Dental Council now allows all dentists to use the courtesy title of Dr			
The Police				
Police Commissioner (Metropolitan forces)	Sir Henry Helmet (followed by any decorations), Commissioner of Police of the Metropolis/for City of Lilliput	Dear Sir Henry/Dear Commis-sioner	Commis-sioner/Sir Henry	Sir Henry Helmet
Deputy or Assistant Commissioner	Trevor Truncheon Esq., Deputy Commissioner of Police of/for the Metropolis/City of Lilliput	Dear Mr Truncheon/ Dear Deputy Commis-sioner	Deputy Commis-sioner/Mr Truncheon	Mr Trevor Truncheon
Commander, Chief Superintend-ent, Superintendent	Chief Superintendent Thomas Tunic MBE, Metropolitan Police	Dear Mr Tunic/Dear Chief Superintend-ent	Chief Super-intendent/Mr Tunic	Mr Thomas Tunic

Chief Inspector, Inspector, Police Sergeant, Police Constable	Police Sergeant Tracey Truncheon (abbreviations, e.g. PS, are often used on envelopes)	Dear Police Sergeant/Dear Mrs Truncheon	Police Sergeant/Mrs Truncheon	Mrs Tracey Truncheon
Chief Constable (other police forces). Assistant chief constables enjoy the same form	Sir Simon Shield (Simon Shield Esq. if not a knight), followed by any decorations, Chief Constable, Middleshire Constabulary	Dear Sir Simon/Dear Chief Constable	Chief Constable/Sir Simon	Sir Simon Shield
All other ranks follow the form of the Metropolitan forces.				

BIBLIOGRAPHY

Ager, Stanley and St Aubyn, Fiona, *Ager's Way to Easy Elegance*, James Wagenvoord Studio, Inc. (New York), 1980

Beyfus, Drusilla, *The Bride's Book*, Allen Lane, 1981

Beyfus, Drusilla, *Modern Manners*, Hamlyn, 1992

Burch Donald, Elsie (ed.), *Debrett's Etiquette & Modern Manners*, Headline, 1981

Devereaux, GRM, *Etiquette for Men*, C Arthur Pearson Ltd, 1906

Hilliard, Elizabeth, *Brides Wedding Book*, Condé Nast Books, 1992

Humbry, Mrs, *Manners for Men*, Pryor Publications, 1993

Humbry, Mrs, *Manners for Women*, Pryor Publications, 1993

Kightly, Charles, *The Customs and Ceremonies of Britain*, Thames & Hudson, 1986

Killen, Mary, *Best Behaviour*, Century, 1990

Martin, Judith, *Miss Manners' Guide to Excruciatingly Correct Behaviour*, Hamish Hamilton, 1983

Mitford, Nancy, *Noblesse Oblige*, Hamish Hamilton, 1956

Montague-Smith, Patrick, *Debrett's Correct Form*, Debrett's Peerage Limited, 1970

Mosley, Charles, *Debrett's Guide to Entertaining*, Headline, 1994

Mosley, Charles, *Debrett's Guide to Bereavement*, Headline, 1995

Nicherson, Joseph, *A Shooting Man's Creed*, Sidgwick & Jackson, 1989

Nicholson, Harold, *Good Behaviour*, Constable, 1955

Noel, Celestria, *The Harpers & Queen Book of the Season*, Headline, 1994

Rees, Nigel, *Guide to Good Manners*, Bloomsbury, 1992

Shackleton, Fiona and Timbs, Olivia, *The Divorce Handbook*, Thorsons, 1992

Sutherland, Douglas, *The English Gentleman*, Debrett, 1978

Troubridge, Lady, *The Book of Etiquette*, Kingswood Press, 1926

Yapp, Nicholas, *Debrett's Guide to Business Etiquette*, Headline, 1994

INDEX

5764